PEDAGOGICAL IMAGINATION
A Conceptual Memoir
by Edmund W. Gordon

VOLUME I
Using the Master's Tools to Change the Subject of the Debate

VOLUME II
Using the Master's Tools to Inform Conceptual Leadership, Engaged Scholarship and Social Action

VOLUME III
Defiance: On Becoming an Agentic Black Male Scholar

PEDAGOGICAL

IMAGINATION

A Conceptual Memoir

– VOLUME II –

Using the Master's Tools to Inform Conceptual Leadership, Engaged Scholarship and Social Action

Edmund W. Gordon

Foreword by
Eleanor Armour Thomas

Progressive Black Publishing Since 1967
Chicago

Third World Press
Publishers since 1967
Chicago

First Edition
16 15 14   6 5 4 3 2 1
Printed in the United States of America
Pedagogical Imagination: Conceptual Memoir, Volume II, Using the Master's Tools to Inform Conceptual Leadership, Engaged Scholarship and Social Action

Cover illustration "Harvest Talk" by Charles W. White
Cover Design by Relana Johnson
Interior layout by Denise Borel Billups

ISBN 13: 978-0-88378-331-3 (Paper)
ISBN 13: 978-0-88378-340-5 (Cloth)

Library of Congress Cataloging-in-Publication Data

Gordon, Edmund W., author.
 Pedagogical imagination : a conceptual memoir / Edmund W. Gordon.
    volumes cm
  Includes bibliographical references and index.
  ISBN 978-0-88378-326-9 (volume 1 : pbk.) -- ISBN 978-0-88378-339-9 (volume 1 : cloth)
  1. Education--Social aspects--United States. 2. Educational equalization--United States. 3. African Americans--Education. 4. School improvement programs--United States. I. Title.
 LC191.4.G67 2012
 306.430973--dc23
                               2012033149

CONTENTS

PART ONE

CONCEPTUAL LEADERSHIP AND ENGAGED SCHOLARSHIP

PART TWO

SOCIAL ACTION

FOREWORD

Eleanor Armour Thomas

It is immoral to begin by measuring outcomes before we have seriously engaged the equitable and sufficient distribution of input-opportunities and resources essential to the development of intellect and competence.

Edmund W. Gordon, 1995

This quotation taken from one of Gordon's essays in these volumes epitomizes the centrality of the principle of equity undergirding much of his scholarly writings over the last four decades. Energized by the civil rights movement of the 1950s and 1960s, his early essays speak to the inequitable distribution of educational resources for children and youth from less advantaged backgrounds that severely limit their striving to reach the same levels of academic achievement as their more privileged peers. Gordon coined the concept of *Compensatory Education* and discusses its principles and strategies for equalizing opportunity of academic achievement for all pupils irrespective of their status as members of diverse social and economic groups. Recognizing the limitations of a compensatory approach to the education of marginalized children, this notion is followed by a host of additional conceptualizations of how a society intent on the education of its children can proceed. In the essays included in *Pedagogical Imagination* we see evidence of a creative mind working ceaselessly to imagine and create strategies by which the academic and personal development of children can be facilitated.

We see that Gordon's scholarly writings consist of essays about the diversity of functional and status characteristics that are found within and among human populations and the implications of this diversity for the design of educational interventions, achievement testing and educational policy. He goes to considerable length to distinguish between the implications, for education, that result from differences in the status that one experiences and differences in the way that one learns. In these writings he articulates a distinction between equality and equity in which the former connotes sameness and the absence of discrimination whereas the latter has more to do with distributional sufficiency and appropriateness. It is from this conception of equity that he laid down a two-pronged challenge to educators. The first is the moral obligation to ensure a fair and just distribution of education resources to all children irrespective of their status as members of race/ethnic, language, class, gender national origin, or special-needs groups. The second is to ensure the appropriateness and sufficiency of the allocation of educational resources in relation to the differential manner in which individuals tend to function. Consonant with his conception of equity is his argument for the achievement of the necessary competences, skills and credentials for all children and youth that will prepare them for meaningful participation in the mainstream of a democratic and pluralistic society. He dismisses with contempt the idea of differential standards for diverse populations of learners. He advocates for intellective competence as the universal currency in modern technologically advanced societies.

Gordon's commitment to making academic excellence independent of the economic, ethnic and social backgrounds of learners continues as a dominant theme throughout this collection of his essays. As he continues his search for appropriate and sufficient intervention he comes at the issue of equity by calling for the *Affirmative Development* of academic ability of all children and youth as an alternative to *Affirmative Action.* He argues cogently that affirmative action is a rational social response to official exclusion of specific groups from the economic and social intercourse of the society, but that affirmative development is a necessary complement to affirmative action under the circumstances of prior exclusion. Unlike much of his early writings, Gordon comes to the point that he is not as convinced that schools alone can do the job of developing intellective competence among their pupils, particularly those from less advantaged backgrounds. Rather, he contends that overcoming the academic underperformance of these pupils requires a sustained and systemic approach of simultaneous interventions by families, communities, teachers, schools and the larger society. His essays on *Supplementary Education* explore the various forms of education-related capital as the wide varieties of non-school based educational conditions and experiences conducive to the development of intellective competence for students in general and students from less advantaged backgrounds in particular.

Foreword

Several of these essays reflect Gordon's explorations in the epistemological implications of changing perspectives, in the production of knowledge, from almost exclusive attention to western culture—as dominated by European cultural traditions—to the deliberate inclusion of more diverse cultural reference groups. He easily moves from the cultural identities of people to the theoretical assumptions that inform different epistemologies. Gordon's thinking ranges from underpinnings in contextualism, interactionism and perspectivism to methodological problems in research. His writings influenced the democratization of membership and programs in national research organizations. He argues that the integrity of academic canons and even our better understanding of the disciplines themselves rest on—broadening the reference points from which we begin our search and ultimately produce and apply knowledge.

Gordon has written about popular youth cultures and their resistance to the status quo. He has written about racial conflict and its roots in classism and communicentric bias. He brings an ecological perspective to bear on counseling and education as instruments of behavior change. As in all of these essays, Gordon can be depended upon to bring considered knowledge, the wisdom of experience, critical reflection and humane values to bear on the problems of education and human development. He closes this reprise, reinterpretation and reflection on more than sixty years of productive scholarly inquiry and scholarly practice with a body of more biographical work. Here he combines reflection and reflexivity to examine his own experiences with some of the people who were important to his development. He terms these people "defiers." They are persons who, through their intentionality and human effort, exercised human agency to defy the odds against success. Having been born into privilege, Gordon declines to identify himself as a defier; he claims not to have overcome great odds. But on careful reading of this, the more biographical volume of his memoir, Gordon reveals that his accomplishments and his life are etched with the evidence of his defiance—defiance of traditions, defiance of theoretical constraints, defiance of socially constructed limitations and exclusion, defiance of the odds against success for a "little black boy from rural and segregated North Carolina."

Eleanor Armour Thomas is Professor and Chairperson of the Department of Education at Queen College of the City University of New York.

PREFACE

Pedagogical Imagination is my conceptual memoir—my attempt to apply reprise of, reflection upon and reflexivity to the ideas that have informed the almost seventy years of my life that have been devoted to the study of the practice and sciences of pedagogy. This is not a biographical work, but I have taken a biographical approach to the final volume of the work. In Volume I, I have addressed different conceptualizations that contribute to our understanding of the challenges that face education and other interventions that are intended to facilitate the development of human beings. In Volume II, I re-visit the several ways in which I have tried to apply behavioral and social science knowledge to education and the improvement of the human condition. Throughout the three volumes, I have tried to remain close to the conceptual and theoretical groundings that form the foundations for my work, but in most instances I have taken the liberty to go beyond the original formulation or application to address the problem on which I have focused. I contend that such is typical of my career. I have freely used my intuition and imagination to adapt the knowledge and techniques that I have acquired to better understand and to act. *Pedagogical Imagination* conjoins the creative use of mind to address selected problems in the improvement of education, similarly to C. Wright Mill's admonition that sociological imagination is brought to bear upon the pursuit of understanding in sociology and of solutions to social problems.

I think it was Dr. Goodwin Watson, a professor at Teachers College, who in the early 1950s first introduced me to the writings of C. Wright Mills. Like so many of my exposures to great minds, I suspect I was not ready for Mills. As I recall, it was some ten years later, as I began my own career as a professor, that I discovered Mills' *Sociological Imagination* (1958). Thinking that appendices carried marginal details, it took me another few years to get beyond the provocative ideas of the main text to my reading of Mills' appendix, an essay on intellectual craftsmanship. To this day I insist that my students read this appendix, even if they cannot find time to read *Sociologi-*

cal Imagination. But it is Mills' notion concerning the importance of creative thought—imagination—that really captured my attention. It is in the appendix that he talks about and illustrates how to do it. Mills was jealous of the time available for thought that he admitted to reservations concerning the time required for the careful gathering and analysis of data, when that time could be used for reflexive thought about the conceptual grounds for; the relationships between phenomena; and the theoretical implications of the findings and problems that emerge from our efforts at inquiry and the production of knowledge. I may have resonated to Mills because his ideas provided a weak rationale for my own approach to knowledge production. I have always favored qualitative over quantitative approaches to the production of knowledge. For as long as I can remember, I have privileged thinking about problems and searching for possible connections between ideas to collecting and analyzing data. To this day, I get more satisfaction out of analyzing and synthesizing the ideas that flow from the research of others, to the design and conduct of well-controlled experiments.

Since I define myself as an applied social scientist and have devoted most of my career to the application of existing knowledge to the improvement of life chances for less privileged populations, it has been possible for me to gain some prominence in education and educational psychology as a "promiscuous conceptual hunter." When the available ideas have not served my purposes, I have tried to adapt or modify the extant to fit the perceived need. In reflection on my career, I have realized that I resonated so to C. Wright Mills because he endorsed my use of my imagination to re-think—re-conceptualize—existing ideas, the work of others, to better serve human needs. I have chosen the general title "Pedagogical Imagination" for my memoir because I believe that whatever success I have achieved is the product of my use of my imaginative use of other people's ideas, and a few of my own, to generate rather common sense notions concerning the meaning of pedagogy and the usages of pedagogy.

In retrospect, I sometimes wish that I could have matched Mills in his contributions to his discipline. In James Traub's (1991) implicit tribute to me in his book *City on the Hill,* Traub acknowledges that my name is associated with no major social science theories, no significant breakthrough in the behavioral sciences, yet in the mid 1990s, the *New York Times* referred to me as, "the premier black psychologist of [my] generation" (2003). Mills complained that the scientific tradition privileges excessive experimentation and empirical validation while it fails to recognize sufficiently the creative work of mind. The late Urie Bronfrenbrenner (1989) used to remind us that the human brain is, perhaps, our most valuable research tool. John Stokes

(1994), on the other hand, praises the privileging of Pasteur's Quadrant—that approach to knowledge production that embraces the conceptual/theoretical and the empirical/practical. If I were to relive my career, I hope that I could have achieved a greater blend of the two. However, as I look at the ideas that I have brought to and nurtured in the field of education, I take pride in my association with the ideas of *Compensatory Education* (1956); *Equality of Educational Opportunity* (1965); *Career Education* (1966); *Comprehensive Education* (2008); *Supplementary Education* (2005); *Human Diversity and Pedagogy* (1986); *Affirmative Development* (2007); *Contextualism, Perspectivism and Broadened Academic Canons* (1987); *Dynamic Pedagogy* (2006); and *Curriculum Embedded Assessment* (2002). My contributions to the advancement of these notions are the product of my having employed pedagogical imagination, an idea that was inspired by C. Wright Mills' little book, *Sociological Imagination.*

I have indicated that the contents of *Pedagogical Imagination* are organized around three mental processing constructs, viz., reprise as in repetition, reflection and reflexion. Volume I is introduced with a drawing by the distinguished American artist, Charles W. White, titled "Move on up a little higher." This drawing was chosen to reflect my concern with using existing knowledge; I metaphorically refer to that knowledge as the master's tools, to raise the level of public thought about education and human development to change the debate. In this volume I have re-printed several of my essays which best represent my repeated effort at re-conceptualizing extant knowledge in ways that enable and inform programs of educational intervention, as well as the conduct of educational research. These essays are organized under subtitles that reflect the varying purposes of these essays, (1) to change the nature and subject of the debate; (2) to interpret and extend the meanings of conceptual foundations; and (3) to address recurring issues in education and public affairs. I wish that these essays had made as much of a difference as I intended when I wrote them. But I discovered, as Du Bois came to realize before I did, knowledge and understanding are important to the solving of the world's problems, but they are not sufficient.

Volume II contains some of my reflections on my experience at going beyond knowing and understanding to taking action. Here, more than repetition, I offer my reflections on my involvement in the conceptual leadership of some of the major developments in education and social action during the twentieth century. To introduce my reflections, I use Charles White's charcoal drawing, "Harvest Talk" in which two sharecroppers use the master's tools to harvest crops, from which they and the dominant society will benefit. I see Charlie's image as symbolic of my own efforts at using the tools available to serve productive ends for our people. In these essays I reflect most on my concern for the achievement of excellence and equity in education, perhaps the most dominant theme in my work. On reflection, it is clear that as much as seventy five percent of my activity, research and writing has been directed at the serving of these dual ends. I reflect on my participation in efforts at desegregation, compensatory education, career education, early childhood education, comprehensive education, human diversity and pedagogy, cultural diversity and knowledge production. I refer to my involvement in these developments and movements as "engaged scholarship and social action."

Volume III of *Pedagogical Imagination* is titled "Defiance: On Becoming an Agentic Black Male Scholar." It is introduced by a charcoal drawing by my friend and fictive brother, Charles W. White, "General Moses and Sojourner" in which two defiant Black women are pictured. This volume, which is the most biographic of the three volumes, opens with my reflexive examination of my experiences, with my models for what it means to be an agentic Black man. In addition to my somewhat idealized images of these men, including my father, I examine their roles in shaping my career and my person. In Part 2 of this volume I draw upon some of my research concerned with Black men who have overcome tremendous odds against their success to become agentic and effective human beings. Defiance is advanced as a more appropriate and useful construct than I think resilience to be. I conclude from my studies of this phenomenon that my search for explanation for the success of these men is not very useful since for each of those identified as winners, we have thousands of losers. Our society is better organized to produce losers than it is to support winners, especially if they are Black and male. Volume III ends with a frankly biographical essay in which I try through both reflectivity and reflexivity to describe and interpret how it is that a little Black boy from rural and segregated North Carolina developed to hold endowed professorships at two Ivy League Universities, using the tools of the hegemonic culture.

Edmund W. Gordon

Acknowledgements

Pedagogical Imagination is a compilation of my reflections on the ideas and experiences that have informed my career in education and psychology. I am fortunate that these ideas and experiences have occurred in the context of cooperative work with my colleagues. Initially, I worked with more mature scholars from whom I learned a great deal—Herbert Birch, Doxey Wilkerson, Stella Chess, Alexander Thomas, Joseph Wortis, and Margaret Lawrence. However, I quickly turned to work with younger scholars who helped me do my work, while they were learning intellectual crafts-personship with me. Practically all of my clinical and research work was shared with these young people and 75 percent of my publications are co-authored works. I owe so much to these young people, many of whom are now senior and leaders in their own right. I am tempted to write the long essay that would be required to do justice to them and their impact on me. It will have to suffice to refer to several essays written by a number of these young scholar colleagues in *Edmund W. Gordon: Producer of Knowledge, Pursuer of Understanding* (edited by Carol Camp Yeakey, 2000).

In the years since my retirement (1991) a few young people have rallied around the old man and have kept me intellectually alive. I am especially indebted to Eleanor Armour Thomas; A. Wade Boykin, Ernest Washington; Ana Mari Cauce; Norris Haynes; Beatrice Bridglall; John Powell; A. J. Franklin; Michael Nettles; Herve Varenne; Howard Everson; Carol Bonilla Bowman; Carol Camp Yeakey; Fayneese Miller; Ronald Ferguson; Ezekiel Dixon Roman, David Wall Rice, Aundra Saa Meroe, Maitrayee Bhattacharyya, Geoffrey Canada; Betina Jean-Louis, Brenda Mejia, Mariana Vegara, Veronica Holly, Paola Andrea Valencia Cadena and Juliana Quintero.. I thank them for their assistance, inspiration and support. For the past fifteen years Susan A. Shurtleff has been administrative and personal assistant to Dr. Susan G. Gordon and myself. She has relieved us of the management of our home and our finances. She has been enormously helpful with the management of our personal lives, even as she has assisted with our professional work. In the process she has grown to be a personal friend and extended family member. It is difficult to overestimate our indebtedness to her. She has been invaluable.

Acknowledgements

In the writing of *Pedagogical Imagination,* I owe an enormous debt to Paola Heincke, my editorial and research assistant, who has also become our friend and fictive daughter. Over the past six years, Paola has created from my books and papers the Edmund W. Gordon Archives, with assistance from Jamila Brathwaite and Stephen Charles. She has begun to make this enormous file of material accessible to us, and others, even as she mined it to retrieve materials necessary to the development of these volumes. She has immersed herself in the substance of my ideas and incorporated much into her own thinking such that she has become expert on my career and the notions that have informed it. She has become efficient and skillful at tracing the emergence and development of my ideas and at documenting the sources of these ideas and where and how I have used them. It is her orderly and logical mind and her insistence on clarity, consistency and the avoidance of redundancy that have made our product more accurate and reader friendly. She has contributed all of this while functioning as doula (or more accurately) as midwife in the delivery of this work of three volumes. With her third hand, she has coordinated my on-going research. She has supervised my bibliographic research. She has participated with me in the collection of data. She has been my constant professional companion. At least I know that I could not have continued to be intellectually and professionally productive into the end of my ninth decade without her help. With hindsight I know very well that I could not have completed Pedagogical Imagination without her contributions and support. If memoirs were co-edited, she would be co-editor. If I had chosen another genre, she could have been my biographer. I am eternally grateful to Paola for her loyalty and support and proudly share this achievement with her.

In several places in these three volumes reference has been made to the place and role of my wife, Susan G. Gordon, M.D. in my life and work. My children attribute all that I have become and much that I have accomplished to their mother's influence. They and I recognize that Susan G. and Edmund W. Gordon have been a team for almost sixty-five years. Our private and our professional lives have been constantly intertwined, even as we have pursued our independent careers. We have spent all of our discretionary time together or together with our children. In these times together we have been blessed with communication and exchange of ideas that have made it difficult to determine which is hers and which is mine. It is Susan G. Gordon who encouraged me to move beyond my somewhat narrow Christian belief system to explore a wider range of perspectives. It is she who introduced me to philosophical materialist thought and progressive political action. It is she who encouraged me to continue my professional education and subsequently to immerse myself in the

Acknowledgements

sciences of behavior. I initially sought better to comprehend the mechanisms by which we understand human behavior and, under her influence, I have turned to the humanities in search of the meanings of the behavior of fellow human beings. I am indebted to her for so many things—our children, a challenging and rewarding life together, more blessings and pleasures than I deserve, and in the writing of my memoir and several other works, I am grateful to her for generous criticism and constant support. Our children are correct. I would be a very different person without her influence and a much less content person without her love.

Our children are correct about a number of things. They have grown to be the most knowledgeable persons alive concerning who Susan and Edmund W. Gordon are. It is true that we conceived and raised them, but they have contributed mightily to the development and maturation of their parents. Presiding over their transition from childhood, through adolescence, to adulthood required that we, their parents, learn so much, and in the process, that we become better persons. I also realize that it was out of that personal growth that Susan and I became more able scholars and more insightful human beings. Having started to write this memoir after they had become adults to whom I listen and for whom I have the greatest respect, as much as I do to and for their mother, I must acknowledge my deep appreciation for their contributions to my development and to my work. There are no critics who are as unrelentingly critical as are one's children, and it was only my parents, my sister and my wife who have been more complimenting and supportive of my work and me than have Edmund T.; Christopher W.; Jessica G. and Johanna S. Gordon. In my lexicon, it is to my own family of birth and to the family to whom Susan and I gave birth and created that I express my greatest thanks.

The development and completion of Pedagogical Imagination was underwritten with the generous support from the Social Investment Fund of the Educational Testing Service (ETS), under the guiding eyes of Eleanor Horne. It was ETS who convened a group of my former students and friends to give us initial advice on the development of this project, and who funded us through the process. I have also been supported for work related to the memoir by the CEJJES Foundation, the College Board and the W. T. Grant Foundation.

INTRODUCTION

By the children of Susan G. and Edmund W. Gordon:
Jessica Gordon Nembhard, Christopher W. Gordon,
Edmund T. Gordon and Johanna S. Gordon

We always knew their values. Our parents, Susan Elizabeth Gitt Gordon and Edmund Wyatt Gordon (EWG), are scholar activists. We, their children, grew up knowing that for all of their lives they fought personal, family, community, national, and global battles for civil rights, human rights, economic and social justice, human dignity and peace. There was no ambiguity in our family, no confusion, concerning these matters. All of us, their children, understood that to be a human being means to be humble, to show compassion, and to work tirelessly against oppression, discrimination and injustice. They communicated their values through words and deeds: during family discussions and shared family reading, at the dinner table, in the car, hiking or at the beach, by having us accompany them to demonstrations and rallies, through the types and caliber of their friends, as well as through the charities they supported. Our parents supported our struggles in school when, for example, we girls insisted on being able to wear pants once in the school building not just outside on a cold day; when we each participated in demonstrations against the Viet Nam War and nuclear proliferation; as we agitated for more content about African Americans in our curriculum and more teachers of color, and for more student representation and educational democracy; and when we morally could not participate in air raid drills because they represented false hope of surviving a nuclear attack.

In every aspect of their lives Edmund and Susan G. Gordon used logical analysis and social commitment to address and subvert oppression and marginalization. They demonstrated their social and intellectual responsibility, as well as their dedication to human perfectibility and systemic change, in their choice of where to live, their professions, their friends, and organizational memberships. We watched them, we participated with them, and we are the products of their social activism, wisdom, dedication and perseverance. We came to learn that our parents were not just busy people with dual careers, always helping out the neighbors while raising four children (and sometimes an additional "foster" child), but they were also servant leaders. We came to understand that they are two people committed to the achievement of social and economic justice for disenfranchised peoples around the world. Mom chose to work through medicine and health maintenance. Dad chose education and psychology with the promotion of intellective competence as his focus.

In some ways we each came to understand their intellectual contributions through different experiences and careers as young adults: Ted (Edmund T.) ended up choosing economic and cultural anthropology, specializing in culture and power in the African Diaspora, race education, and the racialized economy of space and resource distribution. His work often parallels Dad's as they address similar problems such as the development of Black males, and the relationships of access to resources and power to developmental opportunity and schooling. Jessica was a research assistant at the Institute for Urban and Minority Education established by EWG at Columbia Teacher's College, working with Dad while in high school, and then through education courses at Yale University and earning a Master's of Arts in Teaching at Howard University, she became more exposed to our parents' work and ideas. Partly reflecting Mom's undergraduate minor in economics and Dad's embrace of economic determinism, she earned a Ph.D. in economics. Through her specialties in Black Political Economy and cooperative economics, she connects the themes of youth development, educational reform, and community building in ways that parallel Mom's and Dad's work. Johanna studied nursing at Columbia University and earned a Master of Science in Nursing, Women's Health, from the University of Pennsylvania. She and Mom often discuss medicine and public health. She worked with young women as a nurse practitioner, and later worked with Rockland Parent's RYSE, a parent empowerment program developed with Dad. Chris' appreciation of his parents as professional workers came when he entered the world of education, as a second career, specializing in middle school special education in the public schools of North Carolina. He began to develop pedagogy that is consistent with Dad's vision of teaching and learning as continuing inquiry into the cultivation of intellect—and connected to Mom's concerns with health, learning, and well-being.

In addition, we all also heard them talk with each other and their colleagues and friends about their work, and began to read their articles and sometimes to attend their speeches, or events in their honor. We now run into their students and colleagues through our own careers, and have worked on some of their projects with them. As adults we have also been consulted about their professional career decisions. We have also participated in helping them think through Mom's campaigns for school board and for school board president; and Dad frequently consulted concerning his work at City University of NY, the College Board, ETS, Columbia's Teachers College, Yale University, and now Rockland Community College.

Susan and Edmund Gordon have never given up on or ceased their involvement in making change for the good of all; although now in their 80s and 90s, they have slowed down. Mom continues to walk three miles six days a week, to use every activity as a teaching moment, and to read the daily newspaper out loud to whoever may be present. Dad swims five days a week. As always, he still brings work home, to dinner parties and on weekend outings. He has become almost inseparable from his laptop, typing his ideas, answering an email or finishing a paper, lecture, or another section of his memoirs. We, their children, established CEJJES Institute (www.cejjesinstitute.org) to honor their philosophy, lifetime achievements and legacies. As partners with them in this endeavor, we keep learning more about them, their aspirations, activities, passions, and scholarship. We plan to continue to commemorate all their many accomplishments and pass on their values to the next generation.

As you read through our father's selected essays and his reflections on his life and work, first you should know that much of his scholarly activity as well as his political activism has been heavily influenced by our mother, Susan E.G. Gordon, M.D.; as well as by his mentors: W.E.B. Du Bois, Alain Locke, Paul Robeson, Howard Thurman, Doxey Wilkerson, Olive Schreiner, and Max Otto. You should also know that EWG is a prolific writer. He has authored or edited about twenty books and monographs. His three hundred or so essays and reports have been published as book chapters and/or as articles in journals and other published sources. The chapters re-printed in *Pedagogical Imagination* and those written specifically for this memoir are just a small selection of what we think are his most representative writings. We selected these essays, conscious of three interrelated themes that are interwoven throughout his thinking and writing:

- Excellence and Equity in and through Education;
- Using Intelligence—Knowledge and Understanding— to improve the human condition; and
- The Pursuit of Responsible Human Agency.

Introduction

He has divided this memoir into three volumes that roughly correspond to those three themes.

Volume I, "Using the Master's Tools to Change the Subject of the Debate," includes essays concerned with our father's journey through the struggle to achieve equal educational opportunity through desegregation of public schools—the elimination of racial isolation—and the struggle for equality of educational achievement, to his concern with the social marketing of the affirmative development of intellective competence and comprehensive/supplementary education. In these essays Dad uses established ideas and extant research to examine old problems and to think about these problems and old solutions in new ways. He challenges colloquial interpretations of the Audre Lorde admonition that we cannot use the master's tools to destroy the master's house.

In Volumes I and II ("Using the Master's Tools to Inform Conceptual Leadership, Engaged Scholarship, and Social Action"), he demonstrates that subjected to critical analysis and followed to their logical conclusions, much of this knowledge can be used to radically change the life chances of marginalized and socially excluded peoples. In these essays he uses logical analysis to exploit the potential of the dominant system's theories ("the master's tools") to subvert that system's efforts at intellectual marginalization and oppression of low-income people of color. These essays illustrate how he followed respected theoretical constructs to their logical conclusions to challenge hegemonic perspectives and practices. Examples are his use of the theory of interactionism and the notion of epigenetic development to clarify the nature versus nurture debate, and his use of William James' notion of radical empiricism to challenge the more rigid and over generalized applications of positivist thought and empiricism to privilege the scientific method; and use of the ideas of contextualism and perspectivism to challenge the artificial boundaries imposed on academic canons, and the limitations imposed on research methodologies in the production of knowledge. He also has used all these systems of thought to argue for the relevance of Einstein's theory of relativity for humankind's efforts at knowing and understanding social as well as physical phenomena.

The third volume ("Defiance: On Becoming an Agentic Black Male Scholar") consists of essays on the achievement of human agency as examined through the lens of his perceptions of the men who have influenced his life and themes that have recurred throughout his career. In these writings he challenges the notion of resilience as an explanatory construct for Black men who have overcome odds that favor failure to go on to high achievement. Dad rejects the construct resilience as too passive. These

Introduction

men's success is not just the unfolding of fate or some natural tendency to survive, but is more likely the result of the deliberate exercise of defiance and human agency. Edmund W. Gordon continually reminds us in these writings that the production of knowledge is a social and political activity as well as a scientific undertaking, and that the purpose of knowledge pursuit and its production is to interrogate, improve, emancipate, and transform the human condition.

Reading this compilation of Edmund W. Gordon's writings is a reminder to us, his children, of much to which we have been exposed throughout our lives, the stuff we have "cut our teeth on" in some way—ideas we have consistently heard our parents talk about. These are words, phrases, and ideas that we have grown up with and internalized. *Pedagogical Imagination* makes it now possible for others, from all generations, to also grow with these ideas and ponder these insights.

Read, enjoy, learn, and act.

PART ONE

CONCEPTUAL LEADERSHIP
AND ENGAGED SCHOLARSHIP

1
Education, Excellence and Equity

Good evening colleagues and friends. I appreciate more than you can know the fact that I have been asked by the American Educational Research Association (AERA) to present the Inaugural Lecture in the annual commemoration of the 1954 US Supreme Court decision in the matter of *Brown v. Topeka Board of Education.* As you know, this series of annual lectures is concerned with the use of findings from research concerning education to inform professional practice and public policy. Before getting into the body of my lecture, I want to make a few acknowledgments. Few of us achieve much in life without the assistance of others. A personal word of thanks goes to my wife, Dr. Susan G. Gordon for giving me 58 years of her life, four remarkable children, and unending guidance, freedom and support while I have tried to be a scholarly worker in the struggle for justice. I acknowledge with gratitude the financial support for this and related work from the College Board, Learning Point, Associates and the Rockefeller Foundation.

I also acknowledge with deep appreciation the continuing assistance that I receive from my staff colleagues at the Columbia University Teachers College Institute for Urban and Minority Education. I want to offer special thanks to Dr. Beatrice L. Bridglall, my research and editorial associate and coeditor of our two forthcoming books, one on supplementary education and the other on the affirmative development of academic ability. For the aging scholars among us, my advice is to keep going as long as you can. But if you choose to follow my example, it will help greatly if you can find a bright young developing scholar to help you. I am able to continue to be productive in my ninth decade of life because Dr. Bridglall helps me to remember things, to find what I am looking for, to keep up with the reading, to avoid unnecessary redundancy, and to remember to consider perspectives that have escaped my immediate attention.

3

For the past few years, I have been predicting that each of my last few AERA presentations will be my last, as I try harder and harder to retire. I truly believe that this time the prediction will be more accurate. So please permit me to say a few more words of thanks. I want to thank AERA for the ways in which it has grown and changed with the times, and for the many ways it has honored me. I was never able to win election to the presidency of this august body, but you have showered me with your other awards and recognitions. I am, perhaps, most grateful for the fact that many of the ideas that were considered marginal to the values of the Association when I first presented them, are now at the very core of our concerns. Thank you for honoring me by embracing many of my ideas.

TRIBUTE TO KENNETH B. CLARK

I must begin this lecture by paying tribute to Kenneth Bancroft Clark, who led the distinguished group of pedagogical and social scientists that did the intellectual work that was foundational to the judicial, legislative and public policy work of which the Brown decision of 1954 is symbolic. Professor Clark and this group of scholars prepared what has been referred to as the defining brief synthesizing the research findings that became the basis for the 1954 decision. To the best that many of us have been able to determine, this was the first time that social science research concerning education had been used to inform a decision of the United States Supreme Court. You may recall that reference was made to this work in the body of that decision written by the then Chief Justice Earl Warren. I first heard of this work during my first year as a graduate student at Columbia University. The late professor Herbert Birch called to ask if I would join a group of scholars who were helping a young assistant professor named Clark with a literature review he intended to submit to the Supreme Court of the United States in support of the claim that racially segregated schools were unconstitutional. I don't recall my playing a significant role and I certainly was not among the group of scholars who were signatories to the report that Clark prepared. But some members of AERA signed the report. Among them were several names that I readily recognize, such as Jerome Brunner, Isodor Chein, Mamie Clark, Allison Davis, Otto Kleinberg, and Ira Reid.

Please join me in a moment of silence as we honor these scholars and Distinguished Professor Kenneth B. Clark, who, no doubt, were it not for the ravages that age and illness have taken on him, would have been chosen to present this lecture rather than me. I feel honored and humble to stand here in his shoes, and I should add in relation to my career, to have stood on his shoulders.

REPRISE OF THE DECISION AND SOCIAL SCIENCE EVIDENCE

Three lines of argument based on educational and social science research were advanced in the brief that Professor Clark and his associates presented.

They argued that:

1. State sponsored racial segregation in public schooling has a deleterious impact on Black children;
2. State sponsored segregation in public schooling had a less clear but implicitly negative impact on White children; and
3. When structural factors in the social context force changes in human behavior, change in attitudes follow, thus challenging the traditional belief that change in attitudes had to precede change in behavior (Clark, 1950).

These wise educational and social scientists advised the court that science is not always as exact and precise as we would like, and that the evidence in support of these findings was, indeed, uneven. Consequently, they also reported the findings from the survey of the judgments, concerning these issues, of several of the then most prominent social science scholars in the nation. The collective judgment of this group of scholars surveyed supported the conclusions of the scholars who had signed the report.

This synthesis of the knowledge base was completed before 1952, but this work anticipated problems that we face today concerning warrants for the evidence that we offer in support of our research claims. The problem that they faced is reflected in the current debates concerning the privileging of the random assignment of subjects to controlled experimentation as the universal method of choice in knowledge production and decision making relative to policy and practice. Here, some fifty years ago, these scholars respectfully considered the uneven findings drawn from the empirical evidence, and complemented the findings with reflexive human judgment. These scholars were acting in the best expression of an admonition I once heard made by the distinguished Urie Bronfreunbruner, when several of us were confused by the empirical research findings. Urie reminded us that the human brain may be one of our most powerful research tools.

In the middle of the twentieth century the Supreme Court of the United States of America determined that segregation by race for purposes of education in the USA is inconsistent with the rights of citizenship that are protected by the

Constitution of the U.S. By this action it reversed an earlier decision by the court *(Plessey v. Ferguson)* in which the court decided that separate but equal arrangements were consistent with that Constitution. Since that momentous decision in 1954, most of the institutions of our society and most of the practices of government have come to be consistent with the spirit of that declaration that segregation by race creates an inherently unequal condition. So powerfully is that principal imprinted on modern U.S. society, that even a conservative Supreme Court, at the beginning of the twenty-first century, has ruled in favor of race-sensitive affirmative action to redress the imbalance that has been created by the disadvantages associated with caste like ethnic/racial status in this country. But Judge O'Connor, writing for the narrow majority of the court, opinioned the hope that such an interpretation of the law would be unnecessary by the end of another 25 years.

We applaud these 1954 and 2004 decisions in support of social justice. The gains that are associated with the first and the extended opportunities that are protected by the second are cause for the commemoration that we are celebrating this year. Collectively we offer our thanks to whatever God each of us respectively may serve, and to the courageously intelligent human beings who struggled to bring us this far. But the struggle is not over.

A substantial portion of my career has been marked by my involvement in a variety of ways in the effort to improve academic achievement through reductions in racial isolation, especially in schooling. The school desegregation efforts are thought by many to be the most extensive activities of the civil rights movement. Without regard to the proportion of the civil rights effort that was associated with school desegregation, the Supreme Court decision of 1954 in the case *Brown v. Topeka* appears to have had a greater impact on issues related to civil rights throughout the nation than it had on either racial integration in public schools or of the quality of education available to ethnic minorities in those schools. Nonetheless, for a period of about 30 years from 1945 to 1975 the education establishment in the U.S. was preoccupied with questions having to do with equal educational opportunities as largely defined by where Black and Latino children went to school and with whom they studied.

It is a source of sadness for me that this concern with racial and ethnic group isolation took center stage while concern with the appropriateness and quality of opportunities to learn was more or less neglected. Possibly under the influence of Kenneth Clark's lifetime commitment to racial integration as the solution, we seem to have agreed with his wish that Black children be given the same educational experiences that are available to White children. Evidently we thought that if they were in the same schools and classrooms they would have access to similar opportunities to learn. That differences in the academic achievement outcomes persisted after the Supreme Court decision, and even in those schools situations where racial isolation was successfully removed initially appeared paradoxical. However, the fact is that racial mixing proved to be an insufficient intervention.

Perhaps the most serious research effort directed at this problem by the federal government was the 1966 study "Equality of Educational Opportunity" by James Coleman and others. My 1967 commentary on that report remains appropriate.[1]

> Future historians may well conclude that the civil rights movement of the 1950s and 1960s had a more telling impact on public education than on any other single aspect of our society. Not only did this struggle contribute to a mid twentieth century renaissance in education in the United States, as noted by former U.S. Commissioner of Education Francis Keppel, but its concern with further democratizing education led also to the design and conduct of one of our most important pieces of educational research.
>
> Section 402 of the Civil Rights Act of 1964 directed the Commissioner of Education to conduct a survey and report to the president and Congress on "the lack of availability of equal educational opportunities for individuals by reason of race, color, religion or national origin" in public educational institutions at all levels in the United States. The resulting report, Equality of Educational Opportunity, often referred to as the Coleman Report after its senior author and one of the nation's ablest research methodologists, is the most extensive survey of the U.S. public school in the entire history of the institution.
>
> The Coleman Report, nevertheless, has received considerable criticism. Reviewers have commented on the absence of a theoretical basis for the study. Others have criticized problems in design, problems in sampling, and debatable approaches to data analysis. Some of the findings and

---

1. Gordon, E. W. November 1967 *Equalizing Educational Opportunity In the Public School* in IRCD Bulletin Volume III, No.5., Publication of the ERIC Information Retrieval Center on the Disadvantaged. New York: Yeshiva University.

conclusions of the survey, as well, have been at variance with assumptions that previously were widely held. Many of these problems and suggested weaknesses, no doubt, are due to the time limit imposed upon the study. Under requirement of the law, it was planned, designed, and conducted in two years. Additionally, within that same time period, data were analyzed and a final report prepared and published. But in spite of these suggested shortcomings, the fact is that the Coleman survey has produced some valuable data related to the general problem area of equality of educational opportunity. Indeed, there are findings from that report which most reviewers feel would stand tests of reanalysis or reinvestigation should the study be replicated or its data subjected to further analysis.

The four principal questions asked of the analysis of data in the Coleman Report and the findings related to each are summarized below:

1. What is the extent of racial and ethnic group segregation in the public schools of the United States? The great majority of children in this country attend schools in which most of the students are members of the same ethnic group. The assignment of children to schools by ethnic group identification is the dominant practice particularly in the South and, to a large extent, in the metropolitan North, Midwest, and West. "More than 65 percent of all Negro pupils in the first grade attend schools that are between 90 and 100 percent Negro. And 87 percent at grade 1 and 66 percent at grade 12 attend schools that are 50 percent or more Negro. In the South most students attend schools that are 100 percent White or Negro." A similar pattern of segregation is reported for teachers of Negro and White pupils.

2. Are the schools attended by children in the United States equal in their facilities, programs, staff and pupil characteristics? Negro children are likely to attend schools which are inferior to those attended by White children. The quality of schools attended, however, varies by region. "For the nation as whole White children attend elementary schools with a smaller average number of pupils per room (29) than do any of the minorities (30 to 33) ... In the non-metropolitan North and West and Southwest there is a smaller average number of pupils per room for Negroes than for Whites." But for secondary schools in the metropolitan Midwest, the average

for Negroes is 54 pupils per room as compared with 33 per room for Whites. "Nationally, at the high school level the average White has one teacher for every 22 students and the average Negro has one teacher for every 26 students." Nationally, Negro students also have fewer of the facilities, which are thought to be most associated with academic achievement. "They have less access to physics, chemistry, and language laboratories. There are fewer books per pupil in their libraries. Their textbooks are less often in sufficient supply." Just as minority groups tend to have less access to physical facilities that seem to be related to academic achievement, they also have less access to curricular and extracurricular programs that would seem to have such a relationship. Negro high school students are less likely to attend schools that are regionally accredited. Negro and Puerto Rican students have less access to college preparatory programs and accelerated courses. Puerto Rican pupils have less access to vocational curriculums. Moreover, the average Negro pupil attends a school where the average teacher quality is inferior to that of the teacher of the average White child, where type of college, years of experience, salary, extent of travel, educational level of teacher's mother and teacher's vocabulary score are considered. Differences are also to be found in pupil characteristics. "The average Negro has fewer classmates whose mothers graduated from high school, his classmates tend to come from larger families, they are less often enrolled in college preparatory programs, and they have taken fewer courses in English, math, science and foreign language." Differences in school characteristics are considered to be small when considered in the context of national averages, however, for fuller appreciation, regional differences should also be considered. Coleman notes that "in cases where Negroes in the South receive unequal treatment, the significance in terms of actual numbers of individuals involved is very great, since 54 percent of the Negro population of school going age, or approximately 3,200,000 children, live in that region."

3. What are the achievement patterns of children of different backgrounds as measured by their performance on achievement

tests? With the exception of pupils of Asian family background, the average pupil from the minority groups studied scored distinctly lower at every level than the average White pupil. The minority group pupils' scores were as much as one standard deviation below the majority pupils' scores in the first grade. At the twelfth grade level, the scores of minority group pupils were even further below those of the majority group. Of additional significance is the fact that a constant difference in standard deviation over the various grades actually represents a mounting difference in grade level gap as the pupils move toward the twelfth grade. Consequently, schools seem to do little about an initial deficit, which only increases as the minority pupils continue in school.

4. What relationships exist between pupil academic achievement and characteristics of the schools they attend? When differences in socioeconomic background factors for pupils are statistically controlled, differences between schools account for only a small fraction of differences in academic achievement. "The schools do differ, however, in their relation to the various racial and ethnic groups." White pupils seem to be less affected by the quality of their schools than minority group pupils. "The achievement of minority pupils depends more on the schools they attend than does the achievement of majority pupils." In the South, for example, 40 percent more of the achievement of Negro pupils is associated with the particular schools they attend than is the achievement of White pupils. With the exception of children from Asian family backgrounds, this general result is true for all minority groups. Coleman suggests that this finding "indicates that it is for the most disadvantaged children that improvements in school quality will make the most difference in achievement." Although the relationship between school characteristics and pupil achievement is relatively modest, several of the characteristics on which predominantly Negro schools score low are among those, which are related to pupil achievement. The existence of science laboratories in schools, for example, shows a small but consistent relationship to achieve-ment—Negroes attends schools with fewer of these facilities.

Teacher quality shows an even stronger relationship to pupil achievement, and it increases with grade level. Additionally, its impact on achievement is greater for Negroes than for Whites. On measures of verbal skill and educational background, two relatively potent teacher variables, teachers of minority group pupils scored lower than teachers of majority group pupils. Educational background and aspirations of fellow students are also strongly related to pupil achievement. This relationship is less significant for White pupils than for Negro pupils. Coleman found educational backgrounds and aspirations to be lower among pupils in schools Negroes attend than in schools where Whites are in the majority. In addition to the school characteristics that were shown to be related to pupil achievement, Coleman found a pupil characteristic that appears to have a stronger relationship to achievement than all the school factors combined. The extent to which a pupil feels that he has control over his own destiny is strongly related to achievement. This feeling of potency is less prevalent among Negro students, but where it is present, "their achievement is higher than that of White pupils who lack that conviction." Coleman reports "while this characteristic shows little relationship to most school factors, it is related for Negroes to the proportion of Whites in the schools. Those Negroes in schools with a higher proportion of Whites have a greater sense of control."

In trying to draw implications from these findings, it is important to consider that Coleman has produced summary statistics, which describe certain conditions and correlational statistics that, in turn, describe relationships which may be causal or simply coincidental. Causation certainly cannot be inferred from the strength of the relationships reported. When combined with the problems some critics see in the study, we are advised to move with caution in using the Coleman findings to determine public policy. Such caution, however, need not preclude serious thought and considered action. As the major findings of the study are reviewed, empirical experience, logic, and facts provide a context in which Coleman's conclusions may be interpreted.

There are some findings which common sense and clear observation leave us no choice but to accept. Public schooling in the United States is segregated by ethnic group and socioeconomic status. Negro children are more likely to attend schools of poorer quality than White children. Academic achievement for minority group children (except Asians) is inferior to that of majority group children. There simply is no question that these findings correspond to reality as we have experienced it in the area of relationships between factors; nevertheless, there may be little room for debate.

It seems clear, however, that for the development of the young person who comes to school without the advantage of being raised in a privileged or economically and socially secure White family what happens in the school is of great importance. The quality of his school's curriculum, the quality of his teachers, and the background of his fellow pupils are importantly related to the quality of his academic achievement. Additionally, his interpersonal experience in the educational setting appears to influence his sense of power to control his destiny. As pointed out before, this attitudinal factor, even more than all school factors combined, has a significant relationship to quality of achievement and rate of development.

Now, in a sense, whether or not one wants to accept these conclusions and act upon them is not in question. The fact is that the political realities of the present period strongly reflect sensitivity to these conclusions. Indeed, the primary political struggles in public education today have to do with economic and ethnic desegregation and with improved quality of education as the prime vehicles for equalizing educational opportunity. Even the current demand for "Black" schools and "Black" control of schools for "Black" children is but an expression of this struggle. The recently accelerated unionization of teachers and their efforts to improve salaries, working conditions, professional status, and quality of education are another part of the same struggle. It is only unfortunate that these two expressions have not always moved in concert.

A major strategic error in the recent strike in New York City was the teachers' failure to make adequate provision for the education of poor children during the period of the strike. If Coleman is right about the contribution of school factors to minority pupil achievement and given the modest use of the public school by more privileged families in New York City, the teachers were really striking against working class, Negro, Puerto Rican, and poor children. Important and necessary as this strike may have been, this was the effect without the advantage of providing any major inconvenience to the city's power structure and the upper classes as was true in the New York City transit strike when employers were deprived of workers who depended on public transportation. Surely, it is to the credit of the states and men more tolerant in the Negro community that the historic ties between the Negro community and labor unions were not ruptured and that we are not now faced with a sharper cleavage between teachers and the spokesmen of the "Black" community who deeply resented the unavailability of teachers to carry on even the concededly inadequate educational services the schools provide. The "Black" community did not need Coleman to tell them that what happens in school can be important in the development of their children. This they knew, and they have come to expect much from the school.

The contradictions involved in the expectations of the "Black" community for the schools and the schools' obviously low performance in the achievement of academic mastery in minority group children bring into focus the central problem in the Coleman study. The public school was created for the purpose of making certain levels of achievement independent of social origin. Its historic mission has been to enable youngsters whose families could not adequately provide for their private education to acquire the knowledge and skill necessary for full participation in a democratic society. Coleman asked of his data whether or not the schools do this equally well for children from all segments of the population and found the answer to be no. He also asked if the schools' treatment of children from minority backgrounds is equal and found the answer to be no. The inappropriateness of this second question became clearer when he asked why the inequality existed.

When Coleman attempted to establish relationships between factors which help us understand why we do not do equally well with children from a variety of backgrounds, he found that what children come to school with accounts for more of the variation in their achievement than any other factor. Now, if this is true, it suggests that schools should not be providing equal treatment to all children but that treatment should, in fact, be unequal. The schools need to design their programs to meet the special characteristics and needs of the many kinds of children served; and, if a democratizing function is to be adequately served, these special programs must be designed to eventually bring all children to, at least, some common achievement goals. The schools are not doing this, and, furthermore, Coleman did not design his study to get at dimensions of this aspect of the problem.

School factors may have been found to be of relatively modest importance for all pupils not because what the schools can do is not crucial but because Coleman did not look at all of what the schools actually do. He looked at static and status variables; he did not look at process variables. Variations in facilities, offerings and teacher qualifications may be of less importance than variations in pupil teacher interaction, teacher expectation, classroom climate, pupil interaction, and the types and demands of the learning experiences available. Within the context of static and status variables the dimensions studied may be too narrow to pick up the differences. Variations in class size between 26 and 36 may be unimportant. Differences between 18 and 36 may be highly significant. Although information was collected from administrators concerning their schools the nature and quality of school administration was not evaluated. Differences in administrative styles and relationships and school climate resulting from such differences were not identified in the study. Coleman's study did not treat school factors sensitively; rather it approached them with crude measures that identified gross and not subtle characteristics.

When the gross nature of the study is combined with the fact that tradition did not lead Coleman to study the extent to which special pupil characteristics were reflected in the adequacy or the inadequacy of the schools' offerings, it is clear that important as this report is it only begins to suggest the magnitude of the problem. Educational opportunity in the United States is not equal, but it is even more unequal than this landmark study indicates.

The Coleman survey, nevertheless, does provide some leads as to what may be required to make educational opportunity and achievement more equal. An important step toward providing for equality of educational opportunity would be economic or social class integration. Additional data from the Coleman Report and some reanalysis reported in "Racial Isolation in the Public Schools" also indicate that ethnic group integration will be an essential step in this process. Even if racial integration in the schools is not essential in and of itself, it will be required in the achievement of social class integration since the Negro middle class is not large enough to provide an appropriate mix. Significantly, the pool of middle-class Negro children is reduced by the fact that in some areas better than one-fourth of these children are in institutions other than the public school. Despite the general conclusion that school factors are relatively unimportant as determinants of achievement in the total school population, Coleman's data also seem to indicate that enriched curriculum, improved teacher quality, and other improvements in the schools which Negro students attend should make for increased achievement of poor and Negro children.

A program feature that emerges from the study, as well as from other sources, has to do with school organization. Just as Coleman omitted sensitive examination of dynamic aspects of school administration, he also did not look at patterns of parent and community participation in school policy making. It would not be unreasonable, however, to conclude that the important "locus of control" or "control over one's destiny" variable would be influenced by the child's perception of such power or influence in his parents or the adults in the group with which he identifies. The tradition in school administration of discouraging lay people, particularly poor or minority lay people from participating in the determination of school policy will need to be sharply modified. These parents and community spokesmen may be a hidden resource, which the depressed area schools have used inappropriately or not at all. Coleman reminds us that we were wrong about the educational aspirations and interests of minority groups. It also appears that we may have been wrong in excluding them from any meaningful voice in the direction of the schools their children attend.

These beginning efforts at equalizing educational opportunity will certainly not be adequate to the task. What is needed to make educational opportunity and achievement equal for all groups in our population must be the subject of extensive action and research programs. The Coleman study is a beginning, and from it flow many questions that should engage the attention of research investigators and social activists as well.

It is to be remembered that this monumental study was authorized by an act of Congress 10 years after the 1954 decision, in part because of concerns about the failure of that decision to radically change patterns of racial mix in public schools and the differences in academic achievement of different groups of children. My modest expectations have proved to be understated. The efforts at desegregation have not reduced the differentials in academic achievement between ethnic and class groups in our society. Why is this the case?

1. Differential patterns of academic achievement in a racist society are partially attributable to the racist practices of the society. The research of Nancy St. John (1975) demonstrates that rather than racial mix being a sure solution it is a complex condition, which can be bi-directional in its effects. In this important body of research she calls attention to circumstances or racial mix in which negative stereotypes concerning low status students are reinforced and negatively impact the performance of the minority students. Despite the general tendency in mixed status groups for the low status students to gravitate toward the mean of the highest status students thus raising the level of academic achievement of the minority students overall patterns of achievement for the minority students continue to lie behind those patterns established by the majority. In addition, there are extra school factors that operate against the reduction of racial isolation as in the phenomenon of "White flight" as demonstrated in the work that created conflict for Coleman (Coleman 1966). Coleman found that as previously White schools were forced to accept Black students White families withdrew from these schools. Unfortunately, Coleman was severely criticized for this line of work by people who thought that his research undercut support for school desegregation, and it probably did. However, over time Coleman was proved to be right. Since the mid 70s public schools in the United States were perhaps more segregated than they were before the 1954 decision. The racism of the society seemed not only to influence the quality of educational opportunities, but it also influence cultural patterns referable to choice of schools and the use of public schools by higher status families.

2. These differences in achievement are also class related and to the extent to which race becomes synonymous with caste status, patterns of school achievement have been demonstrated to be associated with both class and caste status. Social class moves upward academic achievement follows. This phenomenon is complex. In general, socioeconomic status (SES) is a crude but accurate predictor of academic achievement. However, as

16

achievement and or SES increase the gap between high and low status groups also increases. In Sexton's income and education we find data that show the association between school achievement and family income. So strong is this association that it has been suggested that family income is the most powerful predictor of academic achievement. When we examine the ubiquitous association between race and income we find further evidence in support of the assertion that school achievement is related to class and cast.

Throughout the most active stages of the school desegregation movement I found myself a less than enthusiastic participant and this was a source of conflict for me. I am an integrationist and believe strongly that in a democracy one's ethnic or social status should not limit one's access to get education. Yet through this struggle I had the sense that patterns of racial mix were not the solution and found myself in sympathy with Black nationalists who argued for racial separation in afro-centric schools if for no other reason but to demonstrate that Black people did not have to study with White people in order to learn.

I had other grounds for reservations concerning desegregation. Having lived my personal life in highly segregated as well as significantly integrated racial settings I had and continue to have serious reservation concerning the possibility for the achievement of racial integration in a society where race remains closely tied to economic status. In a reasonably integrated northern suburb I have observed public schools becoming the source of education for ethnic minority students while White students are congregated in private schools. When one examines the quality of pedagogy in these public schools, it becomes clear that the motive for the use of the private schools must be social isolation from low status people rather than a simple search for quality education. If access to education of high quality rest upon our capacity to racially integrate educational institutions, low status people will simply not get access to high quality education.

In my book *Human Diversity and Pedagogy* (1988), we go to great lengths to discuss some of the diverse characteristics of human learners, which could be used to inform the design of pedagogical interventions. In that collection of essays, my colleagues and I argued in favor of differentiation in the organization of learning experiences in response to the differences in learner characteristics that students bring to school. In the section on ethnicity and race we were able to establish few characteristics associated with racial identity that dictated different approaches to pedagogy. It is possible that some members of specific ethnic groups may find particular content more to their liking, but generic differences within the ethnic groups did not adhere to differences in instructional strategies. In that work, we did find differences in cognitive style, affective response tendencies, temperament, etc. This appears to have implication for one's approach to instruction. But these functional differences varied more greatly within each of the ethnic groups than between them. I was forced to conclude that using ethnicity and race as a determinant in the design of teaching and learning experiences was not supported by the science that informs our understanding of these characteristics.

Having been born in the early twentieth century, having been raised in a rural, racially segregated southern state in the United States, and having received my elementary and secondary education in the racially segregated schools of Goldsboro, North Carolina, I have an interesting perspective on issues related to racial isolation in schooling and the efforts at the desegregation of schooling. I experienced the struggle to equalize the quality of schooling available to Negro children in the days when we were trying to force the school systems in North Carolina to equalize pay for Colored and White teachers. I lived through the struggle to equalize facilities for schooling for Negro and White children. When I first studied biology, we had one microscope in our under equipped laboratory which doubled as the chemistry laboratory. Our advocates claimed that there were several microscopes in the high school that was reserved for White children. Those of us who were fortunate enough to complete 11 years of school and attend college, either went to college at the institutions of higher education that were reserved for Blacks in the state, attended historically Black colleges or went north in search of colleges that did not discriminate against Black people. Even that search was compromised by exclusion based on race. I experienced considerable shock when I applied for admission to the Divinity School at Princeton University and received a note in response indicating that the university did not admit Negro students, but that the Presbyterian Church (USA) sponsors two theological seminaries for Negro students: the Lincoln University in Oxford, PA, and the John C. Smith University in Charlotte, NC. Since I was well and supported at Howard and was subsequently admitted to continue my studies there, I did not pursue further study under the sponsorship of the Presbyterian Church. Obviously, even though the Presbyterian Church in the United States of America had separated itself from the southern section of the church over the problems of race and racism, the practice of segregation had deep roots.

The commitment to desegregation was equally deep seated in the value systems of some of our friends from the southern as well as northern states. When I first gave expression to my reservations concerning the wisdom of the decision to give primary attention to the reduction of racial isolation or to the desegregation of public schools, Gordon Foster was visibly distressed. Gordon had been one of our most vigorous defenders of the desegregation movement. He had devoted his professional career to the struggle for racial justice and being a White man, working largely in the southern USA, he had paid a price. His position on the issue had certainly cost him more than my support of the desegregation movement had cost me. Gordon fought back with everything that he had, including a new found bitterness. Not only did he think that I was wrong, but he seemed to feel that he had been betrayed by an intellectual colleague. I was aware of the fact that I was chiseling away at the very foundation of his concept of who he was, but I was struggling with the conflict between my strong political commitment to desegregation and my growing intellectual awareness that racial segregation and its associated inequalities in educational opportunities were insufficient to adequately account for the failure of our democratic society to educate adequately the diverse peoples of this nation.

There is no doubt in my mind that our efforts at the desegregation of public schools and ultimately other sectors of the society were the correct thing to do. State supported and enforced segregation by class, disability, gender, first language, race, religion or any other demographic, in my view, is wrong and inconsistent with the values of a democratic society. I do not regret the efforts or the sacrifices made on the behalf of this struggle. I do regret that the desegregation effort consumed so much of our attention that other efforts at addressing the problem of unequal and effective educational opportunities were neglected. I wish that I had been able to make that point more clearly to Gordon Foster and to other friends and colleagues who may have felt betrayed or unsupported by my expressed reservations concerning desegregation.

Fortunately for the movement, I was not a sufficiently central player to have radically changed its direction. As I recall, it would have been very difficult to change direction once the forces of support for desegregation were set into motion. Many of these forces could trace their origins to aspects of the Reconstruction period when the creation of public schools was a product of poor Blacks and Whites advocating for free public education. Civil rights advocates like Du Bois, Harrison and Randolph had built growing support for the idea that racial segregation was culpable. My friend and mentor, Kenneth B. Clark was unconditionally committed to the idea that racial isolation was dysfunctional and that racial integration was the only answer. Clark was at the epicenter of intellectual support for the movement. Then there was the judgment of legal experts that unequal access to a publicly financed and provided service like education was highly vulnerable to a constitutional test of its legality. That argument resulted in the *Brown v. Topeka* Supreme Court decision of 1954.

My final objection may be better informed by hindsight than foresight. Here at the close of my professional career I am convinced that the preoccupation with race was a mistake. From the beginning we should have given more thoughtful attention to the several factors that influence academic achievement. We should have said more about the contribution that learners and their families make to academic and personal development. I should put it in the context of my objecting to the sole emphasis on desegregation because it places too much emphasis on schooling and neglects two of Coleman's most important findings having to do with: (1) the association between family background and school achievement, and (2) the association between a student's sense of power and academic achievement. We naively believed that schooling could compensate for other factors that were missing in the educational lives of children. I have become much more open to the discussion of the possibility that some of the natural and imposed characteristics of the victims were contributing to the under productivity of these students.

I am writing now, almost 60 years after the U.S. Supreme Court ruled that racially segregated public schools are unconstitutional. Many of us then thought that the decision would make a difference in educational opportunities and outcomes for ethnic minorities. Following modest gains in 1970 and 1980s academic achievement for minority group students has settled into an estimated one standard deviation gap between their performance indicators and those of Asian American and European American Students. Why has the education establishment consistently been ineffective in closing the achievement gap?

I think that we may have been in error in the way we conceptualized the problem. I think that one of the problems has to do with the fact that for many years we have thought of the academic achievement gap as a primarily racial problem. Too many people were comfortable explaining the gap as the result of differences that had to do with genetics; others thought that the gap had to do with racism and racial discrimination; some argued that the achievement gap is more related to socioeconomic status and the disproportionate number of people of color who suffer from low income. However, as important as are SES and income, it is not a sufficient or adequate explanation of the problem. In fact, data indicate that the size of the gap increases as we go up the scale regarding income and achievement. The gap is bigger at the higher income levels where Black students with one parent who has a college degree achieve at a comparable level of White students with a parent who has a high school diploma. These data also show that middle class status for Blacks does not produce the same level of academic achievement as does middle class status for White students (Miller 1995). This is an anomaly that James Coleman reported 44 years ago in a much-neglected part of the 1966 Report.

These differences that appear to be associated with race and SES are important, but they contributed to interventions that were misdirected at class and racial mix in public education and the neglect of a direct attack upon guaranteed access to education of high quality.

First, in the talk that I gave on the 50th anniversary of the 1954 Supreme Court decision concerning the desegregation of schools, I suggested that as important as our attack on segregated schooling was to the society, it may have been a setback for education, because it prevented us from thinking more about the nature of education of high quality. In other words, the Supreme Court decision may have given the impression that solving the problem of racial separation would solve the problem of access to education of high quality. The reality that the data shows is that even in the most racially integrated schools we are still having problems of an academic achievement gap. The opportunity to focus our attention on race may have taken us away from the opportunity to focus on problems of pedagogy.

Second, I think that we have concentrated on schooling to the neglect of the broad complex of educative forces that influence the development of intellective competence. John Dewey (1920), early in the 20th century, and Lawrence Cremin (1975), later in that century, talked about what we now call comprehensive approaches to education or thinking comprehensively about education. Heather Weiss (2009) prefers to call it complementary education and I edited a book in which I called it supplementary education, but all of us are referring to the effective orchestration of the wide range of influences, opportunities and resources by which teaching and learning are enabled and occur. We are looking at the relationships of learning and teaching that occur out-of-school such as health, nutrition, childcare practices, cultural practices in the community and home, expectations, and other supports for academic development to the effectiveness of the teaching and learning that occur in school. Bourdieu (1986) has referred to these resources as education relevant forms of capital that can be invested in education. These are forces that are not under the control of school. Despite this line of thought, throughout the twentieth century and now in the twenty-first century with a radically different approach to national governance, the main focus of intervention addressed at the reduction of the academic achievement gap is focused on school reform.

I think that we cannot afford to get too far away from quality of schooling and especially the quality of the teaching persons to whom students are exposed. Good schools and good teaching are tremendously important! But schooling while necessary may not be sufficient. Since the school reform movement started in 1950 we have achieved some gains in the access to schooling of higher quality. We cannot deny that we have seen some advances in the processes and technologies of instruction. Between 1950 and 1980 we even saw some gains in academic achievement but we have not seen significant gains in the reduction of the academic achievement gap. Obviously there are limits to school reform as the solution.

As I read things today, there are things that happen in our society that enable schools to work and I think that those things are related to what the French philosopher Pierre Bourdieu calls education relevant forms of capital. I have referred to this position. In his use of this construct, Bourdieu goes beyond the specific forms of education relevant capital to talk about "habitus," which I translate to mean attitude, disposition, view of life, a way of thinking, a habit of mind. What he is suggesting is that when one has the privilege of the access to those resources for education and living, one develops the disposition and capacity to use one's self in the interest of the self and in the support of others. It is an approach to life that my colleague Albert Bandura at Stanford University has called "agency." Coleman's sense of personal power is not unrelated, when one's access to those forms of education relevant capital is insufficient it may get in the way of the effectiveness of schooling because the lack of access reduces the quality of habitus—interferes with the development of sense of power—locus of control and human agency. We have not addressed that issue in our efforts to close the achievement gap and we have certainly failed to address this issue in our efforts for school reform.[2]

Education programs may have been too sharply focused in the improvement of schools. I don't want to take anything away from that effort because I think that improving our schools is very important, but I believe that parallel to this effort

---

2. This is a current theme in my career.

there must be increased attention and support for better enabling families and communities to support the academic and personal development of their children. I have begun to talk of parent involvement not so much as parent involvement in the activities of the school but as parents' *engagement in the active support of the academic and personal development of their children.* This will be reflected in what parents do at home with respect to the distractions of TV; what they do in their faith-based institutions; what they do for summer vacation, or field trips, or travel of any sort; and more important, the kinds of conversations that they have at home; the way in which they feed their children; and the kind of people to which they expose their children. It will be reflected in the opportunities for self-expression and guided self-reflection.

Going back to my comment about the relationship of education to the civil right struggle, I think that in a way we have focused on education of high quality as a civil right. A democratic and humane society must ensure adequate education as a basic right of all citizens. But we have neglected the civil liberties with respect to education. We have taken education as a right of citizenship but it is also a liberty of citizenship. As I see the difference, education and learning as a civil right is something that the society does for and to people while education as a civil liberty is something that one does for one's self with the help of others. This means that the society must continue to provide a safety net under the existence of all children, but it must also provide scaffolds on which our children can climb. Scaffolds that enable them to engage in the affairs of the society and that encourage them to learn, to explore, and to seek out for new answers to old and new questions. Jim Comer pointed in this direction when he wrote a very provocative little book, *Waiting for a Miracle: Why Schools Cannot Solve Our Problems and How We Can.* Jim argues that we cannot wait for schools, working alone, to solve this problem. It is a problem of the people and we the people have to solve.

My colleagues and I are currently working with a group of institutions in the New York area to try to give meaning and meaningful practice to this concern. We are doing some work with the Harlem Children's Zone, the Thurgood Marshall Academy, the Eagle Academy for Young Men and the New York Urban League to open Comprehensive Education Resource Centers that have as their primary task the promotion of opportunities for teaching and learning that occur outside of school to complement what happens inside of school. The centers will provide information concerning and access to resources in areas such as health, nutrition, reading and talking with the children, modeling behavior for children, setting reasonable expectations and standards for children, and more important, teaching parents how to actively support the academic and personal development of their children. The core of this Resource Center is concerned with its being a facility in low income communities that teaches parents how to best use the schools and the other education resources available in their communities.

Back in the mid 1950s, my mentor Dr. Wilkerson and I found in a group of mothers in Harlem unrealistically high aspirations for their children's academic development. We concluded that they had high aspirations for their children's educational development but they had low levels of knowledge and skills with respect to how these aspirations into behaviors and experiences would enable children to reach these goals. In 1999 to 2000, the proportion of associate degrees earned by Blacks was greater than the proportion of bachelor's degrees earned by Blacks. Nearly one-quarter of all bachelor's degrees earned by Blacks in 1999 were earned at historically Black colleges and universities. The proportion of Blacks completing college increased between 1975 and 2000; however Blacks still remained less likely than Whites to earn degrees. In 1999, Black instructional faculty in colleges and universities were more likely to be assistant professors than professors or associate professors.

Perhaps, most troublesome is the fact that significant gaps in academic achievement continue to exist between Asian American and European American students on one hand, and students who identify themselves as African American, Latin a/o and Native American. This is the problem that we at the College Board brought to national attention in the 1999 report, *Reaching the Top*.

The problem is especially acute in the sciences and engineering, African American students earned 12,149 bachelor's degrees in Social Science; 4,851 degrees in Biological/Life Sciences; and 4,324 degrees in Engineering for the school-year 2000-2001 (American Council on Education's *Minorities in Higher Education,* 2002-2003. *Twentieth Annual Status Report,* 2003). The figures are even more alarming on the graduate level. With respect to doctoral degrees, African Americans earned only 80 degrees in Physical Science; 190 degrees in Life Science; 299 degrees in Social Science; and 82 degrees in Engineering (American Council on Education's *Minorities in Higher Education,* 2002-2003. *Twentieth Annual Status Report,* 2003). These figures are cause for concern in light of the fact that African American students represent approximately 11 percent of all students enrolled in higher education (American Council on Education's *Minorities in*

Higher Education, 1999-2000. *Seventeenth Annual Status Report,* 2000).

This reality is of particular concern not just for the gifted and talented African American students who do not persist and graduate in the sciences, but also for higher education and the nation, which increasingly privileges those skills and intellective competencies required for meaningful participation in an advanced technological society. These intellective competencies include the ability to bring order to the chaos created by information overload; the ability to reason; uncover relationships between phenomena; and use comparison, context, intent and values in arriving at judgments. Such competencies are respected and sought after in both technologically developed and underdeveloped societies. Indeed, the capacity to function effectively in these domains is the essence of intellective competence, increasingly the universal currency in technologically advanced societies.

LIMITATIONS OF BROWN AND SINGLE ISSUE PUBLIC POLICY

Almost 55 years have passed since the *Brown v. Topeka* decision of 1954, but it is obvious that despite this celebrated decision excellence and equity in educational opportunity and achievement have not been achieved. Despite the enormous gains for our society from the emphasis on racial justice in the *Brown* case and the Civil Rights movement, the attack on racism was a necessary but insufficient solution to the problem of conjoining excellence and equity in education. If the goals were equal access to excellent educational opportunities and equal representation among those who achieve academic excellence, the *Brown* Decision was insufficient and possibly targeted on the wrong variable. Consider for a moment the possibility that W. E. B. Du Bois may have been correct. I recall his arguing in one of his talks that among the destructive things that White America has done to Black people was to get our attention so focused on race that the dominant society has been free to run away with the entire store. In our focus on race, racial isolation and segregation, we have ignored the possibility that the problem may be caste and its concomitant constraints on access to the educationally relevant forms of capital that appear to be correlates of high academic achievement. In the distraction created by the focus on race, we have neglected the also necessary work on the redistribution of access to capital or the deliberate compensation for the absence of such access. The framing of the problem of inequality in education as due to the segregation of the races, I believe, led us to ignore:

- The declining significance of discrete social divisions like ethnicity and gender for policy decisions in societies experiencing the advanced stages of capitalism;
- Du Bois' shift from his primary focus on the "color line" as the problem of the 20th century to his focus on the division of the world's population between the haves and the have nots;
- William Julius Wilson's claim for "The Declining Significance of Race" (Wilson, 1978);
- Bordieu's iteration of the forms of education relevant capital necessary for investment in education and other human resource development enterprises, such as, cultural, fiscal, health, human, and social capitals (Bordieu, 1986), and polity capital Miller (1995);
- James Coleman's (1990), Gerald Jaynes' and Robin Williams' (1989), Frances Pliven's (1971) and Patricia Sexton's (1969) findings showing the association between family income (SES) and academic achievement; and
- Richard Wolf's (1966) and Jane Mercer's (1973) findings concerning the association between family environmental supports for academic learning and quality of academic achievement. Achievement tests data that indicate increases in academic achievement, despite ethnic identity, when quality of life and opportunity to learn are improved.

The affirmative development of intellective competence and academic ability is most universally accorded expression. Intellective competence the universal currency of technologically advanced societies; I take the position that the competencies of critical literacy and orality referenced above, enable the achievement of intellective competence, which I define as developed abilities and dispositions to perceive critically, to explore widely, to bring rational order to chaos, to bring knowledge and technique to bear on the solution of problems, to test ideas against explicit and considered moral values and against empirical data, and to recognize and create real and abstract relationships between concrete and imaginary phenomena. In other words, intellective competence essentially reflects the effective orchestration of affective, cognitive and situative mental processes in the service of sense making and problem solving. These achievements are less focused on what we want learners to know and know how to do, and are more sharply focused on what it is that we want learners to become and be, i.e., compassionate and thinking interdependent members of humane human communities.

I use *intellective* to distinguish our concerns—the variety of cognitive, affective, situative and emotional processes that are integral to daily functioning and problem solving—from both *intelligent* and *intellectual* behavior. I worry that the term *intelligent* is too closely associated with *intelligence,* which is too often thought of as that which is measured by IQ tests. Intellectual behavior seems too easily confused with the work or habits of intellectuals and professional scholars. How then, can we begin to frame the construct intellective competence? We can start by defining pedagogy as the "art and science of teaching." This definition is not incorrect, but it is narrower than the conception we choose to advance. We prefer to think of pedagogy (inclusive of teaching, learning and assessment) as dialectical and transactive components of a maieutic process that enables the development of intellective competence.

From my perspective, "to teach" is to enable and empower through directed learning experiences, guided exploration, structured problem and question posing, mediated problem solving and explicated modeling of examples. In contrast to earlier notions of teaching as primarily involving the transfer of knowledge, skills and values, our perspective casts the teacher as guide, as coach, as model, and as resource person who respects the fact that learning is something that one does for oneself and cannot be done for the student by someone else. Our reference to learning is bi-focal, and references the assimilation and accommodation of that which is old, and the active construction and integration of that which is new. While not rejecting the traditional emphasis on such processes as attending to, associating, memorizing and retrieving other people's data, our vision of human learning privileges situative social processes that require constructive, hermeneutic and transformative engagement, by learning persons, with data that are or become one's own—no matter the source.

AFFIRMATIVE ACTION AND AFFIRMATIVE DEVELOPMENT

Until recently, our society has accepted the assignment of preferential treatment to designated categories of persons as special rewards for service to the nation, as compensation for unusual prior disadvantage, or simply as the entitlement associated with one's status. These various forms of affirmative action are currently under increased attack largely because of their public and colloquial association with minority group membership privilege. In all candor, affirmative

27

action is also under attack because of abuses in its practice. Instead of an effort to ensure that qualified persons are not disqualified because of ethnicity or gender, affirmative action is often perceived as a program to privilege "unqualified" persons over those who are "qualified." The preoccupation with race may be a part of the problem. In a racist society all social arrangements are designed to reflect racist values. And explicit efforts to subvert those values are bound to come up against open resistance.

I propose a few adjustments. Rather than targeting ethnic or gender groups for affirmative action, I propose targeting larger and more diverse groups: those that are low on wealth and wealth-derived capital resources. Education and employment opportunities could be regarded as instruments of human resource development rather than agencies for the credentialing and rewarding of the "ablest." Rather than protecting the opportunity to enter, let us ensure the opportunity to develop and qualify. In addition to a program of affirmative action, we are proposing a program of affirmative development.

The largest affirmative action effort in the history of the USA was our veterans' preference program. This was also an affirmative development program. The components of that program ensured that veterans had ample opportunities to improve their economic, education and health status. They were a protected group with respect to vocational skills development and employment. They were assisted in the acquisition of wealth through subsidized business and home ownership. The social ethos even gave them privileged positions in the political arena where they were enabled to access political capital through the jingoistic and patriotic biases of the populists. This national effort may have begun as a reward for service in the nation's defense establishment, but in reality it was a massive human resource development endeavor that positioned the nation's labor force for the economic and technological expansions of the latter half of the twentieth century. The affirmative development of the nation's underdeveloped human resources proved to be in the best interest of the entire United States.

THE AFFIRMATIVE DEVELOPMENT OF ACADEMIC ABILITY

Almost 75 years ago, Du Bois (1940) warned against the neglect of gifted and talented minority students. Current attention, however, is primarily focused on the overrepresentation of minorities on the left end of the academic achievement distribution to the neglect of those on the right end. These problems include a persistent gap between minority and majority students, in general; a larger gap between high achieving minority and high achieving majority students; and the tendency of traditional indicators of high academic achievement to over-predict the subsequent academic achievement of many minority students. These often ignored findings were first reported by Coleman in Equality of Educational Opportunity (1966) and in the 1980s and 1990s by Willingham (1985), Durán, (1983) and Ramist, Lewis, & McCamley-Jenkins (1994).

The National Task Force on Minority High Achievement concluded that these problems require a national effort at the affirmative development of academic ability. Academic ability is one expression of human intellective competence that, increasingly, is recognized as the universal currency of societies that are technologically advanced. Academic ability references such capabilities as:

- Critical literacy and numeracy;
- Mathematical and verbal reasoning;
- Creating, recognizing, and resolving relationships;
- Classification of information and stimulus material;
- Problem solving from both abstract and concrete situations as in deductive and inductive reasoning;
- Sensitivity to multiple contexts and perspectives;
- Accessing and managing disparate bodies and chunks of information;
- Resource recognition and utilization (help-seeking); and
- Self-regulation (including meta-cognitive competence and meta-componential strategies).

Such capabilities appear to be the products of exposure to the demands of specialized cultural experiences—schooling being the most common—that interact with a wide variety of human potentials (Cole & Scribner, 1974; Cole, Gay, Glick, & Sharp, 1971; Hunt, 1966; Martinez, 2002; Sternberg, 1994). We therefore conclude that academic ability is a developed ability—the quality of which is not primarily a function of one's biological endowment or fixed aptitudes. With the recognition of academic ability as a developed ability, The Study Group on the Affirmative Development of Academic Ability begins with the assumption that closing the gap in academic achievement between groups of students from different social divisions (class, ethnicity, gender and language) will require the affirmative development of such ability in a wide range of individuals through certain interventions in our homes, communities, and schools.

THE MAJOR FINDINGS OF THE STUDY GROUP

Access to various forms of education related capital to be invested in the educational and personal development of the learner. Among these forms of capital that appear to be foundational to academic success are: cultural; financial; health and nutritional; human; institutional; polity; and social capital (Bourdieu, 1986; Bridglall & Gordon, in press):

1. Feelings of trust in the institution in which one is learning and in those who seem to represent the interests of that institution (administrators, staff and especially teachers) (Bryk, 2002; Steele & Aronson, 2000; Mendoza-Denton & Aronson, in press).

2. Early and continuing exposure to pleasurable and progressively more rigorous learning experiences that are relevant to the knowledge, skills and understandings that are part of the repertoire of educated persons. Bloom's Developing Exceptional Talent (1976); Equity 2000, Everson and Dunham (1996); Hunt (1966).

3. Effort and time devoted to and engaged in learning tasks that are relevant to the tasks to be mastered (Carroll, 1989; Resnick, 1987; Lee, in press).

4. Engagement through the processes of academic learning, of the learner's preconceived notions about how the world works and the integration of those ideas into evolving conceptual beliefs that are more like the models being taught (Bransford, Brown, & Cocking, 1999; Lee, in press; Cauce, in press).

5. Acquisition of a deep foundation of factual knowledge, in the context of conceptual frames that enable the organization of knowledge in ways that facilitate retrieval and application (Bransford, Brown, & Cocking, 1999; Lee, in press; Everson & Renzulli, in press; Greeno, 1991).

6. The development of meta-cognitive and meta-componential competencies, and agentic behaviors and dispositions that are focused on academic learning (Flavell, 1979; Sternberg, 1994;

Bandura, 2001; Bridglall & Gordon, in press; Greeno, 1991).

7. Opportunities to engage in teaching and learning encounters that are grounded in one's zone of proximal development—a point just beyond the learner's zone of learning comfort or current level of mastery—combined with guidance in the utilization of instructional scaffolding of the new material to be learned (Vygotsky, 1978; Lee, in press).

8. Engagement in the exchange of distributed knowledge that is made available through cooperative and expeditionary learning in which the learner is encouraged to think about and evaluate what is being experienced (Fullilove &,Treisman, 1990; Cauce, in press; Greeno, 1991).

9. Socialization to and/or explication (giving emphasis to) of the unique demands of scholarly work, and repeated exposures to exemplars of the standards that are operative (Forgione, 1998; Gordon, 1999; Cauce, in press).

10. Access to a wide range of supplementary education experiences that support both intellective and social competencies (Gordon, Bridglall & Meroe, in press; Steinberg, 1996).

11. The politicization of academic learning in the lives of minority student learners so that they can more readily see that academic learning is compatible with the ends that they seek. Learning task engagement, time on task and resource utilization are seen as being related to such compatibility (E.T. Gordon, in press; Ianni, 1989).

12. Freedom to concentrate on academic tasks without constant concern about the relationship between one's cultural identity and 'prejudice apprehension' or 'stereotype confirmation (Gordon & Armour-Thomas, 1991; Steele & Aaronson, 1995; Mendez-Denton & Aronson, in press).

SCIENCE AND HUMAN SOCIETIES

The findings of the Study Group on the Affirmative Development of Academic Ability represent but a sampling of the rich knowledge base that is available to inform public policy and professional practice concerning education. Thanks to the education research community, this knowledge base, increasingly, is readily available but under utilized. None of us believe that extant policies, practices and resources relative to education are adequate or are the best that we can do. At a recent meeting of the National Academy of Education we heard several critiques of the No Child Left Behind Education Act. Criticisms of the general status of education in our nation are ubiquitous. It may be time for those of us who identify with the education research community to emulate Kenneth Clark, Isidor Chein, Stewart Cook and their colleagues. It may be time for us to lock arms with civil and human rights activist, and with them to go back into the courts to assert and defend excellence and equity in education as a civil right.

The challenge to those of us who produce knowledge and utilize it in our professional practice is to find ways to honor in our daily personal, professional and public lives such cardinal values of our profession as agency based on knowledge, technique, judgment, reason, and justice. Given the distortion of information and the corruption of power that we see from the top to the bottom of leadership in our society, I offer a new banner for our campaign—in education, domestic affairs and foreign relations ignorance and misinformation are not tolerable options in public policy or professional practice.

2
Compensatory Education

I could take some unjustified pride in my having written forty-six years ago the concluding chapter in Doxey A. Wilkerson's and my book on Compensatory Education. It is an assessment that could have been written today. For that reason it is included in my memoir. Much of what I wrote in 1966 remains true to or appropriate for 2012. I think the fact that this is the case is much less a credit for Edmund W. Gordon than it is a demerit for the field of education and the society that has enabled, and maybe even encouraged this lack of progress. The chapter is reprinted here as it appeared when the book *Compensatory Education: Preschool through College* was published in 1966.

A Critique of Compensatory Education

If the success of our efforts at facilitating the educational development of disadvantaged youngsters could be evaluated simply on the basis of the amount of enthusiasm and activity generated by those efforts, we would at once declare the majority of the programs studied successful. As was the case with the much-heralded Project Head Start, the wide acceptance of the idea, the involvement of many segments of the community, and the political momentum building lip behind such efforts, combine to give the impression of success. In communities large and small, in schools public and private, in preschool, elementary school, high school and college, and in graduate and professional institutions all across the nation, we find grow¬ing concern reflected in special projects directed at the disadvantaged.

It appears at first glance that the efforts directed at desegregating our schools and improving educational opportunities for children from low-income families have resulted in important and impressive modifications in the work of our schools. A wide variety of ideas for improving the effectiveness of the school has been advanced, hardly anyone of which has not received at least a degree of consideration and trial in some school system during the past few years. In fact, there are some school systems in which practically every serious proposal has been tried with some group of its pupils.

Problems in Program Evaluation

The appropriateness of a practice or the success of a program cannot be adequately judged from the enthusiasm with which it is embraced or the speed with which the practice spreads. Educational innovation, unfortunately, has too long a history of approaching evaluation and decision making on such an inadequate basis. At the very least, evaluation of compensatory education would seem to require a precise description of the newly Introduced educational practices. Of the specific conditions under which they are initiated, and of the populations to whom they are applied; the careful Identification of target population and of appropriate control groups for whom specified criterion measures are established; and the collection and analysis of data appropriate to the measures identified. Despite the almost landslide acceptance of the compensatory education commitment, we find nowhere an effort at evaluating these innovations that approaches the criteria suggested. Where evaluative studies have been conducted, the reports typically show ambiguous outcomes affecting unknown or amorphous educational and social variables.

This unhappy circumstance is likely to encourage premature and contradictory educational planning and decision-making. On the one hand, apparent but meager gains by pupils in pilot projects may give rise to unduly optimistic interpretations, thus encouraging extensive long-term commitment to compensatory programs whose validity has not yet been established. On the other hand, lack of clear evidence that certain programs or practices are improving pupils' development to any significant degree may strengthen tendencies toward their abandonment, and even toward repudiation of the entire compensatory education effort. Neither of these reactions is warranted. It is clear beyond doubt that special problems exist in relation to the education of many children from disadvantaged backgrounds. It is also clear that some of these children are helped immensely by the special efforts of our schools. It is not yet clear exactly what helps which youngsters under what conditions. We do not know why certain practices that seem logically correct do not work. We have yet to determine which aspects of some of our more elaborate programs actually account for the reported changes. There remain unanswered critical questions related to motivation and to the reversibility of learning disabilities, which arise from deprivations in experience. Some of these questions may be approached theoretically. For others, which must be examined empirically, answers may be sought from a critical review of our current experiences in compensatory education.

Assessing the Major Developments and Trends

Viewed as a group, current compensatory programs are surprisingly recent. Of 76 programs for which starting dates were available, 93 percent were begun since 1960, and 43 percent just since 1963. Relatively few of them have been set up on a controlled experimental basis to determine whether specific innovations result in improved school performance; however, a number of them are concerned with the total effect of a multiphase program on the target population. For all their variety of means, the programs have generally suffered from one fundamental difficulty—they are based on sentiment rather than on fact. Or, at best, those facts on which they are based are the obvious ones: that a population exists which is not able to benefit from the education being served up by the schools, that that population has certain common characteristics (the programs are less likely to be sensitive to the differences) among which are low reading ability, low general school achievement, low interest and motivation level, poor health status, and so forth. The great majority of the programs are simply an attempt to "do something" about these problems. Their stated aims are usually couched in unarguable generalities, "to raise achievement level," "to raise the sights of the students," "to enlarge the students' horizons," or "to awaken parents to the value of an education." The urge to do something has been so compelling that many of the programs have been designed without grounding in any systematic study of ends and means.

It is not inappropriate that the programs of special education for the disadvantaged have been described as compensatory. They are attempts to compensate for, or to overcome, the effects of hostile, different, or indifferent backgrounds. Their aim is to bring children from these backgrounds up to a level where they can be reached by existing educational

35

practices. And it is in terms of this aim that we tend to judge their success or lack of it. A compensatory program in the seventh grade would be held successful if it enabled its participants to move into a "regular" eight-grade program. Or, to cite another example, if preschool programs in general might measure their success by how well their graduates adjusted to traditional kindergarten and first-grade activities. In other words, the unexpressed purpose of most compensatory programs is to make disadvantaged children as much as possible like the kinds of children with whom the school has been successful, and our standard of educational success is how well they approximate middle-class children in school performance. It is not at all clear that the concept of compensatory education is one to most appropriately meet the problems of the disadvantaged. These children are not middle-class children, many of them never will be, and they can never be anything but second-rate as long as they are thought of as potentially middle-class children. (They may become middle-class adults, however, and some certainly have middle-class aspirations.) At best they are different, and an approach that views this difference merely as something to be overcome is probably doomed to failure. What is needed is not so much an attempt to fill in the gaps as an approach that asks the question: What kind of educational experience is most appropriate to what these children are and to what our society is becoming?

Once this question has been posed, it brings into focus the really crucial issue, that is, the matter of whom we are trying to change. We have tended until now to concentrate our efforts on the children. Unwilling to abandon what we think we have learned about teaching through our years of educating, with some success, the children of the middle-and upper-classes, we have tried adding and multiplying our existing techniques to arrive at a formula for success with less privileged children. We have tried to help them by giving them more of what we already know how to do-more guidance, more remedial reading, more vocational information, more enrichment activities. We have said to these children, "We will prepare you for our school system, we will help you to catch up when you fall behind, we will show you the kinds of lives other kinds of children already know about, and if you get discouraged and drop out we will try our best to get you back." But what we have not said is, "We will take you as you are, and ourselves assume the burden of finding educational techniques appropriate to your needs." We have asked of them a degree of change far greater than any that we as educators have been willing to make in our own institutions.

It seems significant, for example, that so much of the current work in the education of the disadvantaged has been directed either at preschool children or at youngsters who have dropped out of high school, while so little attention has been given to investigating the overall appropriateness of contemporary educational processes. If school people were not such a decent lot, one would think that these two emphases have been so widely accepted simply because they require the least change in the school itself. It is often easier to add extensions than to change the basic structure of institutions.

There are, of course, logical arguments to support the preschool emphasis. There is no question that children who grow up under different life conditions are likely to show different developmental patterns. Unless experiential input has been designed to produce the same learning readiness end, such readiness will vary. Consequently, it is not inappropriate to assume that children coming from privileged homes enter school with skills and competences different from those of children from less privileged homes. And since all these children, despite the differences present upon entry, must meet common academic standards, the disadvantaged child, it is argued, needs special remedial or enrichment experiences in order to better cope with the traditional school requirements.

Following the logic of this position, educational programs for nursery school-age children from disadvantaged backgrounds have gained wide acceptance, this despite the fact of early evidence suggesting that there is little value in the nursery or preschool educational experience in the absence of continuity and consistent high quality for the nursery, kindergarten, and primary grades experience. Special program gains seem to wash out in the absence of subsequent school experiences that build upon the head start.

The preschool movement, strengthened by massive federal support since the initiation of Project Head Start in the summer of 1965, has become one of the major forces in the nation's war against poverty and in the school's effort at meeting the educational problems of disadvantaged youngsters. The quickly organized national push, however, is not likely to do as well as its experimental precursors, for many of these programs do not consistently meet the needs of the children they enroll. While they rarely fail to provide an atmosphere that is warm and accepting, they are not always as successful in providing an atmosphere that offers psychological support to each child—some of whose needs may run more to order, firmness, and discipline than to a free, unstructured atmosphere and uncritical warmth. Preschool classes, more than any other compensatory programs, have often been started and staffed by ardent, well-meaning but untrained armatures—a shortage of well-trained, professional teachers at the preschool level being only one facet of a personnel shortage that haunts all phases of compensatory educational programs. These amateurs bring to their work many virtues and some skills, but not among them frequently arc the specific techniques for providing the kind of directed pre-academic experiences that will really equip these disadvantaged youngsters to start and move ahead in school. Although relatively little is known about the specific kinds of experiences that are most effective in encouraging language development and language acquisition, certainly more is known than is being widely utilized. Experimental programs that test the efficacy of new approaches to concept formation, to the acquisition of learning set, to the wider utilization of symbols, and so forth, are vital to provide us with continuing insights into the types of activities that should be included in a truly effective preschool program.

Certainly, as advocates of public education, we should welcome this downward extension of public education to include the three-to-five-year aids. However, we should be unprepared to accept this downward extension as a substitute for new, different, and greater effort in those school grades that are now traditional. It is also somewhat arbitrary in the light of some of the work of Piaget and Hunt, to settle for intervention at the third year of life and not at the eighteenth month or during the first year of life. If we are serious about the importance of early encounters with the environment, it may be that we must take greater collective responsibility for influencing life experience from birth and even for controlling the quality of the physical environment before birth. It is unlikely however that our society will be ready for the revolutionary social changes involved in this kind of commitment for a good many years to come.

If preschool programs represent the earliest intervention we have yet become involved with, dropout programs represent the last intervention of the school into the lives of these youth. Unfortunately, their very lateness

38

.

mitigates against their success. Where dropout programs operate on the junior high school level—and are really special educational programs modified to suit particular children rather than anti-dropout programs—they are more likely to be effective. Because the sad fact is that a high school dropout, or a young person who is simply waiting impatiently in school to reach the age when he can drop out, tends to be a youth for whom school has represented perennial failure. If when he drops out of school he does not find a job—which is most likely—his failure has been compounded. It seems highly unlikely that such a youth, lured back to school by the understanding advice of a guidance counselor, has any greater basis for success, whatever the concessions made by the school, than he had when he left. Nothing significant has happened to change his estimate of school, of education, of life, or of himself. Furthermore, in the case of minority group youngsters, the opportunity structure of the job market is, as they often know, such as to make their education almost irrelevant. Negro and Puerto Rican youngsters who graduated from high school were shown in one study to be earning, on the average, only about $5 a week more, seven years after graduation, than those who had dropped out. In addition, the lifetime earnings of Negro college graduates are about equal to those of White high school graduates. This is, of course, if they are employed at all. As one researcher commented, "We are almost in the position of counseling them to stay in school so that they can become unemployed high school graduates." Obviously the answer to the dropout problem lies far back along the educational track—back in grammar school and kindergarten where the failures begin. But for those who have passed through the system and come, frustrated, embittered, demoralized, and uneducated, out the other end, the answer would seem to lie in somehow providing them with experiences in formal education and work from which they can gain both a sense of personal responsibility and a sense of personal success. From such experiences, eventually, they may also gain the courage and motivation to face their previous areas of failure and so resume their commitment to learning. The weakness of so many of the dropout programs that have tried to do just this is that they have been unable, through no particular fault of their own, to provide meaningful work for meaningful pay to the youths they are trying to help. Of even greater significance, however, is the failure of the school to identify those approaches to curriculum content and organization that take into account the special learning problems of persons who are essentially adult but developmentally handicapped. Simple or complex changes in schedule, changes in sequence of material presentation, and changes in the quality or quantity of material presented are inadequate. If we succeed in holding these young people in school or in attracting them back to formal learning situations, and they learn only that we have not yet developed the capability to insure that they achieve literacy, concept mastery, and ability to utilize new knowledge, we cannot claim success for anti-dropout programs.

Even if the school succeeds in combining remunerative work and more appropriate formal learning experiences, it will, unfortunately, not have totally met the problems of potential school dropouts and ex-dropouts. Substantial modifications must indeed be made in curriculum material, content, and methods, but significant innovations will also be required in the job market. Work and formal learning have yet to be integrated in the development of new jobs—including those at the pre-professional or sub-professional level—which provide for upward mobility by making automatic provision for continued training. To settle as so many programs do, for jobs—any jobs—is not only inadequate but also uneconomical and basically dishonest. What do we gain when we invest training and placement resources in solutions that only postpone for a few months or a year the long-term problems of career development? To lure a youngster back into school and to train him for a vanishing job, to place him in that job and to claim that we have been successful, may contribute to the statistical success of a project, but makes no real contribution to the solution of the problems of young adults who drop out or do poorly in school. Programs that follow such practices, and many dropout programs do, are simply practicing rank deception.

It is entirely possible that a successful attack upon the problems of school dropouts and unemployable youth will require not so much a greater effort directed at these young people, but a greater effort at identifying for them and facilitating their assumption of roles in the fiber of our society that have meaning. We know from the rehabilitative influence of military experience on some of these youths that there is a tremendous potential for development and productivity latent in this population. The individual behavior traditionally associated with stability and upward mobility is likely to be most easily achieved as a by-product of involvement in activities on which society places importance and for which it offers tangible rewards. One possible answer might be a Peace Corps or a National Service Corps less oriented. Than the present Peace Corps toward the altruistic concerns of middle-class young adults—an organization in which the pay is good, in which the work is challenging, and in which membership commands respect. Such a corps would come closer to answering the needs of these young people whose conditions of life leave them with little interest in volunteer community service. And, finally, it may not even be sufficient to the problems presented by this segment of the population to provide good pay for respected work. Because these young people tend to be alienated from the values and goals professed by the society at large, it may also be necessary that their work and their opportunities for education and self advancement be directly related to influencing the political social power structure. One of the characteristics of earlier periods in our nation's history when uneducated and alienated people succeeded in the system was the fact that opportunities then existed for these newcomers to move into and influence the power structure of the communities in which they settled. The work they did paid off not only in terms of money, but also in terms of homes, communities, institutions, businesses, and industries in which they had gained or could aspire to varying degrees of control. In other words, the work and the rewards were not artificial, and although they were also not guaranteed, they at least had meaning in a relatively open opportunity structure. It may be that what is critically missing from our programs for unemployable youth is any realistic opportunity for their participation in the decision making processes that control their lives. To provide this opportunity, society may have to reexamine some of its basic economic and political tenets which have thus far precluded consideration of more radical approaches to the creation of new—and the rehabilitation of old—institutions, industries, and communities.

In the last few years it has become an acknowledged fact that teaching the disadvantaged is a specialized task. It cannot be left only to the newest teachers, who may have no choice in their assignments, nor to the older teachers, "left over" in the center-city schools after the pupils whom they knew how to teach have gone elsewhere. The growing recognition of this fact is evidenced by the degree to which teacher training and retraining projects figure in programs of compensatory education. Unfortunately, it is doubtful that any short-range orientation or in-service teacher training courses will move us far toward the long-range goal of providing satisfactory levels of instruction in disadvantaged schools. This is so because the problem of staffing "unpopular" schools is merely the most difficult aspect of an already difficult problem—an overall shortage of qualified personnel. Much of what has been written about teaching the disadvantaged has been written as if such a shortage did not exist. It is all very well to talk about screening teachers for their attitudinal suitability to teach in depressed area schools, but the fact is that in many communities there is almost no one to screen. It may be theoretically sound to propose the effective reduction of classroom size by assigning highly trained and specialized personnel to problem schools, but the fact is that before we can begin to multiply classrooms by reducing their size, we will have to get teachers into the classrooms we now have. This personnel problem is one that time will only intensify. By the early 1970s, one-third of the population will probably be in our educational system somewhere between kindergarten and graduate school. We are going to need teachers to manage all these classrooms and, without some concerted effort on the part of educators and of society in general, it is highly unlikely that we will have them.

Even if we had an unlimited pool of willing candidates from which to choose, we would still have no assurance that we could put into depressed area classrooms teachers qualified to provide the kinds of educational experiences these children need. Training programs have invested time and money in improving teacher competence and teacher behavior but neither research nor practice has yet provided definite guidelines as to what should be emphasized in such training. When Koenigsberg studied teachers who were thought by their administrators to be successful with disadvantaged children, she found no objective evidence of their superiority in this area. Some programs stress the human relations approach, but in our own investigations of this area, we have observed allegedly good teachers who, judged by colloquial standards, seemed to be lacking in the traditional human relation traits like warmth, support, and sympathy. Other programs stress understanding the culture and values of the poor. Yet we know that a good bit of this "awareness of the child's background" gets distorted into gossip about the number of men with whom their mothers sleep, and is seldom reflected in significantly changed teacher attitudes.

42

There is more than adequate justification for concern with the problems of teacher attitude. Unfortunately, much of this concern is expressed in suggestions that teachers be warm, accepting, supportive, non punitive, and so forth, while insufficient attention has been given to the value of an attitude of positive expectation—the expectation that these children can learn, and that teacher activity and curricular design can be effective in the teaching-learning process. There is increasing evidence that the teacher's awareness of the potential of her pupils not only influences her attitude as to what she may expect of them, but influences their performance as well. Clarke and Clarke (1954) in a follow-up study of a group of children who until they were three had been classed as mental retardates, found these children at age 10 to be of normal intelligence. At the age of three these children had been placed with foster parents who were told they were normal. A matched group of children who remained institutionalized were judged at the age of 10 to be essentially mentally subnormal. Rosenthal (1959), among others, has demonstrated that when psychology students are told that the children they are about to test are superior, those children perform significantly better than do other children who have been described as poor learners, although both groups of children are, in fact, equal in ability. In the light of such findings, approaches to teacher retraining focused on improving teacher attitude as a means of improving pupil performance might assume primary importance in compensatory programs.

As far as the problem of staffing depressed-area schools is concerned, the school systems might, as a first step, concern themselves with the functional ability rather than the paper qualifications of potential teaching personnel. If, as former Assistant Secretary for Education Keppel has observed, there are school systems in which teachers with two years of relevant experience in the Peace Corps are technically unqualified to teach, one would doubt the rationality of those systems. The use of volunteer or paid sub-professionals to perform non-teaching functions, and what would seem to be a general overcoming of the antipathy of school systems toward enthusiastic laymen in the classroom, suggests that in some school systems human needs are beginning to outweigh bureaucratic needs. This approach, of course, must be tempered with awareness that good will is not for long an adequate substitute of technical competence.

It is not only movement from the bottom, which has met with hostility in school situations. Many times the introduction at top levels of "specialist" or "resource" personnel has met with a kind of stony resistance on the part of the classroom teachers with a resultant underutilization of the services these auxiliary personnel are offering. It is rarely profitable to introduce into an existing school hierarchy a curriculum expert who is not at the same time a human relations expert, because it takes a particularly sensitive person to provide assistance to experienced personnel without at the same time causing resentment. One suggested approach to this problem is the retiring of the status people already in the school, although one would have to evaluate the degree to which the older, more established teachers are actually susceptible to retraining.

Aside from any hostility derived from a concern for status, some teachers are honestly convinced that given the overcrowding of the classrooms in many of these schools, any additional personnel should be given classroom assignments in order to reduce overall classroom size. In evaluating the Higher Horizons Program, the 10 percent of the teachers who recommended canceling the program felt that the special Higher Horizon's personnel could much better be used in the classroom. And the fact is, that until programs are designed with more effective built-in evaluative procedures, there is no one who can tell them they are wrong.

Probably the most productive approach to change teacher behavior and attitudes is that which emphasizes providing teachers with new and improved tools. It is instructive in this respect to recall the experimental work of K.S. Lashley (1963). In the middle twenties it was a widely held view that laboratory rats were unable to discriminate among geometric forms. They could make brightness discriminations, but experimenters consistently found that rats could not discriminate between, say, a triangle and a circle. Lashley hypothesized that the problem lay not in the rats' inability to discriminate, but in the experimenters' failure to devise an adequate learning situation. So Lashley modified the demands of the learning situation by reducing sources of extraneous stimuli, limiting the range of alternative responses, and increasing the drive state of experimental animals. Under the changed conditions for learning, he was able to teach rats to make discriminations among a variety of geometric forms.

If appropriate learning situations can be designed to enable rats to learn discriminations they are supposedly unable to make, is it not possible that appropriate classroom situations and procedures can be devised to enable all children to learn those things many children are already learning? We cannot expect the teachers in their individual classrooms to find for themselves all of the necessary teaching techniques and learning situations appropriate to these children. Taking a cue from the experience with the new mathematic curriculum, the Zacharias Commission has stressed the importance of new instruments and methods that work in achieving behavioral change in teachers. Is it easy for teachers to slip into attitudes of defeat and indifference when they see littler return for their efforts and it is hard for them to remain indifferent and unchallenged when their efforts begin to meet with success.

A weakness of teacher training programs and of our overall programs of education for the disadvantage is our failure to match the revolutions taking place in society with a revolution in the teaching-learning process. We have not yet removed the burden of proof from the shoulders of the learner and placed the responsibility for the success of the academic venture on the shoulders of the school system, where it belongs.

In no area is this misplaced responsibility more obvious than in the area of curriculum innovation. Remedial education programs have been developed, teacher-pupil ratio has been reduced, new materials have been produced, classroom grouping has been modified all sensible and appropriate changes, but they represent no basic alteration in the teaching-learning process. They are likely to result in increasing the number of children who succeed, but they are unlikely to meet our era's real challenge to the schools, that of insuring that children save those with significant neurological defects achieve competence in the development and use of ideas as well as mastery of the basic academic skills.

Most of what is being done in the area of curriculum change is being done in line with a tradition of unscientific innovation in the school system. Many of the innovations consume considerable time and money. Few of them are based on identifiable theoretical premises or verifiable hypotheses. Very often these innovations appear to have resulted from isolated, poorly controlled trial and error discoveries, and all too often the new practice is supported only by the exhortation of its enthusiasts. For example, there is little empirical evidence or theoretical basis for judging either homogeneous or heterogeneous groupings as providing the more effective learning situation. Homogeneous grouping may indeed provide an easier teaching situation, but in practice it often serves simply to segregate the minority group children from their more privileged peers. Given the evidence suggesting that segregation is, per se, a handicap to the achievement of educational equality, and given, in addition, the social problems of the time, it might be well for school systems to examine the premise on which they have overwhelmingly adopted homogeneous groupings. It is quite possible that the more difficult teaching situation provided by heterogeneous grouping is also the more productive in the total development of the child.

Team teaching is another structural modification for which the justifications are largely those relating to more effective use of personnel rather than to any presumption that is an effective method of handling disadvantage children. Where block-time programming has been introduced at the junior high school level, its introduction has been justified on the basis that these children are not ready to move out of the single-teacher, single classroom situation. If these children at a secondary school level need identification with one teacher, it might be appropriate to assume that the greater flexibility which learn-teaching allows to the administration in the use of personnel does not necessarily results in psychological benefit to the children themselves. On the other hand, perhaps the need for personal identification with the teacher may be better met under team teaching conditions where the higher teacher pupil ratio allows for more meaningful, if not consistent, teacher-pupil interaction.

These structural rearrangements, like a number of other innovations, which have been called compensatory, are really attempts to bring the schools up to date. Such additions as audiovisual aids, science equipment in the elementary schools, and programmed learning, are simply modernizations that may or may not have relevance to providing appropriate education for the disadvantaged.

One of the most interesting things about these efforts at modification and improvement is the absence of anything really new or radically innovative in pedagogy. Most of these programs utilize common sense, or traditional procedures, or both, which are or should be a part of any good educational program. In fact, it is something of an indictment that these practices have not been introduced earlier into the education of the less privileged.

But if curriculum development is to be significantly innovative, we might well give greater attention to the effect of intra-group interaction on the teaching-learning process. Professionals concerned with such fields as decision processes and psychotherapy have developed elaborate systems of theory and practice based upon concepts of group dynamics. This sophistication has not yet been appropriately applied to education. Other advances in curriculum development and modification might well be achieved through exploring different ways of organizing learning experiences to meet individual differences in readiness. This readiness may vary with respect to the functional capacity to discriminate between things seen, heard, tasted, or felt. It may vary with respect to habit patterns that have been established around these sensory functions. Readiness may vary, based upon the dominance of one aspect of sensory function over another. The plea here is for curriculum development that takes into account available knowledge concerning significant variations in the organization and operation of the senses. Work with neurologically impaired subjects has provided insight into the significance of variations in sensory and perceptual function for efficiency in learning. This work has also made us aware of the possibility that normal individuals vary widely with respect to behaviors dependent upon such functions. But of greatest significance is the contribution that work with these neurologically damaged subjects has made to the design of modified procedures for teaching and training. Because man's function is not alone determined by his biological characteristics but also by his encounters with the environment, it may well be that children whose life experiences vary, have significant variations in function. If this is in fact the case, the leads provided by the special education model should be rich with possibilities for curriculum design for socially disadvantaged children. Furthermore, if individuals, independently of experience or station in life, differ with respect to the degree to which they are inclined to respond with one or another of the senses, it may be that one of the significant variables in learning ability and disability may be the quality of support provided for the learning experience when the pattern of the learning task presented docs not complement the sensory organization

47

of the learner. Understanding the interaction between these two phenomena in the learning process will provide a new dimension along which curriculum materials may be designed and content organized.

Our concern with learner-environment interaction provides a new life space for the curriculum. From developments in programmed instruction we have learned something of the usefulness of modifying the rate and sequence in which learning experiences and materials are presented. We have yet to explore the significance of larger scale modifications in sequence, where instead of breaking down and reordering the structure of a single concept, brood categories of curriculum material and content arc subjected to such sequential modifications. However, the formal curriculum elements are not the only elements in the environment that impinge on the learner. Of equal importance are the social, psychological, and physical environments in which learning occurs. This is not to say that educators have heretofore been indifferent to these environments. The importance of the climate for learning is "old hat" in education. But innovation will grow from our awareness of a far broader set of dimensions along which these environments may be manipulated. In recognition of variations in response patterns, within as well as between learners, dependent upon the circumstances and nature of the learning task, the various aspects of these environments may be manipulated to achieve certain learning outcomes.

These examples by no means exhaust the possibilities for new or greatly modified approaches to curriculum design. However, concepts such as these are rarely found in the programs that have been studied. It may be that behavioral scientists will need to assume a greater responsibility for the application of their competencies to theoretical and applied problems in education. In any case, it is probably unreasonable for us to expect that the present generation of professional educators will be able to take the giant strides required for curriculum innovation that will answer the challenge. Growing interest in improving opportunities in higher education for the disadvantaged has led many of our colleges and universities to draw their newest student bodies from an increasingly wide variety of social, ethnic, economic, and cultural groups. Some of these new college students are the first members of their cultural or ethnic groups to attend these institutions, and large numbers of them are succeeding in college, defying pessimistic predictions of their chances for success. Sometimes these achievements are simply the result of discovery programs, which provide an opportunity for college study to young people of ability. In other cases, success follows special remedial and enrichment programs in which youngsters who were functioning at modest levels were helped to correct their weaknesses in preparation and to move ahead. Still other members of this new collegiate population arc counted among those who have taken advantage of the opportunity provided by the growing number of junior or community colleges. Increasingly, the new college group will include young people who have spent their summers and much of their free time during their last few undergraduate school years in special college preparatory programs. In short, it can be said today that any young person of above-average ability can find an opportunity for collegiate study, particularly if he is Negro. Unfortunately, these talent search programs and changed admissions policies have not routinely received a broad enough interpretation to enable them to assist other disadvantaged groups, including poor White youth. Furthermore, they have only skimmed the cream. They have not yet moved far enough from dependence on traditional indices of talent or potential to draw from the mass of youngsters who are academically handicapped because of their socially or economically disadvantaged status.

In facing the many problems involved in weak prior academic preparation the colleges face a substantial challenge. Where the issue has been engaged, emphasis has been placed on remedial work and enrichment experiences, special counseling, guidance and tutorial work, extended time complete requirements, or the selection of students who show pro that this is so. It is quite likely that knowledge of the pupil's life may make the teacher somewhat more at ease or at least somewhat less vulnerable to shock. But few of us are really able to straddle cultures and to utilize knowledge of other cultures creatively. Even fewer of us have the capacity to adapt experiences from our own value systems to alien value systems without being patronizing. Of greater importance, however, is the question of whether good teaching and effective learning can transcend one's identification with a particular set of values or a particular culture. The history of education indicates that they can. The upper class has always received the best education and few upper-class members are educators. Education has been the vehicle of upward mobility for the lower class and certainly, by the time they function as teachers, educators are not members of the lower class. Understanding of differences in culture and values may be helpful in teaching, but such understanding seems to be a noncritical variable and

49

preoccupation with it may be diversionary in the education of the disadvantaged.

The importance of the interview and psychotherapeutic counseling as instruments for change in attitude and behavior has been greatly exaggerated. Although few programs have been developed with an intensive psychotherapeutic emphasis, almost none of the programs studied are without a significant guidance counseling emphasis. These counseling components, which vary from information-dispensing and motivational exhortation to reflection of feeling and the provision of advice and support, tend to be based on the same assumptions as psychotherapy. The heavy dependence on counseling reflects the views that greater insight into factors which seem to be related to the behavior results in a modification of the behavior, that atypical behavior reflects lack of correct information or correct interpretation, that habitual behavior patterns are subject to change under the impact of interaction with a person of higher status. These and a host of other assumptions have some validity. However, the counseling emphasis does not provide for the role of experience—direct confrontation with life upon the development and change of attitudes and behavior.

Where one's life experience, or at least one's perception of the opportunity, corresponds to the values, goals, and behaviors stressed in the counseling situation, one may expect somewhat more positive results. When the major events of one's life and one's awareness of the opportunity structure contradict the hypothetical world of the interview, it is folly to expect positive results.

Too many of the guidance components of compensatory education programs are based upon superficial and infrequent pupil-counselor contact. Most of the encounters with guidance counselors are far removed from meaningful involvement with the real problems in the real world. Too often the guidance counselor represents a degree of sophistication with regard to the priority problems of the pupil that borders on naivete. Usually the guidance focus is on talking about the problem when the need is to do something about it. Too often, unfortunately, the support that the status person could provide is not given because life circumstances often rob these young people of trust in that segment of the population represented by the counselor.

Guidance programs in which the counselor performs an active helping role seem to be more effective. Often the counselor's value is established more readily on the basis of his having taken an action in the pupil's behalf. Arranging for a change of teacher, help in finding a job, mediating a parent-child conflict, coming to the pupil's defense in the face of the police, or taking a correct stand in the civil rights struggle are actions that may do we have more to establish a relationship than months of counseling. For the disadvantage youngster who daily meets and often copes with many concrete difficulties in living, a focus on help with these problems may be the most productive approach to guidance.

It is not suggested here that information, support, reflection of feeling, advice-giving, and verbal reinforcement are to no avail. The importance of relationship therapy and models in guidance are not to be demeaned. The point to be made is that, particularly with this group, guidance efforts directed at control and modification of the environment, efforts directed at positive intervention to change the negative and destructive elements in the lives of these children, are likely to be more productive than efforts directed at change of attitude and behavior through verbal and other vicarious experience.

Ten years ago when one could make a contribution to the situation simply by calling attention to the fact that education for the disadvantaged was a problem, a critical approach to the review of the few real efforts then in existence would have been inappropriate. However, today when work in this field has almost become a fad, it is essential that we do not let our enthusiasm blind us to the limitations of our efforts. The predominantly critical view taken of these programs is born of the fear that quantity of effort may be mistaken for quality of achievement. Weaknesses and limitations in these programs have been stressed in order to call attention to the fact that we have not yet found answers to many of the pressing educational problems of the disadvantaged. To assume that we have the answer is to subject multitudes of children to less than optimal development. More seriously, to settle for the beginning effort now mounted is to lay the basis for the conclusion that, children of low economic, ethnic, or social status cannot be educated to the same levels as other children in the society. This conclusion could be drawn because despite all of our current efforts tremendous gains are not yet being achieved in upgrading educational achievement in socially disadvantaged children. We are probably failing because we have not yet found the right answers to the problem. To act as if the answers were in is to ensure against further progress.

51

Even though we do not know how best to educate socially disadvantaged children, we cannot afford to wait for better answers. The presence of these children in our schools, the demands of increasingly impatient communities, and the requirements of an increasingly complex society demand that we apply the best that is currently available even as we seek to improve. Our current experiences by no means leave us without leads. There are several ideas and practices that show promise.

Effective teaching. None of the programs studied have come up with a substitute for effective teaching. They have also failed to develop the effective approach to teaching. The teachers who are judged to be successful are those who have developed sensitivity to the special needs, the variety of learning patterns, and the learning strengths and weaknesses of their pupils. These teachers have also developed a wide variety of instructional techniques and methodologies by which they communicate knowledge with which they are very familiar, and attitudes of respect and expectations that they strongly hold.

Child-parent-teacher motivation. In the absence of revolutions in educational technology, one of the most promising areas for emphasis is that of motivation. Few programs have generated more enthusiasm for learning or better pupil gains than those, which involved teachers, parents, and children in active and creative motivational campaigns. Utilizing a wide variety of motivational schemes, these programs have raised the level of expectation on the part of teachers, have greatly increased parent participation in the school as well as home-based learning experiences, and have helped youngsters to find pleasure and reward in learning.

New materials and technology. One of the significant developments of the current period is the emergence of instructional materials more widely representative of the variety of ethnic groups that exist in this country. The better material in this category not only includes more appropriate graphic art but the prose is more pertinent to the realities of the pupil's life. The development of improved literacy techniques is worthy of note. Among these are the Initial Teaching Alphabet, Color Coded Words, the Progressive Accelerated Reading Technique, and the Talking Typewriter. Many of the better programs make good use of some of the excellent programmed instructional materials as well as of inexpensive-to-costly teaching machines.

Peer teaching and learning. Drawing upon a long-ignored technique employed by Maria Montessori, some programs have caused children to make significant gains in academic achievement as a result of helping other children learn. Most often the pattern is that of older children serving as tutors for younger children with both showing gains from the experience. The practice not only has many tangential social benefits, it also has the advantage of replicating the naturalistic out-of-school experiences of children, where they generally tend to learn from each other.

Psycho-educational diagnosis and remediation. It is well established that disadvantaged children are a high-risk population with respect to developmental abnormalities. The higher incidence of developmental defects and learning disabilities makes careful psycho-educational diagnosis of crucial significance in programs serving these children. Obviously it is not enough to diagnose; prescription and remedy must follow. Excellent programs will include or at least have access to such staff and facilities.

Learning task specific grouping. Considerable controversy has developed around homogeneous versus heterogeneous grouping. Such a dichotomy clouds the issue. Clearly, there are some learning tasks, which are easier for some children to master and for some teachers to teach, if they are presented to a group who are at much the same level. Mastery of other tasks may proceed faster in heterogeneous groups. There are some tasks that require small group instruction, and others for which small groups are wasteful if not inefficient. Grouping of youngsters for instruction should flow from the nature of the learning task and not from the bias of the teacher or the school system. In work with disadvantaged children, the social gains that may also be derived from flexible grouping should not be ignored.

Extensions of the school. Although school learning is focused in the school, its quality is significantly influenced by factors outside of school. Where competing forces operate outside of school, it is often necessary to extend the school day, week, or year so as to increase the period during which the school's influence may be felt. The All-Day Neighborhood School, weekend activities, and summer programs are among the variations used. In a few instances boarding-type schools are being tried, combining certain status and quality elements to the extended exposure to the school environment.

Staffing. There are few solid guidelines to staffing programs for the disadvantaged. However, the more promising trends give emphasis to:

a. the selection of teachers who have good, basic backgrounds in academic disciplines, combined with particularly good instructional skills. Most programs stress some appreciation for the cultures from which pupils come, but instructional techniques that work seem to provide the best payoff.
b. The use of indigenous nonprofessionals as teacher aides is increasingly stressed although some critics of this development call attention to the possible influence of "negative models," particularly in language usage.
c. In addition to strength of staff, quantity of staff is also stressed. Combined with team teaching, where a master teacher supervises several less skilled teachers, the use of junior-level personnel can be used to advantage.
d. Considerable emphasis in some programs is being given to the use of male role models. Visitors and part-time people are used when men are not in ample supply on the regular staff.
e. A wide variety of supporting staff are being used. These include social workers, psychologists, physicians, nurses, community organizers, remedial specialists, guidance specialists, and home-school liaison officers drawn from the surrounding environment.

Social or peer-group support. Particularly in work with adolescents and college-bound youth the peer group or appropriate social or ethnic reference groups are used to provide morale support, an island for temporary retreat, or reference-group identification. This is particularly important in young people whose upward mobility may appear to be taking them away from the groups with which they identify.

Financial assistance. Many of the administrators of college programs have recognized the necessity for providing some financial assistance for youth from disadvantaged backgrounds. This need is not so readily recognized at the high school and elementary school level. However, many of these children's families simply cannot provide the pocket money, which makes school attendance and social participation possible. The need for stipends is urgent for many of these children. Another unusual pattern of financial assistance consists of modest aid beginning as early as the seventh grade and continuing through college. In one of these programs, college is guaranteed while the student is still in junior high, as long as the pupil continues to demonstrate that he can qualify for this assistance.

Improved Opportunity. Improved opportunities in college as well as in other post high school endeavors is viewed by some programs as a major factor. The view held is that perception of opportunity is in itself enough to move many of these youth from a position of lethargy and alienation to active involvement in their own development.

These several trends have made for considerable improvement in education for the disadvantaged. They flow logically from what is known about these children and from the best traditions in education. Their further development may be expected not only to enhance the quality of the educational experiences our schools and colleges provide for children and youth handicapped by poverty and discrimination, but also to strengthen the profession's competence in serving the needs of learners of all social classes and races.

New Directions

These approaches to improvement in the education of disadvantaged young people, although promising, will not alone suffice to cope with the new demands which rapid social change now poses for our schools and colleges. More fundamental than the task of providing compensatory educatioon with these concerns might appropriately give attention to five specific educational goals. The first of these is a renewed commitment to effective teaching— sufficiently effective to provide for all students the mastery of basic communication skills. A real commitment to the goal of developing universal competence in speech, in reading and writing, and in arithmetic computation has crucial implications for education and for society. For education, it will mean the development of the kind of materials, methods, and conditions for learning that are appropriate to the different background experiences and learning styles of children other than those of children other than those for whom most of our educational practices have been designed. These practices have not even succeeded with all the pupils for whom they were designed, and they have failed completely to meet the needs of most of the children who have been designated "socially disadvantaged." Consequently, a genuine determination on the part of the schools to assure universal mastery of basic communication skills would constitute a self-imposed challenge of some magnitude. The school has no choice about taking on such a challenge. In the agricultural and industrial eras, physical strength and manual skill were sufficient tools for man's survival, but it is increasingly clear that the survival tools of the cybernetic era are communication skills. If the schools cannot universally provide these tools, they will be institutionally dysfunctional in modern society.

Let me remind those who lack the courage to meet the challenge that our concepts of educability have consistently followed society's demand for educated persons. At one time it was only the religious and political nobility from which educable persons were thought to come. When the Reformation and the emerging industrial revolution required that more people be educated, we learned that educability existed in broader categories of humankind. Gradually in the West, there came a general acceptance of the notion that all White people were at least potentially educable, and in this country it was only the Negro who could not be taught. When, at last, out of humanitarian concern and society's need we began to discover that Negroes could learn, we came to accept a tacit responsibility for the education of all people. But though we have accepted the theory of universal educability, we have not attained universal education—at best we have learned how to teach that majority who meet certain rather stereotyped criteria. However, educability is a function of societal definition and societal need, and I submit that in the latter part of the twentieth century educability will be defined in the broadest and most inclusive terms. It is in those terms that the school will be challenged to produce.

A second goal of education, only somewhat less crucial than the mastery of basic skills, involves providing students with an attitude of readiness toward, and an increasing capacity for, continued learning. We must teach people to think of the acquisition of knowledge as a lifetime undertaking, not as a pastime for youth, because accelerating technological innovations are effecting profound changes in our job structure. Occupations are rapidly altering. We are seeing a developing stratification of people on the basis of intellectual function and technological skills. Over the last 10 years the proportion of White-to blue-collar workers has altered radically. Now for the first time White-collar workers outnumber the blue-collar workers, and the trend is not likely to reverse itself. We already have the capacity to install a productive system based primarily on machine power and machine skills. The coming replacement of man by the machine will destroy many more existing jobs and render useless the work contributions of vast numbers now employed. When that time comes, and it is coming rapidly, obtaining employment in one of the new fields will depend largely upon the level of adaptive skill and the quality of education of the applicant. Unemployment rates compiled in 1959 for those with seven years of schooling or less, reached ten percent, compared with just over three percent for those with 13 to 15 years of schooling, and just over one percent for those with 16 years of schooling or more. A willingness to learn, and continued practice in learning, will stand in good stead those who would be employed in such a marketplace.

But motivation for learning is not, of itself, enough. In any given field, or group of related fields, available and necessary knowledge has already outstripped any single individual's capacity to master content. Only the student who by practice, by utilization of techniques of selection, discrimination, and evaluation has honed techniques which will allow him to sort out the worthwhile from the worthless and the significant from the insignificant can escape being inundated in a sea of paper. Those who would succeed tomorrow must learn not only how to acquire, but how to manage knowledge.

And this is the third of the tools with which educators should consider themselves obligated to equip tomorrow's students—the techniques of managing knowledge. Successful functioning on an intellectual level consists not in having a head full of facts, but in problem solving, in knowing how to conceptualize problems, and how to pursue the information which will provide solutions. The intellectual leaders today are those who have mastered the techniques of conceptual analysis and synthesis. And, increasingly, those who would succeed must gain competence in these skills—in the identification and analysis of principles and in their subsequent reassembling around new data to produce newer or more advanced concepts. These are the skills necessary to the successful functioning of today's intellectual elite. Tomorrow, in a highly technical society, they may be necessary for most of us, not only to enable us to do productive work, but also to provide us with armor against the ravages of idle leisure.

Leisure may well be the most important industrial by-product of our coming generation. As an outgrowth of a computerized age in which two percent of the population will be able to produce all the goods and food that the other 98 percent can possibly consume, leisure will replace work as man's most time-consuming activity. At a meeting in 1964 of leading political and social scientists, the president of the American Academy of Political and Social Science recommended such revolutionary measures as the establishment of departments of leisure in the 50 states, and the compulsory teaching of leisure skills in the public schools. He was immediately challenged from the floor as being hopelessly conservative in his approach. An economist at the meeting claimed that we face such an explosive increase in leisure that within a mere 10 years we may have to keep the unemployed portion of our population under sedation unless we can quickly figure out something better for them to do. Unemployment will be concentrated among the older workers and the youngsters entering the labor force and, according to Theobald (1963), "no conceivable rate of economic growth will avoid this result." Of the 26 million people who will enter the job market during this decade, 9.8 million will have less than a complete high school education. Many, if not all of these people, will face a lifetime without market-supported work.

How these people are to be kept solvent is a problem, which we educators are not immediately asked to deal with. How they are to occupy themselves is at the heart of our concern. Even now America is a land of golfers, travelers, bowlers, amateur painters. After finding free time for all the marginal chores of living—mowing the lawn, taking a fishing trip, driving the kids to the library—what will a man do to fill his extra leisure hours?

Americans are ill equipped to absorb leisure in any but the smallest doses. Our education, our informal training, our mores, our Horatio Alger kind of tradition, our puritanical mythology honoring the no-play-hard-work equals-success tradition, have made us a people who feel guilty about "wasting time."

It must, then, become the fourth goal of our new educational system to teach our students just how creative and how elevating the wise use of leisure can be. Such a change may well be among the most difficult asked of us. Our public school system has always been a training ground for its students to "get ahead." It has consistently expounded the principle that only hard work and study will prevent failure after graduation. But it has rarely equated hard work with pleasure or self-satisfaction. It has more enthusiastically taught English as the language of business letters than as the language of Shakespeare, Thoreau, and Du Bois. Our schools will have to start teaching a drastically new philosophy, one appropriate to our new age of abundance. The new educational standards will have to reflect, as well as encourage, a basic alteration in our cultural standards. The pursuit of pleasure will have to be accepted as a virtue. But at the same time, pleasure will have to cease being equated with non-doing and idleness, and come to be associated with self-management, with self-imposed and self-chosen activity. To a people freed from the need to work we shall have to teach the skills of leisure as if our lives depended on it-and indeed they may.

For now, in the latter half of the twentieth century, we have reached a point where the abundance of knowledge and technology available to this country would allow us to create a society based on humanist rather than survival values. In earlier generations, when the hard realities of life seemed on every hand to run counter to copybook maxims about justice, equality, and humanity, the school necessarily based its teaching of these values on exhortation and fabricated example. Now, the school could well take as its fifth goal the education of citizens whose competencies in self-management and human relations render them capable of an appropriate creative response to the fact that we now possess the material potential to create a society truly respectful of human rights, a society where respect for one's fellow man no longer conflicts with his need to provide for his family and himself. The challenge of the new condition is to match the normal learning experience to this new reality and to meet the new opportunity of a freer social system with a new approach to educational methods and to a new organization of society. The great danger is to pretend that there has been no fundamental change and to go on using methods that were not completely useful even in the old days, thus missing an opportunity to advance learning and behavior when such an advance is not only possible but desperately needed. The failure of man to create a humane social order under the new conditions will carry with it the threat of society's suicide, because the same conditions of scientific advance and material plenty that make it possible for man to now be truly human, also make it possible for him to be definitively and conclusively antihuman.

COMMENTARY

If I were writing this chapter today, I would give a less central role to schooling and place much feel that they need the time for work that is unavailable than for people who are freed from the necessity of remunerative work.

When I wrote the compensatory education book, my thinking was much more tuned to the facilitation of academic learning and to finding ways to improve upon the teaching side of teaching and learning. The fact is that with the exception of a period in my life when I was a practicing psychotherapist, I have devoted considerable attention to finding improved technologies and strategies for treating the people I serve more effectively. It is interesting that as I was moving from psychotherapeutic intervention into educational intervention, I was advocating for the enablement of my clients to heal themselves. In my Ed. D. dissertation I argue, "Therapist as servant, helper, and enabler." (Gordon, 1957). I somehow retreated from that position to embrace the teacher or server role, which I now see as problematic. There are many teaching and learning situations where didactic instruction, mediation, modeling and structuring are essential, but I am persuaded that learning often proceeds best when the learner is guided in exploration and inquiry, provided with essential resources, and encouraged to use one's own resources to construct and test possible solutions. This more constructivist approach to teaching and learning shifts the focus from the teaching person to the learning person. In my current thinking about education and compensatory education, it is to the enablement of the instrumentalities of human agency—capacity for appropriate and deliberate activity in the interest of self and others—that I place special attention. My earlier concerns are not displaced or abandoned but joined and possibly superseded by this concern for the enablement of human agency.

3
Individualization and Personalization in Pedagogy

My concern for and almost preoccupation with the phenomena of variations in the characteristics and manifestations of behavior in human subjects led me to spend a considerable number of years thinking and writing about group and individual differences in human behavior. For a period of about 15 years I concentrated my attention on what I called the problem of Human Diversity and Pedagogy. I was convinced for a while that pedagogical practice should be informed by the characteristics of the learning persons, and that the actions and behaviors of teaching persons should be matched to the characteristics of the learner. Even now it is difficult for me to move away from that conviction. The related work of my friends Thomas, Chess & Birch (1971) only reinforced my belief. Their definitive work on behavioral individuality along with that of Jerome Kagen (1998) on temperament provided for me a basis in the science of behavior for a notion that seemed as logically persuasive. The correctness of our position was further reinforced by the very thoughtful work of another friend, Robert Glaser (1977), who designed an elaborate program of pedagogical intervention, *Individually Prescribed Instruction,* that complimented our assumptions concerning the relevance of these variations in human behavior for the design and management of teaching and learning transactions. Even when Lee Chronbach and Richard Snow (1977) published their definitive review of research concerning possible interactions between human traits and educational treatments and found little evidence to support the claim, they and I found it difficult to retreat from the conviction that there was merit in the idea.

The final book that Stella Chess and Alexander Thomas wrote, for which I wrote the introduction in 1998, *Goodness of Fit,* provided further explanation and defense of the notions we had begun to explore some 40 years earlier. I wrote then:

It is not only the origins of behavior that are explained by interactionist conceptions, but the continuing expressions of behavior as well. When interactionist and epigenetic perspectives are combined, three conclusions may be drawn concerning the causes of behavior: (1) Behavior arises from both biological and social origins; (2) The interactions between biological and social phenomena that cause behavior are complex and multiple; and (3) These interactions result in bi-directional transformations, which influence both the social environments and the bio-social behaviors. Behavior—normal and abnormal, adaptive and maladaptive—is the product of these interactions. According to Chess and Thomas those adaptive and normal behavioral responses reflect a high degree of goodness of fit, while those mal-adaptive and abnormal behaviors generally reflect a poorness of fit. In all of these processes interactions are the constant. Goodness of fit is a judgment based on empirical evidence and sometimes on aesthetic value.

By the time that I completed the oversight and coordination of the human Diversity and Pedagogy project and sent our collection of commissioned essays to press, I was beginning to think that the idea of matching instruction with the characteristics of learners was problematic, but as I have indicate, I could not give up the idea. Even here at the close of my career, I remain convinced that the problem is not so much with the idea as it is with our understanding of the relationships between the two categories of variables. Certainly the one to one match with which most of us began no longer makes sense. My former student's notion of "dynamic blending" (Esposito 1965) still has appeal for me. I continue to believe that students find it easier to relate to and learn material when it is presented in ways that complement the learning habits and styles with which they have had prior success. But Stella's, Alex's and my concern with the importance of matching may have been overstated. I have seen students who were effectively challenged by the contradiction between the demands of the new learning and their habitual or stylistic approach. I am impressed by the power of a student's identification with and ownership of the learning problem to be mastered. With the advent of electronic and epistemic games, I am fascinated by the interest and engagement evoked by contradiction, novelty, and paradox. I have come to believe that the problems posed for pedagogy by human diversity are problems of identification with and ownership—what we have come to call personalization.

Individualization and Personalization in Pedagogy

I have argued that intellective competence reflects the effective orchestration of affective, cognitive and situative mental processes in the service of sense making and problem solving. How do we begin to conceptualize the practicalities of reaching this goal with regards to the affective and situative domains? As Brandt (2003), Sternberg (1999) and others confirm, effective learning includes processes broader than cognition alone. These processes are thought of as inherently associated not only with students' social and emotional needs but also with the varying contexts in which they learn, develop and achieve. With respect to academic achievement, we are beginning to see a convergence of various psychological insights and recent neurophysiological findings that one's emotional state seems to determine the level and quality of one's cognitive processes, such as attention to and understanding of the concepts that make up a discipline (how people learn, bridging research and practice (LeDoux 2000) other sources). The thoughtful attempts to integrate these processes in learner-centered and knowledge-centered environments appear to enable the nurturance of academic ability (How people learn 1999).

Recent theoretical and empirical literature indicates that effective learning occurs in personalized learning environments that emphasize high academic standards; rigorous and relevant curriculum and teaching; and continued professional development for administrative and teaching staff. But what exactly is personalized learning and how do we create it, particularly when this conceptualization includes various definitions that depend on the learning context, condition and population? For example, this construct can refer to students' engagement in and attachment to a learning environment, usually the school, and their effort in mastering concepts taught. It also refers to a reflexive and deliberate structuring of the learning environment so that progressively rigorous exposure to curriculum results in student mastery of concepts and ultimately academic excellence. The implication is that learning environments that are sensitive to their students' cognitive styles, temperaments, sources of motivation, identities and cultures are more likely to have students who are engaged in and have positive relationships to school.

Personalization thus includes (1) the individualization of teaching and learning transactions; (2) the casting of academic learning in the context of the relationship between teacher and learner; (3) the internalization of the content and product of the learning; and (4) the learner's ownership of the material learned and the process by which it is learned. In the conceptualization represented in 1 and 2 above, personalization is a pedagogical technique that is used on the student's behalf by the instructor. However, in the conceptualization implicit in 3 and 4 above, personalization is an achievement of the learner, or something that the learner does for herself or himself. The literature on the subject is much richer in reference to this construction as a pedagogical technique than as pedagogical product or learner achievement. Personalization as a customizing pedagogical technique was described half a century ago by George Kelly (1955) who denominated it "Personal Construction Theory (PCT)."

The key message of Personal Construction Theory (PCT) is that the world is "perceived" by a person in terms of whatever "meaning" that person applies to it and the person has the freedom to choose a different "meaning" of whatever he or she wants. In other words, as suggested by George Kelly, the original proponent of the theory, the person has the "freedom" to choose the meaning that one prefers or likes. He called this alternative constructivism. In simple words, the person is capable of applying alternative constructions (meanings) to any events in the past, present or future. The person is not a prisoner of one's "biography or past" and could liberate oneself from the misery of "miserable" events if one desires by reconstruing (reinterpreting and redefining) them. The theory rejects the existing schism between affect, cognition, and action and recommends that they be construed together for developing a fuller understanding of human behavior.

Kelly (1955) suggested that PCT is based on the model of man-the-scientist. Within this model,

- the individual creates his or her own ways of seeing the world in which he lives; the world does not create them for him;
- (s)he builds constructs and tries them on for size;
- the constructs are sometimes organized into systems, group of constructs which embody subordinate and superordinate relationships;
- the same events can often be viewed in the light of two or more systems, yet the events do not belong to any system; and
- the individual's practical systems have particular foci and limited ranges of convenience.

In that same period the concern with Kelly's PCT was prevalent. John Flanagan (1971) advanced notions concerning personalization and individualization through his "Project PLAN." It was Flanagan's idea that learning experiences should be matched to the characteristics of learners, and to achieve this, a dynamic "plan" should be created for each child. The plan was to be dynamic, in that it should change with the changing needs of the learner, and used as the framework for the teaching and learning experiences of the learner. Flanagan (1971) anticipated the advent of the electronic computer, which would be needed to manage the vast amount of information and instructional material that would be necessary to implement hundreds of plans in each school. Glaser (1966) encountered the same problem with his efforts at individually prescribed instruction (IPI). In IPI classrooms, teaching assistants helped teachers produce and manage the voluminous files of instructional materials from which the teacher could choose. Flanagan (1971), Glaser (1966), Kelly (1955) and others who sought to customize teaching and learning encounters in consideration of the specific characteristics and needs of the learner did not emphasize personalization, but the underlying assumption was that individualization made it easier for the learner to identify with and take ownership of experiences and materials that were so adapted. Thus individualization was often used synonymously with personalization.

The use of personalization to refer to an achievement of the student has received more implicit attention in the literature and in practice. The learning process is individualized in part to gain greater learner identification with what is to be learned. The teacher/learner relationship is used as a vehicle for encouraging learner engagement with and internalization of the content and process. In general usage, the term "personalization" suggests an identification with and ownership of the object or stimulus that is being personalized. Personalization refers to the dynamic interaction between learner and elements of the learning situation which results in a sense of ownership, empowerment and gratification for the learner."

From my perspective, personalization is a tri-focal phenomenon that references the extent to which:

1. the teaching and learning process is adapted to or fits with the characteristics of the learner;
2. the processes by which teachers and students relate in transforming what is being learned into the learner's data; and
3. the learner's identification with and ownership of products of the learning transaction.

Thomas and Chess (1977), which I referenced earlier, as well as Bryk and Schneider (2002), also referenced earlier, and Bennett and others (2004) emphasize the importance of trustworthy relationships and environments as the contexts for identifying with and taking ownership of learning processes and learning products. Gardner (2006), Gordon (1992), Greeno (2005), Kornhaber (1994) and Sizer (1973) emphasize the internalization of the learning experience and the products of that experience as habits of mind and intellective character. Similar to the complex construct we call culture, our use of the construct personalization encompasses all of these notions referable to the processes and products of human learning. Like culture, personalization is both a determinant and consequence of particular learning behaviors.

I contend that we can nurture a sense of agency, self-efficacy, effort, interest, motivation, self-regulation and personal control/agency in students by personalizing the teaching and learning transactions. Personalization is bi-directional in that the teacher, with support from administrators, peers, personalizes the experience and the stimulus materials, but it is the learner who must personalize the process and the product. This conceptualization emphasizes that for personalization to be optimally effective, the student must take ownership of the product of that learning and the process by which he or she learns. In my earlier work, I have indicated that this process include experiences of support from teachers and peers; integration into a peer group; student preparation for and level and quality of effort in schoolwork; and efficacy beliefs that doing well in school is personally important. These processes appear to enable the realization of academic knowledge, skills and dispositions (Eccles, Roeser, Wigfield, and Freedman-Doan 1999; Masten et al. 1985; Pianta, Rimm-Kaufman and Cox 1999).

RATIONALE FOR THE PERSONALIZATION OF ACADEMIC LEARNING

Clearly, human learners are more than cognitive beings. Human behavior is variably influenced by affect, motivation, identity, environmental press, and by various manifestations of status, such as race and ethnicity, gender, socioeconomic class, first language and culture. A comprehensive conceptualization of the learning person requires that we understand each learner not only from these seemingly separate dimensions of human diversity but also from the collectivity of these dimensions as they are orchestrated in the lives and behaviors of learners. It becoming increasingly clear that as important as each of these learner characteristics may be, it is not in their unilateral but rather their multi-dimensional impact that their importance for teaching and learning resides. Learners do not bring their unique characteristics singly to bear on teaching and learning transactions. Rather, they bring these characteristics to bear on learning behavior in dynamically orchestrated patterns or clusters. It appears that it is the interactions between these orchestrations and individual attributes that influence the learner's approaches to learning problems; the strategies and skills that are developed in response to learning task demands; the directional deployment of effort; and ultimately, the nature and quality of task engagement, time on task, goal-directed deployment of energy, resource utilization, and efficacious behavior. Thus, while it may be important that the teacher know the dominant features of each students' cognitive style, temperament, sources of motivation, identity, and so forth, it may be more important that the teacher be sensitive to the stimulus conditions and situational constraints under which aspects of these domains emerge and change.

It appears that we may be dealing with learner attributes at three levels: traits (cognitive style or temperament), instrumental behaviors (strategies, directed effort, skills), and intermediate outcome behaviors (time on task, resource utilization). The orchestration of these attributes in the service of academic work appears to result in academic excellence and achievement. Instead of focusing on a specific manifestation of cognitive style, for example, it may be necessary to examine several components of cognitive stylistic preference as they are orchestrated in learning strategies and to focus the manipulation of educational treatment on these strategies rather than style. This strategy argues against single-domain clustering or patterning that may reflect too limited a conceptualization. Messick (1982) suggests that human traits in learning behavior may be best understood as including cross-style and cross-domain (for example, affective or cognitive) patterns that are not necessarily constant across situations. We can interpret this to mean that preoccupation with the learner's tendency to utilize a specific manifestation of a single domain or even the learner's utilization of multiple expressions from a single domain is counterproductive. A more cogent conceptualization includes the principle of behavioral individuality and those dynamic and dialectical relationships within and between domains, selectively integrated into response tendencies.

Hence, it is entirely possible that multiple manifestations of styles or response capabilities may be present simultaneously, with some expressions more readily available, some more actively incorporated into habit patterns, or some attached by prior experience to specific stimuli or situations. Specific instances of learner behavior may then be the product of deliberate or fortuitous selection from the repertoires of possible responses. Leona Tyler (1978) suggested that:

> The core idea is that each individual represents a different sequence of selective acts by means of which only some of the developmental possibilities are chosen and organized.... As Whitehead pointed out, the fundamental realities are actual occasions in which indeterminate possibilities are transformed into determinate actualities. (p. 233)

Our referenced learner behaviors are examples of Tyler's "determinate actualities." They are the results of selective acts through which multiple manifestations of diversity are orchestrated. To seize on unitary components of those orchestrations may be an error, but the adaptation of instruction to those orchestrations may pose a greater challenge than the pedagogical sciences foundational to education currently enable us to meet.

Why is personalization considered so important in teaching and learning transactions? Unlike the factory model which considered children as "raw materials to be efficiently processed by technical workers (the teachers) to reach the end product" (Bennet and LeCompte 1990; Callahan 1962; Kliebard 1975). Students in the current period "need to understand the current state of their knowledge and to build on it, improve it, and make decisions in the face of uncertainty" (Talbert and McLaughlin 1993). One of the ways educators can enable students to meet this standard is to both personalize the learning environment and nurture those psychosocial attitudes and behaviors (including self-efficacy, agency, motivational regulation, internal locus of control) that may be just as crucial in maintaining students' interest, performance, and commitment to academic excellence and achievement.

THEORETICAL GROUNDING

We anchor our conceptualization of the multidimensional interaction between engagement, effort and personalization in several bodies of thought. These include Bourdieu's (1986) idea of social capital; Bandura's (1986, 2001) idea of self-efficacy and agency; Wolters' (2003) idea of the regulation of motivation; and Wolters' idea of an internal locus of control. These theoretical constructs are examined below for their capacity to contribute to our understanding of the structural and student characteristics that may be necessary to reduce the academic achievement gap between majority and minority students and increase student effort; persistence; level of academic and social integration; and academic excellence and achievement.

Social Capital

There are several related approaches to defining the social capital construct. Sociologists such as Ronald Burt (1997), Nan Lin (2001), and Alejandro Portes (1998) define social capital as resources, including information, ideas, and support that individuals are able to procure by virtue of their relationships with others. According to Portes (1998), the first systematic analysis of social capital was produced by Pierre Bourdieu (1986), who defined the concept as "the aggregate of the actual or potential resources which are linked to the possession of a durable network of more or less institutionalized relationships of mutual acquaintance and recognition" (p. 248).

Coleman's (1988) definition is somewhat more practical in that social capital is perceived not as a single entity but a variety of different entities, with two elements in common: they all consist of some aspect of social structures, and they facilitate certain actions of actors within the structure. Coleman (1988) suggests that there are three forms of social capital: obligations and expectations, information channels, and social norms.

Obligations and expectations. This form of social capital depends on two elements: trustworthiness of the social environment, which means that obligations will be repaid, and the actual extent of obligations held. Social structures differ in both these domains. Individuals in social structures with high levels of obligations outstanding at any time have more social capital on which they can draw. This suggests that the usefulness of the actual resources in the social structure may be amplified by their availability when needed.

Information channels. The potential for information that is inherent in social relations is another significant form of social capital. Information is important in providing a basis of action. But acquiring information is costly. At a minimum, it requires attention, which is always in scarce supply. Coleman (1988) suggests that one means by which information can be acquired is by use of social relations that are maintained for other purposes.

Social norms. When a norm exists and is effective, it constitutes a powerful, though sometimes fragile, form of social capital. Norms in a community that support and provide effective rewards for high academic achievement in and out of school greatly facilitates the school's task. A prescriptive norm within a collectivity that constitutes an especially important form of social capital is the norm that one should forgo self-interest and act in the interests of the collectivity. Norms of this sort are reinforced by social support, status, honor and other rewards. As indicated, effective norms can constitute a powerful form of social capital. This social capital, however, not only facilitates certain actions but also constrains others.

Within the context of a high performance learning communities, it could be argued that student self-efficacy (Bandura, 1986) is one of the attitudes that shapes and is shaped by Coleman's ideas of obligation, expectations, access to information, and social norms of reciprocity. In high performance learning communities, where students are expected to take responsibility for themselves and for each other, it could also be argued that high degrees of sel goal. The regulation of motivation occurs through the deliberate intervening in, managing, or controlling one of the underlying processes that determine this willingness. With respect to behavior, the regulation of motivation includes those thoughts, actions, or behaviors students engage in to affect their choice, effort, and persistence for academic work. The regulation of motivation can thus be characterized as processes used in an intentional manner to influence motivation. To the extent that such a strategy is initiated, monitored, and directed by a student, it can be identified as a self-regulation strategy and considered one aspect in deciding whether that student is a self-regulated learner.

In this conceptualization, motivational regulation is one process that operates within the larger system of self-regulated learning. It is thus related to but conceptually distinct from other processes considered essential to self-regulated learning including motivation (Wolters, 2003). Relatively new to the field, the construct of motivational regulation (Wolters, 2003) as conceptually distinct from motivation has recently emerged in the framework of self-regulation. Consequently, relevant literature and empirical validation studies of this construct are lacking. It is, however, an intriguing distinction with respect to its implications for interventions that nurture academic excellence among minority students of color.

An internal locus of personal control

Perceived personal control, in current thinking, appears to be determined by "successful behaviors, achievements and accomplishments," and relative to education, results in increased "effort, motivation and persistence in problem solving" (Mirowsky and Ross 1989; Rosenberg 1989; Ross and Sastry 1999). This conceptualization, however, seems to have evolved during the past half century. In 1966, Rotter posited that a person's internal or external locus of control is determined by experiences of affirming or negative reinforcement while Wallston and Wallston (1978) maintained that perceived control fluctuates depending on the domain or experience. Wheaton's (1980) idea of instrumentalism suggests that "instrumental persons are likely to accumulate resources and to develop skills and habits that prevent avoidable problems and reduce the impact of avoidable problems. Thus, over time, they improve their positions even more, producing a self-amplifying reciprocal effect between achievements and perceived control" (Ross and Broh 2000).

Ross and Broh suggest that "personal control is a learned, generalized expectation that outcomes are contingent on one's choices and actions." What does this really mean? Theoretically, it means that there is congruency between an individual's choices, efforts and outcomes. But it appears that perceived control includes more than simply making choices, and engaging in certain efforts that may lead to particular outcomes. We argue that perceived control may also be contingent on one's ability to plan, and intentionally motivate and regulate one's actions. For adolescents, success in school (as in the work and economic realm for adults) more strongly predicts perceived control, in theory, than do social attachments (Ross and Mirowsky 1992). According to the theory of personal control, the successful performance of a variety of tasks shapes the sense of control (Mirowsky and Ross 1986; 1989). For adolescents, perceived competence and success in school may be most important to beliefs about personal control. Research has found that academic achievement is associated with a high sense of control, whereas dropping out of high school reduces the sense of control (Finch, Shanahan, Mortimer, and Ryu 1991; Garner and Cole 1989; Lewis, Ross and Mirowsky 1999; Mone, Baker and Jeffries 1995).

Although mentioned in passing above, regulation may be a critical component of a learner's personalization of the attitudes and behaviors that contribute to academic success. Self-regulation, within the context of agency, is defined as inclusive of the cognitive and behavioral processes that are concerned with initiating, adapting, modifying, or changing a person's physiological responses, emotions, thoughts, behaviors, or environment (Carver & Scheier, 1998; Compas, Connor, Saltzman, Thomsen, & Wadsworth, 1999; Eisenberg, Fabes, & Guthrie, 1997). These cognitive and behavioral self-regulatory processes have implications for the interaction between personal, social, and environmental factors during the teaching and learning process. Thus the self-regulation of motivation, affect, and action is managed through the self-monitoring of performance, self-guidance through personal standards, and corrective self-reactions (Bandura, 1986, 1991b). (These processes should be closely examined for their relevance to changing student cognitions, learning strategies, attitudes, and behaviors (Bandura, 1986; Zimmerman, 1994).

In addition to regulation and motivation, it appears that a perceived sense of control may depend on whether the goals one engages in are proximal or distant. Bandura suggests that students are motivated by goals that they perceive as challenging but attainable, not by goals that they perceive as too easy or excessively difficult. Similarly, students who perceive their goal progression as acceptable and anticipate satisfaction from accomplishing their goals feel both efficacious about continuing to improve and motivated to complete the task (Bandura, 1986). Goal properties such as specificity, proximity, and difficulty level (Bandura, 1988; Locke & Latham, 1990) seem to influence self-efficacy and control because progress towards a specific goal becomes measurable. Students' negative evaluations of their progress do not necessarily decrease their motivation if they believe they are capable of improving by working harder. Alternatively, motivation may not increase if students believe they lack the ability to improve or to succeed (Locke & Latham, 1990).

There is a status dimension to perceived control as well. Adolescents whose parents have low levels of education and are poor may experience failures disproportionately compared with those of more advantaged parents. Parents who are well-educated and well to do may help their children develop skills and habits that make the children more effective at schoolwork, which indirectly increases the children's sense of control (Mirowsky and Ross 1998). Well-educated parents with high incomes may also raise adolescents' perceptions of control directly because they value self-reliance, personal responsibility, and personal development in children and may encourage and reward independence, whereas working class parents with high school degrees or less may emphasize obedience, conformity, and quiescence (Gerris, Dekovic and Janssens 1997; Kohn 1969). Perceived control is the subjective reflection of objective conditions of control and power in the stratification system, and adolescents whose parents are well-educated and have high incomes may have more actual control than do their less advantaged peers.

Determinant: Social relationships, self-esteem and perceived control: Self-esteem is a function of reflected appraisals of close family members and friends, parents or other close adults like teachers (Rosenberg 1979, 1989; Rosenberg et al. 1989). Perceptions of self-worth, or self-esteem, stem from social attachments to close friends and family members that reflect positively on a person and provide interpersonal support (Schwalbe and Staples 1991). Largely on the basis of research and theory about Black self-esteem, researchers have concluded that self-esteem results from reflected appraisals in one's immediate social network, such as teachers, parents, and friends, not on reflected appraisals in the larger social order (which in this case is a White society that may marginalize and devalue Blacks) (Hughes and Demo 1989; Rosenberg 1979; Rosenberg and Simmons 1972; Wade, Thompson, Tashakkori and Valente 1989). Perceptions of self-esteem stem from social attachments to close friends and family members that reflect positively on a person and provide interpersonal support. Of these close attachments, those with parents are central to children's self-esteem (Yabiku, Axinn and Thornton 1999).

Perceived control and self-esteem are positively correlated (Hughes and Demo 1989). Thus, if research includes self-esteem but not the sense of control, causes and consequences attributed to esteem could really be due to personal control. For example Liu et al (1992) found reciprocal relationships between academic achievement and self-esteem among students in grades 7-12; that is, students who score high on general self-esteem achieve high grades, and high grades, in turn, are associated with high levels of general self-esteem. However, without adjustment for perceived control, these associations could be spurious. In our theory, achievement shapes perceived control more than it does self-esteem and persons with high levels of personal control are effective, active participants in producing desired outcomes, so that the reciprocal effects found are more consistent with personal control theory than with self-esteem theory. Adjustment for both self-esteem and the sense of personal control is necessary to unravel which of the two is having an effect.

It is our contention that we can nurture a sense of agency, self-efficacy, effort, interest, motivation, self-regulation and personal control/agency in students by personalizing the teaching and learning transactions. Personalization is bi-directional in that the teacher, with support from administrators, peers, personalizes the experience and the stimulus materials, but it is the learner who must personalize the process and the product. This conceptualization emphasizes that for personalization to be optimally effective, the student must take ownership of the product of that learning and the process by which he or she learns. We have briefly indicated that this process include experiences of support from teachers and peers; integration into a peer group; student preparation for and level and quality of effort in schoolwork; and efficacy beliefs that doing well in school is personally important. These processes appear to enable the realization of academic knowledge, skills and dispositions (Eccles, Roeser, Wigfield, and Freedman-Doan 1999; Masten et al. 1995; Pianta, Rimm-Kaufman and Cox 1999).

Exemplars of Personalization

Our conceptualization of personalization includes concern for the context, processes of effort, engagement and outcomes. With regards to context, it appears that experiences of support from teachers and peers influence students' persistence, effort and engagement. These experiences take the form of teacher and peer involvement, support for independent thinking, and an adaptable pedagogical structure. Process of engagement in this context includes two aspects of student adjustment in school – ongoing engagement and reaction to challenge. "Ongoing engagement includes the extent to which students exert effort on schoolwork, pay attention in class, prepare for class, and believe doing well in school is personally important. Reaction to challenge includes different ways students may cope with or react to negative school related events. Students may blame negative events on teachers or others (projection). Students may downplay the importance of negative events (denial). Students may perseverate on events and worry about them without taking action to ensure such events do not re-occur (anxiety amplification). Finally, students may examine their behavior and attempt to change to prevent similar negative events from re-occurring (positive coping)." Outcomes include increased student academic performance and school commitment as evidenced in strong test scores and consistent attendance. In the following section, we provide exemplars of high academic achievement of students of color by highlighting a college preparatory school serving students in K-12 and an exemplary student academic development program in higher education.

Summer Bridge Program. Once selected for the program, Meyerhoff students attend a mandatory pre-freshman Summer Bridge Program and take courses in math, science, African American studies, and the humanities. They are also trained in how to study in peer groups and how to engage in rigorous and systematic problem-solving. Students are also exposed to relevant social and cultural events that encourage them to value each other's diversity and commonalities.

A particular strength of the summer bridge program is a committed faculty from different fields and program staff who explicitly prepare students for the new expectations and requirements of rigorous college courses. This component was structured on the basis of Hrabowski's research and earlier experience with directing an Upward Bound (UB) program for students following high school graduation. UB programs are intended to prepare students for rigorous college-level courses; familiarize them with faculty expectations; and provide students with opportunities to interact with peers, staff, and faculty.

The MSP's mandatory summer bridge program is implemented with the expectation that intensive summer academic work, in addition to opportunities for building academic social networks, will prepare students for excelling in university level work. Additionally, academics in the summer bridge program and in the course of students' undergraduate academic career in the MSP are balanced with social opportunities and cultural events that encourage constant interaction with peers, faculty, university leadership, and program staff.

Conversations with program staff suggest that the summer bridge component is one of the more crucial of the components. One of the staff's guiding principles is from Proverbs 22:6 KJV

> Train up a child in the way he should go,
> And when he is old,
> He will not depart from it.

Program staff regard the six weeks they have with pre-freshmen students as a crucial time because it gives them an opportunity to reduce and/or eliminate the bad habits of writing a paper overnight and studying overnight, for example. According to the Mr. Toliver, "Aside from molding them and exposing students to the Meyerhoff way, the greatest things they [the program staff] can give students is compassion and empathy." Ms. Ernestine Baker, executive director of the MSP, acknowledges that she and her staff have "unconditional faith and belief" in the Meyerhoff Scholars. She emphasized that it is important to her that her staff knows their students' strengths and weaknesses, "who they click with, their background, their pet peeves, and their fears" (Toliver, personal communication, 2003). Program staff gains this information in the course of the six weeks of the summer bridge program and through the daily advising and monitoring of students.

During this time and throughout students' careers in the MSP, old-fashioned socialization is also emphasized. Mr. Toliver stressed that "Meyerhoffs have to open doors, pull out chairs, not chew gum in public, and dress in a certain way—girls wear skirts a certain length below their knees." This emphasis is referred to as both "challenging the Meyerhoffs to be better persons and outfitting them to succeed."

Our observations of the program staff's interactions with students suggest that they genuinely care about how well their charges do. Both program staff and students openly admit that the program is intrusive. It is this characteristic, they believe, that partially accounts for the program's effectiveness. According to Mr. Toliver, "males have more trouble with intrusiveness than females" and they (males) "are not open to talking about what's happening to them" (Toliver, personal communication, 2003). Meyerhoff Scholars have to check in almost daily with program staff who are concerned about the students they do not see almost daily. From the perspective of the program staff, they work "well together with students like a family" (Toliver, personal communication, 2003).

How Effective teachers Nurture Student Achievement. From Pressley et al's study of Providence-St. Mel School (PSM) on Chicago's West Side "student and faculty responses to a questionnaire mentioned teacher dedication as important in the success of the school. Students described teachers as "dedicated" and "caring," consistent with Noddings' (1984) vision of effective teachers. There were many mentions in the student questionnaire responses of teacher availability to assist students before, during and after school. Pressley et al. (1982) observed that teachers were available and did provide support before, during and after the school day – in the lunchroom and on the run between classes. Observed that most teachers were on task every minute they were with a class, often teaching from the moment students entered the door and continuing to interact with students meaningfully as they departed for their next class. Teachers' enthusiastic willingness to stay after school and to come to school to do Saturday tutoring was striking. Teachers often suggested to students to come for the supplemental, after hours instruction.

Teachers at PSM know their students well and work with them to achieve goals. After school hours, they take students to activities, for example, the school choirs appeared often in Chicago and surrounding communities.

The teachers welcome contact with their students' families. For example, every day, there were lots of positive discussions between teachers and parents in the first floor corridor as parents came to pick up students at the end of the school day.

A theme that ran through many faculty comments on the survey was that the faculty worked like a team, with each other, the students, the administration, and the parents, consistent with the relational trust identified by Bryk and Schneider (2002) as occurring in effective schools. A high degree of camaraderie among the faculty was evident, for example as grade-level teams coordinated their days, and at celebratory events.

The principal had instituted a "vigorous accountability system for teachers, which includes multiple observations each year by the principal; the directors of the lower, middle and high schools; and the heads of the academic departments at the high school level. These visits are to assess whether a teacher is effective with respect to delivery of the curriculum and classroom management. Pressley et al. documented that all members of the faculty whom they observed to be underperforming relative to the school's expectations were not invited to return to the school for the next school year.

Instruction supporting high and meaningful academic achievement— Although academic demands are high, there are many supports to promote student academic achievement (Strage, Tyler, Rohwer and Thomas 1987). One of the most salient is that all students have agendas (planning books) with homework assignments recorded in them. If a student does not complete homework, after school homework club is required. If a student is absent, work is sent home with the expectation that it will be completed. Teachers told students to study the review sheets and previous quizzes in preparation for exams. Math teachers urged students to practice exactly the kinds of problems that would be on the test; science teachers told students to practice recalling factual information that would be covered on upcoming tests; social studies teachers urged students to go over the review questions assigned in class. Such effort has great potential to pay off at PSM because most exams are aligned with information considered essential by the teachers, with such information covered in previous reviews and quizzes. In short, there is careful thinking throughout the school about what is essential content, with that represented prominently in study aids and exams.

There is also much written feedback on homework and quizzes and much discussion in classes about what students have done wrong on quizzes and how errors can be corrected. Teachers went over exams that had been returned often, providing students with much information about how to avoid the same errors in the future, consistent with the recommendations in the learning literature about how to do academic feedback so that it is effective (Bangert-Drowns, Kulik, Kulik, and Morgan 1991). The teachers also worked hard to reduce anxiety about exams, for example, consistently sending the message that students would be ready if they studied the material that was flagged as important. The teachers made sure that certain students knew that their grades were not entirely a function of exam performance. Thus, one external observer watched as a teacher completed the review for an exam by asking the students not to panic, reminding them that if they did do poorly on a test, they could make it up with a project. These efforts make sense in light of what is known about how to treat exam anxiety (Ergene 2003).

For students who have substantial academic difficulties, there is after school tutoring, as well as Saturday tutoring from 9a.m. to noon, all done by the faculty. If a students' difficulties are so severe that she or he fails a course, PSM offers a summer school that permits students to catch up. The summer school enrolls about 200 on average.

Finally, an important source of support is the students themselves, with the external observers often seeing students providing assistance to one another before school, at lunch, and in the computer lab. There is a huge support network for PSM students when they struggle academically. In summary, there are many ways that the school provides help for students to learn what they need to learn and to do tasks that they need to do to succeed at the school. Much of this effort is the direct result of hard work by the faculty, who align instruction, reviews and exams, provide tutoring and make certain that students know how to use the technology and library resources available to them.

An emphasis on understanding: in almost every class observed, there was substantial emphasis on understanding rather than low-level learning. The PSM teachers insisted that students be thoughtful, that they process material deeply, with most of this processing occurring in discussions. This is significant because there is a growing literature establishing that there is higher achievement in classrooms where understanding is demanded (i.e., through extensive discussion; see Applebee, Langer, Nystrand and Gamoran 2003; Knapp and Associates 1995). In sum, in classroom after classroom, elementary students are very actively involved as part of learning, from cooperative discussion to reflections on material covered in text to doing dramatizations that are much more than reading the words of a script. In class after class, the external observers listened to discussions where teachers demanded not just that students know the facts but that they be able to explain the facts. In sum, active learning, so heavily favored in the educational psychological literature, is present everywhere at PSM (Wiske 1997).

Scaffolding. When curriculum and instruction are demanding, an important mechanism for assuring that learning, achievement, and understanding actually occur is teacher scaffolding of students (Hogan and Pressley 1997; Rogoff 1990; Wood et al. 1976). When teachers scaffold, they monitor individual students to determine who needs help. Then, they provide just enough assistance so that the student can make progress on his or her own, allowing the student to do so. The external observers saw such scaffolding often. The result was that students seldom seemed frustrated.

She moved from student to student, making suggestions as to how to proceed next, explaining to each student just what the student needed to know at the moment or reflecting with each student on some aspect of the project. Instruction was one mini-lesson after another. Part of scaffolding is creating student confidence. As she monitored student progress, she constantly reassured individual students when they lacked confidence in their own work. Urging students to value their creations.

Encouragement of self-regulation. An important point with respect to scaffolding is that the PSM teachers, like effective teachers generally (Pressley, Dolezal et al 2003; Pressley, Roehrig et al., 2003) are determined that students be self-regulated as soon as possible. Thus, the scaffolding is intended to provide just enough support to get the students on track, then working on their own. Teachers aspire for students to work hard all the time, largely directing themselves.

CONCLUSION

At a juncture in this nation when the mantra of "no child left behind" seemingly reflects an attempt to understand and reduce educational achievement gaps and devise the conceptual grounding upon which different strategies and approaches can function individually and interdependently. Assessment cannot only be focused on standardized tests but needs to incorporate quantitative and qualitative as well as individualized measures of student ability. This strategy more accurately captures differential learning patterns and modes of intellectual performance (Gordon 2000). Indeed, understanding that the properties of one set of behaviors may enable even more comprehensive behaviors which is at the core of Gordon's advocacy for the differential analysis of learner characteristics and the design of learning experiences. Such differentiation is thought to be essential to one's understanding of the learner's behavior and status. Gordon advocates that schooling for students in urban communities needs to converge around the criteria of good educational planning, wholesome and purposeful developmental conditions, greater diversity of curricula and goals, and greater attention to the needs of individual learners. He argues that the purposes, goals, and practical strategies informing teaching, learning and assessment need to both value the backgrounds and situations of students of color and to enable them to achieve higher levels of competencies. In order to do so, educators must facilitate the mastery and transfer of culturally-specific as well as hegemonic knowledge, skills, and dispositions. Gordon believes it is toward such developments in our students that we must continue to direct our efforts and our endorsement of education in general. This will enable the shifting of the debate away from majority and minority differences in levels of intellectual functioning to understanding the mechanisms and meanings that exist between the developmental patterns, cultural and learning styles, and temperamental traits of learners and the educational experiences to which they are exposed (Gordon 2000).

4
A Curriculum of Cultural Interdependence and Plural Competence

As a response to the controversy around the content of the social studies curriculum, and the raising concern on the treatment of African American, Latino and Native American content in the social studies curriculum, the New York State Board of Regents appointed a committee to study the problem that was created by the political reaction to a prior report—"A Curriculum of Inclusion" that was prepared by a committee headed by Professor Lenox Jeffries at City College of New York. That committee made the report that encountered considerable resistance, in part because of the vigor with which the case for a more inclusive agenda was advanced, and also because the committee's style was viewed as confrontational. The members of the Board of Regents directed the commissioner to determine whether or not anything could be done to salvage attention to the problem of multicultural under-inclusion without embracing the political "offensiveness" of the original report.

Commissioner Thomas Sobol had appointed a politically and racially balanced group to work with Francis Roberts, a former superintendent from a school district in Long Island, under me to review the report "A Curriculum of Inclusion" and to recommend a course of action for the Board of Regents. The review committee consisted of some persons who were very sympathetic to the Afro-centric perspective that had been advanced in the Jeffrey's report, several persons who were sensitive to the need that the curriculum content should be broadened and some persons like Arthur Schlesinger, who thought that there was no need for the curriculum to be changed and advanced the notion that a more inclusive curriculum ran the risk of supporting cultural disunity. The meetings of this committee were remarkably calm and cooperative as I recall it, there were seldom heated debates. Rather, most discussions preceded with a high level of respect for different perspectives. Early on in the meetings, under the leadership of my

81

colleagues from upstate New York, we agreed that we did not want to refute the arguments and position of the Jeffrey's committee since there was a high degree of consensus that the Social Studies curriculum for New York State should reflect the variety of cultures that are represented in the peoples of the state.

Since we were to release our report at about the same time as the tercentennial of the U.S. Declaration of Independence, we came up with the theme "cultural interdependence" which substantially came to be represented in the title of our report: A Declaration of Cultural Interdependence. Having established as a core value the notion of multiple perspectives and cultural interdependence, the next six months of the committees work were devoted to the generation of arguments in support of these two values and the generation or identification of materials, which could be used in the teaching and learning of such values. In the course of our discussions it became clear to me that there is an argument grounded in theories of cognitive development that support what we were about. One of the salient contributions of Piaget, the French developmentalist, is the notion that perspectives taking, seeing the world through the eyes of others and the capacity to entertain multiple perspectives represents the high stage of cognitive development. The committee enthusiastically embraced my argument that one of the strongest planks in the platform supporting multiculturalism in education is the idea that more than the moral issues involved and more important than the politics of inclusion, for education, the contribution that multi-perspectivist approaches to pedagogy are productive of intellect.

I think it was perhaps this grounding of our recommendations in respected cognitive theory that lead to the standing ovation I received when I made our oral report to the Board of Regents. They saw in our work a logical defense grounded in accepted theory of a political solution that they wanted to embrace. I found it interesting that we had not retreated from the positions advanced by the report "A Curriculum of Inclusion." What we had done was to accept the basic ideas and put them in a language that could be supported by a broader political spectrum. I am not at all convinced that observers others than the members of the Board of Regents were equally receptive of the position advanced in "A Declaration of Cultural Interdependence." The Jeffrey's group was thankful that we had not tried to reject the arguments advanced in their report. Some other Afro-centrist seemed to feel that the traditional Euro-centrists curriculum needed to be confronted by an Afro-centric curriculum. Our report did not do that. Many Afro- and Euro-centrists seemed to agree with the Board of Regents that our report was a masterful compromise and intelligent solution to a messy problem and, of course, the representatives of the status quo were unhappy to have the Board of Regents embrace the notions concerning multiculturalism and multi-perspectivist thinking. Arthur Schlesinger and Kenneth Jackson were so concerned that each of them filed a dissenting opinion. I was respectful of Professor Jackson's position even though he and I disagreed on some key points. Professor Jackson at least read the final draft of "One Nation, Many Peoples: A declaration of cultural inter-dependence" before he wrote his dissent. I cannot say the same for Professor Schlesinger, who indicated to me that he was writing his dissent without the benefit of reading the report of the committee because he was going to be out of the country but wanted his point of view to be represented in the report. Jackson's reaction was unexpected since he had at least participated in several of the meetings of the committee and at times I thought was sympathetic to the prevailing position. Schlesinger's dissent was not unexpected since he had stated his position early in the work of the committee and had not participated in most of our meetings. It is my impression that his position remained unchanged throughout the period.

I do not know whether "A Declaration of Cultural Inter-dependence" made much difference in the field. I have not followed actual practice in the teaching of social studies in New York state but from my casual observations and some other experiences, I suspect that those of us who supported broadening the social studies curriculum found support for our biases in the report and, perhaps, continued movement in this direction with greater confidence. It is my impression, however, that the social studies in New York continued to play "lip service" to human diversity and multiple perspectives but little conviction. In 2009, almost 20 years since writing that report I find the faculty of a college that is committed to teaching about diversity and pluralism is struggling with how to represent these concerns appropriately in its curriculum. Among the strongest advocates for the inclusion of broader content are those who are hung up on the tension between (1) teaching about and celebrating the characteristics of diverse peoples and a somewhat patronizing respect for the same, and (2) emphasis on the development of the intellective capacity to analyze and understand critically the relationships between cultural experience, cultural identity and human agency in a cosmopolitan world. I continue to see the latter as the more important challenge facing multi-cultural education.

The United States is unique in the respect that it is one of the few nations that has deliberately set out to make itself a nation of many people. The United States has always been a country of many diverse peoples, coming from many different cultural backgrounds, attempting to co-mingle as one society. Although as a country we are made up of many different cultures, these separate cultures have been encouraged to recede into the background or blend together. Rather than to hold on to any specific individual culture we have been encouraged as a nation to meld our cultures together to create one culture, all be it, dominated by the cultures of northern Europe.

The blending of diverse cultures into one amalgam has brought about its own unique set of problems. Which cultural elements are to be accepted as components of the hegemonic culture and why? If I become part of the hegemonic culture what happens to my culture and its own distinctive set of variables? The United States started as a nation consisting mostly of immigrants of European descent that tended to ignore the Native American and African American cultures, however in recent history there has been a strong influx of immigrants from non-European countries. Many of these new and old citizens alike feel strongly about their cultures and heritages and they are justifiably concerned about being swallowed up into the dominant culture without the inclusion of identifiable components of their cultures in the amalgam. These facts of diversity in the characteristics of people, and pluralism in the values that guide the society are problems that will increase in their impact on the U.S. society. Consequently any discussion of public policy in the twenty-first century has to be concerned with Multiculturalism as a modern phenomenon.[1]

The components of a multicultural society can be defined as both diverse and plural (Gordon, 1991). If we look at the many different cultures present in the United States today we see much diversity—many different groups of peoples with many different characteristics. There are also present the pluralistic roles that people must fill. We take on many different functions in our multicultural-multilingual society: a man might be a husband, a father, Spanish speaking and a physician, while a woman might be a mother, bi-sexual and a CEO, increasingly called upon to show multiple competencies, i.e., to speak more than one language, to function in multiple settings, to practice female, male or androgynous gender roles.

These diverse and plural roles create a tension between that which is personal and in a sense private, and that which is public. When we were able to live in greater

---

1. Readers concerned with Multiculturalism should see Banks & Banks *Handbook of Research of Multicultural Education, Journal of Negro Education,* One Nation: Many Peoples.

isolation we were free to be just us, and able to function within a narrow range of competencies. Now our world has become a communicatively small global community, due to enhanced communication and the density of our population, we are all living together with a diverse population of people and it has become essential that we be able to function in a number of different contexts and ways. With these many different roles and diverse cultures all commingled it becomes necessary to direct public policy toward equipping people with the ability to accept, understand and interpret each other's commonalities and differences.

Most active public policy responses to human diversity in the nation have been in the desegregation of public facilities and the introduction of multicultural education. Multiculturalism was first seen and taught as an area of pedagogy concerned with knowledge of different cultures and different ethnic groups (Banks, 1992). As it began to evolve, multicultural courses were taught as ethnic studies, primarily concerned with African American and Latin American studies that focused on the characteristics of experiences of these specific groups. In the 1980s the growth of this field turned to greater diversity in the material covered and tended to be more inclusive of material that referenced many different ethnic and gender groups. By the 1990s the languages of perspective and voice were introduced. Here the concern was not so much with facts about groups of people, as it was with developing sensitivity to the perspectives and voices of the different groups or people who populate our nation. Even within specific population studies, celebratory history and the descriptive inventorying of cultures began to give way to contextual analysis and critical interpretation.

In the several iterations of multicultural education, one can see several functions that have been served by this enterprise. In the early period the focus in multicultural education and ethnic studies was on inclusion and assimilation. The concern was with rejecting the amalgam that was emerging as American culture. There was an insistence that specific excluded groups be included and that contributions made by members of these groups somehow be represented and identifiable in the fabric of the national culture.

In the several iterations of multicultural education, one can see several functions that have been served by this enterprise. In the early period the focus in multicultural education and ethnic studies was on inclusion and assimilation. The concern was with rejecting the amalgam that was emerging as American culture. There was an insistence that specific excluded groups be included and that contributions made by members of these groups somehow be represented and identifiable in the fabric of the national culture. The goal was to have the various components integrated in the whole so that they were distinguishable by their origin but accepted as integral to the whole. However, the politics of inclusion forced a concern with accommodation and correction in which the field tried to accommodate these mechanically included new concerns while representatives of the excluded knowledge insisted that greater emphasis be placed on the correction of either distorted and/or omitted knowledge. This period was marked by public debate and protest concerning the extent to which some information concerning some groups in the society was simply missing or that information about these groups was in reality deliberately misrepresented and incorrect.

In response to the distorted images of Latin Americans, Native Americans, African Americans, and Asian Americans, representatives of these groups worked to introduce corrected images and more appropriate representations. As more and more information was included, corrected, and accommodated by the dominant culture and its canon, the shift in attention of these formerly excluded groups moved to appreciation and celebration. This stage is characterized by elements of group pride, and even chauvinism as previously neglected groups achieved a greater degree of appreciation for their own characteristics and contributions. This stage led to a period of nationalistic celebration; for example, in the African American tradition this stage was marked by slogans like "Black is beautiful" and the concern for "Black power." The changes observed throughout this period were largely the result of the political and celebratory activities of the neglected groups. It is generally agreed that such change would not have come about without these actions. However, change breeds change. As new knowledge and perspectives were introduced and recognized our conception of what should be included changed.

As advocates of multicultural education and protectors of the traditional canon, alike, began to struggle with more dynamic conceptions of knowledge and new perspectives, they were forced to view the struggle within the context of postmodern thought. Multiculturalism and postmodernism both require that attention be given to ideational context and situated perspective. Thus the concern with ethnicity and cultural groups moved away from an exclusive emphasis on distinct groups to the relationship of ethnic, gender and national group status to major political and historical developments. For example the Civil War is better understood when its study includes contextual analysis and perspectives of Black and White people, of men's and women's lived experiences, of the differential impacts on the economies of Black people and White people in Northern and Southern communities. This stage which began to emerge in the late 1980s, was characterized by an insistence on the study of people in context, that is, effort was placed on better understanding the relationship between the characteristics and experiences of particular groups and the context out of which their experiences developed. The true integration of multiple cultures in the hegemonic culture could only occur if that integration were sensitive to the context and the conditions that influenced the development.

In the current period the functions to be served by multicultural education have expanded to include critical interpretation and critical understanding. These expanded functions make multicultural education more a process directed at conceptual understanding than a simple matter of factual teaching, and technique and knowledge accumulation. The concern for critical interpretation (Guess, 1981) includes the perspectives that (1) knowledge about a people is best understood in the context of the interests served by the information and its production; (2) that comparative and contextual analysis amplifies descriptive analysis; and (3) that the validity of a phenomenon is in part a function of the context in which it is observed. From the critical perspective it is argued that comprehension of the reported characteristics of one's own or another culture is only possible if that knowledge is understood from the perspective of its contextual origins, purposes and the attributions assigned to them. For example one might make a point of calling attention to the involvement of people of Jewish ancestry in the enslavement of Africans. While this information is factual, if the knowledge interest served has to do with the demeaning of Jewish persons, rather than an understanding the origins of slavery, it is likely that an understanding of the role of profit making in human exploitation would be missed entirely. If one's purpose is to contribute to students' understanding and the prevention of human holocausts, what is more important are the factors that encouraged and enabled human exploitation rather than the isolated identification of one group of participants. The advocates of critical interpretation in multicultural education are trying to move the field of study away from the conveyance of decontextualized information concerning the cultures of human kind, to the use of information and knowledge to develop the capacity for critical understanding in students. Thus the next function of multicultural education is the development of critical and creative understanding by which students understand the interrelatedness of the phenomena of the world and are able to use these advanced perspectives to create understanding that may not have existed previously.

It is through its contribution to critical understanding that multicultural education provides an opportunity to address one of humanity's most critical problems. In an increasingly diverse world, which is rapidly becoming a single world community, the juxtaposition of peoples, cultures, and political economic interests makes it urgent that our knowledge of peoples be used to build bridges and improve communication between diverse cultures. It is in the utilization and application of critical and creative understanding that some of us see the possibility for addressing this problem. This plea for tolerance and openness (Gordon and Roberts 1991) in the examination of ideas and perspectives comes into conflict with another important social value and i.e. nation building.

One of the long recognized functions of the curriculum is to prepare students for citizenship in support of the continuing effort at nation-building. We recognize that nation-building, especially in so diverse a populace, requires that we give attention, not so much to our differences as to our commonalities. Some of us feel strongly that the education in all of its manifestations should stress the nation's common values and traditional conceptions of our history, Others of us feel that those values and conceptions have become truncated as a result of the hegemonic ascendance of cultural elements, values and world views that tend to be associated with our European ancestry alone. Thus the insistence on the inclusion of broader perspectives and non-dominant knowledge sources. But the question arises as to whether we can conjointly serve both pluribus and unum, a critical approach to multiculturalism, suggests that we can. For example, we may be mistaken in our association of the "flowering of human civilization" in Europe as an achievement of European people alone, old, and certainly more recent knowledge sources indicate that what flowered in Europe was the combination and culmination of cultural and technological developments from Africa, Asia and Europe. Thus ethnic cheerleading should be replaced by collective human celebration as we uncouple specific human achievements at one point in history from the immediate and sometimes fortuitous context in which they have been presumptively "first" observed (Gordon and Roberts 1991).

Another line of reasoning, as well, illumines the responsibility of schooling to aid in nation-building by preparing the young for citizenship. We refer to one of the fundamental tenets of democratic government, viz., government with the consent of the governed. We realize today that consent cannot be considered to count unless it is informed consent. We assert that informed consent cannot be based upon ignorance, or even upon simply knowing or believing. Informed consent requires understanding born of critical analysis, synthesis and critical interpretation. Such intellectual competencies do not arise from training in established traditions, values and beliefs, or from the teaching of consensus history. Education to develop intellect capable of informed consent and choice requires exposure to diverse opinions, multiple perspectives and situated histories, where the learning tasks involve comparative analysis, contextual validation, heuristic exploration, and judicious reflection. We want our students to become thinking participants in, rather than trained validators of, decisions concerning the affairs of the nation. Such richly intelligent beings are very likely to recognize and respect the important things that we share in common as well as the unique things that make us different. In a similar manner, they are, perhaps, more likely to choose the common good than are persons with less well-developed intellectual abilities. If society cannot expect such qualities of its educated members, then we are in very serious trouble.

For quite some time, the concept "equal educational opportunity" has dominated educators' thinking. The concept grew out of court litigations around issues related to ethnic segregation in public education and distributive inequality in resource allocation. As a result, the nation has affirmed its commitment to equality of educational opportunity for all and has translated this to mean equal access to the educational resources provided through public funds (Coleman, 1968). But equal opportunity may not adequately reflect the implicit commitments of a democratic, diverse, pluralistic, and humane society. If what we are committed to is to make educational and other achievements independent of ethnic group, social class, sex group, religious group, and/or geographic group origins, then is not a concept such as human diversity with social justice more worthy of our tradition?

The intervention indicated by the answer to the question posed may violate our more narrow conceptions of equality—impartiality—but, given the compelling facts of human diversity, it may be the only way in which we can approach social justice. To honor, then, the implicit commitment to equality of opportunity we may be required to embrace a new commitment to the nurturance of human diversity in the pursuit of social justice.

Concern with human diversity is not new to educators. We have a long history of awareness of individual and group differences. Unfortunately, however, an examination of that history reveals pedagogical concern for such differences has been far more obvious in our verbalizations than in our practice. Most teachers recognize that learners differ greatly in their learning relevant as well as learning non-relevant characteristics. Good teachers go to great lengths to try to make adjustments in the learning experiences of children they know to be unlike other learners. A sizeable body of research has developed around concerns for the individualization of instruction (Glaser) and the exploration of the potential of attribute-treatment-interactions (Cronbach & Snow, 1977). Yet the range of variance in curriculum design and instructional practice is far less rich than is the diversity to be found in the populations of learners available. There are only modest complimentarities between the emerging knowing base referable to functional and status human characteristics, and knowledge concerning theories and technologies, and curriculum development and pedagogy. The best developed of our programs of individualization tend to focus on single aspects of diversity, learning rate, interests, aspects of personality, or combinations of developed abilities, achievement and background experience.

Moreover, we are persuaded that it is not so much a greater sensitivity to differentials in the level of developed intellect that is needed to improve the effectiveness of pedagogy or to increase the degree to which equality of educational opportunities and outcomes are achieved. Rather, what is required is greater sensitivity to and understanding of the multiple factors, which seem to interact with intellect, to influence its development and the effectiveness of its utilization.

This nation's failure to live up to its ideals is made most evident by its educational system; a system that does not make productive use of learner differences or educate for social justice. A well conceived and administered multicultural approach to teaching and learning would contribute to the elimination of the relationship that currently exists between race, gender, socioeconomic status and proficiency in standard English dialect, and educational opportunity and achievement. It would also increase the pool of socially aware and socially responsible United States citizens. Supporters of the multicultural education movement maintain that the changing demographics of this nation require that students develop multicultural literacy; (Gordon & Holmes, 1990) that they acquire the knowledge, attitudes and skills necessary to function in a diverse world. For some, multicultural education can contribute substantially to the uniting of a deeply divided nation (Banks, 1992). Inter-group conflict would be lessened as a result of the more continuous and authentic personal encounters that would result and serve to decrease destructive distancing and categorizing (Greene, 1992). In addition to uniting groups in conflict, multicultural education, according to its supporters, should enhance the self-esteem, self-confidence and consequently, the school performance of children as what is taught becomes more relevant, interesting and positively reinforcing.

90

MULTIPLE PERSPECTIVESM IN TEACHING AND LEARNING

Weaving multiple cultural perspectives into the curriculum is important to the education of all students. By including preparation in multicultural education in its standards, the National Council for the Accreditation of Teacher Education (NCATE) correctly recognized years ago in the late 1970s what we appear to need to "discover" again: that multicultural education has powerful pedagogical repercussions critical to both White students and students of color, quite apart from issues of assimilation and loss of identity. NCATE suggested in 1979 that multicultural education provided:

Preparation for the social, political and economic realities individuals experience in diverse and complex human encounters. These realities have both national and international dimensions. This preparation provides a process by which an individual develops competencies for perceiving, believing, evaluating, and behaving in different cultural setting. Thus, multicultural education is viewed as an intervention and an ongoing assessment process to help institutions and individuals become more responsive to the human condition, individual cultural integrity, and cultural pluralism in society. (Cited in Charles A. Tesconi, Multicultural Education: A Valued But Problematic Ideal, *Theory Into Practice.* 23(2). pp. 87-92, 1983).

Because of the diversity of the world and in order to prepare students to understand and influence the world of which they are a part, we should strive to teach from a multicultural perspective, regardless of whether the school community is itself diverse or whether the local student population is drawn predominantly from one cultural group. To make this possible teachers should have maximum flexibility, within the established curriculum, to adjust to the emphases selected consistent with the immediate and broader cultural contexts. Multicultural education should seek to make clear not only the common concerns, achievements and aspirations that are of the source of national unity, but also the distinctive historical roles, traditions and contributions of the different peoples who together have struggled to create the societies of the world. A multicultural perspective, then, means that all the applicable viewpoints of the historical and social protagonists should be explored paying special attention to the ways in which race, ethnicity, gender, and class generate different ways of understanding, experiencing, and evaluating the events of the world. Because interpretations vary as experiences differ, a multicultural perspective must necessarily be a multiple perspective that takes into account the variety of ways in which any topic can be comprehended.

Each academic area should complement, and be complemented by work in other academic areas. All disciplines should contribute to students' development of cognitive abilities, literacy, and quantitative knowledge and skill. Wherever appropriate, interdisciplinary approaches should be used, for example, relating social studies to the study of language arts, science, mathematics, and the arts. The goal is the development of the intellect, including the ability to find, process, and transfer information, with the study of multiple cultures and their diverse forms of understanding as the vehicle.

The development of the intellect includes the ability to use evidence to test a thesis, to reason inductively and deductively, to test a thesis, to reason inductively and deductively, to discern similarities and differences, and result. An understanding of multiple perspectives includes the capacity to distance oneself from one's beliefs in order to encounter and appreciate the beliefs, behaviors and rationales of others.

The students' ability to use controversy, argument and debate as tools of thinking should be developed by organizing learning so that students can engage in them.

Shared cultures do tend to make for some degree of knowledge consensus. This difference in the conception of what knowledge is, stems from the different cultures in which people live. In the examination of these different cultures, it is apparent that there are strains of knowledge that are common to all people. These common strains represent the stability of knowledge, however we also see a wide range of variance depicting the fluidity of knowledge. It is because of this stability and fluidity that it is important to recognize how and where knowledge is produced, by whom it is produced, and who benefits by its production. If the dominant group in a given society is assessing what knowledge is, we can assume that the substance of this knowledge will be biased to favor the interests of the dominant group. Knowing that the production of knowledge arises from many different contexts and serves different interests it becomes important to enable people to recognize and accept these differences in the nature of knowledge. In multicultural education we realize that most knowledge is relative to the context from which it came and the purposes it serves. But societies cannot function without some common knowledge, some shared reference points, some sense of social consensus. To deal with this need, human societies tend to develop canons—bodies of accepted knowledge to which members of these societies turn. The canon in any particular society has become the standard source of acceptable information. As societies like the USA have become more diverse, the consensus around the canon has declined. This change has led into discussions and debates concerning the nature of the canon as well as the knowledge that it enshrines. A high degree of importance attaches to the integrity of the canon, but problems arise when we consider the boundaries of the canon. Thus questions concerning the validity of various knowledge components constantly stand just beneath the surface of many of our discussions. Some of us are more comfortable with the knowledge and its sources that have been recognized and certified by the academy. Others of us repeatedly call attention to new knowledge, new sources and new voices and their claim, to validity equal to that assigned to the traditional and the hegemonic. The tension between these two positions is not a new phenomenon. The history of human societies, our own nation included, is marked by debates and even wars over different conceptions of truth and views of reality. It is a measure of human progress that we have arrived at the stage of societal development that in democratic societies, these debates are verbal and written and not the subject of physical combat. However, they are none the less critical, in part, because in modern societies the changing conception of what it means to be an educated and intelligent person includes our capacity to entertain and understand phenomena from perspectives different from our own, on our way to arriving at wise judgments and the reconciliation of differences. Without falling into the futile debate concerning whose canon shall be taught, we have elevated the question to include pedagogical problems concerning how we enable learners to respect and deal with multiple perspectives, i.e., multiple ways of seeing things and using different sources of knowledge better to understand experiences and information. This assertion is advanced, in part, because, for much of our knowledge, validity is difficult to establish independent of context.

Some of us are surprised by the depth of feelings concerning diverse renditions of history. Some of us who are comfortable in the belief that the history that we know is valid are offended by the assertion that much of that history is incomplete or false. Some of us who feel that the standard histories have excluded or misrepresented important players, find it difficult to assert our claims dispassionately. In the views represented by some of us, it appears that much of the dominant or traditional information available to us is viewed with doubt, skepticism and distrust because it does not fit comfortably with the experiences of some of us, and, for others of us, it is simply counter intuitive. Deciding what to teach under such existential circumstances confronts us with problems of monumental complexity. What is even more problematic for teaching and learning is the ease with which information, ideology and belief become commingled in the minds of many of those whose interests are served by these ideas. This is sometimes so much the case that these ideas, despite their differential order, come to be interchangeable one for the other. Although we are generally in agreement that histories tend to reflect the interests and perspectives of those who write them, there is a ubiquitous undercurrent of concern for the recognition of historical and other truth.

It may well be that it is this concern for truth that will be most difficult to reconcile with our conception of education as being directed at the development of intellect and understanding. Unlike earlier periods when one demonstrated one's intellect by how much one knew, i.e., how many facts one had at her/his command, increasingly we recognize the mark of intellect to be the capacity independently to analyze, manipulate, synthesize and critically interpret information in the interest of problem solving. It is not that facts, knowledge structures, are unimportant, it is that they are insufficient and often so situation bound as to limit their utility in understanding and problem solving. Thus the concern for multiple truths, situated knowledge, contextual validity and multiple perspectives in our study of most phenomena of the humanities, social sciences and history. This almost contradictory juxtaposition of positivism and relativism in the production, interpretation and understanding of information is one of the fundamental sources of complexity in teaching and learning.

CONCLUSION

It is important to understand the imperative for multiculturalism within the context out of which it has grown, that context is one of the relative political and economic powerlessness of subaltern peoples. Multiculturalism has grown out of those human relationships, which are marked by the distinct absence of social justice in a society where privileged and subordinated cultures exist in close proximity. One of the goals of multiculturalism is directed at achieving a higher degree of social justice in society, particularly for these politically and economically powerless groups whose cultures have been subordinated. This may be why one of the annoying characteristics that we find in the field of multiculturalism is that a good part of the imagery and substance of the field gets directed at those political ends. It could be argued for example that if it were not for the fact of relative political and economic powerlessness and the absence of social justice we would not be as concerned with multiculturalism. Just as the people who control the power in society are seldom the proponents of change. Since multiculturalism is expected to serve these justice ends the field has become particularly susceptible to dogma and ideology, however, the privileging of dogma and ideology always stands in juxtaposition to the optimal development of knowledge and understanding.

Thus one tension in the current press for multicultural education is between this concern for knowledge and understanding and the press toward dogma and ideology. Epistemologically one understands that dogma and ideology arise under the conditions that are identified above, as when you have either political economic instability, or a sense of powerlessness, or even the sense that ones power is under threat. So that the ascendancy of dogma and ideology can happen with the majority group when its members feel that their power is under threat. In defense of that perceived threat, they begin to take dogmatic positions and to develop ideologies that support their own political and status positions. However, the perspectives of the hegemonic group are seldom recognized as ideology and are often accorded the status of facts or theories. They are the counter positions and resistance ideas that are most often referred to pejoratively as dogma. Thus the origins of the multicultural movement almost naturally make it susceptible to the development of "dogma" and "ideology". Another source of the push toward dogma and ideology is the felt need to correct misconceptions and distortions. The proponents of multicultural education have often felt the need to correct these distortions that the dominant group has projected onto lower status groups, the response has been to develop alternative or counter ideologies and dogma. On the other side of the equation is the increasing amount of diverse knowledge that is available concerning people. Consider now the tension between this tendency towards situated dogma and ideology and the increased respect for perspectivist knowledge and understanding. Richer knowledge concerning diverse peoples, subaltern groups, and the presence of subaltern voices—those of women, African Americans, homosexuals and others—is a possible alternative to this trend towards a unitary chauvinistic ideology. Unfortunately, in the reaction against the ideology and dogma of the oppressors, too much focus of much that passes for multicultural education has been packaged as new knowledge when in actuality it is simply new or counter dogma. The substitution of one dogma for another dogma is simply not good education. Multiculturalist and multi-perspectivist education is by contrast concerned with the appreciation of context, perspective and situation as essential to understanding.

Efforts directed at developing and implementing this view of multicultural education will be neither simple nor easy. The issues that will arise as a result of these efforts will be complicated partly because they are simultaneously epistemological, political, and practical. They are epistemological in the sense that they challenge traditional notions of the very nature of knowledge or at least the categories of knowledge which may be included in the canon. Conceptions of the nature of knowledge are indeed changing, with more voices contributing to the canon and being recognized as such. However, for many the introduction of new conceptions of the nature of knowledge is threatening because it challenges knowledge systems with which we have become familiar. It forces new ways of thinking about the world and ourselves. It requires that educators teach across disciplines, across cultures, and with heightened sensitivity to context.

The issues are political in the sense that knowledge is power. Struggles to expand, change, and control knowledge-and access to it-are struggles to change the control and distribution of power and ultimately the distribution of resources. There is a long history of conflict over the control of what is to be included in the canon and reflected in the curriculum (Cremin, 1989). Repeatedly in the history of the nation, questions have been debated concerning the purposes of education and the content with which educators are to pursue their goals. As different segments of the United State's population have gained voice, the values honored by the society have changed, as have the goals of education and the ways in which schools function. The current debate over Africentric, Eurocentric, and multicultural education and about what is to be included in the canon is a continuation of this political struggle concerning who will control knowledge, what students are expected and allowed to know, the ways in which students are enabled to think, and with what resources they will be enabled to participate in society. The manner in which these questions are answered will not only influence what schools do, it will also determine the nature and extent of the power and resources that will be under the control of these students when they become adults.

The political issues are further complicated by the changing demographics of our nation. It may well be that the projected shift from a nation in which persons of European ancestry constitute the majority to a multicultural nation where such persons are a numerical minority is such a psychological threat to the present majority group as to make their rational accommodation to it a political impossibility. Accommodating such change is already viewed by some to mean the disruption of the social order and the disuniting of the nation (Schlesinger, 1991).

There are those who contend that multicultural education leads to diversiveness and racial and ethnic polarization that undermine national unity (D'Souza, 1991;

Schlesinger, 1991). Some see it as a movement to deny the contributions of European Americans. According to Schlesinger, (1991), multicultural education is an attempt to make people feel good about themselves; a responsibility that belongs to mental health professionals, not educators. Even some who are far left on the political spectrum criticize multicultural education because they believe that it reinforces the status quo and contributes to the oppression of those who are already subjugated by society (McCarthy, 1988).

Clearly, multicultural education is not panacea. However, it is politically, socially and pedagogically naive to assume that its only benefit is to make people feel good about themselves. Our schools have become noxious environments for many of our children who defend against assaults to their psyche by choosing not to learn. Our schools have become the battle grounds for a war against group supremacy. Millions of children have become prisoners and casualties of this war. Too many of our children are incarcerated in a system that does not permit them to raise questions about the things that count and does not permit them to develop more than a limited and restricted worldview.

The issues are practical in the sense that the implicit changes will require the development of new instructional materials. The reeducation of a huge teaching staff, and the redesign of much of our existing curricula. These changes in curricula will involve not only their content but also their functions and the nature of the assessment of curriculum outcomes. Such practical changes will not be well served by a political decision to substitute one dogma for another dogma.

What is required is professional and scholarly effort directed at better understanding human cultures, the knowledge and techniques by which they are represented, and their utilization in the processes of education, which is, again, the development of human intelligence and not simply the transfer of information and skill. Multiculturalism then is not an end, rather it is concerned with increased human capacity for recognizing and dealing with multiple perspectives that is to be achieved. Multicultural initiatives are vehicles to be used on the way to a more intellectively competent, and empathetic society, which conditions, we contend are essential to the achievement of a truly democratic and civil society.

Multiculturalism viewed as an essential element in our continuing process of nation building forces the examination of more than our educational institutions—more than the monitoring of the content and nature of the information and messages schools, museums, libraries, media, etc. deliver to the populace. Increasingly, it appears that the circumstances of people's lives influence their ability to profit from experience, to utilize the information, which is available, and to engage in the opportunity to learn. This suggests that the cultural, economic, political and social circumstances of the lives of persons must allow and support the development of intelligent and empathetic behavior. Many years ago, a wise educator/philosopher, Joseph K. Hart, wrote:

> The democratic problem in education is not primarily a problem of training children. It is a problem of making a community in which children cannot help growing up to be democratic, intelligent, disciplined to freedom, reverent of the goods of life—eager to share in the tasks of the age. A school cannot produce this result. Nothing but a community can do so. (Hart 1924)

5
Dynamic Assessment and Pedagogy

From early on in my career, I have been called upon to address the claim that traditional and standardized approaches to assessment were inherently biased against populations whose characteristics deny the hegemony of the dominant culture. I use hegemony to underscore how one perspective is used and generalized to diverse populations despite class, cultural, ethnic, racial, religious, and gender differences. Thus, standardized approaches to assessment presume to be universally valid by assuming commonality of characteristics, standards, and opportunity across different populations. They measure competence by determining what a learner at a specific level can do. Too often, these measures blame the learners when they are unable to achieve at commonly agreed expected levels without consideration of the appropriateness of the measure itself to the population being assessed or educational opportunities.

Earlier in my career I was focused on the psychometric and sociocultural test bias of standardized achievement tests and the deleterious consequences for many students of color. To a large degree I continue to struggle with the question of equitable approaches to educational assessment. In my work, I have sided with scholars and educators who advocated for the need to develop assessment procedures that appropriately measured the ways in which diverse people think, learn, and work and to rely less on memory and simple regurgitation. I worried that traditional approaches to assessment presume that when learners can demonstrate knowledge mastery, they are ready to transfer and apply this knowledge when needed. However, the continuing academic achievement gap, the rates of students who give up on school, the tendency of some tests to over-predict and under-predict achievement, and the ubiquitous association between test scores and the divisions by which we classify students, suggest that our standardized measures may inadequately assess student learning and the ability of diverse students to learn.

Despite my lack of enthusiasm for standardized psychological testing instruments, I recognize that a great deal of work has gone into the development of test items that tap into a variety of intellective functions. These tests and many of the items on them have proved to be very useful in describing the learner's status and predicting future performance in a variety of situations. The problem, however, is that these same items have been grouped, presented, scored, and analyzed to: classify, determine success or failure, place the examinee population within normal distributions, and predict who will succeed or fail under traditional circumstances. We have little systematic data on the use of these tests under different conditions of preparation or different demands of performance. The data from these tests have not been analyzed for different purposes. Some forty years ago, I began to propose alternative approaches to the analysis of standardized test data, which would be more sensitive to the differences among tests takers. I also proposed changes in the purposes from which such tests were used (see Gordon, 1970). I contend that these instruments can be analyzed though logical analysis to:

1. Determine the dimensional or categorical functional demands of selected standardized tests.
2. Establish what dimensions of function appear to be tapped by the instrument as these can be conceptualized from a surface examination of item content.
3. Ascertain the rationale used in the test development and the conceptual categories for which items were written.
4. Determine which item response consistencies might cluster empirically.
5. Reveal the learning task demands represented by the items of selected tests and the classification of those demands into functional categories.
6. Appraise the extent to which selected tests provide adequate coverage of the typical learning task demands found in educational settings.
7. Establish whether the tests are measuring the processes required by important learning tasks and how the types of learning tasks demands correspond to the processes seemingly measured by the test.

Using these same instruments we could additionally:

- Create quantitative reports on the performance of students as well as reports descriptive of the patterns of achievement and function derived from the qualitative analysis of existing tests. For example, response patterns might be prepared differentially for: (a) information recall; (b) rote call; (c) associative recall; e) derivative recall; and (g) vocabulary.

- Explore the development of test items and procedures that lend themselves to descriptive and qualitative analyses of cognitive and affective adaptive functions. For example, we can develop new tests with the goal of evaluating: (a) adaptation in new learning situations; (b) problem solving in situations that require varied cognitive, skills and styles; (c) analysis, search, and synthesis behaviors; (d) information management, processing, and utilization skills; and (e) nonstandard information pools.

Furthermore, in the development of new procedures, attention could be given to the appraisal of:

1. Comprehension using experiential, auditory, and visual methods.
2. Expression through artistic, oral, nonverbal, and graphic, as well as written symbolization.
3. Sources and status of motivation.
4. Temperament characteristics.
5. Habits of work and task involvement under varying conditions of demand.

In the development of tests and procedures designed to get at specific achievements, attention should be given to:

- Broadening the varieties of subject matter, competencies, and the skills assessed.
- Evaluating these achievements in a variety of contexts. Open-ended and unstructured probes of achievement to allow for atypical patterns and varieties of achievement.
- Assessing nonacademic achievements such as social competence, coping skills, avocational skills, and artistic, athletic, political, or mechanical skills.

As these points illustrate, test development should be focused on helping educators to help all their students. From this approach, assessment can reveal what students know and do not know as well as how the instructor's teaching should proceed. Thus, the objective of the assessment is to obtain information about the learners' status and the difficulties he or she is encountering in mastering specific skills, as well as the conditions in which the child can perform specific tasks. Additionally, the assessment process and procedures can be more sensitive to students' diverse characteristics and enhancing the expression of latent abilities.

My quest for equitable assessments for diverse human populations led me into two directions in my work. Initially, my attention was focused on the qualitative analysis of adaptive and learning behaviors. I was greatly influenced by Hausserman's (1958) descriptive work on the assessment of developmental potential in preschool children with neurological insults. A teacher and cognitive-developmental psychologist, Hausserman conducted semi-structured series of examinations to evaluate a child's performance for the purpose of educational intervention. She was convinced that the goal of assessment was to determine the conditions in which a child can accomplish particular tasks and those in which it is difficult or impossible for him or her to do these tasks. In other words, it was less important to simply determine whether the child could accomplish tasks in the standard condition and more important to reveal the conditional correlates of the child's potential. In addition, Hausserman was trying to make the point that issues or concerns of descriptive analysis of behavior could be used to infer assessment information. Through careful examination and analysis, her work illuminated the importance of alternatives in the nature and modes of assessment. However, due to the fact that that descriptive analysis was very labor intensive and it did not lend itself to standardization, her innovations were never broadly accepted. My late friend, Herbert Birch (1958), captured well what this approach to assessment is all about. I extend this reference to include children who are specifically challenged to their rehabilitation, and to education (i.e., pedagogy as the integration of assessment, teaching, and learning).

> The use of a method for intellectual evaluation as an instrument that has positive value for the promotion of training and education is an essential feature of rehabilitation. In this area of work one is far less concerned with predicting whether one given child will achieve success in competition with a group of age-mates drawn from the

general population, than with the problem determining the kinds of training and experience that will best promote his own adaptive functional abilities. From this point of view one becomes concerned with the laws of perceptual-motor functioning in a certain seven-year-old child rather than with the question of whether or not he can copy a geometric figure from a model as well as can other children of the same age. In short, the objective of the examination is to provide information about the special circumstances which are needed to create appropriate conditions for learning in the handicapped child. Such an approach, as Miss Haeussermann so aptly puts it, shifts 'the burden of proof.... from the child who is being examined, to the items which test the level of his comprehension.' (p. ix)

I had been sensitized to the importance and utility of B. F. Skinner's behavior analysis (1957; 1969). Skinner argued that behavior could be modified by using reinforcement and failure to reinforce to increase the frequency of desired behaviors and extinguish or diminish problematic ones. He called this behavioral modification strategy contingency management. Even though Skinner's concern for conditioning slowly gained traction, I was always more interested in his advocacy for behavioral analysis, which he recognized as being instrumental to conditioning or contingency management. I saw in Haeussermann and Skinner's different approaches to the analysis of behavior a model for educational assessment. I continue to regret that I did not personally give more attention to the development and perfection of this approach to educational assessment.

Those early behavior explorations with a view to the generation of prescriptions for educational and pedagogical intervention dominated my concern for alternatives to educational assessments. It gained its best expression in the exploration of the notion of *dynamic pedagogy* in which the assessment and instructional functions were combined— integrated with the facilitation of learning. Briefly, dynamic pedagogy describes the process of teaching and learning in which assessment, teaching and learning are inseparable processes in pedagogy (Gordon & Armour-Thomas, 2006). By the term "dynamic" I mean the constant adaptation of these three processes in response to the demonstrated learner strengths and needs. Before describing dynamic pedagogy in more detail, it may be helpful to discuss what I mean by dynamic assessment.

Dynamic Assessment

I use dynamic assessment to describe an approach to measurement that is as much concerned with uncovering the mental processes that examinees use in their performance as it is with the product of their performance. Dynamic assessment seeks to determine the status of examinees or learners and the processes of learning by which the status is achieved or manifested. It is dynamic in the sense that it is adaptive to the performance of the examinee/learner and it has no fixed entry or exit points. In this way, assessment begins where the learner is, follows the learner's lead, and it ends at the limit of the learner's demonstrated ability or willingness to try.

Instead of standardized procedures, the assessments are tailored to the characteristics of the person being examined. Thus, the primary task is not simply to understand what the student or learner knows and can do but to elucidate the processes and conditions that the learner uses to demonstrate her/his status. In the dynamic approach, we seek to determine the conditions under which the examinee can demonstrate what she knows or the processes by which he draws from the zone of proximal development or new learning to demonstrate both intent and consolidated competence. I feel that the dynamic assessment approach is preferable to standardized assessment, which can misrepresent the constantly changing nature of the processes by which knowledge and skill are acquired and utilized.

Additionally, I believe that the increasing concern for equity and fairness in testing requires that responsible approaches to educational assessment include attention to the quality of teaching and learning transactions and to the sufficiency of learner access to these experiences as part of the assessment process. If one is assessing ability to learn it may not be sufficient to simply assume that one has had or availed appropriate and sufficient opportunity to learn.

My colleagues Chatterji, Koh, Everson, and Solomon (2008) describe a useful assessment technique that is designed to help students deconstruct the learning for tasks in any content (e.g., mathematics) area. Similar to dynamic assessment, their concept of "proximal assessment," is also embedded in the instruction and it is used as a diagnostic and instructional process during student-teacher interactions. It is continuous and useful in planning instruction. In their research, Chatterji and her co-researchers trained teachers to use proximal assessment by categorizing math problem solving (e.g., division) into specific targeted student skills. For example, they state that by arranging problems in order of difficulty, teachers can evaluate student learning and understanding at various steps and more precisely reveal where the student misunderstanding begins. In this way, the purpose of their assessment is to diagnose problems during the instructional process instead of at the end of the lesson.

CONCEPTUAL UNDERPINNINGS OF DYNAMIC PEDAGOGY (DP)

My concern for assessment and instructional procedures that are sensitive to the diverse characteristics of learners led me to the design of an intervention that my colleague, Eleanor Armour-Thomas, and I described as dynamic pedagogy (Gordon & Armour-Thomas, 2006; Armour-Thomas, Walker, Dixon-Roman, Mejia, & Gordon, 2006). The term "dynamic" underscores the deliberately dialectical variation and gradation in the teaching—assessment—learning transactions that occur between the learner and the teacher within and beyond the classroom.

Our conceptual framework for the dynamic pedagogy intervention was guided by several theories and concepts of teaching, learning, and child development including Vygotsky's (1978) concept of the "zone of proximal development," Campione's (1989) concept of "on-line diagnosis," Slavin's (2001) "learning probes," Skinner's (1957, 1969) behavior analysis, and Glickling and Havertape's (1981) curriculum-embedded assessments. These constructs are integrated into the three (teaching, assessment, and learning), areas of dynamic pedagogy discussed below.

Teaching

In dynamic pedagogy, the teacher uses various instructional strategies that are adaptive to the developed cognitive strengths and expressed needs of the learner (Gordon & Armour-Thomas, 2006). These strengths and needs have been determined through the use of diagnostic assessment data. For instance, instructional strategies may be associated with behavioral principles (e.g., direct instruction) or with constructivist principles, scaffolding, and metacognition). Dynamic pedagogy may include direct instructional strategies, scaffolding strategies, mediation, discovery, and demonstration. What is unique is the integration of assessment, teaching, and learning such that these components of pedagogy are expressed on a bidirectional continuum. In practice, one sees movement back and forth across the three modalities whether through direct instruction, mediated learning, or scaffolding.

In direct instructional strategies, information is transmitted directly to the student and class time is structured to foster students' acquisition of basic knowledge and skills (Gordon & Armour-Thomas, 2006). Based on Slavin's (2001) direct instruction strategies, it is hypothesized that teachers can implement the following to help students to learn more complex skills: (1) state learning objectives explicitly, and orient students to the lesson; (2) review perquisites; (3) provide independent practice; (4) provide distributed practice and review; and (5) provide feedback.

Feuerstein (1979) first used the concept of mediated learning to describe an interactive clinical involvement during dynamic assessment in which the examiner teaches the child how to find and use the rules underlying a task. During this interactive relationship, the examiner behaves like a teacher in selecting examples for clarifying the task, asking for and giving explanation summarizing progress, resulting in a change in cognitive functioning.

According to Vygotsky's sociocultural theory of cognitive development, children use complex mental processes in social activities through conversations and collaborations with other individuals. As such, cognitive development and learning occur when children engage in problem solving and learning activities within their zone of proximal development (ZPD) or within their actual and potential cognitive level under the guidance of adults. Vygotsky's ideas suggests that teachers can use scaffolding instructional strategies to help students to access their prior knowledge and skills to advance and develop new knowledge and skills. Social scaffolding is similar in function to mediated learning in that it involves the guidance and support for learning by more competent peers or adults.

In contrast to earlier notions of teaching as involving the transfer of knowledge, skills and values, the dynamic pedagogy approach, views the teacher as a guide, a coach, a model, and a resource person. Consequently, there are several intentional tasks that the teacher must engage when instructing students. To begin, teachers must make explicit the objectives, conditions and criteria for student performance. In addition, teaching can be most effective when the teacher:

1. Establishes student readiness for learning.

2. Helps students to make connections with their own prior knowledge and skills.

3. Enables learners to integrate and extend their learning to new contexts.

4. Uses multiple representations to facilitate clarity of content and enable student understanding.

5. Provides various tasks to capture students' interest and attention in ways that are culturally relevant to their lives.

6. Encourages learner behaviors such as the deployment of effort, task engagement, time on task, and resource utilization.

7. Recognizes the differential requirements of learning in the academic domain of interest.

8. Facilitates student progress in cumulative understanding of content.

9. Assists students to make progress in the development of knowledge, metacognitive, thinking and learning skills.

10. Links tasks of a lesson with instructional goals and objectives.

11. Models the desired learning behaviors.

12. Recognizes the important of supplementary learning experiences.

13. Gives special attention to the roles of attitudes, disposition, confidence and efficacy.

Assessment

To develop the assessment component of dynamic pedagogy, we drew from Campione's (1989) concept of "on-line probe," Slavin's (2001) "learning probes" and Glickling and Havertape's (1981) curriculum-embedded assessments. One way to assess the learner's knowledge and skills is (1) to probe their prior knowledge, skills, and readiness for new learning, (2) to check their emerging understanding of new concepts and procedures as well as misconceptions; (3) to check whether they have acquired the new knowledge and skills; (4) to check how well they are able to demonstrate their knowledge and skills with automaticity; (5) to check how well they have consolidated their new learning, and (6) how well they are able to transfer it to other contexts. Teachers can engage in an iterative dynamic loop in which they assess, instruct, and assess to design instruction that is sensitive to changes in student learning and performance.

Although assessment has various purposes, one primary goal is to provide diagnostic information about students' strengths and weaknesses in relation to the attainment of explicit instructional objectives (Gordon & Armour-Thomas, 2006). Therefore, assessment is consistent with the instructional objectives. In addition, it is thought that assessment should:

- Allow for appraisal of discipline-based knowledge of content and procedures, discipline and situation—based tacit knowledge and metacognitive knowledge, understanding and skill.

- Be representative of the actual learning experiences and the meta-products of those experiences.

- Probe for progress toward the attainment of discipline-based content knowledge, metacognitive thinking and learning sills.

- Provide information that informs instruction and learning.

- Use multiple methods, modalities, and formats to appraise learning.

- Be embedded in the curriculum, teaching, and learning experiences.

As noted above, teaching, assessment, and learning are dialectical and transactive components of the pedagogical process. Increasingly, these components are viewed as functioning in a symbiotic relationship to one another. Although each of these components has an independent history and a separate constituency, they are, perhaps, best viewed as parts of a whole cloth, which parts are differentially emphasized at various times for different purposes.

Learning

In addition to the teaching and assessment strands, it is important to consider the curriculum that will be used to guide and mediate student learning. In dynamic pedagogy, the curriculum consists of a wide range of materials (e.g., text, media, and workbooks) that represent the concepts, principles, and procedures of a discipline (Gordon & Armour-Thomas, 2006). The degree to which students learn the content of a discipline significantly depends on whether tasks can motivate students to learn and use their minds. For example, it is important that tasks not only allow students to make connections to their prior knowledge and skills, but also build new knowledge. Further, learning tasks should be relevant to students' personal interests to arouse and sustain their motivation until they are successfully completed.

Sternberg's theory of intelligence (1985, 1988) is useful in thinking about a curriculum that can draw on the learner's analytic, creative and practical intelligence in the process of learning. According to Sternberg, analytical ability is activated when learners use information processing components for relatively familiar tasks that require them to analyze, judge, evaluate, compare and contrast. Learners apply their creative abilities (e.g. ability to discover, invent, create, explore) when they approach relatively novel tasks or familiar tasks in a novel way. Finally, learners use their practical ability which includes the ability to put into practice, apply, use and implement knowledge and skills, to solve either familiar or novel tasks in every day contexts or settings. Therefore, it is argued that if students are exposed to tasks that require them to think about concepts and procedures in analytical, creative, and practical ways, they are likely to learn more deeply about the content of a discipline. Sternberg contends that the use of these thinking processes is partly, indicative of intelligent behavior.

In order for students to successfully master and transfer new knowledge, learning is facilitated when it involves the learners' adaptive capacity and disposition to use mental processes to solve everyday and novel problems. Learners must understand the information with which they are engaging and use critical skills so that they can assimilate what is familiar and accommodate that which is new. In dynamic pedagogy, it is assumed that learning is most effective when:

1. New information is linked with prior knowledge and skills.

2. Differential development of the whole child is recognized (emotional, cognitive and social, and physical).

3. Differential requirements and conditions for learning are recognized.

4. It involves the active construction of new knowledge and meaning from information and experience.

5. It is facilitated through social and political interactions with others.

6. Experiences are mediated through the instructional scaffolding of concepts and ideas and student participation in apprenticeships.

7. Teachers are motivated to teach and students are motivated to learn.

8. It is facilitated through guided and independent practice.

9. When learner characteristics such as learning style, cultural style, and cognitive and affective response tendencies are recognized and incorporated into the teaching and learning transaction.

The core processes of dynamic pedagogy can be summarized as consisting of the integration of teaching, assessment, and learning. The instructor can use probing to:

- Expose not only what the leaner knows but what he or she does not understand.
- Reveal the capacity to use and apply what is known in different contexts.
- Encourage the use of secure knowledge to generate additional knowledge.
- Reveal a learner's capacity to process new learning.
- Enable identification of patterns of errors and detect errors.
- Assess the capacity to use both deductive and inductive reasoning.
- Correct the work of students.
- Determine how the leaner constructs responses from different contexts and perspectives.
- Evaluate contextualized and de-contextualized knowledge and skill.

The instructor can also conduct various types of analyses to assess, teach, and help students learn:

- Qualitative analysis of teaching and learning to reveal knowledge and technique (skill) demands of the exercise.
- Hyper and hypo-textual analysis–constructed responses from partial or over supply of information
- Examine portfolios and other records of self presentation.
- Distill assessment data from records of teaching and learning transactions.

The data from the probes and analysis of teaching and learning can then inform the tasks that the instructor develops such as:

- Analogical reasoning tasks.
- Tasks that reveal the processes by which the learner produces or fails to produce responses.

While not rejecting the traditional emphasis on associative and retrieval endogenous processes, the new vision of learning privileges constructive, and interactive social processes which are both exogenous and situative. I argue that the product of the teaching and learning endeavors are reflected in the achievement of *intellective competence* which references the developed abilities and dispositions to perceive critically, to explore widely, to bring rational order to chaos, to bring knowledge and technique to the solution of problems, to test ideas against explicit and considered moral values, as well as, against empirical data, and to recognize and create real and abstract relationships between concrete and imaginary phenomena. In other words, teaching and learning are less focused on what we want learners to know and do, and are more sharply focused on what it is that we want learners to be and become (i.e., thinking persons).

These three core components of dynamic pedagogy are brought together in the curriculum, which guides and provides the structural context for the instructional activities. The curriculum is the mechanism that the teacher uses to mediate the teaching, assessment, and learning transactions or what occurs between the teaching persons and learning persons. In dynamic pedagogy, the assessment is integrated with the teaching and learning, all three of which are directed at such assessment, teaching and learning outcomes.

Dynamic Pedagogy Project Implementation

Following the conceptualization of the dynamic pedagogy intervention, my colleagues (Eleanor Armour-Thomas & Erica Walker) and I convened a research team and implemented the project in two separate phases with the goal of improving the mathematics performance of children at the third and fourth grade levels enrolled in schools in the suburban district of New York (Armour-Thomas, Chatterji, Walker, Obe, Moore, & Gordon, 2005; Armour-Thomas, Walker, Dixon-Roman, Mejia, & Gordon, 2006; Amour-Thomas, Walker, Mejia, & Gordon, 2004; Gordon & Armour-Thomas, 2006; Walker, 2007). The intervention was first piloted in five K-3 elementary schools during the 2003-2004 academic years. In the first year, two teachers from each of the five schools participated in the intervention. For the second year, eight 3rd grade teachers (two returning teachers and two new teachers) from two schools and two 4th grade teachers participated in the study.

We began by delivering a series of professional development workshops (see Armour-Thomas, 2008; Armour-Thomas, Walker, Manoff, & Goldfischer, 2006; Walker, 2007) for the participating teachers which included: discussions about the principles of dynamic pedagogy, provision of templates for recording pre-planning thoughts and lesson plans, and a self-administered measure of' experiences with the mode. Following the professional development workshops, teachers returned to their classrooms to deliver four lesson plans in mathematics according to the dynamic pedagogy model. During the evaluation phase, research assistants observed and later transcribed the delivery of these dynamic pedagogy lessons. After teaching each lesson, teachers compiled student portfolios, which would later be analyzed for student understanding (Armour-Thomas, Walker, Mejia, Toro, Gordon, 2005; Armour-Thomas, Walker, Obe, Toro, Mejia, & Gordon, 2007). We believe that the dynamic pedagogy model holds promise for not only adding to our knowledge base about the multidimensionality of teacher pedagogical content knowledge but also for contributing to our understanding of the mechanisms by which such knowledge impacts student motivation, learning and achievement (Gordon & Armour-Thomas, 2006; Armour-Thomas, Walker, Dixon-Roman, Mejia, & Gordon, 2006; Walker, Armour-Thomas, E., & Gordon, 2007).

CONCLUSION

To a large degree, the subject of test bias and inequitable assessment approaches is still alive today. For those of us who worry about the disparities in academic achievement, the problems with the standardized achievement testing in schools are of primary concern. In my discussion, I have primarily discussed equitable assessment approaches and have focused less on the psychometric theory and socio-cultural problems of standardized educational assessments. Specifically, I contend that educational assessment has two specific purposes. The first is to *inform* instruction and learning; the second, purpose is its use as an *instrument* for teaching and learning in which the learner and teacher engage in bi-directional assessment, teaching, and learning transactions, in the spirit of Socratic dialogue.

To elaborate on the first purpose, it seems that we have come to use assessment to determine the learner's status and/or level of function. I describe this as the accountability function, and while it is an important function, it seems that it is only one of the many functions in pedagogy. Moreover, it seems that the accountability function is excessively privileged in standardized assessment where status is assessed to help determine placement and certification. However, this process largely ignores the dynamic instrumental and developmental functions of learning and teaching.

Assessment can be embedded in the curriculum as a tool for teaching and learning. By embedding the assessment in the curriculum, the teacher can determine the student's status during the assessment teaching and learning processes and continually tailor the curriculum to meet the learner's progress, needs and style of learning. Thus, the curriculum becomes the vehicle that guides the assessment, teaching and learning transaction. The instructor can use a Socratic type of inquiry or probes that progress from concrete to more abstract to illuminate the learner's mental processes, level of (mis)understanding, and capacity for critical thinking. By engaging in a Socratic dialogue with the learner, the instructor can deepen the evaluation and the student's learning while enhancing instruction. These exchanges can be recorded, paying particular attention to the learner's responses, which can be reviewed later to determine the learners' understanding and mental processes.

This iterative use of diagnostic and stimulating probes followed by instruction, mediation, evaluation and re-assessment have the advantage of providing a richly descriptive record of the assessment, teaching, and learning transactions. This record then can be used by the teaching person as a guide for further instruction and, interestingly enough, could be used by a psychometrician as a source of assessment data. With an understanding of the conceptual demands of the assessment, teaching, and learning transactions, the psychometrician could then distill from this record assessment data necessary to make evaluative judgments concerning the processes used by the learner, the level of the learners' mastery, and the relative status of the learner's achievement.

One of my students, Carol Bonilla-Bowman, did her dissertation on the documentation of such instructional transactions in the student portfolio (see Bonilla-Bowman, 1999). She alluded to the potential value of such a procedure for assessment purposes but did not develop an assessment model for doing so. Nonetheless, our model for dynamic pedagogy is bifocal in that it has utility for the conduct of instruction and assessment without additional demands on the learning time.

6
Thinking Comprehensively About Education

For a good part of my life I was convinced that there was a direct relationship between poverty and the academic under-productivity of some students. I believed that the confluence of low-income status and low ethnic status at least helped to explain the high correlation between low academic achievement and children of color. When I encountered the Bourdieu (1986), and later Coleman (1966), work on education related forms of capital that they claimed was necessary for investment in education, I found conceptual reinforcement for my simple notion that the elimination of poverty would take us far toward the removal of the gap in academic achievement between Blacks and Whites. But there is a flaw in this mechanical conceptualization. At the same time that I was convinced that the ubiquitous association between income and academic achievement was the culprit, I was also trying to explain the finding by Coleman (1966) and Miller (1995) that as socioeconomical status (SES) improves the academic achievement gap increases. According to my assumptions, the academic achievement gap between income groups should decrease as SES increases, if income were the determining factor.

Birch and Gussow (1968), Gordon and Wilkerson (1966) Frazier (1965) and Proctor (1966) documented differences in the experiences, access to resources and life styles of Blacks and Whites who were identified as middle class or who had access to similar incomes. Bourdieu's use of the construct 'habitus' turned out to provide a useful explanatory mechanism, as did Steele's notion of 'fear of stereotype confirmation' and Clark's (1954) and Coleman's (1966) findings of differential access to effective schools.

In contrast to Bourdieu's focus on the attitudes and dispositions associated with habitus, Claude Steele and Aronson (2000) have focused on an aspect of personality also intrinsic to persons that operates to influence behavioral adaptation in some subjects, working primarily with African American subjects.

115

The reports have indicated that academic achievement and test performance can be influenced by the responding subjects perception with respect to how their performance would be evaluated or judged. In experiments conducted by them, they were able to demonstrate that Black students who were informed that their performance would be compared to the performances of White students ended up performing at a lower level than when they were told that their performance would be compared to that of Black students.

Katz (1964) reported similar findings when he compared the performance of Black students when examined in racially mixed settings or by White examiners. In the experimental condition Katz found that his Black students performed less well in racially integrated settings or when the examiners were of a different race. Steele and Aronson (2000) interpreted these findings to suggest that human performance can be impaired when the respondent feels that he/she runs the risk of confirming stereotype of his or her reference group that is held by the dominant society. These Black students performed as if they thought that they run a chance of demonstrating Black inferiority by the test scores. This perception seems to have been exacerbated by the knowledge that others will compare them to the dominant group.

Other possible explanations that contributed to my understanding of the failure of my original association made between income and achievement is the notion of access to appropriate opportunities to learn. In this conceptualization of the problem, differences in academic achievement independent of one's SES can be predicted by one's access to weak or strong, or adequate or inadequate opportunities to learn. We have a long history of research that relates the quality of school to academic achievement. When Coleman studied this problem in 1966 he initially reported a higher association between family background and achievement than between quality of schooling and achievement. In a secondary analysis of his data, he found that when he controlled for SES background of students the quality of opportunity to learn rose to the top. That is for low income, socially disadvantaged and minority students' quality of schooling outdistanced family background as a predictor of school achievement. I interpret this to mean that if you are poor and/or Black, the quality of schooling is more important than if you are White and come from a reasonable adequately resourced background. Thus it is that the confused relationship between family resources and school achievement can be influenced by the richness or poorness of access to appropriate opportunities to learn.

116

All of these explanations must be considered in the context of the consistent finding that SES remains the best overall predictor of achievement in school. When we fail to disaggregate the data to account for other influences upon academic performance but we know the income of the family we are reasonably safe in assuming that academic achievement will be closer to being adequate if family income is high rather than low. However, I have consistently tried to avoid contributing to the tendency to blame these families for the consequences of their lack of resources. This blaming of the victims has greatly complicated efforts at correcting the academic underproductivity of low income and socially disadvantaged learners.

It is the experience with Black-White middle class comparisons that contradicts these associations and, of course, contributes to the paradox in the history of my thinking about the subject. I am forced to conclude that the most adequate explanation is to be found in the relationship between the prior experience of the person and that person's resulting developed ability. So that when we look at the extent to which one's life experiences are actively supportive of academic development, academic achievement tends to be high. Studies by Wolff (1966) and Mercer (1973) in families where environmental supports for academic development are plentiful academic achievement tends to be high across ethnic and class groups. Low-income children whose families happen to be able to provide rich support for academic development tend to perform more like more affluent families. I am less convinced than I once was that it is the financial resources available to a family what makes the difference. Rather, it is the effective management of family resources, even in the presence of poverty, what is less debilitating than resource management that results in the social deprivations and dislocations often associated with poverty.

I have also come to realize that my conceptualization about the problems of education for the poor and other low status populations is in part a self-imposed limitation, born of the manner in which I have permitted aspects of my ideology to constrain the way in which I have conceptualized the problem. In an article I published concerning the education of disadvantaged students, I discussed some of the model characteristics of this population. It was my view at the time that many of the characteristics of the population were inconsistent with high levels of academic achievement and/or that those characteristics created special challenges for educators. Resonating to Frank Riessman's book, *The Culturally Deprived Child,* I argued that the children with whom we are concerned are not without culture; rather, they had different cultural experiences from majority group children with whom the schools were more effective. At the time, these characteristics were viewed as deficits that these children and their schools needed to overcome. (Gordon, 1965) We later realized that these "deficits" may appropriately be referred to as differences. This emphasis on differences rather than deficiencies came to dominate the discussion of the problems of educating the poor. I resonated to the parallel arguments that a focus on the deficiencies of the group was to "blame the victims." while a focus on differences shared the responsibility with the school and the society. I somehow managed to avoid romanticizing the fact of difference and many of the actual characteristics and correctly turned my attention to how those characteristics might be utilized in the education of low status children. This need for the adaptation of schooling to the characteristics of learners continues to be a central tenet in my approach to pedagogy. Increasingly, however, it has become clear to me that while adapting to the characteristics of learners and building on students' strengths (many of these characteristics should be viewed as potential sources of strength) is appropriate, it is clearly not sufficient to their effective education.

In my first book length treatment of the education of low status persons I introduced the term "compensatory education." The late Doxey Wilkerson and I argued that for education to be effective with students disadvantaged by economic and ethnic status, pedagogy should not only compensate for the deficits and disadvantages our children had suffered, but also be adapted to the differences in their characteristics. And while we recognized the importance of culture, we also viewed cultural experiences as phenomena to be celebrated and utilized in the education of our children. We eschewed the deprivation construct and privileged the differentiation construct.

More specific than Riessman in his conceptualization of the problem of cultural experience, Reuven Feuerstein's Instrumental Enrichment (1980) viewed cultural deprivation as referring to students being deprived of aspects of the hegemonic culture that provided the foundations for academic learning. Feuerstein described how many educated parents mediate personal, social, and environmental encounters in ways that provide their children with many of the instrumentalities essential to academic learning. Those children without this clear advantage were not deprived of culture; rather, their cultures did not emphasize those attitudes, behaviors, experiences and values that are instrumental to high levels of academic learning. His curriculum called "instrumental enrichment" was an attempt at integrating the demands of academic excellence and acculturation to the habits of intellective competence into explicit learning experiences for children for whom such learnings were not acquired incidentally. Hence, instrumental enrichment continues to be a concept that I emphasize as necessary in the education of low status populations. Going beyond the rather formal structure of Feuerstein's focus on the intellective tasks of Raven's Matrices, I have come to recognize the importance of behavioral analysis, mediation, explication, exposure and structure in the lives of those who would become academically sophisticated. It seems to me, thus, that the following instrumentalities of academic learning may be essential for persons whose natural life experiences may not enable the development of high levels of academic ability. These include:

- The functional analysis of the prior knowledge and academic behavior of the learner as a basis for the design of instruction and, especially, the acceleration of learning as opposed to remediation;
- The explication of the principal features of the stimulus material, the salient components of the process and the critical demands of the criterion standard;
- The explication of the critical importance of situative and tacit knowledge referable to content and procedure;
- Repeated, structured and incidental exposure to progressively more rigorous on- demand-performance experiences; and
- The explication of names, meanings the relevance of common features of the content and skills to be learned and their contexts.

What is important about these instrumentalities is that they are not routinely addressed in school, perhaps because schooling was designed on the assumption that most of these learning needs are met, incidentally, in the home and community. Some years ago, Frederick Strodbeck, through his research on decision making in lower class and middle class families, suggested that there appeared to be greater parity in decision making in the middle class families than in the lower class families. He argued that lower class children learned from family decision making to listen for explanations, directions, signals and the subtleties of the arguments made by the discussants so that they could anticipate which side to team up with (Strodtbeck, 1964). Strodtbeck argued that these children became more analytic and reflective listeners, and were thus better prepared for the demands of school. Bernstein (1961) came to similar conclusions concerning language differences between working class and upper class children. Since the number of words used and the complexities of the vocabulary were greater in upper class families, their children had stronger language skills and hegemonic language habits than children from working class families. While these habits and skills are in keeping with the demands of the academic learning, they are however, not the products of formal instruction but of informal learning experiences that are incidental to quotidian exposure to educated or otherwise sophisticated persons. This is a more subtle expression of supplementary education. Strodtbeck (1964) called it the "hidden curriculum of the middle-class."

Part of the problem we face these days is that we have concentrated on schooling to the neglect of the broad complex of educative forces that influence the development of intellective competence. Informed parents, scholars, and educators have known for some time now that schools alone cannot enable or ensure high academic achievement (Coleman et al., 1966; Gordon & Bridglall, 2001; Wilkerson, 1979). James Comer asserts this position more forcefully in *Waiting for a Miracle: Why Our Schools Cannot Solve our Problems and How We Can* (1997) in which he makes the argument that we cannot wait for schools to solve the problems of children of color and poverty. Hugh Price in his book *Achievement Matters* (2002) makes the case for our giving much more serious attention to high academic achievement. Both of these authors turn attention to how parents and other interested adults can do something about high academic achievement in minority student populations. Colloquial knowledge among many parents "in the know" reflects awareness that there are a number of things that occur outside of school that appear to enable schooling to work. Examples can be found in the many education related opportunities that affluent and academically sophisticated parents make available to their children, i.e., travel, dance lessons, scouting, tutoring, summer camp.

I think that we cannot afford to get too far away from quality of schooling and especially the quality of the teaching persons to whom students are exposed. Good schools and good teaching are tremendously important, but schooling while necessary may not be sufficient. Since the school reform started in 1950 we have achieved some gains in the access to schooling of higher quality. We cannot deny that we have seen some advances in the processes and technologies of instruction. Between 1950 and 1980 we even saw some gains in academic achievement; but we have not seen significant gains in the reduction of the academic achievement gap. Obviously there are limits to school reform as the solution. If the problem can be traced to communities, families and schools, the focus on school reform will not be sufficient. Even the best schools may not be able to reverse all the ravishes of poverty and injustice. The very best of instructional and managerial systems, combined with the excellence of teachers and their teaching, together with orderliness and safety are necessary components of good education and should be demanded in our schools, but such ideal educational institutions may fall short of achieving excellence in academic achievement in ways similar to the failure of limitations of excellent hospitals and medical schools in this country to achieve excellence in health maintenance. These institutions have contributed to the improvement of health care and medical service in the United States, but there are the improvements in provision for public health that are thought to account for the nation's major strides forward in health maintenance: modern systems of garbage and sewage removal; the elimination of stagnant swamps and other mosquito breeders; the availability of potable water and non-polluted air; improvements in personal hygiene; changes in diet to favor health producing and to exclude health demeaning foods; and the recognition of the importance of exercise are all now recognized as major contributors to health maintenance.

Without demeaning the importance of adequate and appropriate school resources, the focus of my work toward the end of my career is directed to the crucial importance of access to educational resources that are supplementary to what is available in school. What I have called "Supplementary Education." The idea of supplementary education (Gordon, 1999) is based on the premise that beyond exposure to the school's formal academic curriculum, high academic achievement is closely associated with exposure to family and community-based activities and learning experiences in support of academic and personal development that occur outside of school. For low-SES and non-Asian students of color, these opportunities are generally underutilized. In the home environment, for example, high achieving students benefit from literate adults, home computers, books, magazines, journals, adult conversations and the academic assistance and encouragement of older siblings and parents. In terms of community resources, the combination of local library and museum privileges, mentoring and tutoring programs, peer-based study groups, summer camp, Saturday and/or after-school academies, and participation in various folk and "high" cultural events and faith-based activities, influence the development of proactive and engaged dispositions toward engagement and systematic academic learning.

I define supplementary education as the formal and informal learning and

developmental enrichment opportunities provided for students outside of school
and beyond the regular school day or year. Some of these activities may occur
inside the school building but are beyond those included in the formal curriculum
of the school. After-school care, perhaps the most widespread form of
supplementary education, includes the special efforts that parents exert in support
of the intellective and personal development of their children (Gordon, 1999).
These efforts may range from provisions for good health and nutrition to extensive
travel and deliberate exposure to socialization to life in the academy, as well as to
mediated exposure to selected aspects of both indigenous and hegemonic cultures.
Many activities, considered routine in the settings in which they occur, are
nonetheless thought to be implicitly and deliberately engaged in to ensure
adequate intellective and academic development of young people. These routines
include reading to and with one's children; dinner table talk and inclusion in
other family discussions of important issues; exposure to adult models of behaviors
supportive of academic learning; active use of the library, museums, community
and religious centers as sources of information; help seeking from appropriate
sources; and investments in reference and other education materials (Gordon,
1999).

When I first started writing about supplementary education my wife, who
was then president of a public sch (200) and Lawrence Cremin (1975). Those
who are familiar with the sociological literature will recognize Pierre Bourdieu
(1986) in association with the idea that education is enabled by the learner's access
to educational relevant forms of capital:

> *Cultural capital:* the collected knowledge, techniques and beliefs of people.
> *Financial capital:* income and wealth, and family, community and societal
> economic resources available for human resource development and
> education.
> *Health capital:* physical developmental integrity, health and nutritional
> condition, etc.
> *Human capital:* social competence, tacit knowledge and other education-
> derived abilities as personal or family assets.
> *Institutional capital:* access to political, education and socializing
> institutions.
> *Pedagogical capital:* supports for appropriate educational experiences in
> home, school, and community.

122

Personal capital: dispositions, attitudes, aspirations, efficacy, and sense of power.

Polity capital: societal membership, social concern, public commitment, and participation in the political economy.

Social capital: social networks and relationships, social norms, cultural styles, and values.

Miller & Gordon added to Bourdieu's list the technological and informational capitals defined as the access to the capabilities and instrumentalities by which people communicate, by which people collect information, by which people process that information and exchange it in technologically advanced modern societies.

We cannot stress too much the importance of these resources to the developmental outcomes, including linguistic competence; habits of mind, dispositions, acquisition skills, information, and identity and purpose to which they are related. Health and nutrition are of crucial importance, children can function and survive in the presence of ill health and poor nutrition, but impairments in these domains take their toll on the efficiency with which humans function and the quality of the human effort invested in learning. Poor health and nutrition impede attention, attendance and energy deployment. Some conditions so compromise the integrity of the organism as to interfere with learning.

One of the most intriguing varieties of Bourdieu's forms of capital is the conception of "polity capital." We use the term to refer to the sense of membership in and by the social order as reflected in social commitment, concern and participation. In other words, if I do not feel that I belong in the group, I am not likely to take the group's standards and values seriously. If the group does not consider that I belong, it is not likely to take my needs or my development seriously. Banks (1977) makes a telling point in research that suggests that when one sees inappropriate behavior in a person considered to be like-minded or related to the observer, the cause of the behavior is attributed to the context or environment. When the same behavior is observed in one who is considered "other than me" or "unlike me" the cause of the negative behavior is attributed to the non-belonging person. This reciprocal sense of membership—polity capital— is an often ignored but critically important resource for learning and survival. Unfortunately, all children do not have easy access to this important resource.

With comprehensive education we try to compensate for the fact that access to these forms of capital is unequally distributed. All people don't have access to these forms of capital and Comprehensive Education makes them either available or finds alternatives for them. In other words, if these forms of capital are what effective education must depend upon, then one cannot think of an adequate education or an adequate system of education that does not address them.

The second theoretical frame that supports the idea of comprehensiveness is J. McV Hunt's notion of intelligence as a function of the richness of the learner's experiences. Some of those experiences are directly related to academic learning, others are enabling of it. Still others create a climate, a context out of which ones investment effort in the pursuit of academic learning grows. Something like disposition, attitude toward learning, effort. What Hunt was arguing is that if we can design learning experiences that are appropriate to the learning characteristics' and the learning needs of the persons that we are trying to teach, the achievement of developed abilities increases. To the extent that the variety and quality of those experiences are limited, achievement declines. Hunt believed that if we can design appropriate matches between the characteristics of learners and the necessary learner experiences, levels of intellective development could be increased significantly.

The third frame of support comes from Michael Martinez. In Martinez's work *Education as the Cultivation of Intelligence* he argues that too much attention may be given to the mastery of the specific content of the academic experience and insufficient attention to the cultivation of mental ability - the capacity to solve problems and the capacity to use the information. Martinez correctly reminds us that along the way of learning how to solve problems and how to use one's intellect efficiently we must also master chunks of knowledge and the content of the academic experience. But if one views the academic experience solely as the mastery of content and not as the cultivation of the intellect one is missing the point.

Martinez's mentor, the late Professor Richard Snow and I believe that the study of the content, processes and techniques associated with the academic disciplines in instrumental to the development of mental abilities. The development of intellect does not require academic studies but intellective competence appears to be greatly facilitated by the acquisition of the knowledge and skills stressed in school or other systematic exposuretions of excellence and structure have made them the preferred choice. In addition to this more formal

124

settings for academic learning faith-based institutions have become a major source for the incidental learning of attitude, habits, mores and values that are associated with believes propagated by these institutions.[1]

People differ greatly in their ways of learning and, to some extent, even in the capacity to learn or their capacity to learn in standard environments. The broader domain of teaching and learning that we call comprehensive education provides greater and redundant opportunities to learn so that if one doesn't get it in one place he/she will get it in another place. One will get the exposure, and all of those exposures, Martinez would argue, contribute to the development of intellectual capacities; the developed intellective competence of persons.

The last theoretical frame that I want to refer to is Lawrence Cremin's notion that John Dewey was incorrect to separate schooling and life as dual sources of education. He talked about schooling and life as the primary educative forces and Cremin argued that they should be brought together because when we think of education in a bifocal way we miss the point. What education really has to represent is the complementarities between these two forces. Therefore, education must be thought of comprehensively, relationally and publicly. (Cremin 1975)

I read Cremin to be arguing that thinking comprehensively with respect to education must include concern for all the opportunities in life to learn and to teach, for the ways in which they complement each other, and for the proper orchestration of opportunities to learn wherever they may occur, and I want to underline the notion of orchestration. The richness of educational opportunities in life is important but the way in which they are orchestrated in the life of the individual who needs them is critical. When we think about Comprehensive Education we are also thinking about the ways in which they are net together. When Cremin talks about thinking relationally about education he is talking about the ways in which these pieces fit together in the lives of particular individuals.

In general, high degrees of congruency between the values promulgated at school, at home, and in a student's immediate community are associated with high academic achievement. What may be equally critical are students' perceptions that what happens at school matters and is consistent with what

---

1. Cole and Schriebner have investigated the differential manifestations of intellect that are associated with exposure to school and other settings for learning. Ole & Schreibner (1968)

parents and other family members consider important (Wilkerson, 1979). This is conveyed through expectations, physical provisions for academic pursuits, attitudes toward intellectual activity, and the models that are available for children to emulate. Participation in comprehensive education activities contributes to the development of a sense of membership in high performance learning communities and shared values for the importance of academic achievement for personal fulfillment, community development, and social and political upward mobility (Gordon, 1999).

The values that are privileged by parents and the experiences that parents and communities provide are so critical to the mix that I am convinced that teaching parents how to be advocates for their children's academic and personal development needs much greater emphasis. In my own research three related efforts are included in our program of work: (1) strengthening the capacity of families and parents to support the academic and personal development of children; (2) educating and supporting parents and other interested adults as advocates for the academic and personal develop of students; and (3) better enabling parents to function as competent adults who are capable of directing and supporting the optimal development of children. We argue that it takes a well-developed adult to support the optimal development of a child. In the first of these activities the emphasis is on better enabling parents to function effectively as persons, as parents and as supporters of academic and personal development. The second activity is more sharply focused on assisting, demonstrating, and enabling parents to interact with school people and programs and to advocate for the best interest of children. In the third set of activities, we are seeking to better enable parents to function as competent adults do—at home, at work, in their communities. We are convinced that the absence of such competence is one of the problems faced by teenaged parents. We have also observed adults trying to function as parents when their own development has been so arrested that they are incapable of providing for themselves or their children. In cases such as these, the support for the academic and personal development of children rests on very week reeds. The optimal development of children requires that well-developed adults mediate and orchestrate the developmental experiences of children.

Comprehensive education is about the scaffolding that caring members of our families and communities create around "the mainstream of society that" enables our children "to move up" (Blackwell, 2002, p. 28). The essence of what we call supplementary, complementary or comprehensive education is as much about the ethos of caring and concern, and the acts of enablement, nurturance and protection, as it is about the institutions, resources and services that should be available for families and communities. The a la carte or supplemental components of education include attitudes and expectations. Included are the demands, the routine provisions, the things that are done for fun, and even things that are forced under duress in the effort to ensure that optimal development and effective education are achieved.

Redundancy is another important element for education. Most complex systems that achieve effectiveness and stability are characterized by redundancy— that is, systems in which all critical mechanisms have back-up alternative components in case of failure in the primary system. We routinely see such redundancy in biological, electronic, and mechanical systems. It is possible that the educative systems of human societies also require redundancy—multi-layered mechanisms by which the developmental tasks of human learning are engaged, supported, and mastered. At best these compensate or take over when one mechanism or another fails. Supplementary education just may be a part of that ubiquitously redundant system concerned with motivating, preparing, enabling, mediating, facilitating, consolidating, and ensuring that high levels of academic learning and personal development are achieved.

In the context advanced by Brice-Heath and Mclaughlin (1993), Rebell and Wolff (2008), Stenberg (1999), Weiss (et.al.2005, 2006), Varenne (2007), and I (Gordon et.al. 2005), emphasis is given to family/home, school and community, but comprehensive education is not co-terminus with these institutions. It also occurs in peer and intergenerational relationships. It is ubiquitous to one's personal and public efforts at making sense of the world. It is a function of commercial enterprise, gang-life, political participation, fun seeking and making love. It happens in the solitary practice of shooting baskets on the basketball court. One of my students cautions that we are ignoring the learning involved in epistemic games.

When Teideman (1965) distinguished between "other people's data and one's personal data" as competing concerns of school learners, he was referring to the tension between our concentration on the mastery of the academic content of schooling and the pressing learning demands of peer relations, dating, pursuit of reputation, athletic and social competition, and the adjudication of the relationships in family as well as community politics. Schooling privileges teaching and learning related to the demands of academic knowledge and process mastery, but it competes with the learning and teaching related to learning to live and survive. Thinking comprehensively about education requires that we privilege both and the ways in which the two are conjoined and dialectically-related. If we follow Cremin, logic requires that these processes be thought of as a whole, and that they be thought of publicly, i.e., as in the public domain and as part of the public responsibility for education.

VARIETIES OF OPPORTUNITIES FOR TEACHING AND LEARNING

Our society has developed a wide variety of educative institutions and resources from which opportunities for teaching and learning can be chosen. Some of these institutions have long histories and colloquial familiarity. Among these institutions and services are:

Settlement Houses and Community Centers: Organizations which offered social services to address the inability of low income, immigrant and highly movable families to provide the structure and supports that are associated with family life like: health, recreation, child care, employment, personal development, and counseling. Some examples of these organizations are: The British Association of Settlements and Social Action Centers (BASSAC) in the United Kingdom; the Hull House in Chicago and the University Settlement House in New York.

Faith-based Institutions: Churches, Synagogues and Mosques emerged very early as institutions concerned with teaching and learning. Initially, they ran educational activities directed at the development of their leaders. Most of the efforts went into the religious training of followers. For a long time, faith based institutions have sponsored k-16 education. In many communities the colloquial perceptions of excellence and structure have made them the preferred choice. In addition to this more formal settings for academic learning faith-based institutions have become a major source for the incidental learning of attitude, habits, mores and values that are associated with believes propagated by these institutions.

Youth development Services: There are organizations that offer different kinds of learning experiences for the development of the young people. The following are some examples:

1. Pre-vocational education. Variety of organized experiences design to introduce and orient knowledge to live and work of a given profession. Children are early introduced to vocational education. For example: 4H, Future Farmers, Future teachers.
2. Scouting (also known as the Scout Movement) is a worldwide youth movement with the stated aim of supporting young people in their physical, mental and spiritual development, so that they may play constructive roles in society.
3. Big Brother/Sister mentoring organization with a mission to help children ages 6 through 18, in communities across the country to reach their potential through professionally-supported one-to-one relationships with mentors that have a measurable impact on youth.
4. Apprenticeships. Supervised learning experience that involves the engagements in the activities of the craft skill or profession, usually under the supervision of an expert who cultures the learning person in the tacit knowledge associated with the area of expertise.

Coaching, mentoring and tutoring: Mentoring and tutoring are more widely recognized as academic resources than is coaching, but all three place their emphasis on individualization, customization and personalization. In mentoring the relationship between the teaching person and the learning person is sometimes thought of as primary and the content of the experience tend to be more focus on socialization and psychological development. We associate the coaching function with the learning and homing a particular skill or set of skills, while the tutoring function is often dominated by a purpose on academic content and academic skill development. However, the product of each of the three functions is the development in the learner of competences comparable to those of the teacher and the achievement in the novice that often surpasses the achievement of the expert.

The Posse model for admission to and success in college: Unique program of selection and support for admission to and competition of college for culturally diverse and low-income students whose backgrounds would normally make them less likely to be admitted to highly selective colleges. The Posse Foundation program responds to the three main challenges that this population face:

recruitment, retention and integration to the college life. For recruitment, Posse identifies students who represent leadership talent, high status among their peers and communities, and demonstrated ambition and desire to succeed, in addition to academic competence. The program presents these students to participating institutions and advocates for their admission to college as a group. Once the students are in the college, the program tackles both the retention and integration issues through the recruitment, selection, preparation and support of multi-cultural teams of students (Posses), and places these Posses at participating institutions. At each college the Posse functions as a support group for the academic and personal development of its members, as a model of cultural diversity in student life, and as an agent for social change toward democratic integration on its campus.

The Black Star Project parent and student development (BSP): A program that provides educational services that help preschool through college low-income Black and Latino students in Chicago to succeed academically and become knowledgeable and productive citizens with the support of their parents, families, schools and communities. The BSP conducts its programming primarily through parent and student leadership development and advocacy. Among its programs, TBSP offers mentoring, tutoring, Parents University, the Fathers' march, the Fathers club, and the Parent of the Year Award.

Boarding families and Boarding Schools: Alternative for families who want to offer their children the out-of-home life experiences that they consider more appropriate for their development. Boarding families are more likely to be used by low income parents who want their kids to be exposed to the experiences of people with better resources and opportunities; while boarding schools may be more used by high income families who send their kids to attend and live in a school that offers particular type of education in which they are interested.

The Folk School Movement: Organization of schools lead by lay persons and communities with a primary focus on life skills and academic studies. Besides meeting the requirements of the traditional curriculum, these schools respond to the characteristics and needs of the community who co-sponsor them. Folk schools have emerged in modern times as ethnic-centered or culture-centered schools. One example is the Children's Defense Fund.

We are deliberately excluding from this inventory formal school settings where teaching and learning are given priority. However, there is emerging a set of institutions called "schools" which incorporate into their missions a broader range of experiences than those typically available in schools. Two specific illustrations follow along with an overview of the community schools movement:

The Harlem Children's Zone: Project with a unique, holistic approach to rebuilding a community so that its children can stay on track through college and go on to the job market. The agency located in Harlem offers innovative, efficiently run programs that are aimed at doing nothing less than breaking the cycle of generational poverty for the thousands of children and families it serves in a 100 block radius. Currently HCZ serves 7,400 students and 4,100 parents. The two fundamental principles of The Zone Project are to help kids as early in their lives as possible and to create a critical mass of adults around them who understand what it takes to help children succeed. HCZ offers early childhood programs for children and their parents like: Baby College, Three Year Old Journey and Harlem Gems. The Zone also runs two charter schools (elementary and middle school) called The Promise Academy. It also offers family, community and health programs to the parents of the children as well as the surrounding community through projects like the Beacon Community Centers.

The Eagle Academy for Young Men: A public school founded in 2004 that is designed to optimize the academic and social success of Black and Hispanic young men. According to its mission, the Eagle Academy for young men is "a nurturing learning environment where students, faculty and community work together to develop academic excellence, ethical behavior, and personal responsibility. Guided by our core values--academic excellence, leadership, character development, mentoring, integrity, and community service, the Eagle Academy will make a difference, not only in our lives, but in our communities." This institution is, perhaps, an exemplar of schools that exploit the complementarities between the learning and teaching that can occur out-of-school and the teaching and learning that can occur in-schools. The comprehensiveness of its program is suggestive of the schools in the community school movement. The deep involvement of parents and other community people in the support of the academic and personal development of children represents the best of what we do in our efforts to coordinate the inputs from family, community and school.

Community Schools: A community school is a school that combines best educational practices with in-house youth development, health and social services to ensure that children are physically, emotionally and socially prepared to learn. Active, long-term partnerships between school personnel, parents and community agencies are prioritized. Children, youth, families and communities receive a range of support and opportunities before, during and after regular school days, six or seven days a week. Community schools deliver integrated services in the context of traditional academic programs. In her book, *Full-Service Schools,* Joy Dryfoos singled out the Children's Aid Society's Community Schools approach as a model of "how to put together both sides of the fundamental full-service equation: restructuring of education, plus helping children and their families by providing health, mental health and social services on site." The core components of community schools like the Children's Aid Society's are: An extended-day program that offers educational enrichment before school, after school, weekends and summers; medical, dental, mental health and social services; a comprehensive parent involvement program; early childhood education; adult education; and community-wide events.

Places of Learning, Places of Joy: In most of these settings for learning the opportunity to privilege the "for fun" aspects of the activity is greater than in more formal academic learning situations were typically greater emphasis is placed on accountability or mastery of a particular skill or content. In Ted Seizer's Places of Learning, Places of Joy, the case is made for more deliberate distinctions being made between the opportunities to serve these two ends. Seizer argues for the importance of the fun dimension of all learning but concedes an inferior position for joyfulness in most academic learning settings. In his book he associates the opportunity for joy with cultural and social celebration and learning. In our discussion of alternative settings for learning, celebration and playfulness tend to be integrated into all of these settings. Unlike Seizer's model it is not so much the isolation of these two conditions for learning as it is the integration of these two conditions in all teaching and learning experiences, while recognizing that the alternative settings do provide greater flexibility for adaptation of the teaching and learning transaction to the situational demands of the setting. I find it useful to think of the complementarities between the more formal and less formal—the more intentional and less intentional settings—depending on the purpose of the transaction.

POLICY IMPLICATIONS FLOWING FROM THINKING COMPREHENSIVELY ABOUT EDUCATION

Several implications for public policy flow from a serious commitment to the concern for thinking comprehensively about education. Suggested categories of public policy include:

- More democratic access to the various forms of education relevant capital;
- Harnessing the power of popular culture in support of the cultivation of intellective competence;
- Tax credits for documented investment of family and personal resources in comprehensive education and supplements to schooling;
- Pedagogical enrichment of and universal access to on-line information resources;
- Deliberate development of academic socialization and intellective competence in young adults and especially in parents and interested adults;
- Universal access to academic tutoring, coaching in personal agency and academic remediation;
- Community based centers for professional development, information resources and technical assistance for families, faith-based institutions and community agencies concerning Comprehensive Education; and
- Comprehensive Education Development Banks from which community-based groups, family or worker cooperatives and private groups and individuals can borrow investment and/or seed money with which to sponsor supplementary education agencies and services.

Public policies that support and ensure *universal access to education relevant forms of capital* is, perhaps, the most rational policy implication and it is also the most problematic. Available research findings almost unanimously support the conclusion that adequacy of family resources and associated conditions of life (income and wealth) are correlated with academic achievement. This suggests that significantly improving the conditions of life for under-resourced families might well be the first line of attack on the problems of under academic achievement in the United States. The idea of eliminating poverty is by no means new, but except for an aborted effort during the Lyndon Johnson administration our society has not even approached a serious effort at significantly reducing poverty. My first candidate policy issue then is for more democratic access to the various forms of education relevant capital of which financial capital is foundational.

We have been successful at *harnessing the power of popular culture* and the various forms of media in support of the values that inform capitalist corporate America. Would that we could harness that power in support of the crucial importance of intellective competence and the instrumental roles of the variety of educative forces available in our communities to influence its achievement. In my report to the Montgomery County Public Schools in Maryland I made the recommendation, with no expectation that it would be heard, that the Board of Education should control the various media sources in Montgomery County. It was not a practical recommendation. It runs counter to the traditions of free speech, freedom of the press and free enterprise. However the point of the recommendation is so obvious that it need not be expressed. Popular culture is a powerful educative force and it has come to be heavily mediated by electronic and print media. When corporate America dragged its feet in its support of the military demands of World War II, Franklin Roosevelt practically conscripted the emerging defense industry to produce the arms needed for that war. Our government, as a matter of policy, moved to make the production of arms and related military equipment so profitable that for the last sixty years corporate USA has led the effort to maintain what Eisenhower called the "Military Industrial Complex." A strong defense posture politically supported by corporate America has become a prime characteristic of the popular culture. Would that we could secure that kind of support for thinking about education comprehensively. With adequate leadership we can work toward that kind of public policy.

The weight of government can be placed behind ideas we seek to support by making available *tax credit for related expenditures* that are consistent with the idea. I am proposing a wide variety of expenditures for which families, which meet specified income limits would be given tax credit for documented costs associated with education. Among these could be:

134

1. Books and school supplies,
2. Education related travel;
3. Supplementary education services;
4. Time off from work for parental involvement in support of child's education;
5. Tax credit for time volunteered for education related community service; and
6. Some education subsidy for low-income families who could not benefit from tax credits with money that could be used to pay for supplementary education services or comprehensive education essentials.

The advent of digitalization of the information technologies, in democratic societies, demands universal access to on-line information resources. Just as clean air, potable water, uncontaminated food and sewage disposal are required for modern life, so is the capacity to access and process information in digitalized form rapidly becoming a necessity of life. The clear policy implication of this circumstance is the public assumption of responsibility for universal access to this essential human resource. If broadband technology is the medium of information exchange, it and the electricity with which to access it must be made available as a matter of democratic public policy.

I believe that in modern technologically developed societies intellective competence and the academic abilities by which it is achieved must be affirmatively developed in all people. Since I also believe that reasonably well developed adults are required to mediate the learning and developmental experiences of children, public policy should support efforts directed at *socialization to intellective competence through academic achievement* especially in parents and interested adults. We have a model for such policies in the field of public health where increased attention is being given to the social marketing of and socialization to health maintenance. Such policy may need to give special attention to the population of young unwed parents who may not yet have had the opportunity to fully develop, but find themselves responsible for orchestrating the development of children.

Access to schooling is widely protected, even required in the USA, as a matter of public policy, yet *access to academic coaching, remediation, and tutorial services* remains ubiquitous in more affluent families and underutilized in under-resourced families. We have good reason to believe that it is the access that children from more affluent families have to such services and other forms of supplemental/complementary education that is the "hidden curriculum" that is associated with serious differences in the patterns of academic achievement seen in high status and low status children. I fully embrace Robert Moses' claim that access to education of high quality is a civil right, and I argue that access to coaching, remediation and tutoring should be included in that basic right of citizens to education.

In some more affluent and culturally attuned communities, formal opportunities for complementary/supplementary education are plentiful. In less affluent and some ethnic minority communities such opportunities are scarce. As a matter of policy, government will need to create and support *community-based centers for professional development, information resources and technical assistance for families, faith-based institutions and community agencies concerning* Comprehensive Education. These Resource Centers will seek to:

1. Strengthen parents and families in their capacity to advocate for, encourage and support academic and personal development of their members.
2. Strengthen Community Infrastructure for family and parent surrogate functions and community resources and services for the provision and support of the academic and personal development of children.
3. Identify comprehensive/supplementary education resources and disseminate relevant information.
4. Provide access to Information Resources and Referral Services.
5. Promote the Social Marketing of Comprehensive/supplementary education, i.e., building community and family awareness of and support for comprehensive/supplementary education.
6. Develop a Program of Research and Development concerning Comprehensive Education.

The program of the Comprehensive Education Resource Center is informed by a public health approach to education through which we seek to think comprehensively and relationally about education. It would be comprehensively and relationally in the sense that all of the education relevant forms of necessary capital are considered in their dialectical interactions each with the other. As in modern approaches to public health, the resource center will promote the orchestrated availability and utilization of these various forms of education relevant resources in the lives of children and their families in Harlem. We propose to create an education center that will guide the Harlem community in the development of an approach to education that is both comprehensive and relational, and is supplemental to an excellent public school.

To better enable and more greatly ensure that less affluent communities and their families are able to create resource centers and complementary/supplementary services, I have proposed that a federal *Comprehensive Education Development Bank* be created and charged with providing the investment capital and seed money for the creation and initial support of complementary/supplementary education agencies and services in communities where they do not exists and where the resource base makes it less likely that they will emerge. Long-term loans should be available at reduced interest rates. Preference should be given to the cooperative and not-for-profit sectors, but for-profit enterprises should not be excluded.

7
Democratizing the American Educational Research Association

The journalist of public affairs, James Traub described me as having gained considerable prominence in his field without having discovered a major theory or his being associated with some great movement. I think of myself as an applied scientist who has devoted his career, not so much to my own conduct of empirical research as to the examination and interpretation of the work of other scientists for its possible applications to and implications for the real problems of people. Thus it is that much of my work is focused critique and hermeneutic analysis of research done by others, and of the synthesis of ideas derived from bodies of extant research. Not only have I tried to use my resultant sophistication to re-conceptualize approaches to pressing problems, I have also tried to re-shape the culture of the pedagogical and psychological professions. In my Doctor of education project, I wrote of shifting the purpose of the field of counseling and guidance from a focus on serving clients to the goal of enabling.

As chairperson of the Task Force on the Role and Future of Minorities of the American Educational Research Association (AERA) I tried to provide leadership to that association as it became better democratized in its inclusion of diverse populations in its membership, and broadened significantly the epistemologies and methodologies by which knowledge production is informed. I served as co-chairperson for two additional groups whose work was directed at changing the profession of pedagogy. When the New York State Board of Regents was confronted with demand for making the social studies curriculum of the schools in NY State more inclusive, Francis Roberts and I were asked to lead the commission that was convened to resolve the controversy. At the College Entrance Examination Board I was able to convince Donald Stewart, president at that time, to have the board sponsor the National Task Force on Minority High Achievement. An interesting example of these efforts on my part is provided by my work as chairperson of the American Educational Research Association's Task

Force on the Role and Future of Minorities. The following is an adaptation of the report my AERA colleagues and I prepared in 1997 as a part of my effort at democratizing the American Educational Research Association.

The Task Force on the Role and Future of
Minorities of the American Educational Research Association

The Task Force on the Role and Future of Minorities of the American Educational Research Association is pleased to submit its final report to the AERA Council. The report consists of four sections:

- Introduction
- Historical Context of Diversity Efforts in AERA—A section setting forth an historical context for is¬sues having to do with ethnic mi¬nority group members' roles and participation in AERA and some of the issues of epistemology that are sometimes confused with or that confound issues concerning ethnic group identity.
- Changing Demographics, Epistemologies, and Ideologies—The changing character of AERA as an organization and the changing conceptual, demographic, social, and political context in which the association must function.
- Task Force Recommendations—Six recommendations from the task force for action by the AERA Council.

Introduction

In December 1995, Linda Darling-Hammond, then president of the American Educational Research Association, appointed the following members of the association to serve as members of a presidential Task Force on the Role and Future of Minorities in AERA: Beatriz Arias, David Berliner, Edmund W. Gordon, Chairperson, Grace Pung Guthrie, Vernon C. Polite, Richard Ruiz, and Christine Sleeter.

In her letter of appointment, President Darling-Hammond indicated that the Task Force on the Role and Future of Minorities should examine the ways in which scholars of color are currently involved in the life and operations of the association, its functions, and the educational research, development, and utilization profession as a whole; the extent to which full opportunity has been achieved in the various dimensions of scholarly activity, such as participation in research definition, conduct, interpretation, and publishing; and the obstacles and barriers to full participation that may continue to exist for some of our members. She expressed the hope that "the Task Force will provide recommendations to the AERA Council about ways in which the Association can further reduce barriers to full involvement, and can act affirmatively to increase participation and leadership among scholars of color in all of its major activities and functions."

The letter of appointment indicated that:

> The impetus for this task force is twofold. The process of creating a fully inclusive profession is necessarily a continuous one that requires periodic assessment and recommit¬ment to the goals and aspirations the Association holds. Given both the important steps AERA has taken and the need for continued progress in today's world, this is a useful time for stock taking and proactive assessment of where we are vis-a-vis where we want to be as an Association that represents the adults and children in the education community we serve. In addition, some recent events have resurfaced concerns about the historical underrep¬resentation of scholars of color as authors and editors in AERA publications as well as the limited presence of scholarship on issues of concern to communities of color in AERA journals. While the Publications Committee has addressed some specific concerns relating to the Committee's policies and practices, the roots of these concerns go far beyond the boundaries of any Single committee and deserve the attention of the entire AERA community.

In response to this charge, the members of the task force, beginning with their initial meeting, agreed that their work would have a dual focus on issues related to the integration of peoples from diverse backgrounds in the association and on issues related to the increasing coexistence of diverse epistemologies and perspectives in an association where a traditional set of values relative to knowledge production has gained hegemony. Although there are several social divisions into which the members of the association can be assigned (age, ethnicity, gender, language, religion, sexual orientation, social class, as examples) the members of the task force have given primary attention to ethnic and language group identity in this report. However, because it is becoming clear that the problem that the association is having with the increased salience of ethnic and gender diversity in its membership may be a surrogate for deeper problems with diversity in the epistemologies and perspectives that inform knowledge production, development, and utilization, the task force has devoted considerable attention in this report to the implications of changing demographics, epistemologies, and perspectives. It is to be noted that while the report calls for greater inclusiveness with respect to these diverse ways of knowing and viewing the world, the task force members are not suggesting that established and traditional epistemologies and perspectives be discarded. Rather, in the interest of authenticity, fairness, representativeness, and validity, the task force members assert the critical importance of respect for the diverse peoples. Perspectives and epistemologies that are apart of the association and the society in which it operates.

The members of the Task Force on the Role and Future of Minorities have met (1) Once to deliberate the issues and plan the work of the task force; (2) In two public hearings at the 1996 AERA annual meeting to receive testimony from AERA members; (3) Once to review and interpret available information, to formulate initial recommendations, and to consider the content of a progress report; (4) Once to review the council's reaction to the progress report of the task force and to make appropriate revisions; and (5) Once in joint session with the AERA Strategic Planning Committee to contribute to the discussion of the mission of the association.

Historical Context of Diversity Efforts in AERA

This year marks the 80th anniversary of the establishment of AERA, originally called the National Association of Directors of Education. It was a department of the National Education Association until 1967, when it became a separate nonprofit corporation. Since early in its development, AERA has shown concern for issues of equity and inclusion. Beginning in 1972, its council has adopted resolutions that declare its commitment to diversity. The following is the first of these:

Be it resolved that all persons, regardless of race ethnicity, age, sex religion, national origin, marital status, sexual orientation, or any other characteristics not related to the person's qualifications have full opportunity to participate in the activities of AERA.

In August 1977, although divisional affirmative action committees and several Special Interest Groups (SIGs) on minority issues had already been established, a group of members (LaMar P. Miller, John Egermeier, Edmund W. Gordon, Sylvia T. Johnson, and Fernie Baa-Moore) expressed concern in a letter to President James Popham about "the problem of poor utilization of potential available talent for solving educational problems and in increasing the credibility of research, especially in groups that are most underrepresented in the education research community." They called for an ad-hoc committee to study the role and status of minorities in educational research. In December of that year, William J. Russell, executive officer, informed the group that the council had voted to establish such a committee with Romeria Tidwell as chair; the committee was to continue through the annual meeting of 1980. In January of 1980, the council designated it a standing committee of the organization.

The Standing Committee on the Role and Status of Minorities in Educational Research and Development (CRSMERD) was very active in formulating goals and objectives in its first few years. It facilitated communication about its activities thorough a newsletter, first published in 1982 when Robert K. Murphy was chair. Its major goals involved improving general participation of minorities in the organization, increasing the number of minorities serving on AERA editorial boards, improving communication within the organization on minority issues by holding open meetings and coordinating the activities of minority SIGs, monitoring affirmative-action activities in the divisions, sponsoring professional development opportunities for minority researchers through fellow¬ships and mentoring workshops, recognizing the achievements of minority members and others who study minority issues through annual awards and invited addresses, and working with research and development organizations, centers, and universities to increase the possibilities for minority employment.

More recently, in addition to continuing with these and other activities, CRSMERD has spearheaded the development of a directory and data bank of minority scholars that can be used by AERA presidents, editors, committee chairs, and others with authority to choose reviewers and appoint editorial boards and committees. This was impelled by a sense of the CRSMERD that AERA journals tend not to publish minority topics and minority authors, at least in part because of a lack of sensitivity to the variety of interests and modes of knowledge production among the members of the organization. In the late 1980s and early 1990s, members of the committee conducted preliminary investigations on the numbers of minority scholars whose work had appeared in AERA publications. The study was inconclusive in part because of a lack of available data on submissions and in part because it was difficult to know what factors affected submissions. Until this point, there has not been a follow-up or refinement to this study.

The most recent developments in AERA on diversity and equity testify to the fact that, while various committees and officers have been actively involved in promoting minority concerns, there is still widespread concern that the organization still has great needs in these areas. At the 1992 annual meeting, Christine Sleeter and Olga Welch organized a panel discussion on issues of inclusion with chairs of 12 SiGs and standing committees. That session generated a long list of concerns that once again demonstrated strong negative sentiment toward the organization. Especially salient was the feeling that minority issues and the SIGs and committees associated with them are peripheral in AERA.

Currently, there is a widespread perception that, in spite of all these important activities, very little real change has occurred. In 1993, in large part because of concerns expressed by several members of the CRSMERD that structural reform was needed to address these issues adequately, the council established a diversity officer for AERA. In 1995, the council established the Council of Affinitive Action Officers, which met at the annual meeting in New York in 1996 for the first time. Also in 1995, the council was confronted with a problem in connection with one of the association's publications that suggests that issues concerning the participation of minority members in AERA persists. The appointment of the present task force is further testimony to the association's continuing efforts to develop policies, practices, and. structures in AERA that can reduce, if not eliminate, problems referable to the association's diverse membership.

As is suggested by this brief history of the association's concern for the diverse populations represented among its members, much of the focus has been placed on the social divisions by which humans tend to be classified, i.e., ethnic, gender, and language groups. Interestingly enough, concern for class divisions has not been prominent in these deliberations. However, it is the judgment of the members of the task force that as important as these cultural and political identities may be, it is also ideologies and epistemologies that are contributing to the tensions within the association. AERA, like the society of which it is a part, has experienced important changes in the composition of its membership at the same time that we have experienced significant changes in our conceptions of knowledge and the legitimacy of different perspectives with respect to specific knowledge domains. AERA and our society have begun to hear the voices of segments of the population that previously have been less visible and less audible in mainstream discourse. The fact that some of those new voices have been quite strident and that some of those perspectives have seemed to some to be counter-intuitive (if not just wrong) have led some who might otherwise be more sympathetic to become anxious about the integrity of the association and its standards.

It is to be remembered that the American Educational Research Association traditionally has consisted of pedagogical scientists and scholars of educational theory and practice who, like other social and behavioral scientists, model their approach to knowledge production after natural and physical scientists. The standards that have been privileged in our association are grounded in the empiricism and positivism that is typical of these sciences. For some 25 years, AERA has been trying to accommodate the presence of contextualist, perspectivist, and other expressions of nontraditional thought and workers. Many AERA members who joined the association during this period may not represent this new epistemology, but they also are not as firmly identified with the traditional scientific methodologies. The association has made considerable progress in these efforts at accommodation and inclusion of diverse populations and, to a lesser extent, diverse ways of knowing. We believe that the shifting ideological and epistemological ground is as much a part of the association's problem as are the changing demographics of our membership. The tensions we are experiencing around the cultural and ethnic identities of our members maybe the symptoms of deeper concerns about the changing nature of the association and, more broadly, about the changing nature of the knowledge production enterprise. In the recommendations in this report, we have placed greater emphasis on the implications of these demographic changes, however, it is the judgment of the members of this task force that issues related to the role and future of our minority members will not be adequately addressed independently of attention being given to the implications of these accompanying changes in ideologies and epistemologies for the future of the organization.

CHANGING DEMOGRAPHICS, EPISTEMOLOGIES AND IDEOLOGIES
Demographic Changes in Our, Schools and Society

Like the population of our nation, the population of children in our schools continues to be predominantly of European American ancestry, but by constantly declining proportions. Our society and our schools are steadily becoming more diverse in the characteristics and identities of their peoples. The increasing diversity of America's children is a reality that has affected virtually every state and major city in the nation. During the decade spanning 1980-1990, the child population under five years of age rose 13.8 percent, the largest growth for that group since 1966. Of the approximately 19.2 million children below five years of age, American Indian, Eskimo and Aleut, Asian and Pacific Islander, and Hispanic children were the fastest growing ethnic groups. As this cohort of children ages, it will bring increasing diversity to an already diverse group of school-age students (Statistical Record of Children, 1990).

In 1980, the population of children age 5-13 was approximately 31.1 million (US Bureau of Census, Current Population Reports, pp. 25-1095). By 1991, that population had increased to 32.5 million with growth reported for every racial/ethnic group except Whites. During this decade, there was a decline in the White population of approximately 683,000 children.

What the population reports show is that during this decade the growth of all racial/ethnic groups has increased with the exception of the White children. In 1980, there were approximately 475 mil lion children ages 5-13. By 1991, that number had increased to 51.7 million. The increase of 42 million children is largely accounted for by an increase of racial and ethnic minority groups. The population of White children ages 0-13 actually declined during this decade. In 1980, White children comprised 73.6 percent of the total 475 million children ages 0-13. In 1991, the percentage of White children in this age cohort had declined to 68 percent with a corresponding increase in Black, Hispanic, American Indian and Asian and Pacific Islander groups.

This increase in diversity has been accompanied by an increase in the isolation of Black and Hispanic students in our schools. A report by the Harvard Project on School Desegregation noted that the number of Black and Hispanic students attending predominately minority schools has been on the rise. Minority schools are defined as those with more than 50 percent of their enrollment composed of either of Black or Hispanic students or both.. Out of the total five million Hispanic students in the country's public schools, 74.3 percent attended predominately minority schools in predominately minority communities in 1991-1992. The most segregated states for both Black and Hispanic students are New York, New Jersey, Illinois, Connecticut, and Pennsylvania. Additionally, the most segregated states for Hispanics are Texas, California, Florida, and Indiana. The most segregated states for Blacks include Michigan, Tennessee, Alabama, Maryland, and Mississippi.

Compounding the increasing diversity and segregation of students since the 1980s was also an increase in the rate of child poverty. Children are more likely than any other age group to be living in poverty. In 1987, nearly 21 percent of all children and more than 22 percent of preschool children were living below the poverty line. Black and Hispanic children are two to three times more likely to be living in poverty than are White children. The poverty rate for children living in female-headed households continued to be more than twice that of children in general. Increases in poverty rates in the 1970s and 1980s corresponded with periods of recession in the national economy. However, during periods of economic growth, child poverty rates declined only slightly, and for Hispanic children, they did not decline at all (Statistical Record of Children, 1990; Center for the Study of Social Policy, Kids Count Data Book, 1993).

Who these disadvantaged and marginalized students are affects what issues related to education are most relevant. Not only have the demographics changed, but the ability of schools to serve all children well has not been greatly improved, and challenges are concentrated particularly in schools with historically underserved populations. Miller (1995) refers to the urgent need to improve schooling in urban areas. In his book An American Imperative, he argues forcefully that the future of the US will depend on its ability to close gaps between racial groups. Working vigorously to improve schooling for children from racial minority and/or low-income backgrounds is obviously in the nation's best interest. This interest and the needs of these segments of the population have important implications for the mission and work of AERA.

DEMOGRAPHIC CHANGES IN AERA

The demographics of AERA are also changing as Table 1 illustrates. However, AERA membership is by no means reflective of the changing demographic characteristics of students in our schools or of the population at large. This mis¬match in characteristics between our members and the characteristics of our public schools' population could mean that AERA members are likely to frame education issues differently from the ways in which minority educators and professionals most directly connected with underserved populations in these schools are likely to frame issues.

TABLE 1	DEMOGRAPHIC CHANGES IN AERA MEMBERSHIP			
AERA membership	1980	1984-1985	1989-1990	1994-1995
African American	3%	4%	4%	5%
Asian or Pacific Islander	3%	3%	4%	5%
Native American	0.50%	0.4%	0.5%	0.5%
Latina/o	2%	3%	3%	3.5%
Caucasian	89%	86%	87%	82%

These differences between the AERA membership and public school communities can also lead to a gap between issues that tend to receive most attention within AERA and those that are of greatest concern to these schools and communities. Some measure of this difference is reflected in the titles of the works of minority scholars that have been published in AERA publications. More important, the demographic differences between members of the association and the demographic patterns extant in public schools alone the modest representation of minority group persons in the membership of the association make it difficult for members of underrepresented groups to feel that AERA represents their interests.

These demographic changes in schools and within AERA connect with very fundamental challenges to the knowledge production process itself. AERA is experiencing internal conflicts not only because of these demographic changes, but also because historically its role as guardian of the traditional canons and methodologies of knowledge production related to education have sometimes resulted in maintenance at conditions and processes that often operate in ways that are exclusionary of some of the diversity that is characteristic of its members- and even more so of the society of which the association is a part. Because, historically, professional organizations such as AERA have served as the primary arbiters for defining and determining what counts as knowledge in academic settings, those who are challenging AERA from culturally and racially different perspectives are challenging not only established traditions and processes in AERA but also the narrowness of existing cannons and the processes by which knowledge and technique within those cannons are produced.

CHANGING EPOSTEMOLOGIES AND PERSPECTIVES

The dominant paradigms for educational research originated within European and European American experiences and realities and are thought by many to have the effect of colonizing as others" those peoples who do not share that background, whether this effect is intended or not. Approaches to knowledge construction that are ethnically and culturally sensitive are often grounded in very different realities, sometimes using different rules for judging what knowledge is of most worth, how knowledge is to be generated, by whom, and for what purposes. Discussions of profound cultural and political differences in knowledge construction are proliferating leading to a healthy crisis within AERA regarding what counts as knowledge, who validates it, and based on what reference points (e.g., Banks, 1993; Eisner, 1993; E. W. Gordon, 1995; Cordon &t: Meroe, 1991; Heshusius, 1994; Ladson-Billings, 1995; Ladson-Billings & Tate, 1995; Rosaldo, 1989; Scheurich & Young in press; Stanfield, 1985).

Mainstream social science knowledge is grounded in the standards for knowledge production that have developed in the physical sciences (Keto, 1989), in which the main purpose of research is seen as seeking universal "'truths,'" generalizations one can apply to all-"'totalizing schemas'" (Said, 1919; Young.. 199). These truths have been presumed to reflect "natural laws," and the role of the research scientist is to discover these natural and universal laws (Magee. 1973). As James Banks (1993) noted recently in *Educational Researcher.* An important tenet within the mainstream academic paradigm is that there is a set of objective truths that can be verified through rigorous and objective research procedures that are uninfluenced by human interests, values, and perspectives.

The main purpose of the research process is to enable the accumulation of knowledge about human behavior. As Donald Campbell and Julian Stanley (1963) explained, this rests on "an evolutionary perspective, in which applied practice and scientific knowledge are seen as the resultant of an accumulation of selectively retained tentatives, remaining from the hosts that have been weeded out by experience" (p. 4).

Campbell and Stanley (1963) situated the role of scientific research within the broad process of the accumulation of human wisdom. They argued that research serves Has the means of sharpening the relevance of the testing probing selection process.... It is ... a refining process superimposed upon the probably valuable accumulations of wise practice'" (p. 4). In other words, through every day observation and application, humans discover knowledge, but in rather imprecise ways. Knowledge that is produced through research is partially based on and connects with that informally accumulated knowledge, but is thought to be more reliable and valid and thus is usually judged to have more truth probability.

The research methods that have been taught most commonly in Ph.D.-granting institutions derive from this paradigm and are very familiar to the members of AERA. These methods commonly include

- Choosing samples that represent some larger human universe "so that findings are as" generalizable as possible;
- Using data-collection and data-analysis methods that are replicable;
- Controlling for bias through various methods for validity and reliability;
- Subjecting research to review processes within the academy that ensure that published findings adhere to the academy's rules for knowledge production, such as that the findings are objective, verifiable, generalizable, and have been controlled for bias.

Experimental research designs offer the most classic application of physical science research models to the social sciences. Campbell and Stanley (1963) explained that "good experimental design ... is the art of achieving interpretable comparisons .... In all such cases, the interpretability of the results depends upon control over the factors we have been describing" (p. 22). The careful selection of samples, design of experimental and control conditions and design of procedures for data collection and analysis represent attempts to control and manipulate variables to derive generalizable patterns in human behavior.

Some common social science research designs lack the controls of experimental research, but serve other related purposes in generating knowledge about human behavior. Survey research attempts to define patterns in the behavior of large groups. Correlational research attempts to identify variables in human behavior that likely have some relationship to each other. Case studies probe into one or a small number of cases to generate variables and relationships that may

149

apply more broadly and that can be tested using experimental or quasi-experimental research design. In his critique of the knowledge production process Rosaldo (1989) captured the main tenets of mainstream social science research as it has applied to anthropology: Once upon a time, the Lone Ethnographer rode off into the sunset in search of "his native." After undergoing a series of trials, he encountered the objects of his quest in a distant land. There he underwent his rite of passage by enduring the ultimate ordeal of "fieldwork." After collecting "the data," the Lone Ethnographer returned home and wrote a "true" account of "the culture" (p. 30).

What all these research designs have in common is the search for "truth" by an individual who is trained in a set of research methods claiming to maximize objectivity, who studies a sample of human beings to collect data about their behavior, analyzes and interprets that data, and draws conclusions that purport to contribute to a body of accumulated knowledge about human behavior. And what Campbell and Stanley (1963) pointed out that often goes unstated is that this research is intimately connected with the researcher's everyday suppositions and beliefs about what counts as "truth, what human nature is like, what different kinds of people are like, and so forth. In other words, this research process is not divorced from the every day social context in which it emerges, but is a part of that context.

This knowledge production process is limited in its ability to self-critique which deepens the crisis in which the social sciences and AERA find themselves. Within the canons of mainstream knowledge are specific procedures for critique. However, those procedures tend not to critique canonized knowledge and technique. On what basis can we claim that knowledge is generalizable? On what basis can we claim that these procedures yield "truth"? On what basis can we claim that there is such a state as objectivity? Who has the power to define what counts as objective? Who benefits from knowledge claims? To what degree does the knowledge traditionally supported by AERA relate to the diverse communities attending public schools?

These epistemological questions have produced raging debates on a number of fronts. For example, Elliot Eisner (1993) questioned how we know what "meaning" means and why rationality as a way of knowing is so often privileged in the construction of meaning. He challenged researchers to think deeply about "how we think about mind, the enlargement of human understanding, and what counts as meaning" (p. 10). Lois Heshusius (1994) questioned the "objectivity-subjectivity dichotomy" which assumes that something exists "out there: She argues that in methodological debates about how to become more objective, the crucial questions facing schools and kids become lost, and our inability to think with and communicate to others flounders.

Racially and culturally sensitive paradigms, although perhaps new to AERA, are not new in social science scholarship (Banks, 1995). These paradigms challenge many of the assumptions that are foundational to some mainstream knowledge–production processes that are described above (Banks, 1993; Collins, 1991; B. M Gordon, 1990; Ladson-Billings ok Tate, 1995; Rosaldo, 1989). The challenges are similar and. related to those expressed by cities such as Eisner and Heshusius, but also derive partly from the marginalized experiences of communities of color. At issue is the too often unquestioned privileging of European and European American male experiences, in which people other than those of European descent have become incorporated into research in ways that distort and colonize. Educators of color have argued for years that mainstream research, despite claims to objectivity, is biased and almost always frames communities of color as "deficient." In his discussion of the construction of history in relationship to the process of colonization in *White Mythologies*, Robert Young (1990) argues that "the construction of knowledge which all operate through forms of expropriation and incorporation of the other mimics, at a conceptual level, the geographical and economic absorption of the non-European by the West (p. 3). By attempting to incorporate all people into its world view and conceptual universe–while at the same time incorporating non-Europeans into its geographic and economic universe of control–Europeans and European Americans developed a knowledge construction process that at its very core is colonizing. James Scheurich and Michelle Young (in press) refer to this as "civilization racism," which includes "our current range of epistemologies positivism to postmodernism post structuralism [which] arise out of the civilization level of the social history and culture of the dominant race."

Critiques of mainstream research question not just the methodologies used, but also how the context in which a knower views the world shapes what he or she sees (e.g., Harding. 1991). Advocates of racially and culturally sensitive paradigms are not necessarily dismissing mainstream research conducted by, for, and on mainstream populations, but rather the mindless application of such research across cultural and racial boundaries.

Racially and culturally sensitive research challenges the claim of universality and political neutrality of knowledge. For example, Asante (1990) grounds his work in Afrocentrism on the premise that people of African descent should be their own subjects of their own history rather than someone else's objects of study and that the place of people of African descent in the knowledge production process matters epistemologically. One raises the question of place and grounding specifically to orient one to the culture, history, and cosmological frame of reference one is using. As Asante points out, all research is historically situated, "there is no antiplace" (p. 5). Thus, it is important to explicate one's cultural and historical frame of reference and work to deve10p that frame of reference, rather than presuming to move beyond context and standpoint (Gordon, Miller, &: Rollack, 1990).

Research has many purposes, only one of which might be to search for generalizable "truths." A different purpose that has great relevance to racially and culturally sensitive research is to contribute to the improvement of peoples' lives. Patricia Hill Collins (1991) referred to this as an "ethic of caring," which to Gloria Ladson-Billings means "the articulation of a greater sense of commitment to what scholarship and/or pedagogy can mean in the lives of people'" (Ladson-Billings, 1995, p. 474) indeed, much of the scholarship from the "margins" is oriented very explicitly toward the transformation of schools to benefit historically oppressed communities. In this way, knowledge has emancipatory power (B. M. Gordon, 1990) that explicitly challenges what some call the colonizing function of much mainstream knowledge and research.

Unlike most mainstream knowledge production, racially and culturally sensitive research often explicates its political purpose, which then leads to the charge by mainstream researchers that it is "biased" and "politicized." Neither mainstream research nor racially and culturally sensitive research is non-political. Both can and often are used for political purposes, despite the explicit intent of the investigator. It is argued that given the fact that the thinking and methods of research scientists are not independent of their life circumstances, it is impossible to engage in the production of knowledge without some degree of bias. Gordon, Miller, and Rollock (1990) argue that "if we cannot be objective, we can at least be honest" (p. 19). At issue, then, is the degree to which a scholar explicates and interrogates the politics of her/his bias and work.

Racially and culturally sensitive research justifies knowledge claims on less narrow perspectives than does mainstream research. Rather than relying excessively on complex statistical procedures and validation by traditional "experts," Collins (1991) argues that concrete experience be used as a criterion of meaning, that dialogue be used in assessing knowledge claims, and that researchers adhere to an ethic of personal accountability—i.e., personal accountability to the subjects being studied, as well as to the knowledge production enterprise for the authenticity of one's data and their interpretation. Because mainstream research that has been conducted "on" oppressed communities has produced so many damaging distortions, the tenets of mainstream research are thought by some to have little value in judging knowledge claims. Paula Gunn Allen (1989), for example, in her discussion of Native American feminist scholarship, pointed out that her inner voice and her own experiences have been much more reliable touchstones for judging truth than Eurocentric claims about Indian people. Ladson-Billings and Tate (1995) applied Collins' principles in her own research by generating designations of excellent teachers of African American children from African American communities, co-constructing knowledge about pedagogy with teachers, and reflecting on her own accountability to the community in her scholarly work. By grounding her research in the community context and listening to the voice of her own experience as an African American educator, she very self.— consciously worked to produce knowledge that would improve the teaching of African American children. The African American community, then, becomes the final arbiter of her knowledge claims. These indigenous criteria for epistemologic and methodolegic validity are by no means a guarantee of authenticity, but they do add important perspectives that often are more context sensitive than are some of the hegemonic criteria.

This final point brings us back to the significance of demographic changes in schools. Because of the historic inequities in education and the profound demographic shifts our schools and society are experiencing, the need for racially and culturally sensitive research is becoming more pronounced. A slowly growing proportion of the members of AERA is attempting to conduct this research. But working within a different set of assumptions, commitments, and principles from the mainstream, their work is both explicitly challenging the mainstream and putting forth very different principles for knowledge claims than those AERA has historically lauded. The epistemological crisis within AERA will not go away because it is so directly connected with the educational crisis in many schools and the social crisis of a society that is racially and culturally very diverse and structured very unequally.

This epistemological crisis also has the potential for healthy dialogue and growth within the profession as well as in the knowledge production process. Edmund Gordon (1995) notes that professionals need "culturally relevant and situated knowledge rather than (being limited to) decontextualized disciplines separated from the cultures in which they are embedded." He continues: I do not want to suggest that psychology or sociology or anthropology for Black folks is different from the psychology or sociology of White folks. But somehow the study of these disciplines must be approached with sensitivity to diverse cultural contexts" (p. 44). In the long run, opening up AERA to a wider diversity of ways of knowing and to scholarship that connects with the very different realities of different segments of American society, has the potential to strengthen what all of us do by helping all of us become more cognizant of the contingent nature of our knowledge and the rich possibilities for understanding diverse human experiences.

RECOMMENDATIONS FOR ACTION BY THE AERA COUNCIL

The recommendations of the Task Force on the Role and Future of Minorities are presented below in three categories. These categories are:

Support for diverse peoples. epistemologies, and perspectives;

Support for changes in the programs and the functioning of AERA to ensure opportunities for the democratic participation for all members of the association; and

Support for changes in the behavior of members of AERA.

The members of the task force respectfully submit the following recommendations for consideration by the council:

Support for Diverse Peoples, Epistemologies, and Perspectives

The task force recommends that the association adopt and promulgate a normative statement of its mission and commit-ment to support attention to and inclusion of diverse populations, epistemologies, and perspectives and the pursuit of social justice in its organization and its work.

154

The increasing importance of concern for global and diverse perspectives in human enterprises makes it essential that our association, which has as its mission the advancement of the quality of knowledge production, transformation, and utilization in education, make concerns for sensitivity to both common and diverse human characteristics and conditions and multiple epistemologies, perspectives, levels of analysis, and investigative methodologies central to the structure and functioning of the association. In the calculus by which these several values are served, ethical concern for democratic participation, fairness, and social justice must be given privilege equal to that that the association historically, has accorded to traditional standards of scholarly excellence. The association is also committed to the nurturance and development of the potential for leadership in individual members of the association. The same concerns for democratic participation, fairness, and social justice apply to the development of education research leaders as we apply to the production of knowledge and technique concerning education. As the nation's leading organization concerned with the production of knowledge related to education, AERA should exercise leadership in the development and dissemination of knowledge that supports and advances the education of all people, taking full account of the diverse histories, strengths, resources, and needs of those peoples and their communities. Thus the American Educational Research Association serves as a crucible for scholarly debate that draws upon diverse .epistemologies and perspectives in the production, validation, and utilization of knowledge that advances education policy, practice, and theory.

The task force recommends that the association select and appoint a senior scholar as ombudsperson and advocate for the interests of underrepresented epistemologies, peoples, perspectives, and problems within the association. It is recommended that this scholar serve 40 percent to 60 percent time for a three-year experimental term to be evaluated before the end of the sixth month of the third year of service.

AERA has no instrumentality through which a relatively high degree of priority can be given to the continuing need that the association be sensitive to the relationship between the diverse populations and perspectives within the association and the AERA commitment to inclusion and social justice. Although the executive director currently serves as the association's affirmative action officer, it is our judgment that the diversity and social justice concerns of the association

155

require different and. more attention than that officer can provide, given his other responsibilities. The task force therefore recommends that the association appoint an ombudsperson for a three-years experimental period to serve as advocate for the interests of underrepresented epistemologies, peoples, problems, and perspectives in the policy deliberations and functioning of the association. It is recommended that this position be created on a part-time basis, perhaps 40 percent to 60 percent time of a relatively senior scholar who would not give up her/his regular position, but would be partially relieved of regular institutional responsibilities. The appointment should be made with the advice and consent of representatives of the several relevant SIGS. We recommend further that the work of this new officer be monitored by an appropriate committee appointed for that purpose and that the contribution of this initiative be evaluated as a basis for informing the decision to continue this position after the three years' experiment. It is recommended that this evaluation occur before the end of the sixth month before the end of the initial term. During the term of the ombudsperson, he/she should participate in the meetings of the council, ex officio.

Support for Changes in the Programs and the Functioning of AERA to Ensure Opportunities for the Democratic Participation for All Members of the Association.

The task force recommends that the association take several steps to improve communication and reduce the sense of alienation among some of its underrepresented members.

Within the ethnic minority membership of the association, there appears to be a high degree of alienation, frustration, hostility (even anger) felt toward the association and its leadership. Our feedback from this segment of membership points in part to problems in communication within the association and between the leadership of AERA and its ethnic minority members. To address this problem several steps are suggested:

    a. The association should provide clear criteria and guidelines concerning diversity and social justice issues for all AERA divisions, SIGS, committees, and publications. All units of the association and members of AERA should be encouraged to use these criteria for the self-evaluation of relevant work. In an approach to the initiation of these practices, the council might designate 1997-1998 as a year of reflection on issues related to self-evaluation relative to diversity. During this year, all units of the association would be expected to examine its progress and work at inclusion and social justice. The task force hopes such formative self-evaluation will lead to increased representation of diverse perspectives and minority groups in all relevant aspects of the functioning of AERA.

b. AERA should promulgate its criteria as standards of ethics and excellence that are generic to the field of educational research and development and should share these criteria with universities, foundations, OERI, and discipline-based associations.

c. To better acquaint unfamiliar members with information concerning how the association works and how one accesses its resources; the association should consider producing instructional video or other materials on the structure and functioning of AERA, its committees, and the annual meetings. This material should be made available to all interested members and could be shown continuously at the annual meetings.

d. To ensure that all members are fully aware of the vision/mission of AERA and the need to promote diversity and social justice within AERA, the association should conduct diversity training/awareness sessions for all incoming division vice presidents, publications editors, program officers, members-at large and standing committee members.

The task force recommends that the association develop mechanisms of deliberate socialization for underrepresented groups within its membership.

Because socialization to membership in the association tends to occur through natural networks in which minorities are underrepresented, the association should develop mechanisms that facilitate the participation and socialization of members from these groups.

a. To encourage talented minority students to enter the field of educational research, the association should seek funding from foundations and elsewhere to provide training, workshops, and other initiatives designed to achieve this purpose.

b. To encourage that greater attention be given to issues and questions concerning ethnic minority groups, the annual meeting committee should provide incentives (such as additional session slots) to divisions that devote sessions to diversity and minority issues.

c. To give greater prominence to the association's concern for and commitment to diversity and social justice, invited distinguished lecturers who reflect the wide variety of perspectives and possible contributions to knowledge production, transformation, and utilization should be regularly included in the annual program.

The task force recommends that a program of mentoring for younger and underrepresented group members be developed and institutionalized within the association.

Some members of the association seem to benefit from naturally occurring opportunities to be mentored and have their career development encouraged, as a function of the networks that exists. Minority group members appear to be underrepresented in these networks. To ensure that all members have opportunities to become well socialized to the traditional and changing standards that are implicit in the association, it is recommended that a program of mentoring for younger and underrepresented groups be created and institutionalized within the association.

Support for Changes in the Behavior of Members;

The task force recommends that the following changes in the behavior of the members of AERA be encouraged.

While the above categories indicate actions that the association should take, we believe that all AERA members have the responsibility to avail themselves of all opportunities provided by the association. Because meaningful participation in the association in large measure depends on the availability of adequate numbers and qualities of members who produce strong research products, all members should assume greater responsibility for increasing the quality of their preparation and of their research and development products. To address this issue, appropriate members of the association should consider such initiatives as those that follow.

All AERA members should take advantage of various opportunities for gaining knowledge about and access into the governance structure of the association.

All AERA-members should take advantage of all relevant opportunities, such as mentorships and institutes offered by AERA and members' home institutions, to hone investigative and reporting skills.

AERA members are responsible to actively educate one another and themselves concerning the diverse cultures represented in the society and associated issues so that the association may betterment the challenges facing education and educational research in the present and in the future.

AERA scholars are responsible to ensure that they have appropriate and sufficient familiarity and competence to work with populations studied or to team with colleagues who have that competence and familiarity. Similarly, in the review of this work for publication similar criteria should be met.

Underrepresented group members should confirm the accuracy of their perceptions of the association and its procedures, challenge those negative conditions that are confirmed, and be more assertive in the pursuit of opportunities that are sometimes mistakenly perceived to be unavailable.

These recommendations were revised and approved by task force members at the meeting of the task force on November 16, 1996.

The names of members of the task force and its staff are listed below: Beatriz Arias. David Berliner,* Edmund W. Gordon Chairperson, Grace Pung Guthrie, Vernon C Polite. Richard Ruiz, Christine Sleeter. Staff: William Russell. Carmen Arroyo, Charlotte Ramsey.*

---

*These persons were not present for the November 16, 1996 meeting of the task force.

PART TWO

SOCIAL ACTION

8
Diverse Human Populations and Problems in Educational Program Evaluation via Achievement Testing

Considerable static has been raised over the past several years around two related but distinct problems. I call it static because the disturbance signals have been fairly constant and loud, but not very clear. We know some things are not right but we are not quite sure what they are and are even less certain about what ought to be done. The two related problems have to do with:

1. the appropriateness of existing standardized tests of achievement for the assessment of academic function in minority and disadvantaged group member students; and
2. the appropriateness of such instruments to the assessment of the impact of large scale educational programs.

Let us turn our attention first to the problems posed for normative approaches to assessment when we try to apply these assessment strategies and instruments to the appraisal of educational achievement in disadvantaged and low status minority populations. Concern with this problem dates back at least to the work of Davis and Eells in the 1940s as they sought first to look for approaches to assessment which were free of cultural loadings. As they discovered the futility of their efforts at developing tests, which were culture free, they directed their search at the development of tests that were culture fair. These efforts, as you may recall, were more successful, but the instruments, which resulted from their work had low predictive value when subsequent achievement in academic settings was the referent.

As the civil and human rights movements of the fifties and sixties advanced, additional attention was focused on the inappropriateness of standardized tests for the assessment of minority group members. In this period, it was not unusual for psychometricians to add five to fifteen points to the scores of minority subjects to compensate for the assumed artificial depression in test scores resulting from the inappropriateness of the test. However, these added points were arrived at arbitrarily and reflected an assumed common and uniform depression in scores despite known differentials in the minority subjects' exposure to and involvement in the majority culture. The practice subsided as its illogic and patronizing character became better recognized.

Other efforts have been directed at insuring the inclusion of minority group members in the populations on which the instruments are normed. This procedure, however, only slightly reduces the impact of the majority group's dominance in the norming procedure. A more sensitive accommodation, of course, is the development of population-specific norms and the use of such norms in the interpretation of the data. However, this practice has been questioned since the reality standard is performance in competitive academic and work situations with majority group members. This is also the criticism, which has been raised against population-specific instrumentation. The speaker who follows me, Brother Bob Williams (1975), has done pioneering work in the development of a test of "Black intelligence," or rather an achievement test, with Black culture as the referent. I think Bob's data lead into the same problems we have with population-specific norms. Unless and until the curricula and their criteria for mastery are made more congruent with content, purposes and values of the target populations, these changed foci of assessment will continue to have low predictive value. Or, to be more accurate, these traditional curricula will continue to be inappropriate to the assessed behavior and potentials of the target groups. With all of these efforts proving to be somewhat unsuccessful, it is not surprising that by the early 1970s some of us are calling for a moratorium on the use of standardized tests with minority group members.

One could argue that these efforts directed at doing something about the use of standardized tests in the appraisal of minority group members is a political problem rather than a psychometric problem. This is especially likely to be the case so long as it appears that the objection to these tests is based on the fact that minority group members tend to score less well than do majority group members. It is not so much the differential in minority group-majority group scores that leads me to question the appropriateness of standardized achievement tests and the normative approach to their interpretation. Increasingly, I am persuaded that such instruments and procedures are not only inappropriate for the assessment of achievement in minority and disadvantaged populations, but that traditional standardized tests and normative approaches to assessment are dysfunctional and counterproductive to the purposes of pedagogy whenever we are confronted with the problem of educating populations with diverse characteristics.

When we first turned attention to the problems of educating educationally and socially disadvantaged children, a great deal of attention was given to the special characteristics of this population. The notions that dominated this new field were largely determined by conceptions of this population as homogeneous with respect to conditions of life and behavioral characteristics. We assumed a pervasive "culture of poverty." The population has largely identified by it deficits in comparison to characteristics assumed to be typical of the White middle class. Subsequent work and more careful study reveal that minority and disadvantaged children are not a homogeneous mass. In fact, there appears to be so much variation within populations to designate as there is between disadvantaged and more privileged groups. As our attention again turns to the problems posed by, and the ubiquitous prevalence of, individual differences, diversity and heterogeneity rather than deficiency and homogeneity present the challenge. And, it is not only challenge presented by children of low status peoples; diversity in human characteristics increasingly is recognized as the central problem in pedagogical design for all peoples.

Learners differ in interests, in cognitive style, in rate of learning, in patterns of developed abilities, in motivation, in work habits, and in tempera¬ment as well as in ethnicity, sex and social class. In fact, it may well be that our preoccupation with such status and indicator variables is SES, sex and ethnicity have retarded the scientific development of pedagogy. The differences that are associated with these status groups may have much less relevance for the design of educational treatments than do those differences in behavioral function. When we refer to SES, we are using an indicator variable to imply the presence or absence of certain functional characteristics or conditions of circumstance which are presumed to influence learning and development. But the exchange of socialization strategies across SES designations makes social class a much less reliable indicator than we used to think it to be. As sex roles change and are interchanged, and as ethnicity is confounded by social class, the specific characteristics of conditional and behavioral individuality provide better levers for, or guides to, educational planning. It is these characteristics of conditional and behavioral individuality that make for the pedagogically relevant dimensions of human diversity. It is these educationally relevant dimensions of diversity to which education must be responsive. Yet, it is the fact of conditional and behavioral individuality and diversity that normative and standardized approaches to assessment ignore and, in large measure, are designed to avoid. For example, test items are selected with a view toward their capacity to tap stable functions, and by stable we usually mean those functions less likely to be influenced by situational or personalistic variability. We demand that the items be presented in standardized and uniform conditions, which are insensitive to differential response tendencies. The data of these tests are analyzed to reflect one's position in relation to a group norm rather than to reflect one's mastery of the task or the process by which one engages the task. It almost looks as if our tests were designed to be of no use to teachers since it is these processes of engagement, these differential response tendencies, the situational and personalistic variables that are of crucial importance in the design and management of teaching and learning transactions. I, therefore, assert that normative and standardized approaches to assessment are not only inappropriate for the assessment of achievement in minority and disadvantaged populations, but they are also dysfunctional and counterproductive to pedagogy.

In a recent paper, Glaser (1976) has identified several reasons for the current dis-satisfaction with standardized testing. He refers more specifically to tests of intelligence, but his argument is relevant here particularly since I view intelligence tests as slightly more refined tests of achievement. Glaser writes:

1. The present operational definition of intelligence (achievement) measures seems to have reached a plateau or asymptote of efficiency with our present technology. The predictive validity of tests has not increased for some time.

2. Since tests essentially measure general scholastic aptitude, they have not adequately recognized the discontinuity between the backgrounds and cultures of certain groups in our society and the requirements for succeeding in the conventional educational system.

3. Tests reflect a restrictive over selective view of intelligence (achievement) that limits the educational system in adapting to students in order to maximize their achievement. In essence, the tests give go/no-go selective decisions but do not provide much deeper diagnosis for the conduct of education.

4. There is recognition that test theory and technique have not made contact with modern psychological theories of learning and cognition, and that test development should be influenced by new developments in these areas. Modern theory brings us close to understanding the components of cognitive functioning and can help us succeed in analyzing and understanding the detailed processes underlying intellectual abilities--the initial task that Binet set for himself, but had to abandon.

Why has this circumstance come about and why does it persist? Much of the impetus for the development of a technology of assessment related to intellective function and achievement resulted from, and has been maintained by, a supply and demand approach to access to education and the distribution of educational opportunities. Access to a limited supply of educational opportunities has been guarded by selection procedures, which, prior to the twentieth century, were based upon the prospective student's social status. In the pre-Reformation period, access to education was limited to the political and religious nobility and later to other privileged classes, while twentieth century selection procedures have come to be dominated by the student's demonstrated or predicted intellectual status. Where the supply of opportunities has been limited, great emphasis has been placed on the selection of students and the prediction of their performance when exposed to those opportunities (1916). Binet's work in intelligence test development was directed toward the creation of an instrument to which could be used to identify those pupils who were likely to benefit from schooling. His admonition that we also turn to treatment of those expected not to succeed were generally ignored. In a period of scarce educational opportunities, Binet's concern for the educability of intelligence did not gain favor. Society found greater utility in the promise of the predictive and selective validity of his new test.

This emphasis on selection and prediction has continued even though the social conditions, which gave rise to it, have changed. In recent years, we have seen in the United States a growing concern with universal access to education. The educational product requirements of the nation are more frequently coming to be defined in terms of our capability to provide post-secondary educational opportunities for the majority of our youth and a continued program of learning for most of our citizens. If this trend continues, selection and prediction can no longer be allowed to dominate in the technology of psycho educational appraisal; rather, the stage must be shared with an emphasis on *description* and *prescription* (i.e., the qualitative description of intellective function leading, not to the selection of those most likely to succeed, but to the prescription of the learning experiences required to more adequately insure that academic success is possible).

The position being advanced here is that psychological testing obviously can be used to measure achieved development. From those achievements patterns we can predict, with reasonable validity, subsequent achievement in the same dimensions of behavior under similar learning experience conditions. Thus, persons who have learned an average amount during one learning period (high school) may be expected to learn an average amount in the next learning period (college). However, we have not given adequate attention to the facts that psychological testing can be used to describe and qualitatively analyze behavior function to better understand the processes by which achievement is developed, to describe non-standard achievements which may be equally as functional in subsequent situations requiring adaptation, or to specify those conditions in the interaction between learner and learning experience which may be necessary to change the quality of future achievements.

If we are to approach such goals in achievement testing, we will need to redress the imbalance made more obvious by the growing recognition of individual and group differences in function, on the one hand, contrasted with a fairly undifferentiated measurement technology on the other. Until such time as such progress is made, the logic of my position force me to endorse the call for a moratorium on the traditional usages of standardized achievement has ting and its normative interpretation as not in the best educational interests of minorityand disadvantaged populations.

Let me turn quickly to the second issue, that is, the appropriateness of the use of standardized and normative approaches to testing in the assessment of the impact of large-scale educational programs. There are several interrelated problems here. Before discussing them, I need to make certain that the record shows that I am consistent. Since I have argued that these tests should not be used in traditional ways with minority and disadvantaged populations, I must also argue that they not be used to assess large scale educational programs directed at these populations. In his academic lecture at the 1973 American Psychological Association annual meeting, Donald Hebb quoted one of his favorite admonitions. "If something is not worth doing, it is also not worth doing well!" To paraphrase, if these tests are not worth using, they are also not worth using on a large scale to make decisions about children's lives and to inform public policy. But the problems of the evaluation of these programs are much bigger than the question of whether to test or not to test, or as to what tests to use.

I estimate that we have invested since 1965 between one-half and three-fourths of a billion dollars in evaluations of educational programs for the disadvantaged. There are currently two major studies underway–a five million dollar National Institute of Education (NIE) study and an Office of Education study that I once heard estimated as possibly costing twenty-one million dollars over a seven-year period. Those are big sums of money even in periods of inflation. Yet, having examined the RFP for the OE study and having been rather close to the NIE study, I am not at all confident that either will provide the kind of guidance to the relevant policy decisions that is needed or expected. Like, their predecessor studies, they, are likely to produce equivocal findings. It is not because we do not have good and intelligent people designing and conducting these studies. When I came to Washington in 1965 to provide leadership in the development of the research and evaluation program for Project Head Start, a friend and one of our most distinguished authorities in educational measurement and research declined to assist me. He indicated that he would not touch such an evaluation as Head Start or Title I with a fifty-foot pole because it has an impossible task in the absence of better agreement on what the treatment is, the conditions under which it is delivered, and in the absence of assessment instruments appropriate to those treatments, those conditions and the populations served. Nonetheless, I went ahead and I found good people to advise and to help, but no single one of us was, nor together were, good enough to overcome the constraining problems to which my friend called my attention as he sympathetically refused to join me in my folly. You know, it is my belief that if I was to ask him again today, he would still refuse because we have not adequately addressed the problems he raised. Yet, we continue large scale evaluations and continue to make the same errors and continue to produce negative or confusing results. One wonders if there is a conspiracy to prove that such programs cannot succeed, that minority and disadvantaged people cannot be educated, that it is poor policy to continue to heavily invest public funds in efforts at the equalization of educational opportunity. When one puts these evaluations together with the race and genetics debate and with the "schooling doesn't make a difference" pronouncements, it is exceedingly difficult to keep the faith.

I know that this meeting was not called to discuss the problems of large scale evaluation, but it is important that we understand that the problem is larger than one of what kind of achievement tests we use. It may be that we could endure the problems related to the tests if we were better able to deal with such problems as:

1. the nebulousness and variability of treatments
2. the complex economic, political and social context in which the treatment are set
3. the diversity of populations served and goals sought
4. the reconciliation of necessary and sufficient conditions for change and growth
5. such limitations of evaluative research technology as:
   • program and population specification
   • program and population sampling
   • interchangeable and dialectical nature of the dependent and independent variables
   • inappropriateness of extant statistical analyses to the study of the dynamic blending of variables by which effects may be explained
   • the policy of the best generic treatment
   • normative approaches to aggregate data in search of relation-ships which may be idiosyncratically expressed

It may be that some of these problems will be the focus of our next conference. For the present, let us return to achievement testing. What are the limitations of these tests for educational program evaluation? Suchman (1969) has described five levels of evaluation research:

• Evaluation should answer questions as to quantity and quality of treatment. Was treatment delivered, how much and how good?
• Evaluation should answer questions relative to performance or

impact. Did any change occur that can be inferred to have resulted from the treatment? What are the intended as well as unintended consequences?

- Evaluation should address the question of adequacy. To what degree are the results adequate to relieve the problem to which the treatment was applied?
- Evaluation should address questions of efficiency. Is there a better way to achieve equivalent results?
- Evaluation should address questions of process and explanation. How and why did the treatment work or fail?

Obviously, questions as to the nature and quantity of treatment or its efficiency cannot be directly addressed by achievement test data. However, questions of performance/impact, of adequacy and of process/explanation could and should be addressed by achievement data. The problem is that standardized norm-based testing contributes very little to these questions. In their present state, these tests tell us something about performance in relation to some reference group. The data from these tests enable us to make crude go/no-go decisions. They provide data, which in the aggregate inform us with respect to positive, zero or negative impact. We may infer adequacy of treatment from the relative position of the respondents, but since the tests tend not to be specifically related to the criteria of competence, they tell us little about the adequacy of the performance or treatment in relation to need. Similarly, these tests are not directed at illuminating aspects of process. Although underlying processes can be inferred from the analysis of some of the items, assessment of the process variables by which performance treatment interactions can be judged is not the current purpose or capability of these tests. In fact, the very processes by which we develop these tests are counterproductive of data, which speak to questions of adequacy, process, and explanation. As we strive to achieve reliability and validity, these processes force us to eliminate those items which are sensitive to situational and personalistic variance or which are otherwise unstable. What we look for are items that are least influenced by variations in instruction or in pupils. In sum, I am asserting that if good evaluation data are needed to inform policy decision-making, then good evaluation procedure; and instrumentation must be applied. Since the achievement tests which are available to us fail to address crucial evaluation questions, they are inadequate to the task at hand. In commenting on a related point, Calfee (1976) has written: "If a principal, superintendent or program director (or legislator) is to make informed, rational decisions about the strengths and weaknesses of the teaching and learning that take place under his supervision, something more than a gross characterization of success or failure is necessary." I think I cannot be accused of overstating the case when I claim that traditional approaches to norm-based standardized testing fail to provide more than gross characterizations of success and failure. This is true of their use with all children. When they are used then to assess achievement and programs in and for the poor, the disadvantaged and the discriminated against, the problem is simply compounded.

Given this low estimate of the utility of normative and standardized approaches to achievement testing and the equally low likelihood that the call for a moratorium will he heeded, what can be done to improve upon the current state of the art?

Despite my criticisms of the extant standardized instruments they need not be immediately discarded. A great deal of work has gone into the development of item pools, which tap a variety of intellective functions. The problem is that these items have been grouped, presented, scored and analyzed with a view toward gross classification, with respect to success or failure, with a view toward distributing the examinee population over the bell shaped curve, and with a view toward predicting who will succeed. These same instruments can be analyzed:

1. To identify, through logical analysis, the dimensional or categorical functional demands of selected standardized tests. What dimensions of function appear to be tapped by the instrument as these can be conceptualized from a surface examination of item content?

2. To determine the rationale utilized in the development of each of several tests in order to identify the conceptual categories for which items were, written and into which item response consistencies might cluster empirically.

3. To determine the learning task demands represented by the items of selected tests and the classification of those demands into functional categories. The extent to which selected tests provide adequate coverage of the typical learning task demands found in educational settings might also be appraised. Are the tests

measuring the processes required by important, learning tasks? What types of learning task demands correspond to the processes ostensibly measured by the test? and,

4. To utilize the categories produced by any or all of the above strategies in the metric and non-metric factorial analysis of test data in order to uncover empirical dimensions of test responses. These dimensions could be interpreted in the context of item clusters derived from the conceptual and task analytic strategies described above to ascertain the context to which they provide an empirical foundation for those clusters or require a re-conceptualization of response processes. The empirical dimensions could then be used to produce individual and group profiles reflecting across the several categories or factors.

Task 1, 2, and 3 are intended to unbundle existing standardized tests and to reveal their factorial demand structure. These steps are utilitarian to task it which involves the analysis of performance data to reveal diagnostic patterns which become the basis for the profiles to which I have referred.

In addition, to with these same instruments we could:

1. Explore possibilities for adding to their quantitative reports on the performance of students, reports descriptive of the patterns of achievement and function derived from the qualitative analysis of existing tests. Existing instruments should be examined with a view to categorization, factorial analysis, and interpretation to determine whether or not the data of these instruments can be reported in descriptive and qualitative ways in addition to the traditional quantitative report. For example, response patterns might be prepared differentially for:

A. Information recall
   1) Rote call
   2) Associative recall
   3) Derivative recall

B. Vocabulary
  1) Absolute
  2) Contextual

2. Moving away from existing instruments, we can explore the development of test items and procedures that lend themselves to descriptive and qualitative analyses of cognitive and affective adaptive functions, in addition to wider specific achievements.
  A. In the development of new tests, attention should be given to the, appraisal of
    1) Adaptation in new learning situations
    2) Problem solving in situations that require varied cognitive, skills and styles
    3) Analysis, search, and synthesis behaviors,
    4) Information management, processing, and utilization skills
    5) Nonstandard information pools

  B. In the development of new procedures, attention should be given to the appraisal of
    1) Comprehension through experiences, listening, and looking, as well as reading
    2) Expression through artistic, oral, nonverbal, and graphic, as well as written symbolization
    3) Sources and status of motivation
    4) Characteristics of temperament
    5) Habits of work and task involvement under varying conditions of demand

  C. In the development of tests and procedures designed to get at specific achievements, attention should be given to
    1) Broadening the varieties of subject matter, competencies, and the skills assessed
    2) Examining these achievements in a variety of contexts
    3) Open-ended and unstructured probes of achievement to allow for atypical patterns and varieties of achievement

4) Assessing nonacademic achievements such as social competence, coping skills, avocational skills, and artistic, athletic, political, or mechanical skills

Calfee (1976) and others have been experimenting with some alternative approaches to prediction based on "all-or-none tests." They assert that there are some indicator skills, the mastery of which are essential to next steps in learning. Knowledge of the alphabet is an example of such a skill. It is known to be predictive of subsequent performance on reading achievement tests. Calfee asserts, "alphabet knowledge is an indicator, not a cause, of reading success and failure." On the basis of empirical data, one can determine "cut off points" by which we can predict success or failure in reading mastery. It is basically a criterion-referenced test procedure in which the criterion is based upon specific skills or competencies known to be indicative of readiness for the next level of work. It can be used as a diagnostic screening device, as a tool of pupil evaluation, as an instrument of program evaluation, or in needs assessment. The procedure does not identify process, but is an indicator of success or failure in a crucial element in process.

Another alternative is represented by Project TORQUE (Hayden, 1976), which claims to develop tests that help teachers help students. TORQUE can also be used to evaluate large groups of students or to assess the impact of particular curriculum materials. The developers of the test claim that their instrument is diagnostic, that they identify what children know and do well, as well as pinpoint children's problems closely enough to help guide further instruction. They claim sensitivity to children's varied characteristics: All of this is made available through a criterion-referenced model, which is easily administered by teachers.

Obviously, criterion-referenced testing is one of the alternatives available to us. Since there is a session scheduled on this subject, I will not discuss the approach further except for a cautionary note.

Tradition weighs heavily on all of us. We tend to try to legitimatize the new by reference to the old. In a number of instances, we try to demonstrate the goodness or, validity of a criterion-referenced test by showing that it correlates well with an achievement or intelligence test. That may be necessary to gain respectability or acceptance, but it can be defeating of the purpose behind our movement away from norm-based standardized testing. For example, when we were selecting instruments with when to assess the impact of the early Head Start

175

efforts, we asked Bettye Caldwell to develop an idea she had for a criterion-referenced test of mastery of those developmental and pre-literacy skills judged to be associated with successful school entry– the Caldwell Preschool Inventory was the result. However, in an effort to gain credibility for the Inventory and later for the impact data generated there from, we added standardized tests of intelligence and achievement to the battery. As the pressure to demonstrate Head Start's effectiveness mounted, the criterion-referenced test was dropped and the standardized tests remained, even though it was the Caldwell Inventory which best addressed the growth in skills which was the goal of the special program. Else Haeussermann (1958) went into retirement regretting that her excellent procedures for assessing learning processes in children with cerebral damage had not been standardized and age group norms established. So heavily did tradition weigh on her conception of what she was doing that she never was convinced that her criterion-referenced techniques derived a great part of their value from the fact that they were not constrained by standardization, nor was the interpretation of the data limited by norm-based scoring.

One final example. In a highly diagnostic mode, Glaser (1976) has described a performance analytic approach to the assessment of memory function. Drawing upon a conceptualization of the processes involved in short term memory for sequences of items, he suggests that analyses of performance based upon such conceptualizations may have implications for assessing individual differences as well as for improving performance. Glaser writes:

A young or mentally retarded child might fail the test because of insufficient familiarity with the sequence of ordinal numbers, or because of inexperience in using the number sequence to order other materials. An individual may, not perform well because he has not developed the grouping and chunking strategy characteristic of his age level, although he might utilize grouping when prompted by the examiner. Another individual may not be able to accomplish the coding process necessary to take advantage of chunking. Others might lack the capacity for holding back their working memory storage long enough to order their output properly. With the advantage of this kind of added theoretical insight to augment the con¬ventional intelligence test digit span sub-test, it might be possible to localize the source of difficulty for an individual who fails under the standard procedure. This could be of considerable help in indicating how deficient performance in this and related tasks night be remedied.

Studies like those just described raise the possibility that measures of intelligence and aptitude, analyzed in terms of cognitive processes, (will move intelligence and aptitude test predictions from static statements about the probability of success to dynamic statements about what can be done to increase the likelihood of school success. Hopefully, this viewpoint will lead to measuring instruments which are diagnostic, in the sense that they tell us how educational institutions should adjust to the person, instead of simply telling us, as most intelligence tests do, which people already are adjusted to the institution

Educational assessment of individuals and programs greatly influences what happens in the delivery of educational services. Whether we like it or not, whether we intend it or not what teachers teach and the way they teach are in large measure determined by the characteristics of the assessment instruments and programs. In addition, the results of what we do in evaluation no longer remain hidden away in dusty files. Our findings are more frequently used to support the biases and purposes of public policy makers. Thus, what we measure and the way He measure it impinge heavily on the lives of individuals and on the society in general. These observations seem to suggest that the problems we face are not only technical, but involve philosophical and moral issues:

- What is it that we want education to be?
- What are the behaviors and goals of educators and learners that we are willing to encourage?
- What priorities in public policy are we willing to support?
- What is the contribution of our work to the achievement of social justice?

9
Education of the Disadvantaged: A Problem of Human Diversity

Once again, we find ourselves considering problems of educating low-income and low-status persons, with a sense of *deja vu* and an even greater sense of embarrassment, which borders on shame. I feel *deja vu* because I know that we have done this before. I sense embarrassment in part because of the contrast between the affluence of this resort area and the conditions of life in which the people we have come to talk about struggle hour after hour, day after day. That embarrassment changes to shame as I recall that it was fifteen years ago when I first started attending meetings like this and more than twenty years ago that I began professionally to try to do something about changing the life chances of the children of the poor. In those fifteen, twenty, twenty-five years my life circumstances have greatly improved—as have yours, largely as a result of the fact that helping the poor has become a respectable professional and research pursuit. Yet, the life chances of the people we are supposed to be helping have changed very little. In the early 1960s we did not know what needed to be done to make school achievement independent of social class and social caste. Most of us thought that more money, extra effort, improved technology would solve the problems of educating the minority poor. Here in the mid-seventies most of us agree that to the extent that these things have been tried, they have not solved the problems. Despite cumulative appropriations of what must be nearly $30 billion dollars and an enormous amount of sometimes misdirected effort and equivocal research we still do not know how to make school achievement and developmental opportunity independent of social position. Our best general predictor of success in school is successful birth into a middle- or upper-class Caucasian family.

I am ashamed that our efforts have been so futile. I am not so much ashamed that we have not succeeded but that we have not sufficiently tried. Ten years ago, I predicted that we might not succeed, that we might not try hard enough and that some of us would try to blame the victims for our lack of success. Permit me to be so immodest as to quote from my own writing (see Gordon, 1965), published in the *American Journal of Orthopsychiatry,* vol. 35, no. 3, April 1965.

It is tempting to anticipate that the current outbreak of enthusiasm will produce results consistent with the quality of time, energy, money and concern being expended. However, in dealing with problems for which solutions are based upon significant social and scientific advances, popularity and productivity do not necessarily go hand in hand. In the present situation there is grave danger that work with the unfortunate may, unfortunately, become a fad. So great is the danger that it may not be out of place to suggest that the appropriate attitude at this time for those truly concerned with the long-range goal of significantly improving the life chances of disadvantaged populations, is one of restraint and considered action. It is obviously not the quantity of effort that will solve the problems here involved. Work of high quality, which more correctly reflects scientific and social reality finally, will give this result.

Having recently reviewed much of the research and most of the current programs concerned with the disadvantaged, I am impressed by the pitifully small though growing body of knowledge available as a guide to work in this area. The paucity of serious research attention to these problems has left us with little hard data, many impressions, and a few firm leads. What is distressing, however, is the slight representation of even this research in the rapidly proliferating programs. Much of what is being done for and to the disadvantaged seems to be guided by the conviction that what is needed is more of those things we feel we know how to do. Despite the fact that much of our knowledge and techniques of behavioral change have proved to be of dubious value in our work with more disadvantaged populations, these same procedures and services now are being poured into the new programs. Although service to the disadvantaged has become popular, there remains a serious lack of basic research on the developmental needs of such children as well as on the applicability of specific techniques of behavioral change to their directed development.

It is not intended to suggest that the extension of known techniques to these previously neglected populations is entirely negative. Humanitarian concern calls for the use of all possible resources to relieve human suffering. What is suggested is that there may be vast differences between what we feel we know how to do and that which must be done. To settle for what we "know" while we ignore new concepts and the exploration of new leads renders us less humanitarian, less scientific, and less professional. Unfortunately, our society has permitted us to place the-burden of proof of the worth of our services on the beneficiaries of these services rather than on the professional worker or the system in which he functions. This has permitted us to ignore or rationalize our failures. If real progress is to be made, we as professionals must assume greater responsibility for the success of our work, recognizing that it is our role to better understand these problems and to design techniques and measures more appropriate to their solution. It must be clear to all of us that more counseling is not going to solve the problems of a population we have defined as nonverbal. Reading texts in Technicolor are not going to solve the reading problems of youngsters who we claim are deficient in symbolic representational skills. Reduced demand curricula and work study programs are not going to advance the conceptual development of youth whose conditions of life may have produced differential patterns of intellectual function which are so frequently interpreted as evidence of mental retardation rather than as challenges to improved teaching. Occupational information and inspirational exhortation are not going to provide motivation for youth who have yet to see employment opportunities, employed models with whom they can identify and accessible routes to achievement. Intensive psychotherapy is going to have little impact on the neurotic mother whose energies are consumed by the struggle to meet the minimum physical needs of herself and her children. Similarly, preschool programs which capture the form but not the content of some of the more advanced models are doomed to failure. Nor will good programs which are not followed by greatly strengthened primary, elementary and secondary school programs make a major difference in the lives of these children. Improved and expanded mental health services will mean little unless our nation comes to grips with the problems of economic, political and social opportunities for masses of disfranchised and alienated persons.

To honor our traditional concern and for the sake of the disadvantaged, it is essential to recognize the limitations of the current effort. If the products of serious research were as well represented in this effort as the good intentions, the enthusiasm, the "band-wagon hopping" and the grant hunting, we could be more hopeful that meaningful solutions would be found to the problems of the disadvantaged. Unfortunately, some of us viewing the current efforts are left with a nagging suspicion that the net result of many of these programs will be to provide (for those who choose to interpret it so) empirical evidence of fundamental inferiority in these populations we are trying so hard to help. When five or ten years from now the populations we now call disadvantaged are still at the bottom of the heap, those who only reluctantly acceded to the current attempts to help may revive their now dormant notions of inherent inferiority to explain why all the money and all the effort have failed to produce results. The more likely fact will be that we shall have failed to produce the desired results simply because we shall have failed to develop and apply the knowledge and the skill necessary to the task. Unless the issues are more sharply drawn we may not even then recognize the nature of our incompetencies. We see in retrospect that bleeding was an ineffective cure for the plague, not because the barber-surgeons did not know how to draw blood, but because they did not sufficiently understand the nature of the disease with which they were dealing.

To honor our commitments to science and professional service, we must understand the limitations of our knowledge and our practice. Much of what we do is based on the hopeful assumption that all human beings with normal neurological endowment can be developed for participation in the mainstream of our society. We believe this because we have seen many people from a great variety of backgrounds participate and because we want to believe it. But we do not yet have definite evidence to support our belief. We operate out of an egalitarian faith without knowing whether our goals are really achievable. Yet it must be our aim, not only as scientists and professional workers, but also as humanitarians as well to determine the potential of human beings for equality of achievement. If in the light of our most sophisticated and subtle evaluations, we conclude that such equality is not generally achievable, if in spite of the best we can do it seems likely that some of our citizens will remain differentiated by their own biology, then we shall merely have answered a persistent question. We will still have no evidence that group differences, per se, imply any inability on the part of particular individuals to meet the demands of society. We will then be able to turn our energies to helping individuals meet those demands. And if, on the other hand, as we believe, true equality of opportunity and appropriate learning experiences will result in equality of achievement, then we must so organize our professional services and our society that no person is kept from achieving that potential by our indifference to his condition, by the inadequacy or inappropriateness of our service, or by the impediments of our society deliberately or accidentally placed in his path. It is not an unhopeful paradox that the only way we shall ever know whether equality of human achievement is possible is through providing for all our citizens, privileged and underprivileged, the kind of service and society that assumes it is possible and makes adequate provision for the same. As we pursue the "Great Society" let us not be misled by the plethora of activity or companions in the cause.[1]

A great deal has happened in the United States since 1965. Even though we do not have final answers, we know somewhat more in 1975 than we knew in 1965.

---

1. Reprinted with permission of the American Journal of Orthopsychiatry. New York: Orthopsychiatric Association, Inc.

Now as then, it may be beneficial to think more about what we know and to try to generate better conceptions of what needs to be done.

Research related to the education of the disadvantaged has covered a wide variety of approaches and issues. However, most of the work can be classified under two broad categories: (1) the study of population characteristics, and (2) the description and evaluation of programs and practices. In the first category, investigators have focused on eliciting deficits in the conditions or behaviors of the target population— the ways the groups studied differ from alleged "normal" populations. In the second category, which is only now beginning to build a body of theoretical and descriptive material, investigators have attempted to describe what goes on in the schools and to relate such variables as school structure, teaching methods, or a myriad of special services, to student achievement. While the first type of study has been conducted largely by educational psychologists, specialists in testing and measurement, and developmental psychologists, the second has been the product of anthropologists, sociologists, social psychologists and, on a more informal level, of teachers who have worked in the school system. Studies in the former group precede those in the latter and have tended to place responsibility for failure on the children and their background. Although studies in the latter group grew out of the same philosophy and were developed with the goal of designing compensatory experiences for identified deficiencies, newer research in this group has begun to emphasize the role of the educational experience in producing the observed dysfunctions in performance.

POPULATION CHARACTERISTICS

Studies within this category can be further divided between investigations of performance and life conditions. The largest body of research concerns what is called "intellectual performance." Most studies in this area have concentrated on IQ test results and consistently support the hypothesis that high economic, ethnic or social status is associated with average or high IQ scores, while the reverse–low economic, ethnic or social status–is associated with low IQ scores relative to the other group (Kennedy, Van De Riet, & White, 1963).

A by-product of descriptions of the relationship between SES and/or ethnic groups and intellectual performance has been the attempt to interpret results with speculations as to causes. On the other extreme, investigators have seen their work as supporting genetic determinants of intelligence (Jensen, 1968; Jensen, 1969; Shuey, 1966); at the other end of the spectrum, researchers have viewed their findings as support for environmental determinants of intelligence (Hunt, 1961; Hunt, 1969).

However, the majority of investigators now interpret the data as reflecting a complex and continuous interaction between heredity and environmental forces (Hirsch, 1969)

In contrast to the huge body of statistics and analyses concerning intellectual status as judged by standardized tests, only limited effort has been directed at differences in cognitive style. There has been some attempt to factor-analyze standardized tests (Cleary & Thomas, 1966) and one substantial investigation deals with differential strengths and deficits in the intellectual functioning of different ethnic groups (Stodolsky & Lesser, 1967).

Another area of research is that of the plasticity of intellectual development. The work has been conducted by both investigators that would support the dominance of genetic determinants of intelligence and those who adhere to the importance of environmental factors in determining the quality of intellectual functioning (Bloom, 1965). Building on Binet's (1916) early concern with trainability of intellectual functioning and Montessori's effort to modify intellectual performance in children with subnormal performance levels, investigators have worked with all but the most gifted children (e.g., Bereiter & Englemann, 1966; Hurley, 1969; Schwebel, 1968). There is only one longitudinal study that attempts to relate intellectual development to differences in environmental conditions: this investigation traces the development of a sample of twins reared in dramatically different environments over a period of 25 years, and shows significant variations in their level of intellectual functioning (Skodak & Skeels, 1945).

Short-term studies dealing with the plasticity of intellectual development have led to mixed findings. Some reports show intervention to be associated with no significant change in intellect as measured by intelligence test scores (Westinghouse Learning Corporation & Ohio University, 1969). Others have shown only modest change, and many of these results have been interpreted as reflecting a normal fluctuation in intellectual function from one test period to another (Thorndike, 1967). On the other hand, some studies have demonstrated significant increases when pre and post treatment scores are compared (Smilansky, 1965). Unfortunately, these improvements have not yet been tested in large populations, and no follow-up studies have been made after a long enough period to justify the conclusion of permanent change.

However uncertain these data may be, there remains among many researchers the conviction that intelligence is largely a trainable function. A number of studies have attempted to relate trainability to age (Thorndike, 1927). On of the more pessimistic positions is that, due to the lack of powerful and positive environments, the processes underlying intellectual functioning rapidly lose their plasticity after three years of age (Bloom, 1965). More optimistic reports slow typical I.Q. gains of 10 points with adolescents; however, such gains are still only half as much as can be generated with younger subjects (Smilansky, 1966). Studies of such programs as Harlem Prep and Upward Bound support the hypothesis that big changes in achievement, if not in intellectual functioning, can be affected in adolescence (Guerriero, 1968; Hawkridge et al., 1968).

In general, the data leads one to conclude that, as measured by standardized tests, significant changes in the quality of intellectual function are more likely to occur to the extent that there are powerful positive changes in environmental interactions, and that the changes occur early in the life of the individual. The fact that malleability may decrease with age, however, may not reflect a recalcitrant character of intellectual functioning. Rather, what may be operating is the tendency to rely on earlier patterns of stimulus processing in the absence of exposure to powerful and different environmental input. It has been suggested, for example, that the decrease malleability of intellectual functioning among the urban disadvantaged may be the result of prevailing school practices, which do not provide new positive inputs and which may even reinforce previous maladaptive patterns of functioning (Leacock, 1969).

As measured by grades, standardized tests, and high school attrition, there is an abundance of data showing that disadvantaged populations do not do as well academically as do more advantaged populations. Their lower achievement and higher dropout rates have been related to such environmental factors as low income (resulting from limited education and occupational level of parents) (e.g., Goldstein, 1967); health and nutritional deficits (Birch, 1967; Birch & Gussow, 1970); childrearing patterns that do not prepare the children for school (Goldstein, 1967); cultural differences between disadvantaged children and their teachers (as discussed by James Guthrie, Stephen Michelson, Eric Hanushek, Henry Levin, George Mayeske, & Alexander Mood in a recent U.S. Office of Education Conference); and racial isolation and discrimination as well as other school-related variables (US Commission on Civil Rights, 1967).

Demographic studies have fallen into several categories. The more traditional type has concentrated on simply on economic, employment and educational levels of the family as they relate to the children's school performance (Goldstein, 1967). A new type attempts to go beyond a strictly economic kind of data, and centering its interest in what has become known as the "culture of poverty," examines various aspects of family disorganization such as consensual marriage, out-of- wedlock children, divorce rates, broken homes and matriarchal or female-dominated households (e.g., Lewis, 1966; Moynihan & Barton, 1965; Valentine, 1968). One or more of these configurations are then related to children's performance in school. However, the concept of the "culture of poverty" has recently been highly criticized, and a few investigators have begun to focus on those patterns, which may be adaptive within the school environment.

The relationship between specific childrearing practices and academic achievement has been copiously studied. Concentrating particularly on mother-child interaction, investigators have identified maternal influences, which may create such characteristics as language behavior, task orientation and value commitment in the disadvantaged child. Implicit in these studies is the assumption of a middle-class norm, as most studies compare interactions in disadvantaged families with those in more privileged households (e.g., Hess, 1966). So far, there has been little attempt to describe the variations in childrearing practices among lower-class or minority group families, and there has been scant research on those elements in these families which lead to academic success (Davidson, 1967 is an exception).

A neglected area in educational research has been the investigation of the relationship between health status and school performance. Data on the effects of poverty on health and nutrition are substantial, all showing that disadvantaged populations suffer from poorer health care, a greater proportion of premature deliveries, higher mortality rates, poor nutrition, etc (e.g., Scrimpshaw, Nevin, & Gordon, 1967). There is also some research indicating the possible effects of the health of the pregnant mother on the intellectual functioning of the developing child (e.g., Lilienfeld, Pasamanick, & Rogers, 1955; Pasamanick & Lilienfeld, 1955). However, there is little data on the relationship between the individual's own health and nutritional condition and his/her cognitive development or academic performance in school. There is also little research showing the mechanism by which poor health affects performance. Most investigators assume this to be the case, however, and conclude that poor health may result in lowered performance through impaired efficiency or reduced energy levels, or, in more serious conditions, through impairment of the nervous system (Birch & Gussow, 1970).

With the concentration still on demographic characteristics, racial and economic segregation of a disadvantaged population as it relates to school performance is one of the most heavily researched areas (e.g., St. John, 1968). Investigations have consistently led to the conclusion that slow school achievement is associated with the concentration of low-income and minority group students in separate school situations (the one possible exception being Oriental students in segregated situations) (Coleman, Campbell, Hobson, McPartland, Mood, Weinfeld, et al., 1966). A small group of studies have focused on separating out the effects of economic from racial or ethnic isolation and the predominating view has been that economic segregation is even more deleterious to school performance than is racial segregation. However, the point has often been made that it is impossible to draw strictly comparable socio-economic groups across racial or ethnic lines (St. John, 1968).

Related to this research on economic and racial isolation have been those investigations, which focus on the effects of desegregation on school achievement. Studies in this area take two forms: those that measure achievement before and after desegregation, and those that examine the relationship between the degree of ethnic or economic mix and the level of achievement. Research in the former group has arrived at the conclusion that differential responsibility to desegregation is based on such factors as the reasons for desegregation, students' expectations on how they are going to be evaluated in the integrated setting, and the degree of organization or disorganization in the integrated as compared to the segregated setting (e.g., Katz, 1967; McPartland, 1968; St. John, 1968). Studies in the latter group, which are usually based on larger populations than the former, show that desegregation is more likely to be associated with heightened achievement for the minority-group child when the receiving school population is predominantly White and middle-class (Coleman et al., 1966). However, caution, is often expressed about applying these findings to smaller populations and individual cases because of the intervening variables, such as student expectations or school disorganization (St. John, 1968; Weinberg, 1968).

An area of research which is crucial to the interpretation of any results on population characteristics is that of testing and measurement. Most of the effort in this area has been directed toward validation of the content and construction of existing standardized tests and the predictive value of test scores (see the 1966 Testimony of Dr. Roger T. Lennon as Expert Witness on Psychological Testing in the Case of Hobson, et al., vs. Hansen, et al. in Washington, D.C. published in by New York by Harcourt, Brace, and World). Research on testing and measurement of disadvantaged populations has been largely concerned with the relative predictability of specific tests for minority group versus White students, the efficiency of traditional as opposed to culture-fair and other innovative tests, and the problems inherent in testing minority-group populations (Campbell, 1964). More recently, there has been interest in factorial analyses of test data; the aim of this research is to identify patterns of functioning in different populations in order to understand variations in skills as well as deficits

(Stodolsky & Lesser, 1967). A small group of investigators has also begun to research the effects of intelligence and achievement tests on such variables as teacher attitudes, student expectations, and school administrative policy (Rosenthal & Jacobson, 1968).

PROGRAMS AND PRACTICES

In contrast to the rather well-designed and detailed research into the characteristics of disadvantaged groups, the description and evaluation of educational programs and practices for these children have generally been superficial. There has been little effort at matching treatment efforts with the nature and needs of the subject population. Programs are often designed on the basis of long-standing theoretical models or the special biases of researchers. Program evaluations stress little more than the fact or the magnitude of the intervention and a general assessment of the impact. What is lacking are detailed descriptions of the nature of the intervention, the interaction between the intervention and the learner, and the outcome of a particular treatment or intervention program when used with specific kinds of learners. Research on programs and practices can be grouped into four types on the basis of the scope of the subject treated. Most prominent are studies, which report on large-scale projects such as Head Start, Title I, More Effective Schools, Project Talent and Upward Bound. A second group of studies reports on specific programs and services in the schools. A third attempts to relate administrative and organizational change to student progress. Changes in attitudes and orientations of school personnel are the subject of the fourth type. Large-scale projects run the gamut from preschool to college. The aim of these programs has been to provide intensive compensatory education–school readiness, remediation of lagging achievement levels, or supply of the necessary skills for success in higher education–to disadvantaged students. With the exception of preschool projects, where centers have developed experimental programs, most of the large-scale programs have been more intensive versions of standard curriculum and teaching methods (the work of Gray & Klaus, 1965 at George Peabody College and the American Institutes for Research for the Behavioral Sciences' (1969b) work at the Perry Preschool Project in Ypsilanti, Michigan are notable exceptions). The projects have been evaluated by pre-and post-treatment test scores and subjective evaluations of student progress; little research has focused on describing the exact nature of program input or on following the subjects' longitudinal development once the treatment is completed (Klaus, Gray, 1968; Wolf & Stein, 1966a; Wolf

& Stein, 1966b are exceptions to this generalization).

Project evaluations, in general, indicate that compensatory education has failed. In those cases where positive findings are reported, it has been difficult to identify or separate treatment effects responsible for the result from Hawthorne effects (the impact of a changed situation itself) or from Rosenthal effects (the result of changed expectations). However, recent reviews of the research criticize evaluation methods and indicate that the tests used may be insensitive instruments for tapping whatever progress might be made (Scrimpshaw & Gordon, 1967).

Evaluations of specific programs and services in the schools include studies of such elements as counseling programs, tutoring projects, special service personnel (bilingual teachers, reading specialists, paraprofessionals, etc.), curricular innovations, such as bilingual or ethnically-oriented studies and teacher-student developed materials, and changes in teaching techniques (individualized instruction, teaching machines, team teaching, etc.) (American Institutes for Research in the Behavioral Sciences, 1969a; Channon, 1967; Jablonsky, 1969; Khanna, 1969; Rigrodsky, 1967; Shaw& Rector, 1968). Here too, much of the intervention has been a continuation of traditional programs and services, and little effort has been given to matching the specific needs of the population with the intervention instituted. Only projects focusing on curriculum relevance and individualized instruction have been directed toward matching learner and the learning experience (Glasser, 1966; Glasser, 1967). Adequate evaluations of these programs have also been scarce. Programs tend to introduce a number of services simultaneously, and it has been difficult to identify, even in successful programs, the element or elements, which are most instrumental in causing change. For example, in the Title I, ESEA project in Camden in 1966-67, a number of global variables including class size, teaching conditions, corrective reading, medical services, audio-visual programs, and teachers aides were introduced simultaneously, preventing isolation and evaluation of those specific variables which actually had impact (see Board of Education, 1967).

Until recently, studies of administrative and organizational change in the schools have been directed primarily at desegregation. Research on desegregation in Southern school districts describes the politics and process of desegregation, including the implementation of federal guidelines and community resistance to change (Orfield, 1969). Literature on Northern desegregation deals with the same issues, but also describes the development and implementation of specific desegregation plans such as bussing and transfer programs, school zoning, or the creation of the middle school and education parks (Weinbert, 1968). As reported earlier, findings on the effects of desegregation tend to show that the single most important school factor influencing academic achievement for Black and other minority-group children (as well as low-income students) is that the classroom be made up predominantly of White middle-class students (Coleman et al., 1966).

More recent organizational and administrative changes in the schools include experiments with homogeneous and heterogeneous groupings, changes in pupil-teacher ratio, and the implementation of parent and community involvement. Major research on ability grouping shows that it has no measurable effect on student achievement (Passow, Goldberg, Tannenbaum, 1967). When homogeneous grouping causes de facto segregation, it may, in fact, lower the achievement of minority-group and low-income students (Esposito, in press). Changes in pupil-teacher ratio have been studied by a number of investigators with differing viewpoints; and as might be expected, the conclusions reached vary according to the point of view of the researcher (Hawkridge, 1968; Kravetz, 1966; Schwager, 1967). Since extensive parent and community involvement are still relatively new areas for investigation, there is no definitive work on this subject. However, a number of researchers have hypothesized that the influence of parent and community forces in the schools may provide a powerful force for instituting needed changes in both the children and the schools (see Lopate, Flaxman, Bynum & Gordon, 1970). Several investigators have linked the "sense of fate control," which has been found necessary for school achievement, with parental involvement in the schools (Coleman et al., 1966). One major research project concludes that the only hope for narrowing the spatial, cultural and emotional gap between school personnel and school children is through introducing parents and other community members into the schools (Leacock, 19690.

There is a rapidly growing body of research which relates teacher attitudes and expectations to student performance. Studies in this area point to the debilitating effect of low teacher expectations (Rosenthal & Jacobson, 1968). A number of investigations have been aimed at identifying factors which form teacher attitudes and behavior (e.g., Flaxman, 1969; Webster, 1966). So far, this research is inconclusive, but indications are that it is not social class background alone, as previously thought, which creates either positive or negative attitudes and behaviors toward disadvantaged children (Webster, 1966). Without any clear indications of what causes teachers' negative attitudes toward low-income and minority group children, a few studies have focused on the possibilities of changing teacher attitudes. Research in this area is difficult to interpret, since positive changes are usually measured by answers to a questionnaire (Flaxman, 1969) and thus indicate little more than the fact that teachers have learned more "acceptable" responses. It has been hypothesized that artificially changing teachers' expectations of student performance can create measurable change in student achievement; but data on this subject also remains inconclusive (Rosenthal & Jacobson, 1968).

A brief examination of the work which has been done over the past few years indicates that many investigators are turning their attention to the vitally important problem of quality education for the many disadvantaged youngsters in our society. These concerned educators are directing their efforts to a variety of problems. But the variety of questions to be answered only serves to indicate the complexity of the problems, and there remain, in addition to the many unanswered questions, many problems with the answers which we do have and the methods which are used in obtaining them.

1. A common fault among those investigators concerned with population characteristics among disadvantaged groups has been the tendency to view all the many groups involved as constituting one homogeneous population, with a common set of problems and deficits, and a common set of needs. The *real* problem may lie in the degrees and types of differences between groups.

2. A result of this hasty attitude on the part of one set of researchers has been the tendency of those educators concerned with compensatory program design to search for *the* program or *the* remedial approach which will prove to be the magic answer to this problem which is called "the disadvantaged learner." Attention is diverted from the problem of designing specific approaches to benefit specific learner characteristics.

3. The tendency in past research has been to concentrate on quantitative data to the neglect of those qualitative analyses and process variables, which may provide more useful keys to successful individual treatments.

4. Much of the research evaluation has simplistically tended to relate single variables, avoiding the more realistic conclusion that the complex process of behavior determination must be the result of

complicated interactions of many variables and conditions.

5. In a failure to maintain the traditional research stance of objectivity, investigators too often have yielded to the assumption that those variations from the assumed norm, which their research discovers constitute deficits to be overcome in the education of the groups being studied. There has been an almost general neglect of the possibility that these differences, once carefully defined and determined, may be used as helpful features in the design of new educational treatments which are more appropriate for the children to whom they are applied.

6. Far too frequently, evaluators of specific programs or practices have gone no further than to look for certain improvements in the program's subjects; when these changes are not noted, the immediate assumption is that the compensatory practice does not work; some have even gone so far as to assert that compensatory education as a whole cannot work. These kinds of assertions have been made with no attempt to determine the quality of the program used, or even if the program as described was actually implemented. Often the *fact* of intervention is assumed to be sufficient effort to merit results, and when those results are not forth coming, the tendency is to place the blame on the pupils, not on those responsible for assuring the quality of the program.

7. Sloppy experimental design is a frequent fault in research to date, and with the increasing complexity of our society, improvement in the use of controls cannot be expected unless a great deal of expert attention is turned to the problem.

8. Too much of educational research has been turned to the purpose of proving a hypothesis, and too little research effort has been spent in that kind of systematic observation, which leads to theory generation. Given our lack of success so far in this vital field, all our efforts should be bent toward the fostering of new ideas; instead of the re-working of old and tired arguments and failures.

In reviewing briefly, as we have done here, the progress to date in research on the disadvantaged, I think we find in our list of weaknesses several important insights, which not only apply to future research, but also have valuable implications for those of us who are more concerned with practice. Although it is certainly important to bring increased technical competence to research issues, improved research design simply cannot compensate for the lack of programs or material available for study. This is the problem we cannot avoid facing: if we can gain any general impression of the field, it is that not one program of demonstrated effectiveness has yet been successfully implemented on a large scale.

Two basic problems lie behind this disturbing failure. The first is the crippling lack of funds for meaningful large-scale innovation. In a report prepared for the Civil Rights Commission recently, Jablonsky and I estimated that the cost of an effective effort would be $100 billion dollars a year, which is just about double what we are presently spending on education in the United States (Gordon & Jablonsky, 1967). In a more modest estimate, prepared for the same body, David Cohen (1967) suggested that it would be necessary to spend $10 billion dollars more each year then we now are spending. Even this lower figure contrasts dramatically with the $1 to $2 billion dollars yearly, which in actuality are allotted to the effort to bring about quality education for disadvantaged children and youth.

However, even when money is available, we face another critical shortage: a lack of effective ideas for the best utilization of available funds. By 1966, when I worked with Wilkerson (Gordon & Wilkerson, 1966) on a national survey of compensatory education programs, we found very little that was substantially different from traditional approaches to education. In 1968, conducting a similar survey with Adelaide Jablonsky, I did observe some few programs with promise, but their reflection in widely accepted practice was minimal (Gordon & Jablonsky, 1968). Still another study, conducted by Hawkridge in 1969, found few programs associated with significant changes in the level of achievement. In review of his data, it becomes clear that he was no more successful than my colleagues and I in identification of substantive innovations in this field so desperately in need of change.

Obviously, then, we are not putting highly creative conceptions or the necessary national resources into this task. I am not impressed that we are utilizing the valuable research information, which is available to us. What are some of the conceptions and research leads which we can use immediately to improve the outlook for the attainment of a higher level of effort?

Upon completing the study with Wilkerson (1966), I concluded that more effort was needed to improve technical educational procedures designed to change cognitive function. I felt then that we greatly needed to improve formal teaching behavior. I am certainly not ready to back away from this position now, but I do think there is increasing evidence that this cognitive emphasis may not really be the most productive pursuit at this time; the field of education and its supporting sciences may not be able to move quickly enough to make meaningful modification in cognitive functions a viable goal. Zigler has suggested that affective processes may be more malleable and that we may better be able to modify affective than cognitive functions. In addition, we have good reason to believe that appropriate changes in affective state are likely to result in significant changes in the quality of cognitive function. I must emphasize that I do not mean to abandon a concern for understanding and improving teaching. I do believe that most aspects of the teaching-learning process can be identified and refined, that this process can be systematized, and that educability is primarily a function of the quality of the learning experiences to which pupils are exposed. However, although I believe that teaching may become scientifically based, I think we may not at present be able to sufficiently identify and apply those underlying scientific principles to the task at hand. However, we do seem to have better leads toward levers for involving ourselves and pupil environments in the changing of attitudes, feelings, motivation, and task involvement.

Without demeaning the cognitive aspect, I think we may still conclude that effort directed at better understanding and more appropriately designing and controlling the social-psychological conditions in which learning occurs may, in the present period, be a more appropriate strategy. The rationale, viewed in light of the current socio-political scene, is obvious, and lends additional support for this position. Many argue that formal education divorced from the main currents of the life experiences of our pupils, is perceived by them as irrelevant and functions to retard academic development. As a result, such issues as ethnic studies, participatory democracy, and decentralization are seen as possible levers for making the learning experience more relevant to the conditions of life and more conducive to success for greater numbers and varieties of students.

Once we have conceded the importance of social and psychological conditions to success in learning, we will find ourselves with a valuable tool if we extend our use of it far enough. In the past, our concern with analysis of pupils has been characterized by a heavy emphasis on identification of levels of achievement. What we need now is greater qualitative analysis of learning behaviors, combined with the matching of this broader range of characteristics to the design of appropriate learning environments and experiences. Of course, this is not a simple task, since we know very little about the ecological or psychological environments of our pupils. Clinical psychology has at least provided us with models for investigating psychological environments, that is, the way in which the individual perceives his effective environment; but this expertise has not yet been systematically applied to education. The study of ecological environments, that is, the physical, social, and political conditions of the surroundings in which, learning occurs, is still in its infancy. Yet, it is increasingly clear to me that differences in achievement are more related to the circumstances and conditions in which learning occurs and the extent to which the environment supports the mastery of the learning task than they are a function of variations in measured intelligence. Looking at these variations in intelligence we do not see a sufficient relationship between alleged potential and actual performance to say that intelligence, as we know how to measure it, is the sole or most important factor; but the conditions under which learning occurs, the degree of support they provide for learning–these appear to be very important indeed.

Now if we agree that there exists wide variance in the character and quality of the learning behaviors that children bring to school and if we agree that the conditions under which learning and development occur can influence the quality of achievement, then it is possible to conclude that relationships between quality of learning behaviors and quality of learning conditions may be of importance as determinants of quality of achievement. If this somewhat, complex statement of a rather simple concept holds, it has critical significance for conceptualizing the central issue in the education of the poor or disadvantaged.

For more than a score of years the concept "equal educational opportunity" has dominated our thinking. The concept grew out of court litigations around issues related to ethnic segregation in public education. As a nation we have affirmed our commitment to equality of educational opportunity for all and have translated this to mean equal access to the educational resources provided to the populus through public funds. But if my little paradigm is permitted to stand, equal opportunity may not adequately reflect the implicit commitments of a democratic, diverse and pluralistic society. If what we are committed to is to make educational and other achievements independent of ethnic group, social class, sex group, religious group or geographic origins, a concept such as diversity and justice may be more worthy of our tradition. Diversity focuses our attention on those aspects of difference or variance in human characteristics, which have relevance for pedagogical and developmental intervention. Justice moves beyond a concern for distributive equality to a concern for distributive sufficiency. When we speak of distributive sufficiency we are immediately forced to look to questions of need rather than share. The functional education question becomes "what do the special characteristics of this person suggest that the intervening institutions of society do to enable this individual to function with adequacy and satisfaction?" The answer to that question should dictate the quality and quantity of the educational or developmental intervention. The program indicated may be violative of our more narrow conceptions of equality but given the compelling facts of diversity in our people it may be the only way in which we approach justice. For the next period in the history of our nation, let us build on our commitment to equality of opportunity with a new commitment to the nurturance of human diversity and the achievement of social justice.

Paper Presented at the Policy Conference on Education and Inequality, June 5-8, 1975. Sponsored by Rhode Island University, Newport, Rhode Island. Copyright ©1976. Published in N. F. Ashline, T. R. Pezzullo, & C. I. Norris (Eds.), *Education, Inequality, and National Policy* (pp. 101-123). Lexington, MA: Lexington Books.

10
Educational Reforms for Students At Risk: Cultural Diversity as a Risk Factor in the Development of Students

In human social organization, when one's characteristics are at variance in significant ways from the modal characteristics of the social group, which has achieved hegemony, one is likely to find little correspondence between the developmental supports provided by the dominant group and the developmental needs of the persons whose characteristics are different. This is a function of the operation of a principle of social economy whereby social orders design and allocate social resources in accord with the modal or otherwise valued characteristics of the social order. Thus we have schools, public facilities, media, etc., designed and allocated to fit the needs of persons whose vision and hearing are intact rather than to serve the needs of persons with sensory impairments. Consequently, persons with impairment in these sensory modalities are at risk of developmental and educational failure, not necessarily as a function of the impairment but because the society is not organized to adequately support the developmental needs of persons whose characteristics are at variance with those which are modal.

Following this line of reasoning, the identification of a population as being at risk of failure is always situational and relative. In its early usage, "at risk" status was used to refer to persons with identifiable sensory, physical or intellectual disabilities, which were likely to result in their failure to benefit from the normal range of developmental resources generally available. Their risk of failure was related to the goals or objectives the society expected most children to achieve even in the absence of specialized resources, and the implicit recognition that without such resources, expected achievement was unlikely. It is in the latter half of the 20th century that we began to think of persons as being "at risk" of failure to achieve an adequate education because of their social circumstances as includable in the "at risk" population. Thus we see in the group of papers published together here, little attention is called to persons with physical or sensory disabilities, and major attention is directed at persons whose "at-risk" status is based upon their ethnicity, culture, language or economic status.

This shift in emphasis from one class of indicators to another may be a reflection of a decline in the relative number of persons with mental, physical and sensory disabilities, the society's enhanced capacity to address the problems of this group, an increase in the number of persons whose social status places them at a disadvantage in the society, and the increasing recognition of the society's lack of success in meeting the developmental needs of this newly recognized group.

In the identification of populations of children at risk of failure to be adequately developed or educated, it is important that both the old and the new categories of persons be included. It is also important that we recognize the special at risk status of persons who are doubly or triply placed at risk, i.e., those who fall into two or three of the at risk categories. An example of such a person is a language minority group member who is female, hard of hearing and black. For the purposes of our discussions however, these will be treated as extreme cases, and the more common patterns of at risk status will be our focus. Traditionally, at risk status has referenced the characteristics of the persons so designated. Typical of this approach is Rosehan's (1967) list of attributes of "at risk" students.

1. They commonly come from broken homes;
2. They are nonverbal and concrete minded;
3. They are physically less healthy than their middle-class peers;
4. They lack stable identification figures or role models;
5. They lack stable community ties because of their constant migration;
6. They are often handicapped by their color, which provides them with a negative self image;
7. They are handicapped in the expression and comprehension of language; and
8. They tend to be extroverted rather than introverted.

It may be more useful to utilize a more dynamic conception of the construct. We hold that at risk status refers not simply to the characteristics of persons but to an interaction between the traits of such persons and the contexts in which they live their lives. Being at risk of failure may be an iatrogenic condition, i.e., it may be more appropriately conceptualized as a condition or circumstance brought on failure or in capacity of the developmental environment to support the needs of the developing person. Consider the fact that all persons who show the characteristics that we have targeted do not show other evidences of being at risk. All persons for whom English is a second language or who claim African American identity or who have a physical disability do not flounder. In fact, some such persons have relatively uneventful courses of development and achieve quite adequately. In our work (Gordon and Song, 1992) we have found that many such persons develop in environments, which have been specially structured to insure that appropriate supports are available and that incapacitating barriers are eliminated or circumvented. We conclude that at risk status is a function of the inappropriateness of developmental environments to the needs of the person and that a focus on these deficient environments may be more productive than is a focus on the characteristics of the persons. We can then define at risk as referring to a category of persons whose personal characteristics, conditions of life and situational circumstances, in their interactions with each other, make it likely that their development and/or education will be less than optimal.

To better understand the interactions between these characteristics and life situations, it is important to make still another distinction. Gordon (1988) distinguishes between the status and functional characteristics of persons. Status characteristics like ethnicity, gender, class and language generally define one's status in the social order. Status is likely to influence one's access to resources, the nature of one's opportunities and rewards, what is expected, as well as the character and quality of society's investment in one's development. Functional characteristics refer to the hows of behavior and generally refer to the ways in which persons function. Functional characteristics, often culturally determined, include belief systems, cognitive styles dispositions, language systems, mores, skills and technologies (ways of doing things). Obviously there are interactions and overlappings between status and functional characteristics, but either set of traits can facilitate or frustrate development and education by virtue of its primary characteristics. However, there is a secondary characteristic, which adheres to each category, which may be of greater consequence for development than is the influence of status on the distribution of resources or the influence of function on the organization of behavior. We refer to the personal identification and attribution, which derive from one's status as well as from one's way of functioning. Both help to define one's concept of self and the manner in which one identifies one's self. Ultimately, even though status and functional characteristics may be the developmental antecedents of identity, it may be identity, which provides the energy behind behavioral adaptation. How then do human characteristics in interaction with social circumstances influence the development of identity and what is the relationship between sources of one's identity and one's being at risk of developmental and educational failure to thrive? We submit that culture is the context and the ubiquitous vehicle.

CULTURAL AND HUMAN DEVELOPMENT

Psychologists and anthropologists such as Cole, Gay, Glick, and Sharp (1971), have concluded that regardless of cultural, ethnic, gender or class differences among human groups, there are no corresponding differences in cognitive and affective processes. Rather, it is held that the basic processes of mentation in the human species are common—e.g., association, recall, perception, inference, discrimination, etc.—and it is the prior experiences, situations and meanings which form the context for the development and expression of these processes. Because experiences, situations and meanings are culturally determined, the quality of the development of a process, the conditions under which it is expressed and even our ability to recognize its manifestations are dependant upon cultural phenomenon which are often mediated through ethnic, gender or class identity.

Our conception of risk factors offers an example of the importance of discussing the culturally embedded nature of human experience and meaning. In the past, we have framed our conception of at-risk status or vulnerability in terms of risk factors, such as gender, demographic status, social and intellectual resources, genetic history, mobility patterns and negative or traumatic life events. What we have not accounted for in this conception of at risk status is the fact that over half of the individuals who may experience the most severe stressors do not report psychological or social dysfunction. (Waxman et al., 1992) Gordon, Rollock and Miller (1990) have suggested that threats to the integrity of behavioral development and adaptation may exist along a continuum, with the degree of threat better defined by existential meaning than by "reality" factors; the individual's reaction to the threat may depend upon the actual perception or the connotation which is permitted by the context in which the phenomenon is experienced.

It is becoming clear, then, that culture is a construct with a wide variety of definitions and conceptions. Authors have often sought to distinguish between material and non-material aspects of culture. Belief systems, attitudes, and attributions are examples of non-material culture, while tools, skills and artifacts serve as examples of material culture. We hold however, that at its core culture is responsible for all human behavior. That is, when we speak of culture we are speaking of both the cause and the product of human affect and cognition.

Both Geertz (1973) and Tyler (1949) have provided us with widely accepted indices and definitions for culture. In his perception of culture, Tyler (1949) included "knowledge, beliefs, art, law, custom and any other capabilities and habits acquired by man as a member of society," while Geertz viewed culture as: "historically transmitted pattern of meanings embodied in symbolic form by means of which men communicate, perpetuate and develop their knowledge about and attitudes toward life" (Geertsz, 1973, p. 89).

We see then, an effort to discuss culture in terms of objects or tools as well as language and shared conceptual schemata. In joining these perceptions of culture, we can derive five fundamental dimensions of the construct:

1. The judgmental or normative is a reflection of society's standards and values, which often provides the constraints within which thought is facilitated;
2. The cognitive dimension consists of categories (such as social perceptions, conceptions, attribution and connotations) of mentation, which are often expressed through language;
3. The affective dimension refers to the emotional structure of a social unit and its common feelings, sources of motivation, etc;
4. The skill dimension relates to those special capabilities the members of a culture develop in order to meet the demands of their social and techno-economic environment (Ogbu, 1978); and finally
5. The technological dimension refers not only to different, or more highly developed technological practices, but more importantly it refers to the impact of the different information inherent in these practices on cognitive and affective behavior.

These dimensions serve to emphasize those characteristics by which a culture may be identified or by which the culture of a group may be characterized. It is in this descriptive definition of culture that we begin to see the reference points for one's social or group identity, as well as the experiences which provide a context for one's conception of his or her own (as well as other's) patterns of behavior.

The function of culture in human activity, however, does not end with its role as a descriptive concept. In addition to providing the referents for group identity, culture also provides the stimuli and the consequences of human behavioral patterns. Thus, culture also serves as an explanatory construct. As mentioned earlier, when we discuss cultural information in terms of description, we are articulating the status phenomenon of culture, and in general are referring both to the social identity of individuals (Goffman, 1963)—the group to which I belong—as well as describing the effect of this identity on an individual's access to resources. When we seek to explain behavior, however, and discuss the influence of one's personal identity—the group to which I feel that I belong—we begin to wonder how particular language and belief systems, specific objects and tools, not to mention technological advances, influence or enable the behavior of individuals. When we examine ways of thinking—such as linear and sequential thought, tendency to generate abstractions, field dependence and independence, connotations and taxonomies as well as allowable metaphors—we are becoming aware of culture as a vehicle for cognition. Ultimately, culture provides the constraints within which mentation and affect are enabled.

Furthermore, culture serves as a mediator for learning in two fundamental respects. According to Vygotsky's (1978) notions of cognitive development, learning occurs within social interaction. That is, in contrast to the Piagetian conception of self-constructed knowledge, Vygotsky (1978) argued that the development of higher psychological functions is rooted in children's primary social interactions. Learning, based on the cultural-historical theory, consists of four fundamental activities: transmission of knowledge and cognitive skills, cultivation of cognitive abilities and the encouragement of these cognitive abilities. According to this conception, knowledge in one's culture is socially transmitted by adults and capable peers to children. The adult or capable peer, in joint activity, serves as a role model or expert tutor on a task, which allows for cognitive processes to be demonstrated and then practiced and learned. New cognitive abilities emerge as the adult works with the child on tasks, which may have originally been too demanding for the child. As the pair work in collaboration, with the adult providing encouragement as well as appropriate feedback, the child gradually begins to take on the responsibility of the task. While initiating the activity within the child's "zone of proximal development," with time the adult begins to remove support as the child becomes more competent at the task. It is in this form of social scaffolding that we see the mechanism for growth and development in cognitive functioning.

We cannot overstate the importance of an individual's group and personal identity in the social interaction, which comprises the learning process. A secondary human characteristic to status and functional characteristics, one's sense of self—mediated by culture—provides the fuel for the social interaction inherent in learning behavior. It is not only through cultural encounters that human cognition develops, but it is also through these same social interactions that we begin to recognize and identify our identity. Culture provides the reference points that allow me to recognize myself not only in terms of my gender, class, and ethnicity, but also to acknowledge that I am separate from others. It is this complex sense of self which I bring to the classrooms, that must in turn be met and integrated into dynamic culture of the learning environment in order for true development to occur. This interaction between self and learning environment id dialectical in nature: not only will the learning process enable me to grow and change fundamental ways, but my development will clearly impact on culture of the learning environment.

We have discussed in detail the impact of culture on what one does and how one does it. Similarly, we have also addressed the manner in which culture frames as well as enables one's feelings and thoughts concerning what one does. The question arises, however, by what mechanism does culture serve as the vehicle and context from human activity? This question can be answered across several levels of understanding—biological, psychological and social. We will begin at the cellular level and work our way up to the arena of social institutions.

Work in the field of cell assemblies and synaptogensis provide new perspectives on the interrelationship between neutral activity, experience and behavior. Specifically, Hebb (1949) has discussed a model for understanding the relationship between brain function and experience. Neural cells differentiate, and based on experience associate with each other in a manner which he calls "cell assemblies." While a single cell may be associated with several assemblies, under appropriate stimulations, specific assemblies are activated. It is possible to argue, then, that it is culture, which provides the stimuli and the context through which experience actively shapes the organization of brain cells. Further, with respect to reinforcement, it is certainly culture which serves to give meaning to the overt expressions in behavioral products of these cell assemblies, meanings their and reinforcements which in turn allow behavioral products to become established patterns of behavior activity.

In addition to the association of differentiated patterns of cells, the density of synaptic connections is determined by experience during the late prenatal and early post-natal periods of development. During the process of synaptogenesis, synaptic connections are first over produced, followed by a later period of selective degeneration. Greenough et al. (1987) has theorized that experience, in its role as activator of neural activity is responsible both for the organization of synapses, as well as for the selection of which synapsis will degenerate.

Greenough et al. (1987) further advanced a theory of experience-expectant and experience-dependent processes to account for the relationship between synaptic connections and experience. Briefly, the experience-expectant theory hypothesizes that relevant or normal experience results in normal neural activity, which in turn maintains typical synaptic connections. Conversely, an absence of experience or atypical experience may lead to irregular synaptic connections. In Greenough's second theory, the experience-dependent hypothesis states that specific neural activity, which results in the formation of synapsis, is the result of new information processing on the part of the organism.

It is clear, then, on the biological level we see a dynamic interaction between the environment and human development. This is also true for the interaction between social institutions and human behavioral patterns. Socio-cultural context is mediated through institutional structures as well as personal interaction. This socio-cultural context, in the form of family, religious institutions, schools, etc, provide the stimuli (e. g., values, norms, skills and technological devices) that serve to organize cognitive and affective behavior in much the same way that experience shapes synaptic connections. It should be understood, however that the relationship between culture and social institutions is a reciprocal one. The relations between education and culture serve to exemplify the dialectical nature of change. Our educational system exists as a subset of our broader social context. Over the course of time, our society has moved to embrace the concept of education for all citizens. In turn, however, this educated citizenry is now capable of creating tremendous change within our culture.

On the micro level, the socio-cultural context is mediated through personal social interactions. It is here, in teaching interactions that take the form of social scaffolding, that learners develop a system of knowledge structures and affective cognitive skills that are congruent with the values, beliefs and conventions of their socio-cultural group. The interaction between learner and significant other is premised on reciprocity; while it provides the learner with the opportunity to develop personal attributions, dispositions and motivations to behave in existentially appropriate ways, the growth of the learner creates new demands for the tutor.

Ultimately, it is the social institution, which may come to replace or function in parallel with the significant other, both as a source of reinforcement as well as a vehicle for the normative dimension of culture. It is through the processes of accommodation and adaption, in the form of schematization, that cultural transmission occurs. Schematization represents the mechanism by which conceptual structures come to represent cognitive, conative and affective components of phenomena experienced. In accommodation, then, the acquisition and replication of stimulus/response/situation triads is related to existing schemata, while in adaption the existing schemata or emerging conceptual frames are adapted to the demands of currently perceived or changing conditions.

It is in the relationship between social institutions and the learner that high degrees of dissonance can result in failure to learn or a distortion of the learning process. In a society with tremendous cultural diversity and a culturally hegemonic educational system, dissonance between what is learned in personal interaction with the significant other often may come into conflict with demands and expectations of the social institution. Precision of language offers an example of such dissonance. It is not uncommon in some cultures for individuals to use a single word to imply several meanings, or to invoke numbers in the form of estimation rather than precise calculations. In the context of an educational system which allows only for the precision of exact calculation, and which does not appreciate the potential for cultural differences in learning, this demand for exactness may place a child at risk for school failure. It should be understood that while some cultures may place a greater emphasis on technological development than other cultures, the notion of a "culturally deprived" people is a misnomer. The challenge for education thus becomes the enablement of bridging between cultures and of the learning of multiple cultures in all students.

IMPLICATIONS FOR EDUCATIONAL REFORM

Several implications for educational reform flow from this way of thinking about at-risk status. Among these are:

1. The limitations of reform in school governance alone;
2. The limitations of the manipulation of standards and accountability based upon educational achievement tests data;
3. The applicability of principles of social justice; just savings and the needs of the weakest as bases for distributional inequalities;
4. The pedagogical principles of adaptability and complementarity; and
5. The principles of diversity, contextualism, perspectivism and pluralism.

The limitations of reform in school governance alone: Most of the action on the school reform front has been directed at changes in the organizational structure and governance of schools. In what is perhaps the largest current effort, Chicago has devoted all of its attention to governance issues even in the presence of a consent decree, which requires that academic underachievement be reduced by 50 percent in five years (Gordon, Chicago 1991). Site-based management has become the fad, despite the finding that such efforts to date have done more for teacher morale than for student achievement (Miami study, 1990). Most advocates for this approach to school reform argue that real change cannot occur without support from staff, and site based management is the supposed route to such involvement and support. Nonetheless, if the primary goal is to reduce the incidence of school failure in a variety of students who present very diverse characteristics to the school and who are currently served poorly by our schools, the current reforms in school governance hardly seem to be the treatment of choice.

The limitations of the manipulation of standards and accountability based upon educational achievement tests data: Many of the states and certainly the federal government have staked their hopes for school reforms and improvement of education for children at risk of failure on the imposition of higher standards of academic achievement. Now there is no question but that the standards by which we judge academic achievement and to which we consistently fail to hold schools

205

accountable, are too low. They compare poorly to the standards achieved in other technologically advanced countries. However, it can be argued that our standards and achievement are low, not simply because our sights are too low, but because our practice of and provision for education are inappropriate to the requirements of educational excellence. Among the most prominent efforts at goals and standards setting are President George H. Bush' National Education Goals and the non-government New Standards Project. Both have begun with prime attention being given to the achievement outcomes of schooling. While the National Goals would be measured by a new educational achievement test, New Standards promises a new system of educational assessment. The latter is headed in the right direction with respect to assessment, but both give woefully little attention to the importance if educational inputs.

In the NYC Chancellor's Commission on Minimum Standards (Gordon, 1986) the case was made for the importance of symmetry in the pursuit of accountability in schooling. After identifying achievement level targets as standards, the report proposed that standards also be set for professional practice and for institutional capacity. New York City, other school districts, the federal government and New Standards have yet to seriously engage standards for practice and institutional capacity. Yet if we are to expect that children at risk of failure and other children as well will experience great improvements in their academic performance, it is more likely to come from holding to higher standards those of us to manage their education and as teachers, guide their learning.

The applicability of principles of social justice as bases for distributional inequality: As we turn to the actual distribution of resources, we encounter different kinds of problems. In his now classic report, Coleman (1966) challenged the society to separate school achievement from such social origins as class and race. The nation responded with several efforts directed at the equalization of educational opportunity. "Enlightened as these efforts were and despite considerable expenditure of money and effort, educational achievement has continued to adhere to the social divisions by which status in our society is allocated. One of the reasons why this problem may be so recalcitrant is the confusion of distributional equality (insuring that all have equal access to the educational resources of the society) and distributional equity, which requires that resources be sufficient to need. Persons who need more educational resources can not be said to have been treated with equity upon receiving an equal share, when what is needed is a share equal to their need. What is required here is a more appropriate conception of justice. Rawls (1971) has advanced a theory of justice in which the unequal distribution of social goods is justified by the principle of "just savings" through which the future claims of persons as yet unborn are protected, and unequal distribution, which favors the weakest members of the society. Our concern for resource distribution sufficient to the needs of persons most at risk of failure meets one of Rawls principles of social justice.

The pedagogical principles of adaptability and complementarity as conditions for effective teaching and learning: If we recognize that children come to our schools with varying degrees of readiness for academic learning and differential patterns of support for educational pursuits, it is necessary that schools be adaptable to these different circumstances as they guide students toward the goals of schooling. When we add the fact that students have been differentially acculturated and socialized, giving them quite different cultural schemata, cultural styles and related attitudes and dispositions, schools have the added task of developing the capacity to complement much of what students bring to school in the process of bridging from where these children are to where they will need to go in the process of gaining a sound, basic education and becoming effective adult members of society. In the service of adaptation, both our students and our schools give and take as we try to reconcile differences between worlds of home and school. In the service of complementarity, the focus is on conserving the respective strengths of both students and schools as we construct connections (bridges) between the two. Complementarity assumes that beneath the surface differences between groups and institutions the basic human needs and goals are quite similar, and when made explicit, can be brought into complementary relationships with each other. For example, my colleagues and I have been investigating the acquisition of higher order thinking skills and strategies by inner city high school students. After considerable effort at teaching such skills, we discovered that many of these young people already know and use "executive strategies" in their daily lives but were unaware of their applicability to academic problems. Rather than teaching new skills and strategies, we turned to making the utility of such skills explicit in their application in academic settings. Success in using something you already know from an old setting to solve problems in a new setting proved to be easier than teaching what appeared to be new skills in a new (academic) setting.

The principles of diversity, pluralism, contextualism, and perspectivism. Concern with the cultural backgrounds out of which learners come forces us to give attention in education to such philosophical constructs as diversity, contextualism, perspectivism and pluralism. Each of these notions has its complexed meanings, but in education each has special significance. Attention to diversity requires that differences, which adhere to individuals and groups be factored in the design and delivery of teaching and learning encounters. This is often reflected in the individualization or at least the customization of education in relation to these idiosyncratic characteristics. However, pluralism refers to the increasing demand that learners develop competencies in common with learners who may differ from them. Thus the requirement that they become multi-lingual, multi-cultural, multi-skilled, and capable of functioning in multiple environments and settings. So that while education is influenced by and must be responsive to the differences with which learners enter, the exit characteristics of its students must reflect the pluralistic demands of the society in which they live.

In a similar manner, education must be sensitive to variations in the contexts from which students come and in which schooling occurs. Here values and belief systems provide important examples. Engagement in schooling and effectiveness of learning seem to proceed best when there is congruence between the home context and the school context, when the values of the community are not contradicted by the values of the school. Our concern for parent involvement in the school is often misplaced on actual presence or participation in school activities We are increasingly persuaded that the critical variable is not participation but the absence of dissonance between home and school. Where both are about support for common values, participation on the part of parents may be a by-product. But participation is not essential, while complimentarity congruencies. Context specificity cannot be permitted to preclude the school's attention to perspectivism. In our concern for perspectivism we recognize that diverse characteristics and contexts are associated with differences in worldviews. People who live their lives differently are likely to have different perspectives on things. However, it is dysfunctional for education if students are not able to see the world from the perspectives of persons and peoples who differ from themselves, and from ones own perspectives which may differ as a function of different disciplines, different instruments of measurement, and different environmental conditions. Cultural variation in populations is associated with people with different characteristics, who come out of different contexts, and who may have different perspectives. These differences may place them at risk of school failure if education does not function effectively to build upon these differences to enable pluralistic competencies and the capacity for multi-perspectivist thought and problem solving.

11

Some Theoretical and Practical Problems in Compensatory Education as an Antidote to Poverty

Society has always considered educable those categories of persons thought to be needed for participation in its affairs. At one time in the history of man, it was only the religious and political nobility who were considered capable of academic learning. Under the dual pressures of the Reformation and the Industrial Revolution, this category of persons was greatly expanded. In the early nineteenth century in this country, during the period of slavery, the "educable" had been expanded to include most Caucasians, but it excluded most Negroes. With the end of slavery and the incorporation of the enslaved populations into the available labor force, they too were declared educable. Of course, the schools did not succeed in educating all of these new candidates, but the once narrowly defied concept of educability was now more broadly defined.

For a time even in the twentieth century, the uneducated, endowed only with strong backs or skillful hands, were eagerly sought by the economy. In contrast, the economy of the late twentieth century is requiring the ability to manage vast categories of knowledge, to identify and solve highly complicated interdisciplinary, problems, and to arrive at infinitely complex conceptualizations and judgments. Students with this quality of intellect and conceptual competence are not routinely produced in today's schools. In fact, we school people are constantly embarrassed by the large numbers of young people whom we have failed to prepare for much less complex intellectual and social functioning than what is required today. We are also under attack in many quarters for our failure to prepare adequately even more of those who seem to succeed in our system. Witness the large number of "successful" people who read inefficiently and without pleasure. Think of those among us whose skills in arithmetic are limited to simple computation. Consider the large number of high school and college graduates who have difficulty in recognizing a concept and are practically incapable of producing a clear one.

A social revolution has for some time been emerging which is not unrelated to the growing crisis in the use of intellectual resources and the management of knowledge. This time the battle is being waged by Negroes and their allies; soon, no doubt, the poverty-stricken will join them. What they are demanding is nothing less than total and meaningful integration into mainstream of our society. Equality of educational achievement (together with equal opportunity to share in the nation's wealth) is looked upon as a major means of attaining such integrated status. The production of compensatory education has grown out of a recognition that learners who do not begin at the same point many not have comparable opportunities for achieving the same goal, even when they are provided equal educational experiences. To make the opportunity equal for youngsters who have been handicapped, it may be necessary to make their education something more than equal: we may have to compensate for their handicaps before, or at least while, we are providing them with an education of equal quality.

Programs of compensatory education have existed for more than a decade. Although by now they vary widely in size and scope throughout the country, they have in common the dual goals of remediating and of preventing academic, social and cultural handicaps. Unfortunately—and I should say this at the onset—their most common feature of these programs has been their tendency to fail. A brief review of some of their usual strands may help to set in relief a few reasons for their failure.

The principal focus in compensatory programs has been reading and language development. New reading methods and materials, the training of teachers to use them, and the extensive employment of remedial reading teachers or reading specialist are all evidence of primacy of reading in the school learning hierarchy. The assumed relationship between the quality of oral language and skill in reading has sometimes led to emphasis on practice in speaking and listening. Where youngsters do not speak English, there are special methods and materials for developing bilingualism. Finally, some projects have worked to develop primers featuring racially integrated characters and naturalistic speech patterns, which reflect inner-city life.

Other curricular innovations have been inaugurated with the dual aim of individualizing instruction and increasing the relevance of classroom materials to the realities of life. Two major types of structural modification, team teaching and ungraded and transitional classes, have been widely used to ease children into school or facilitate their shift from one school situation to another. Various programs have provided individual instruction and generally greater flexibility in the teacher's time. The use of extra classroom teachers, specialists in such areas as music, science, art or mathematics, and volunteer aids have all relieved the teacher of much of her burden.

A number of projects have become involved in what might best be called extracurricular innovation. After-school or Saturday study centers are widely used, as are clubs organized around sports, science, music, or reading for pleasure. Cultural events, hobby groups, picnics and camping trips have been used to enlarge the experience of disadvantaged children during the afternoon, evening, and weekend hours. Where schools have continued their programs into summer, remediation and enrichment have emphasized.

Almost every sizeable program of compensatory education now includes some effort to increase *parental involvement* in its goals. As more and more schools serving disadvantaged neighborhoods have moved toward breaking down the barrier that has separated school and home, project schools have used home visits by teachers, community aids, or social workers. These visitors interpret the school program to families, provide information about school events, suggest ways in which parents may assist the school program, counsel them about behavioral or school problems, or put them in contact with appropriate community agencies for such counseling. When meetings are held at school, they tend to be small and informal, and are often conducted by the staff persons responsible for home visits or for augmenting school-family contacts. Adult education courses, clubs, and hobby groups have also been attempted to bring adults into the school.

The question of community involvement has concerned a number of project schools as they have reached out beyond the parents into the total surrounding community both to offer and to seek help. School doors have been opened to various community groups as well as for adult education courses. In return, schools have benefited from community volunteers, financial assistance for enrichment programs, and vocational opportunities for their students.

Teacher recruitment and training has given rise to a wide variety of practices designed to attract teachers to disadvantaged schools and to modify their attitude toward low-income families and communities. Intern programs at problem schools for teacher trainees or locally-based college education majors, orientation programs to acquaint new teachers to the neighborhood, extra consultative personnel or specially qualified teachers, inservice training courses and workshops—all of these practices are designed to give teachers a greater chance of being at ease, and therefore performing better, with their students.

Guidance is the one approach almost universally included in projects for the disadvantaged. Although guidance personnel are unfortunately still hampered by their traditional preoccupation with the misfit, increasing emphasis is being placed on providing counseling to all students. A typical, well-run compensatory guidance program will combine individual counseling, vocationally oriented group guidance, and, not infrequently, extensive enrichment activities to widen the student's view of the world.

Finally, three new groups of special personnel (many of whose roles are described above) have been added to the project schools. Instructional staff has been employed to provide their particular knowledge in such subject areas as language arts, science or mathematics, or to offer their special training in work with the disadvantaged. Service personnel are being used increasingly in the areas of guidance and health; counselors, psychologists, psychiatrists, social workers, physicians, nurses, and dental technicians are the most frequent additions in this area. Nonprofessionals have become important, filling such positions as community liaison, teacher assistant, tutor, and study hall supervisor.

These then are eight areas in which innovation has taken place in current compensatory education programs. Probably the most interesting thing about them is the absence of really new or radical innovation in pedagogy. Remedial education programs have been developed, teacher-pupil ratio has been reduced, new materials have been generated, and classroom grouping has been modified. All are sensible and appropriate changes, which should be part of any good education program, but they represent no basic alteration in the teacher-learning process. Significantly, much of the current work in the education of the disadvantaged has been directed at preschool children and at high school dropout, two groups who stand outside the mainstream of the educational process. At times, in fact, one is inclined to think that emphasis on these two groups has been widely accepted simply because they require the least change in the school itself.

I suspect that compensatory education has not worked for a variety of reasons, but one of the main ones is theoretical: the conceptualization has been inappropriate or incorrect. Learning invoices at least there categories of function: the first might be identified as basic cognitive processes, the second as affective processes, and the third as achievement systems including the mastery of content or skills. Using traditional methods, much of our work in compensatory education has focused on a modification of basic cognitive processes. But according to work by Zigler and others, it appears that basic cognitive processes are the least plastic or malleable of the three functions. Compensatory education, in putting its emphasis here, may therefore have chosen the very hardest and most impractical of the systems to modify. Zigler, for one, would argue that the motivational or affective system would be more easily modified. In his paper, Dr. Gurin (1970), points out that what happens in the formal learning situation may be less important than what happens in the individual's total life experience in terms of shifts, changes, and modifications of attitude, of motivation, of expectation in terms of past involvement. He would thus argue that more attention should be paid to modifying affective processes. I am not certain, however, that I would agree that the affective area is the one in which it is easiest for the schools to operate. I would, in fact, place the emphasis on the mastery of skills and content.

However, if we look at developments in educational and industrial technology, and the increasing applicability of the computer, it is conceivable that our traditional concepts concerning the mastery of content and skills may have to shift. Compensatory education, or a good education of any kind, may not involve trying to pour into unready and sometimes unwilling minds a great deal of information, but rather on developing skills for processing, managing, handling, and manipulating that information. I do not think it is a surprise to anyone that the newspaper and the television industry, the directions on appliances—most of the media that uses and seeks information in the society— require a quality of technical skills that might well be the test of a good education. If we are trying to prepare people efficiently to move and function in the mainstream, we must first get across the basic communication skills that are presently requires for functioning in this society. For many reasons I would also like to see the school not turn its back on the development of an appreciation for art and literature and history. But, if the principal focus of compensatory education now is as an antidote to poverty, I suspect those appreciations are of a second order of priority. The first order of priority is to decrease this lack of basic skills.

In one publication, Doxey Wilkerson (1966) and I suggested that there are certain requirements for survival in the emerging society that the school might use to identify goals, or at least establish a floor that every child in the school should reach. Included among these mastery goals are basic communication skills, problem-solving, the ordering and management of knowledge, management of self and of interpersonal relations, and a category that has to do with respect for continued learning and self expression that is discussed within the context of the growing need for competence in the use of leisure time. In developing that position, we were suggesting that, since the number of persons in our society who are truly mentally defective is probably not more than three to five percent, there are certain levels of academic achievement that we ought to expect for every youngster except that three to five percent. At that time I felt that since the lack of prerequisite skills and competencies and entry credentials are serious impediments to upward mobility, we would have gone a long way towards solving the problems of poverty if we could somehow reach this goal.

In rethinking the problem, however, it seems to me that, while this position is appropriate as long-term goal for meaningful living, I am not sure it is appropriate as an antidote to poverty. A brief look at the variety of programs across the country (including Head Start) shows that the educational establishment is not entirely prepared to produce quickly and efficiently enough to achieve the goals that some of us have assumed would be a way out of poverty. It is probably a mistake, therefore, to say to the disadvantaged, "The school is your hope because it is there that you will learn the skills and the competencies that will get you out."

Another issue concerns what it takes to get ahead in this society. As one who has been concerned with the development of competencies and skills, it is become more and more clear to me that although greater skills and competencies are being demanded, they may not be as important in this society as are the entry credentials. If we look at some of the people who occupy high positions in politics, in the commerce and industry, or in social areas, and examine the quality of their day-to-day functioning, I am beginning to be convinced that we have been misleading the poor when we tell them, "You've got to meet this high level of achievement." I still believe in it as a human being and a humanitarian, but I am less convinced that these ideals are the rules of the game that the rest of the world is playing. It may even be that some of our efforts at dealing with certain segments of the population are designed to keep them from really catching on to what the game is about. And the school becomes somewhat immoral when it continues to hold the attainment of these skills as the goal. Those of us who have an opportunity to see how people function in this country realize that is essential for at least some few to understand what is going on, to be able to solve problems, and to point the direction; unfortunately, most of us are not exercising this quality of intellectual and social leadership.

S.M. Miller has raised the question as to whether or not our society is prepared to absorb roughly a third of our population—sixty million additional people—into its mainstream. If we succeed in keeping all these youngsters in school, through high school and college, and if we succeed in having them come out as intelligent, well informed, creative, productive individuals, is the society prepared to absorb them into the mainstream in some meaningful way? I suspect Miller is right in suggesting that we are not. But I suppose the economists, political scientists, and other experts will argue this point. In any case, I do not think that we, as educators, should deceive a group of people into participating in the educational process because it is antidote to poverty. It is not. I think it is a way to a better life. By the year 2000, we will probably be less concerned with problems of economic insufficiency than with those of social insufficiency. Hopefully, we will have been forced to arrive at some manner of distributing the wealth so that people at least do not starve in this country. The disadvantaged of that period will probably be the persons who are incapable of relating meaningful to others, who are inept at using their time in ways that are personally satisfying, unable to relate creatively to nature, to the world of art, or the world of ideas. I would defend compensatory education or equality of educational opportunity, or a good education, on that basis. As an antidote to poverty, I simply do not see it as a solution.

There is a final note on which I would like to comment, and it has to do with the possibility that if we open the doors to everybody, giving all persons an opportunity to function in the society, many will fail just as some have failed who have already had this kind of freedom and have gotten into the mainstream. But I also think that there is something about producing and being an active part of a process that develops people. Rather than letting people spend months or years in developing the skills and competencies, it might be more appropriate to take a direct approach and simply let them in. In other words, it might be more appropriate as an immediate antidote to poverty to give the credentials and let the people act as if they were mainstream members. If we look at two and three generations of development in this country, we see that this is a common course. A family that was poor has acquired a bit of wealth by hard work, or stealing, or good luck, and they have moved to the suburbs. While one see traces of the earlier deficits in their functioning, they have rapidly picked up the characteristics, even some of the skills and competencies, of the people who are already there. The weaknesses I see in this system are that it tends to settle for and encourage a high degree of mediocrity. It is for this reason that I would prefer to hold to somewhat higher goals for education—understanding once again that they are probably not antidotes to poverty. But again, if one is talking about a way out of poverty, I suspect that we ought to begin to admit that in terms of performance, of skill, and of competency, there is an awful lot of mediocrity in our society; there are an awful lot of people who can function on this level, and we should not kid them or ourselves about it.

12
Commentary: Group Differences versus Individual Development in Education Design

By means of an extremely interesting and important line of research, Lesser, Fifer, and Clark (1965) have produced evidence to support the assertion that specific cultural groups tend to be characterized by particular patterns of intellective behavior. Lesser and others have referred to these tendencies as being indicative of stylistic differences in basic cognitive functioning. Probably out of his own biases, as well as out of sensitivity to certain political realities, Lesser gives emphasis in his interpretation of these trends to an association between culture and cognitive function and thus avoids questions as to any possible relationship between genetic factors and cognitive style. As he moves further to discuss possible implications of these trends, he suggests that schooling might well be made more sensitive to group differences in cognitive style by directing learners toward those learning activities and developmental-vocational goals which are most dependent upon the respective cognitive styles. Finally, Professor Lesser and his colleagues turn to the political context in which his work must be viewed and finds himself in conflict with respect to the behavior of research scientists concerned with the problems of cultural and ethnic differences in mental function. I will direct my remarks to each of these issues.

In response to concern with the development of more sensitive analyses of intellectual behavior in human subjects, several investigators have proposed procedures for factorial analysis of standardized tests of intelligence. Each of these procedures permits us to use data from standardized tests of mental ability, collected under standardized conditions, to categorize patterns of intellectual function and the relative strengths of persons tested. It appears that Lesser et al. (1965), have used this work as the basis for his approach to the determination of stylistic variation in the mental behavior of several ethnic groups. This clearly must be regarded as an advance in the development of the field of psychometry.

Before one draws implications from these findings that are too specific, however, the limitations of these efforts must be considered. Standardized tests have been criticized from many sources on the basis of their inappropriateness or insensitivity to the assessment of groups with differential patterns of intellectual function. In response to these criticisms, I have advocated a qualitative, as opposed to a quantitative, approach to assessment. I have argued that a detailed description of cognitive and affective functions in a variety of performance situations is essential to what I consider to be the major pedagogical purpose of assessment: to understand learning behavior in ways sufficient to allow for individually prescribed instruction.

What seems to be missing in Lesser's and his colleagues' psychometric procedures is sensitivity to the qualitative aspects of behavioral analysis, as opposed to the quantitative characterization of demonstrated status. For example, using items that seem to require a relatively high level of competence in spatial relationships as do his indicators; he assigns high status in this modality to examinees performing well on these items. Since no attention is given to analysis of the process by which mastery of these items is achieved, the characterization of function can only be inferred, based upon the status of the examinee's responses. If cognitive style is considered to be an important aspect of intellectual function, and particularly if we are to draw implications from such stylistic variations, cognitive style as reflected in the processes of mentation must be more sensitively analyzed.

There is a long tradition in psychometrics of attention to the assessment of the more stable aspects of human function. Since our concern has focused primarily on the predictive value of assessment data, our instruments of measurement have been designed to tap those achievements which reflect relatively stable functions and from which we can infer status with respect to the intellective categories represented by those functions. Our concern with relative position and prediction of future achievements has resulted in a heavy dependence on the numeric value and normative position assigned to demonstrated achievement and inferred status. Although I do not question the administrative utility of these quantitative data, I seriously question their value in understanding human behavior in learning, or their value in the design of learning experiences. It is for these reasons that even though I welcome the advance in the application of psychometry represented by Lesser's work, cannot view it as an important contribution to the advancement of pedagogy. I want to make it clear that I have no problem with his assertion that persons who share common cultural backgrounds may also share common patterns of intellectual behavior. I fully support the idea that differences in learning style may be due to difference in cultural experience. I'll even go further than Lesser and his colleagues seem willing to go and assert that differences in patterns of intellectual function may be, in part, a reflection of differences in genotype. We know that all children do not grow alike or look alike and that these differences are based in part on genetic differences. I concede that it is entirely possible--even likely--that children's differences with respect to mental function are based in part on genetics. But that is another issue. Let us return to differences attributable to cultural variation. There is increasing evidence to support the conclusion that patterns of cognitive function are associated with cultural group experience.

Greenfield and Bruner (1969), Witkin (1978a), and others have found differing patterns of intellectual function in a variety of cultural groups in the United States and in other countries. Greenfield and Bruner point out that culture can affect the very basic functions of perception and sensation as well as more complex behaviors such as conservation. So powerful is the relationship that these investigators have been led to conclude that "intelligence is to a great extent the internalization of 'tools' provided by a given culture" (1969, p. 634). While I support the findings that differences in learning patterns may be due to culture, gene pool, or some other characteristic, I do not feel that the pejorative connotation usually assigned to the fact of difference is either appropriate or useful. Learning differences are important, and in spite of political and social consequences, they must be recognized in the educational process. It is only when these differences are ignored or dealt with inappropriately that certain groups may suffer. The problem for education, then, is to find an appropriate match between differential learner characteristics and differential characteristics of the learning experience. Lesser tends to focus on a match between the dominant pattern of intellectual characteristics and the outcome, rather than the process, of the learning experience, emphasizing a relationship between preferred mental modalities and vocational choice. He suggests that it is maximally efficient to have students choose those careers that are related to their special abilities or preferred cognitive styles. This relationship, however, is a questionable one and represents a weakness in Lesser's and others' position. In drawing implications from the characteristics of learners, we may find that the nature of the learning experience is more important than its goal. The issue is not whether Chinese-Americans are likely to make better architects or engineers, but whether the functional advantage that some Chinese-Americans may have in dealing with spatial relationships ought to be utilized in the learning processes that allow them to achieve an educational or vocational end of their own choosing, rather than an end dictated by that particular proclivity.

In speaking of the relationship between preferred mental modality and vocational choice, it is important to consider the role and importance of the level of criterion mastery necessary for adequate function, as opposed to excess competence or potential. Abstract thinking, for example, is a necessary ability in law and in some aspect of medicine, but it is not necessarily true that one has to be superb in that area of function in order to master these fields and excel in them. Berg's (1970) work clearly demonstrates that superiority with respect to entry requirements bears little or no relationship to on the job criterion mastery. Analyses of college admissions data and subsequent achievement produce similar findings. In many fields, there may be an essential level of competence beyond which any excess potential contributes very little. Until we have dealt with this problem in teaching, learning, and vocational development, the determination of educational and vocational choice based on some identifiable preferred cognitive style will be dangerous; there will be a tendency to select only those people who function best in an area when people who are functioning adequately in the area could achieve the goal just as well. In planning for groups of people in relation to their preferred cognitive style or the cognitive styles in which they show the greatest strength, we may be ignoring the fact that the height of one's competence in that area may not be as important as the fact of adequate competence.

Another consideration: one ought to explore the possibility that level of ability an individual has attained may be related to the opportunity he or she has had to develop it. Given Lesser's interpretation that cognitive abilities are probably culturally determined, it seems that the opportunity to function in an area may contribute to the quality of subsequent functioning in that area. Whether one argues as a genetic determinist or as a cultural determinist, it seems clear that the interaction of the individual's basic cognitive pattern with the opportunity to express that pattern may enhance its function. Further, the opportunity to utilize an alternative function may result in the alternative's accelerated development. A prediction made simply from having determined status at a particular point in time may not be adequate. One needs to look at the interaction of the basic pattern with the environmental support for its expression and its possible subsequent level of expression.

Lesser's and his coauthors' work seems to have neglected the noncognitive factors involved in learning. Without demeaning or deprecating Lesser's and his colleagues' contributions, I feel that it is important to recognize that the strictly cognitive aspect of intellectual functioning is only one aspect of such functioning and that all behavior, including cognitive behavior, occurs in the context of an integration of affective and cognitive factors. There is some evidence to suggest that the quality and nature of cognitive function is influenced by the quality and nature of the affective experience; thus in investigating stylistic differences in cognitive function, it may be a mistake to isolate them from the context of the affective conditions in which they are called into play. More specifically, Lesser and his collaborators fail to consider the compensatory role of motivation. Even though an individual's ability to perform certain cognitive tasks may not be extremely high, his or her desire to excel may be strong enough to enable him or her to persevere and master the field requiring the particular skill. In vocational choice, interest and motivation are frequently as significant as are ability and aptitude.

In educational planning as well, one has to consider other factors in addition to the child's cognitive ability. Lesser states that since cognitive abilities are determined by culture, the schools, in grouping youngsters according to abilities, have isolated cultural groups from each other. This situation would be rectified if the separation of youngsters were related to self determined goals so that the grouping is functional and purposive with respect to those self-determined goals. The role of cognitive styles in the planning of learning experience is an important consideration; it is not, however, the only consideration in planning the ways in which we group people; and it ought to represent only one element in the learning equation. Lesser implies that grouping people according to their particular cognitive strengths and weaknesses has been the most efficient way to educate them. To achieve humanistic goals, however, the easiest or most efficient route may not be adequate justification for the choice of treatment. If our goal is to develop all people in a society, we must consider in our educational planning the relationship between the ease of program implementation and the goals we are trying to achieve. For some people, we may have to take a harder route because the goal we are trying to achieve requires it.

Related to this problem of the easiest or the hardest choice is the issue of group development versus personal development. Although we are concerned with the development of both individuals and groups, the relative weight given to one or the other at different times is a function of the social values in operation. There may be times in history when we would place the greatest emphasis on development of unique individuals because of some long-term goal of the society. At other times we would place the greatest emphasis on the development of groups, again because of some societal goal. In early periods, for example, when resources were much scarcer, it was very important that societies, particularly in their developmental stages, produce at least a few people who had exceptional leadership ability. We may now be reaching a period in which there is little need for such leadership development; instead the society may need to assure itself that there are not large numbers of people who are underdeveloped. In highly complex societies, survival of the society and the people may depend on everyone's functioning at what we might call a social-intellectual survival level. If that is the principal need, then group development becomes the primary issue. Under such circumstances, the choice with respect to the easier or the harder route can better be made. If it is most essential that a few members of the society function at a particular level, certainly we will take the easiest route to get there. But if the goal is to ensure that everyone functions at an adequate level, it may be that we are going to have to take the harder route to achieve that goal.

Allow me to return to an earlier point. Although group data are important to policy decisions and total group planning, group data are contraindicated in prescriptive curricular design. Individual, not group, differences are important for this purpose. Lesser's and his colleagues' data speak to the characteristics of groups, and if one is primarily concerned with policy decisions for the total society, it probably is useful to understand different trends in the several groups in the society. But if one believes, as I do, that in this particular period in the history of education the primary problems have to do with individual differences and their implications for the prescriptive design of learning experiences, then this work becomes less important in its implications for groups and has to be examined in the light of its contribution to helping us to better understand the functioning of individuals. As we make more progress in solving learning problems relating to individuals and in better understanding the mechanisms of attribute-treatment interactions, we may be able to generalize to groups of people. But it is probable that those generalizations will be more appropriate to groups that share learning characteristics than to groups that share racial traits, social class, or culture. For the differences within cultural groups with respect to patterns of intellectual functioning are probably more extensive and more important than the differences among cultural groups. I suspect Lesser's and his collaborators' data would substantiate this, since there is no uniformity in the patterning of functioning within his groups. His data simply show that there are group trends, but the range of functioning within these groups varies, suggesting, for example, that within the Chinese-American group some people may be functioning much more like Puerto Rican, Black, or Jewish children. It is not really at issue, then, which ethnic group an individual belongs to or resembles; nor is it essential that his or her pattern of functioning indicate what his or her educational or vocational goal should be. The essential question is, what does the nature of the individual's pattern of functioning tell us about helping him or her to develop and learn?

I would like to conclude with a few remarks about the moratorium on the investigation of cultural differences. I can sympathize with Lesser's and his colleagues' anguish on this point, but I think he was poorly advised in his decision not to publish, particularly if he was reasonably certain that his work reflected the best he could do with current knowledge and techniques. What his experience, and that of others, indicates is that things are tough out here, and there are fewer and fewer places for serious workers to hide. I see no alternative for investigators but to carefully examine their own motives to be sure that they are willing to stand with them, to apply the greatest competence, skill, and compassion that they can muster, and then to come out prepared to fight. Research on cultural and individual differences is terribly important, and we need Lesser's and his colleagues' contributions. It is true that some people, for the wrong motives, have seized upon the issue and have tried to use the results to political advantage. But despite this, the area remains an important one, and it is incorrect to discourage research or to refuse to publish good research simply because it is politically sensitive. It is essential that we not quit or hide, that we join in the humanizing task of creating the conditions that make such research and the social environment in which it should occur both possible and respectable. Maybe we can no longer afford to separate science and politics. For honor and science are not alone at stake—for some, what is at stake is a more equitable chance to live and to learn.

13
Characteristics of Learning Persons and the Adaptation of Learning Environments

One of my most vivid recollections as a child is of my country doctor father standing next to a seriously ill old Black woman, who was lying on her sickbed with a stream of blood arching from the blood vessel in her left arm that my father had just lanced. The cuff from his sphygmomanometer was still attached to her right arm, and he was watching its gauge as closely as he watched her. After what seemed like an eternity, he stopped the bleeding and placed a cool, wet towel on her head. Her breathing became easier. The mild jerk in her right foot subsided and she slowly opened her eyes. The crisis had passed. Later that day, as we drove back home, my father explained that the woman's blood pressure was dangerously high, and that he had to let some of the blood out to relieve the pressure. "If we could have gotten her to a hospital, we might have tried something else, but out here we have to be adaptive," he explained.

I often think of my father traveling through the countryside, adapting what he knew about the healing art to the needs and conditions he encountered in his patients. I think about the other country doctors of that period, letting blood to get rid of impurities in the system and performing other procedures we now know to be useless if not dangerous. And I think about us, their counterparts in education, as we seek to practice the art of teaching, adapting what we know—often under less than optimal conditions—to the needs of our pupils. I dream about the day when we shall know more about teaching and learning and be able to look back with amazement that we were able to do as much good and as little harm as we did, in a profession that has yet to establish its bases firmly in the sciences of behavior and pedagogy.

I have been asked to write about adaptive learning environments from the perspective of the learner. Most teachers recognize that learners differ greatly in their learner-relevant and learner-non-relevant characteristics. Good teachers go to great lengths to try to make adjustments in the learning experiences of children

225

whom they know to be unlike other learners. A sizable body of research has developed around concerns for the individualization of instruction and for the exploration of the potential of Attribute-Treatment-Interactions (ATIs). Yet the range of variance in curriculum design and instructional practice is far less rich than is the diversity to be found in the populations of learners. Only modest complementarities exist between our emerging knowledge of the characteristics of learners and our knowledge of curriculum development and pedagogy. Our best-developed adaptations to individual differences are concerned with learning rate, interests, or combinations of developed abilities, achievement, and background experiences.

In the United States, the oldest and most common approach to dealing with individual differences is homogeneous grouping by age, sex, race, and general ability in school, grade, classroom, and activity units. Although grouping by age remains the norm, grouping by sex, race, and general ability has become less common at the school, grade, and classroom levels. This is partly due to democratic concerns regarding the unequal allocation of resources and academic stimulation among such groupings. It is recognized that grouping by these latter categories into classroom units does not result in homogeneous groups; it simply reduces variation in a classroom on one dimension. Lately, grouping by ability into autonomous classes has come under attack because most of the research on grouping practices has shown no universal academic benefits to low-, medium-, or high-ability groups over what they would have achieved in similar but mixed-ability classes. In addition, some of the affective outcomes from such groupings have been rather insidious, stemming from the social-class character of the resulting structure, especially when confounded with race and sex segregation (Esposito, 1971). Thus, education programming has turned to individualized learning systems that serve children of a wide variety of ability groupings in the same classroom.

Gagne's (1974) system of identifying the hierarchical cognitive requirements of an educational task has had a tremendous impact on the best of these individualized learning systems. In stressing the importance of a careful analysis of the steps in learning, he laid the groundwork for teaching a child any concept or skill for which prerequisites can be carefully identified. In learning hierarchically arranged information and skills, it is presumed that the individual characteristics of importance are achievement of the prerequisite skills and information. Gagne recognized different kinds of learning (signal, stimulus-response, chaining, verbal association, discrimination, concept and role learning, and problem solving), each requiring different modes of presentation and teacher prompts and/or direction to be most effective.

This process, then, is an example of transforming the task to meet the demands of both the kind of learning involved and the student characteristics considered most relevant to the task at hand, regardless of the child's performance on some measure of intelligence or a more global type of achievement measure. The assumption is that children fail at an educational task only because it is inappropriately presented or it is mistakenly assumed that the children have the identifiable prerequisites. Thus children take a pretest on the material to be mastered and, according to the information received regarding their acquisition of the prerequisites, they follow the universal sequence of steps for that material, although they may start at earlier or later steps than their peers. Gagne has formed highly precise but generalizable rules for teaching particular "bits" of learning within any hierarchically structured topic relative to the particular "bits" of learning the child has already acquired, thus creating a system for individualizing education on the basis of prior achievement.

A few centers have used this concept of individualizing education according to prior achievement as the basis for large-scale federally supported individual-ization programs (many of which are mentioned in this book) that are implemented in school systems across the nation. Although the emphases of these programs differ with regard to the different ages of the target group, all lean heavily on the goal of individual mastery of behaviorally prescribed objectives, the choice of alternative presentations of instructional material, frequent pre-and post-testing with regard to achievement level, the special training of teachers, administrators, and support personnel for data management and for counseling and diagnostic services, and integrated teamwork in administrative and management procedures. The intent of each program is to improve student achievement outcomes and interest in schooling. After the two or more years required to complete implementation and adjustment, all programs appear to do very well, especially in regard to the achievement of their low- and middle- ability groups. Cost varies, since many of the testing and data processing functions require the use of computer terminals for the efficient use of personnel time (Talmage, 1975). But despite the relative success of many of the programs that plan learning experiences based on prior achievement, findings from a three-year study introduced by Wang and her associates suggest that further delineation of student learning characteristics is a critical need in individualizing instruction and adapting learning environments (Nojan, Strom, & Wang, 1982). Ideally, in addition to prior achievement, learning environments that are truly adaptive should be systematically sensitive to a variety of learning behaviors associated with individual pupil characteristics such as affective response tendencies, cognitive style, motivation, and identity.

Periodically, articles by teachers appear in applied education journals describing how they have met the call for individualization within their classrooms. A hodge-podge of methods and theories has emerged out of the pragmatic quest to deal adequately with the obvious range of individual pupil characteristics with which teachers are confronted. Presumably these arc highly sensitive and conscientious teachers who, whether they do or do not read the educational psychology journals, are making systematic observations and judgments concerning their pupils that are congruent with the findings of educational research. Hunt (1975) is convinced that good teachers have an intuitive sense for the differential characteristics of their pupils and adapt their teaching behavior to their perceptions of those characteristics. Unfortunately, we must conclude that these teachers depict rather uncommon classroom procedures, and that most public education in this country is individualized only to the extent of providing readers with texts on a few different reading levels, combined with some separate instruction for small reading groups within a classroom unit.

It is not surprising that educators have put into practice so little of their knowledge regarding learner characteristics. Not only is this knowledge complex and contradictory, but the major recent efforts at systematizing, clarifying, and interpreting the many related studies have provided little empirical basis for optimism and no guidelines for its application. Bracht's (1970) extensive review led him to conclude that the empirical evidence does not support the expectation that the matching of learner traits and learning experiences will result in significantly improved learning. After some twelve years of exploration and contemplation, Cronbach and Snow (1977) go to great lengths in their most recent book to report the limited utility and the complicated problems of the empirical evidence in support of attribute-treatment-interactions (ATIs) as an approach to the improvement of education. But there continues to exist a persuasive logical relationship between learner characteristics (attributes), learning experiences (treatments), and learning outcomes (interaction results). Several of us, including Cronbach and Snow (1977), Endler and Magnusson (1976), Glaser

228

(1977), Hunt (1975), McV. Hunt (1961), and Messick (1970), find it hard to dismiss the promise of the paradigm despite the missing evidence of its validity. But the tenuous nature of the paradigm does help explain why it is not more strongly represented in curriculum development.

ATI research has been *the* expression of concern regarding the importance of individual differences for learning and teaching. It is best characterized statistically as the comparison of the regression slopes of a variable from individual behavior onto an educational outcome variable under two or more contrasting educational treatments of the kinds of interaction are defined by plotting the calculated slopes, for the range of the ability measured, on the same graph. In the *ordinal interactions,* one treatment is associated with significantly higher criterion scores than the other treatment for a section of the aptitude range, with an insignificant difference between the two treatments at another part of the range. In the *disordinal interactions,* the slopes actually cross so that at one section of the aptitude range, one treatment produces significantly higher results, whereas the other treatment produces better results at a different part of the aptitude range.

Cronbach and Snow (1977) presented a thorough review of the substantial amount of research conducted over the last decade that attempted to discover ATIs using this, and less powerful, statistical methods. They moderated Bracht's (1970) and others' conclusions that there was no evidence for meaningful ATIs with the observations that, for the great majority of the studies they reviewed, (a) small sample sizes militated against respectable power in the statistical tests and encouraged chance effects; (b) person and treatment variables were paired speculatively without a sound theoretical background for generating hypotheses; and (c) treatments were usually short, ill-defined, or un-naturalistic. Moreover, they pointed out that inconsistencies across "replications" are likely because of unanticipated interactions with variables considered too irrelevant to document and, therefore, are un-researchable or un-examinable.

Why is the Attribute-Treatment-Interaction knowledge base so confused? In a very provocative article, Messick (1970) suggested that one of the problems is that we are trying to tally up the score before we have learned the rules of the game. The interactions that have so far been studied are sometimes based on human traits for which the assessment technology is quite limited. Treatments are used that may be too simplistic in their design, and that therefore provide an insufficient complement to the trait under study. Our conceptions of the interactions studied are usually tied to methodological or programmatic

229

constraints rather than based on comprehensive theoretical models.

One of the most serious problems produced by the ATI scoreboard approach is the assumption that studies using the same independent and dependent variables are studying the same interactions between independent variables. The crucial distinction is that ATIs are dynamic; multiply determined events only partially describable or investigateable by present statistical methods Even recognizing that some factors may be more crucial than others in determining (or predicting) a particular behavioral event, the one-on-one independent and dependent variables model is inadequate to explain specific behaviors in complex, partially controlled, real-life situations or settings. The major problem in treating these studies as multiple replications is that although we know that many factors affect school performance, this often overlapping interaction of identified factors or variables is not controlled or accounted for when the findings of these research studies are aggregated and compared.

When looking for main effects, it is legitimate to expect that the effect isolated should be operative in every instance that exemplified the unhampered operation of that effect. On the other hand, when investigating interactions, that is, the complicating or mediating influences of independent variables on dependent variables, the door is open to numerous *unmonitored* independent variables to affect either the action of the monitored variables or the mediating effects of their own interactions. This possibility of unmonitored variables in the research situation affecting observed interactions between monitored variables leads to what Snow (1977) called "locale specificity of effects," which without further experimental controls on environmental factors, restricts our generalizations concerning either main or interaction effects to the particular sample studied. Several situations can affect the results in this way. Study samples, students, teachers, or classrooms can differ in their overall categorization on some dimension on which there is no or little variability within samples (for example, classroom climate, teacher characteristics, neighborhood median income, and so forth); student characteristics can vary in range, standard deviation, or shape of distribution, as well as by their mean values (each of these affecting the likelihood of statistically significant results); and, perhaps most unfortunately, researchers may differ in their conceptions and measurements of the variables presumably under their common investigation.

A basic limiting factor in ATI research is that it forces a search for techniques that produce flattened regression lines over the range of variability of concern.

The model allows conclusions about interactions to be drawn only from comparing the slopes of simple regression lines, using one input and one outcome variable per comparison. Unfortunately, this glosses over some important sources of interactions. The model should be considered as a simple methodological variability is highly related to input variability and is of a similar range, then education has had little effect other than that of maintaining rank position from entry. Reducing the relationship between input and outcome variables reduces the caste character of achievement level and allows schooling a stronger influence, but it does not guarantee optimization of school learning for the individual.

There are other factors that limit the usefulness of what we know about individual differences and the design of learning experiences. These include the following:

1. ATIs are far more complex than the study of them so far would indicate. The study of these interactions has failed to take into account such factors as teacher and treatment interactions, the complexity of educational tasks as phenomena, the fact that tasks can be approached and solved with differing strategies and combinations of traits, or that the traits may function differentially across subjects and situations.

2. A part of the complexity of which we speak is to be found in situational variance. Relatively little work has been done on characterizing environments and situations and their functional properties. In addition, a few of us are only beginning to talk about the interpenetration of ecologic, person logic, and existential phenomena in situational variance. Environments' traits, and treatments have their characteristics, but they also have their meanings. It is, in part, the neglect of the influence of situations and attributions that makes difficult a better understanding of ATIs.

3. Psychological and scientific works in general are based on a search for laws applicable in most instances; but in the behavioral and social sciences, and education in particular, we do, not know enough about the nature and function of the specific instances to generate laws with respect to how the larger constructs, of which they are a part, operate. We may be prematurely copying

the hard sciences as we try to bring comparable precision to our work, forgetting that those sciences developed over hundreds of years. During those developing years, much time was devoted to the generation of descriptions and taxonomies. ATI may be in need of better descriptions and taxonomics before we proceed with further tests of its validity and utility in education.

4. We have not yet developed appropriate categories and labels by which to study ATIs. We tend to identify people by qualities such as socioeconomic status, developed intellect, ethnicity, language, and sex, rather than characterizing them by such functional characteristics as specific manifestations of cognitive style, temperament, and motivation, the dynamic patterning of which tells us much about how individuals approach certain tasks or respond to specific stimulus situations.

The above factors, and still others, make difficult our understanding of individual and group differences and ultimately our appreciation of the value to pedagogy of the ATI paradigm. These same factors help explain why there appears to be little empirical support for the very logical and commonsense notion that differences in human characteristics should be associated with differences in the effectiveness of various educational treatments. In addition to these methodological, operational, and technical reasons for the lack of clarity in this area, one of the reasons why the empirical evidence in support of this notion is so limited may be that the conceptual work in support of the logic of the relationship has not yet been done. As Rothkopf (1978) has observed, "It would be a mistake to expect too much from methodological reform alone. Both hands, the statistical and the conceptual, are needed to plow the field of aptitude x treatment interactions in teaching. The reasons for weak studies and incoherent results derive chiefly from our inadequate conception of the learning person. We need more psychological insights to provide us with working hypotheses about significant aspects of teaching and how they interact with personal abilities" (p. 708).

Glaser (1977) in some ways anticipated the Rothkopf criticism in a little book that is pregnant with pedagogical ideas. In his *Adaptive Education,* Glaser recognizes that the combination of available alternatives provided in systems of schooling and the decision-making procedures used to place individuals in these

232

alternatives are the fundamental characteristics by which educational enterprise can be described and analyzed. He then uses these characteristics to describe the ways in which aspects of teaching can be adapted to individual diversity.

Glaser outlines five models of educational enterprise, which are not mutually exclusive and which are combined in a variety of ways at different levels of education.

Model One: Selective with Limited Alternatives

Individuals come to an educational setting with an initial state of competence. Through informal and formal means, this state is assessed and on the basis of that assessment a decision is made to place the student in the standard educational environment or to designate the student as a poor learner for which some special treatment is required. The activities carried out in the standard learning environment are generally limited in the alternative modes of learning provided and emphasize the particular abilities addressed in the initial assessment, to the exclusion of other abilities. Because the selection process is geared to include those students with a relatively high performance in the abilities required to succeed in the given educational environment, the environment can remain fairly rigid.

Model Two: Development of Initial Competence

The second model has the same characteristics as model one: selection procedures and a learning environment. In model two, however, not only are individuals assessed with respect to presence or absence of abilities that allow participation in the program, but also some diagnostic decision is made about the nature of those abilities. For individuals whose initial state of competence is not sufficient for selection, an educational environment is provided to develop their competence to a point where participation in the program is maximized. In this way, through some combination of prior and continued monitoring and instruction, entry abilities are modified so that the number of individuals who succeed is maximized. A student is forced to adjust to the standard program with the help of supplemental instruction, implying that the deficit lies in the learner rather than in the learning environment.

Model Three: Accommodation to Different Styles of Learning

Model three attempts to respond to the limitations of model two by providing alternative, flexible educational environments and instructional methods that accommodate to different learners' abilities at entry into the program and throughout the course of learning. As information is obtained about the learner, decisions are made to enhance probabilities of success in alternative instructional environments with various learning opportunities. The procedures by which instructional methods are altered for different students is based largely on teachers' intuition and expertise. This process can be improved by increasing the range of diagnostic, instructional, and organizational resources available to teachers.

Model Four: Development of Initial Competence and Accommodation to Different Styles of Learning

The fourth model considers the combination of the second and third models. In this case, achievement is maximized both by improving the initial state of competence and by providing multiple environments so that abilities and instructional environments can be matched and there can be movement across the alternate environments as the individual develops the skills useful to learn in each context.

Model Five: Alternative Attainment Possibilities

In the previous four models, the educational goal reflected the emphases of the elementary school, that is, to teach basic literacy to all students. Model five contains a variety of educational outcomes usually associated with higher education. Multiple goals encourage the development of different constellations of human abilities and reward many different ways of succeeding.

It is not unreasonable to identify the selective, limited-alternative model one with past and prevailing educational practice. Currently, intelligence and aptitude have emerged as the significant entering abilities that are assessed to the exclusion of most other individual characteristics. The assessment instruments used are not designed to determine different ways in which students learn best or to identify basic competencies necessary to learn various kinds of tasks in various environments. Model two attempts to introduce flexibility and seeks success for a greater number of students by developing initial competence.

It is not until model three, however, that the concern for the interaction between instruction and individuals, which is the crux of the Rothkopf criticism, becomes apparent. Glaser indicates that model four—providing for development of initial competence and accommodation to different ways of learning—offers maximum adaptability of aspects of teaching to individual diversity in the elementary years, while model five—offering multiple educational outcomes—maximizes success in the upper grades. A cognitive psychologist who is uniquely sensitive to many of the practical concerns of classroom teachers, Glaser goes on to describe and give specifications for the design, delivery, and management of teaching and learning transactions consistent with these models. However, even Glaser's very advanced concepts fail to provide adequate conceptions of the learning person.

Human learners are more than cognitive beings. Human behavior is also influenced by affect, by motivation, by identity, by environmental press, and, indeed, by various manifestations of status, for example, sex and gender, social and economic status, ethnicity and race, and language and culture. An adequate conception of the learning person requires that we understand each learner from each of these dimensions of human diversity as well as from the collectivity of the dimensions. Our efforts at isolating significant treatment effects in relation to differential aptitudes or attributes, as well as the limited effectiveness of adaptive and individualized education, may simply reflect our continuing insensitivity to such single and collective dimensions of the person whose learning we seek to affect. What do we know about these dimensions of human diversity in learners, and what relevance have they for the design and management of teaching and learning transactions?

Socioeconomic status accounts for that component of subjective recognition of shared similarities that is related to income, style of life, education, occupation, and the acquisition of corresponding modes of life, or prestige of birth, for an aggregate of individuals. The realization that socioeconomic status dictates class in a hierarchical society is an essential component of human history. For Marx, much of human history is rooted in the class struggle. It is this struggle that gives rise to class consciousness. This concept allows for changes in the individual, since the subjective component of consciousness of socioeconomic status makes class an active, emergent force in history. Empirical sociologists concerned with the relationship between class and educational achievement do not give emphasis to this notion of class. Rather, they use class to designate a relatively fixed set of assumed characteristics and social hierarchical positions. This latter use of the term has made for rather dubious causal assumptions since class as an indicator of social hierarchical position points to how one is likely to be perceived and treated but provides little information about the functional dimensions of one's experience and behavior. The works of Mercer (1973) and Wolf (1966) suggest

235

that it is the functional dimensions that make differences in educational achievement, and socioeconomic status is not a reliable indicator of these dimensions.

Sex and gender are often colloquially used interchangeably but are used here to refer to the biological (sex) and social role (gender) characteristics by which distinctions are made in the identification and socialization of females and males. In discussing sex differences, we refer only to those characteristics that can be directly linked to the biological structures and functions of one of the two sexes, whereas gender is used in the discussion of socially assigned or adopted role functions. There appear to be few if any educationally relevant behaviors that can be traced to the biological aspects of sex. However, several of the behavioral differences observable in the learning behavior of boys and girls can readily be attributed to differences in gender. In addition, these differences in sex-related, socially assigned or adopted role functions also serve to influence the ways in which boys and girls are treated, what is expected of them, and what is allowed. Thus the educationally relevant characteristic is gender rather than sex.

Ethnicity is used to refer to one's belonging to and identification with a group that is characterized by such attributes in common as physical characteristics, genetic and cultural history, belief systems, and sometimes language. Although often used synonymously with race, it does not specify biological race (Caucasian, Mongolian, or Negro) but may be used to refer to a group that shares, among other things, a common gene pool. Ethnicity may be assumed, inherited, or assigned. As used in this report, ethnicity includes the growing concern with the self-interest of a group as a manifestation of ethnicity. As Ogbu (1978) has indicated, ethnicity often functions like caste, in that it determines a position in the social order from which its members cannot escape. Since ethnicity is so often associated with status, it is the status phenomenon that has the greatest implications for education. In the United States, ethnic status determines in large measure the nature of one's access to educational opportunities. Because of stereotypic thinking, it influences what is expected of the ethnic group member and, because of biases born of the caste-like nature of ethnicity, how one is treated in educational settings *is* significantly influenced by one's ethnicity. Thus, although ethnicity provides us with few leads for pedagogical intervention, it does strongly suggest the nature of some aspects of educational conditions and circumstances.

Culture is that complex experiential whole that includes knowledge, belief, art, morals, custom, and any other capabilities and habits acquired by humans as members of society. The total pattern of human behavior and its products embodied in thought, speech, action, and artifacts are dependent upon man's capacity for learning and transmitting knowledge to succeeding generations through the use of tools, language, and systems of abstract thought. As a descriptive concept, culture is a product of human action; as an explanatory concept, it is seen as a dialectical cause of human action. In a more colloquial sense, culture is the mores and way of life of a people. Cultures differ. Some are more influenced by technological developments than others and some are more complex; but no people is without its culture. The culturally "deprived" is a misnomer. With respect to education, the culture of the school may complement or be alien to that of some of its students. Bridging and second-culture learning present the largest challenge for education; failure to achieve an effective level of complementarity is the greatest threat.

Motivation has been traditionally defined as a personalistic variable reflecting the ability of a person to sustain effort in the absence of extrinsic rewards, or as a prompting force or an incitement working, on a person to influence violation and action. It is the second definition, which gives emphasis to forces acting *on* a person that better reflects the definitional emphasis utilized here. We see the prompting force as residing *within persons* and *within stimuli.* The process is reinterpreted to refer to the acquired *ability of stimuli* contained within situations to sustain the performance capability of certain individuals. It is in the nature of human organisms to act and react. The ability of stimuli to arouse and sustain human action is the motivating force. In the context of this definition, in education it is the responsibility of the learning experience to be motivating and not of the learner to be motivated. Obviously, the conditions and sources of motivation differ for different learners.

Language, conceptually defined, is a systematic means of communicating ideas or feelings by the use of conventionalized signals, sounds, gestures, or marks having understood meanings. In a deeper sense, however, languages are collections of symbolic, representational repertoires and their appropriate milieu (setting, topic, social status of participants) for realization in speech or other communication modes. The language system' or systems used are thus the vehicles for expressive and receptive communication. In addition, the language system provides the schemata around which mental functions gain meaning. Language competence, then, is a necessary condition for effective education. Educational experiences are more effective when there is congruence between the language of the school and that of the learner. However, learning is not rendered impossible simply because there is a lack of congruence.

Identity, in common parlance, refers to what stands out about a person and how the person defines himself or herself. It has been defined as the unity and persistence of personality reflecting the individual comprehensiveness of a life or character. Here a distinction is drawn between basic and qualitative identity. Basic identity is the non-reflective state in which existence is taken for granted, or in which the sense of existence leads to feelings that all is well. Qualitative identity refers to the sense of completeness, synthesis, and continuity by which persons perceive in themselves a character of a particular kind. Of the characteristics that learners bring to learning situations, it is, perhaps, identity by which most of the components of individuality are integrated. To the extent that one's characteristics are consciously orchestrated in the interest of learning, it is probably around identity that such patterning occurs. Operating at the core of sense of self, identity is the wellspring for sense of efficacy and ultimately for effort applied to learning.

Cognitive response tendency, usually called cognitive style, is used to refer to relatively consistent patterns characteristic of an individual in the manner and form rather than the level of perceiving, remembering, and thinking. The most commonly utilized categories are abstract and concrete functioning and field-independent and field-dependent styles. Since style connotes a higher degree of stability than is supported by the evidence, the term *tendency* is frequently used in preference to the term *style.*

Affective response tendency, identified generally as temperament, is used to refer to relatively consistent patterns, characteristic of an individual, of emotional responses to a specific stimulus situation. Aspects of temperament such as characteristic tempo, rhythmicity, adaptability, energy expenditure, mood, and focus of attention are most often referred to in the literature, and are given emphasis in most discussions. However, affective responses also include stylistic variation in processes such as attribution, personalization, projection, and cathexis. Cognitive response tendency and temperament speak to the how of behavior, defining for the most part the manner in which behavior is deployed in response to stimulus situations. It is the relative consistency in these response tendencies that leads us to type individuals and to anticipate reactions. In learning and other developmental situations, it is thought that the complement between response tendency and situational demands facilitates development while conflict and contradiction tend to challenge and may distort the course of development.

Shipman and Shipman (in press 1988) argue that one of the purposes of education is to extend the repertoire of response tendencies available to the learning person.

Health and nutrition refer to the status of the biophysiological equilibrium of the organism in its environment. Often underestimated as variables of importance to education, health and nutrition influence attentional behavior, available energy, and stability of response potential, as well as such ordinary factors as school attendance and availability for instruction.

Environmental press refers to the influence of living and nonliving phenomena that surround the individual. Specifically, press is what these phenomena can do *to the subject or for the subject* - the power that they have to affect the well-being of the subject in one way or another. There is a distinction between the press that exists objectively for a subject (alpha press) and the press that a subject perceives (beta press). The environment may be thought of as objective or subjective. The objective environment can be defined to include, but not necessarily be exhausted by, the alpha press. However, it may be the attributed character (beta press) that is projected onto the environment by the perceiver that gives environmental press its special role as a determinant of the individual's engagement in and response to educational intervention. Thus, the ecology of learning situations is being increasingly viewed as important. However, it is the social and personal dimension that may be of greatest importance to the learning person.

In a recent National Institute of Education report (Gordon, 1985), the knowledge base relevant to understanding these dimensions of diversity was explored and the possible implications for education were explicated. In the course of the completion of this work, it became clear that, as important as each of these learner characteristics may be, it is not in their unilateral but in their multilateral impact that their importance for teaching and learning resides. Learners do not bring their unique characteristics singly to bear on teaching and learning transactions. Rather, they bring these characteristics to bear on learning behavior in dynamically orchestrated patterns or clusters. It appears that it is these orchestrations, and not the individual attributes, that influence the learner's approaches to learning problems, the strategies and skills that are developed in response to learning task demands, the directional deployment of effort, and, ultimately, the nature and quality of task engagement, time on task, goal-directed deployment of energy, resource utilization, and efficacious behavior. Thus, it may be important that the teacher know the dominant features of each pupil's cognitive style, temperament, sources of motivation, identity, and so forth, but even more important that the teacher be sensitive to the stimulus conditions and situational constraints under which aspects of each of these domains change.

One could say that we are dealing with learner attributes at three levels: traits (cognitive style or temperament), instrumental behaviors (strategies, directed effort, skills), and intermediate outcome behaviors (time on task, resource utilization), the product of all of which is achievement. Instead of focusing on a specific manifestation of cognitive style, for example, it may be necessary to study several components of cognitive stylistic preference as they are orchestrated in learning strategies and to focus the manipulation of educational treatment on these strategies rather than on style. We have earlier suggested (Gordon, Wang, & DeStefano, 1982) that it should be noted that even single-domain clustering or patterning may reflect too limited a conceptualization. Messick (1982) suggests that human traits in learning behavior may be best understood as encompassing cross-style and cross-domain (for example, affective or cognitive) patternings that are not necessarily constant across situations. What is being suggested here is the real possibility that preoccupation with the learner's tendency to utilize a specific manifestation of a single domain or even the learner's utilization of multiple expressions from a single domain is counterproductive. Rather, a better conceptualization of the principle of behavioral individuality must include dynamic and dialectical relationships, within and between domains, selectively integrated into response tendencies.

It is entirely possible that multiple manifestations of styles or response capabilities may be present simultaneously, with some expressions more readily available, some more actively incorporated into habit patterns, or some attached by prior experience to specific stimuli or situations. Specific instances of learner behavior may then be the product of deliberate or fortuitous selection from the repertoires of possible responses. Leona Tyler (1978) has written: "The core idea is that each individual represents a different sequence of selective acts by means of which only some of the developmental possibilities are chosen and organized.... As Whitehead pointed out, the fundamental realities are actual occasions in which indeterminate possibilities are transformed into determinate actualities." Our learner behaviors are examples of Whitehead's "determinate actualities." They are the results of selective acts through which multiple manifestations of diversity (Tyler would say individuality) are orchestrated. To seize upon unitary components of those orchestrations may be an error. But the adaptation of instruction to those orchestrations may pose a greater challenge than the pedagogical sciences foundational to education currently enable us to meet. In what directions, then, do our current knowledge and experience enable us to move?

In answering this question, let us examine three issues: (1) What needs are served by existing models? (2) To what should education be adaptive? and (3) What are the demands placed on teachers of an appropriately adaptive education?

What needs are served by extant models of adaptive education?

The spirit of adaptive education seems to provide greater support greater humanistic approaches to instruction. Its focus on individuals rather than on groups seems to insure that individual pupils are less likely to be ignored, whether their individual learning needs are addressed or not. The customization that we have achieved does seem to serve the needs of some pupils, since individualization tends to broaden the achievement spectrum.

Yet extant models are still too narrowly prescriptive in that they are sensitive singly to pupil characteristics. In many cases, diagnostic information on pupil characteristics reflects a concern for curriculum rather than for the functional nature of the learning person. We have not fully exploited the area of cognitive psychology that addresses the affective and cognitive processes by which pupils mediate their own learning or by which learning can be mediated. This knowledge base may offer us a greater understanding of the learning person and, through that understanding, the development of an appropriately adaptive education.

From the perspective of learners, to what should education be adapted and for what purpose?

Clearly, these questions cannot be answered independently. That to which education should be adaptive depends upon the purposes to be served and the characteristics of the learner.

One can use current theory and common sense to hypothesize about the relative importance of different learner characteristics as the purpose of educational tasks changes. For example, when the primary purpose is to enable mastery of content and skills, adaptation to developed abilities and prior achievement may be most important. Interest, motivation, and affective response tendency may not be as salient, but probably should not be ignored. Adaptation to sex, ethnicity, and social class may be marginally helpful but probably would not be crucial. On the other hand, when the purpose is to learn how to learn and to systematize mentation in problem solving, adaptation to affective response tendencies and cognitive style may be highly important while prior achievement, developed abilities, and status characteristics may be less important. When the purpose is to develop appreciations and a sense of efficacy, it may be that interests, motivation, and identity are the salient learner characteristics to which adaptation must be responsive and that, in some cases, such as when the purpose is to develop understanding of process, relationships, and meanings, blending of all learner characteristics may be required.

Unfortunately, it is unlikely that the matching process is that simple. What is to be adapted to as well as the purposes for which education should be adaptive are not static phenomena. They can change over time and across learning situations, making it essential that adaptive education be recognized as dynamic, dialectical, and transactional in response to Whitehead's "determinate actualities."

What are the demands on teachers of an appropriately adaptive education?

If adaptive education is to serve learners rather than teachers and if, to do so, it must be dynamic, dialectical, and transactional to deliver adaptive education may place responsibilities on teachers that are far greater than they are currently prepared to assume. It becomes necessary to speculate about the qualities such teachers should possess and what regimen of training might facilitate these qualities.

Let us return to the example of the "country doctor," the best of whom were prepared in the tradition of the Viennese physician broadly educated, richly cultured, with a good knowledge of human anatomy, some appreciation of physiology and biochemistry, and a keenly attuned medical intuition. Using limited diagnostic technology, they had to depend upon judgment and wisdom informed by considerable experience. It may be that the teachers we need for adaptive education must be broadly educated, sensitized to diverse cultures, with a good knowledge of human behavior and its development, some appreciation of the science of pedagogy, and a keenly attuned pedagogical intuition. Using limited diagnostic technology, they may, like country doctors, have to depend on their judgment and wisdom informed by experience.

But, given the requirements of a truly adaptive education, these professional practitioners of the art of teaching may not be good enough. They may now stand where the country doctor stood, soon to be replaced by scientifically educated pedagogues. For while teaching will forever be in part an art, its foundations can and should rest on the sciences of human behavior. Pedagogical practice and adaptive education in particular must be informed by those foundational sciences. The orchestrations that we have suggested as being at the core of adaptive education cannot otherwise be systematically arranged.

Edmund W. Gordon, Lizanne DeStefano, and Stephanie Shipman. Copyright ©1985. Published in C. Wang and H. J. Walberg (Eds.), *Adapting Instruction to Individual Differences.* Berkeley: McCutchan Publishing Corp.

14
Culture and Ethnicity

Modern developmentalists no longer give serious attention to the old nature/nurture debate concerning the genesis of organized behavioral development. We no longer ask whether heredity or environment determines the course of an individual's development. With the increased acceptance of a broader perspective regarding development, the focus is now on the nature of the interaction between genetic and environmental forces. However, considerable attention has been given to attributing a "percentage of causation" to each of these factors (Jensen, 1965). Although this line of investigation has received a fair degree of exposure, efforts directed toward describing and analyzing the nature of the genetic-environmental interaction seem to offer greater promise for improving our understanding of both behavioral-developmental processes and intervention procedures. With respect to living organisms, short of alterations in *genotype,* i.e., the genetic potential of the organism, it is an individual's *phenotype*, i.e., the structural or behavioral manifestation of the organism that is the product of this interaction and that can be modified. In our attempt to elucidate this interaction, it is the organism's environmental encounters that provide our primary data. No aspects of the child's encounters are more important than those that are a function of the cultural and ethnic contexts in which they occur.

Most human beings are raised in families with specific cultural and ethnic identities. Even persons raised in nonfamily-centered institutions are assigned an ethnic identity and are socialized to the culture that is dominant in that institution. Thus, mastery of such primary developmental tasks as acquiring a sense of trust, autonomy, and, ultimately, identity (Erikson, 1950) occurs within the context of the cultural and ethnic group characteristics of the child's primary care providers. The influence of these early encounters and the ubiquitous character of their continuing presence on the developing person are probably second only to gender socialization in the shaping of attitudes and behavior.

DEFINITIONS

The concept of *culture* has a wide variety of definitions. It is an abstraction. Its interpretations vary widely, perhaps because it constitutes collective customs inferred from behavioral patterns. The fact that these patterns are transmitted by symbols renders language and the communicative structure of a social unit of paramount importance in our understanding of culture.

Writers such as Berry (1951) treat culture as acquired and learned behavior:

> We are born, ignorant and helpless into a group... We proceed immediately to imitate and acquire these 'group habits' of thought, feeling and behavior, and the members of the group, at the same time, set about to indoctrinate us with those behavior patterns which they regard as right, proper, and natural.

Some authors distinguish between "material" and "nonmaterial" aspects of a culture. Artifacts structures and concrete products of a culture are examples of the material culture, while belief systems, attitudes, attributions, and skills are examples of the nonmaterial culture. In his indices of culture, Tylor (1891) includes "knowledge, beliefs, art, law, custom and any other capabilities and habits acquired by man as a member of society. If we consider these perceptions together, we can conceptualize five basic dimensions or levels of culture" (p. 1).

1. The judgmental or *normative dimension,* which reflects social standards and values, i.e., those behavior patterns which, according to Berry, people regard as "right, proper, and natural."

2. The *cognitive dimension,* which relates to social perceptions, conceptions, and attributions, all of which may be thought of as categories of mentation expressed through the medium of language. This dimension therefore involves the communicative functions and structure of a social unit and is exemplified by what Berry describes as group habits of thought.

3. The *affective dimension,* the emotional structure of a social unit, including its common feelings, sources of motivation, joy and sorrow, and sense of value—Berry's group habits of feeling.

4. The *skills dimension,* signifying those special capabilities people develop to meet the demands of their social and technoeconomic environment (Ogbu, 1978).
5. Remaining is the *technological dimension,* the notion of culture as accumulated artifacts, instrumentation, and techniques, which includes things made and used as well as the manner in which they are used.

So far our definition emphasizes those characteristics by which a culture may be identified or by which the culture of a group may be characterized. But culture is not just a descriptive concept, or as Harrington (1982) has cautioned, not simply a "product of human action: observe the action and you can label the culture." Culture also influences human action and therefore must be regarded as an explanatory as well as descriptive concept. This dual nature of culture not only is important to our understanding of it as a phenomenon but is crucial to use of information concerning culture to inform knowledge production and knowledge utilization.

When we use cultural information to describe and identify, we are being sensitive to culture as a *status phenomenon.* Such information can help us determine a person's position, place, and role in the social order, and to some extent, how the person or group is perceived. From such information we might even predict how the person or group is likely to behave. However, in order to make more accurate predictions and to understand behavior, we might use information relative to culture as an explanatory concept, as a *functional phenomenon.* We want to know what this information tells us not simply about status but about consequences of the phenomenon for the functioning of the person. How does a particular aspect of culture influence the behavior of the person? What does the symbol of the tool enable the person to do? What societal capabilities are provided by the existence of the language? How do specific belief systems influence the patterns of social organization? Questions like these explore the ways culture functions to shape individual and group behaviors rather than to describe the culture or the status of specific members. Kluckholn (1965) has captured the dual nature of culture in the following statement:

Culture consists of patterns, explicit and implicit, of and for behavior acquired and transmitted by symbol, constituting the distinctive achievement of human groups... Culture systems may, on the one hand be considered as products of action, on the other as influences upon action.

Culture is commonly associated with a related but distinct indicator of social group—*ethnicity*, the dictionary definition of which is "a community of physical and mental traits possessed by members of a group as a product of their common heredity and cultural traditions." According to Isajiw (1974), the most common attributes characterizing an ethnic group are (a) common ancestral origin, (b) same culture, (c) same religion, (d) same language, and (e) same race. Earlier, we noted that belief systems and languages are aspects of culture. In addition, our reference to "same race" and "common ancestral origin" seems redundant. These considerations led Isajiw to use the term ethnicity to define

an involuntary group of people who share the same culture or to descendants of such people who identify themselves and/or are identified by others as belonging to the same involuntary group.

Ethnicity, then, refers to one's belonging to and identification with a group with common attributes referable to cultural traditions, belief systems, genetic history, and language and sometimes with common physical characteristics and identification systems. Although ethnicity is often used as a synonym for race, such use does not necessarily specify biological race but may indicate membership in a group that draws from the same gene pool. An example of this is an ethnic group we call Puerto Ricans, in which two racial groups or gene pools (Caucasian and Negro) are drawn upon in varying degrees of concentration or mixture. Another example is found in Nigeria, where the two ethnic groups Ibo and Hausa draw from the same race. In this country, the most widely encountered example is of English, French, and German ethnic groups all drawn from the Caucasian race. There are three races of mankind: Negro, Mongolian, and Caucasian; the ethnicities of mankind number in the hundreds or even thousands.

Because of the tendencies toward within-group mating and procreational insulation, ethnicity has come to reflect biocultural kinship systems rooted in the common, acquired and/or inherited characteristics and identities of the members

247

of these systems. A child may be born or adopted into such a system early in life, although adoptive ethnicity can be limited by the presence of tell-tale "alien" characteristics such as physiognomy. At the same time, ethnicity is a function of societal perception of and attribution from the fact of group differences. These perceptions and attributions then form the basis for the choice or assignment of subgroup membership. In the latter case, ethnic identification (the group to which I am assigned) may differ from ethnic identity (the group to which I feel that I belong). Goffman (1971) has used "social identity" and "personal identity" to distinguish between the identificatory perceptions of others and those of the individual, respectively.

Like the status/function distinction discussed in reference to culture, one's ethnicity in part defines one's status. This is particularly likely in societies in which positions in the hierarchy are determined by ethnic *identification*. However, one's ethnic *identity* influences the manner in which one functions, the way in which one responds to environmental encounters. Thus, ethnicity can determine the way a society treats the individual or group, as in permitting access to and control over resources and power. In this case, it is a *status characteristic*. Ethnicity can also determine how one utilizes the resources and power available, and thus it operates as a *functional characteristic*. For example, being Black in the United States automatically relegates one to a lower status in the social order. At the same time, identifying oneself as Black is likely to influence the manner in which one behaves.

PRACTICAL IMPORTANCE OF CULTURE AND ETHNICITY FOR DEVELOPMENT AND BEHAVIOR

In terms of the relevance of culture and ethnicity to research, practice, and policy in developmental-behavioral pediatrics, this distinction between status and function is of crucial importance. In fact, it may have greater practical importance than the distinctions between culture and ethnicity, since both of these social-group indicators influence the manner in which persons are treated by the social order and define the way a person functions within the social order.

All societies, certainly all technologically developed societies, are organized hierarchically in terms of the diverse groups of which they are composed. Since none of these societies has achieved social justice in its allocation of power or its distribution of resources, position within the hierarchy greatly influences an individual's or a group's access to the power (social influence and control) and utilization of the resources (means of subsistence, human services, and means of production) intrinsic to the social order. Since we tend to develop stereotyped assumptions concerning the functional characteristics of status groups, a status designation not only defines the relation to power and resources but also signals (1) what society expects of the person, (2) the nature of available opportunities, and (3) the degree of participation in the reward structure. For example, we anticipate limited intellectual behavior from a low-status group like Blacks despite the fact that many Blacks show high levels of intellectual productivity. It is common knowledge that in the United States employment opportunities for Black youths are 30 to 40 percent lower than those for White youths. Ogbu (1978) reports that a Black youth may expect to be paid about 25 percent less than a White youth for the same job requiring the same amount of education.

This relationship between status and expectation, opportunity and reward exists for other groups as well. Often, one's status defines the manner in which one will be treated. Persons whose ethnic "status" is low but whose social position is high may experience dramatic reversals in the way others approach them if they do not "fit the stereotype." Even in the absence of superior achievement, such generalized expectations are more likely than not to be an error. Status signaled by one's culture or ethnicity can be helpful but can also be misleading when distorted by stereotypes or thoughtlessly applied.

To supplement information concerning status, one can examine these two group indicators—culture and ethnicity—as vehicles of self-definition and identification. They provide clues to an individual's affiliation and serve as frames of reference as we define our orientation, make judgments, and set standards. They often provide a source of aspiration for behavior models. They also transmit technique, grant or deny legitimacy, and convey social meaning.

Since most socialization experiences are perceived in reference to one's gender role, culture, and ethnicity, these three contexts for development are powerful forces in the definition of self and the development of personal identity. Even the structure of one's gender role is influenced by the culture in which it is developed and the ethnic group to which an individual belongs. Relative degrees of aggression, assertiveness, independence, nurturance, and the like tend to vary in different cultures and ethnic groups. As such, different groups encourage and support varying degrees of these characteristics in gender-role socialization. Likewise, parental role, the nature of childhood, role as breadwinner, and socialization to work and to leisure are influenced by these contexts. Thus, the emerging personal identity and elements of self-definition are rooted in cultural and ethnic experiences. Similarly, after family, which cannot be separated from culture and ethnicity, these social-group indicators are primary reference points for affiliation. The individual's tie to his or her ethnic group and identification with the indigenous culture are among the most deeply entrenched human associations. So strong is this identity that when one is isolated from one's cultural or ethnic group, there is a tendency to use symbols of cultural or ethnic affiliation, and for members of the same group we seek each other out in alien environments. Witness the previously unacquainted "Americans" who greet each other as long-lost relatives on a chance encounter in Accra.

PROBLEMS IN CROSS-CULTURAL AND CROSS-ETHNIC PROFESSIONAL INTERACTION

Language Barrier—Meanings

The salience, strength and ubiquity of culture as forces shaping the behavior of individuals and groups may either facilitate or complicate social adaptation. In isolated or insulated cultures the potential for provincialism and recalcitrance is great and precludes the adoption of new models, values, and behaviors. On the other hand, in situations of cultural and ethnic heterogeneity and pluralism, we confront problems in communication and in evaluation and in trying to reconcile contradictions. We are accustomed to dual language situations, in which we may not recognize or know the meanings of the word symbols a patient uses, and even to some instances where a word is familiar but the meaning is different. We are less accustomed to the situation in which a person's customs, ritual behaviors, and underlying values are different not understood, and not appreciated. Communication under these circumstances is, more often than not, miscommunication. The intent and significance of a message may be missed because it contradicts our own indigenous customs or values. Under such circumstances, we try to reduce this dissonance but may, in the process, distort what is being communicated. For example, introducing infant formula to feed babies in cultures where food processing and handling routines are quite different or less technologically advanced may have deleterious effects on these babies health because of errors or their measurement or use. These errors often result when traditional practices are applied by the mother to whom these materials and procedures are alien and not fully understood. Similarly, in less affluent and medically uninformed families, medications may be diluted or the dosage reduced in order to make them last because the user does not appreciate the need for a certain level of dosage for the drug to be effective. Such frugality may be appropriate to the indigenous culture and circumstances but inappropriate when applied to carefully prescribed and calibrated medication.

Language Barrier—Functional Significance

It is not only form and meaning of language but *function* of language that may vary from one culture or ethnic group to another. Miscommunication is more likely when a message used in the culture of the sender to pass on information or instructions is interpreted in the culture of the receiver as an indication of status or authority. Under such circumstances, as much attention may need to be given to the one who conveys the message as to the content of the message. As the responsibilities of paramedical personnel increase, we should be mindful that a patient may disregard a directive or prescriptive procedure unless it comes from the doctor. Similarly, with our increased effort to have patients assume greater responsibility for their own health, our efforts at providing options from which patients may choose may result, in certain populations, in the judgment that systemic intervention may not be necessary, since the doctor has left so much to the discretion of the patient or the family.

Thus, since specific cultures may attach different functions as well as different meanings to the language, it is imperative that the impact of culture on language be considered in cross-cultural professional contacts. My non-English speaking patient may know enough English to understand the meaning of the words but may misunderstand the intent of the language or the function I intended the language to serve. Since in health care we depend so heavily on the ability to of the patient or the family to through, problems in cross-cultural and cross ethnic communication loom large unless care is taken to ensure that transposition as well as translation of the language is accurate.

SOCIAL STEREOTYPES

Another source of communicative error rests with our tendency to develop stereotyped notions concerning what other people are like and what they mean as result of extensive or intensive contact. We may then appropriately generalize our insights or impressions and apply them to an entire group of people, as if they were homogeneous masses. Instead, we must be aware of the diversity of racial or ethnic groups. For example, although Puerto Ricans and Cubans may share some elements of language and culture, they strongly distinguish themselves from one another, sometimes to the extent of showing open hostility toward the others and toward those who lump them together. Students of cultural and ethnic groups increasingly assert that ethnic differences within groups are as important as differences *between* them. Consequently, if one is to be sensitive to cultural and ethnic variety, one must take the time to identify and understand the specific identity held by the person or persons rather than the general identity assigned by others to the person.

DIFFERENCES IN DIALECT

Occasionally we may incorrectly assume that people share the same culture and language when they in fact use different dialects or have different cultural styles (variations on the same culture). One may tend to consider the dominant culture as the norm and to interpret the language or behavior according to the meaning ascribed to it by those in the dominant culture. However, this approach often leads to a misunderstanding about what is being expressed. One striking illustration of this is the use by young Black males of the verbal exchange called the "dozens." Both the language and its expression have special meanings that may be interpreted by an outsider as hostile and belligerent but to the initiated is recognized as friendly competition, seldom if ever used between enemies. In this case the dominant culture norm actually contradicts the meaning of this "specialized" behavior.

PROBLEMS IN EVALUATION

Problems in miscommunication are also reflected in problems of evaluation. When we judge members of a culture or ethnic group other than our own, we confront several sources of distortion.

Evaluative Bias. Banks (1975) noted that when we are called upon to evaluate a person's behavior that is judged to be negative, we tend to look for external causative factors if that person is a member of the same group. If the individual comes from an alien group, however, we tend to look for internal causative factors–within the person. Thus, when the lower-class Black mother is late for or misses an appointment the tendency is to conclude that "these people are like that, irresponsible and chronically late." When the middle class, Caucasian mother shows the same behavior, we are likely to conclude that something has prevented her from arriving on time. Similarly, the popularly held notion is that low-status outgroup parents are more likely to be child abusers while higher status ingroup parents have problems that may sometimes drive them to abuse or neglect their children.

Chauvinistic Models. All of us tend to suffer from provincialism, which makes us chauvinistic. The models we know and have experienced are usually the models we look toward for ourselves and others. When called upon to make judgments about behavior, we rely on the models that we are familiar with. Since few of us are genuinely bicultural or multicultural, we refer to models from the culture with which we identify. Thus, our conceptions of and judgments about, say, good parenting or wholesome development, responsible patients or adequate males, are likely to be biased in favor of idiosyncratic or chauvinistic models that bear little relationship to the realities of the lives of people from another culture.

Idiosyncratic Values. Evaluative judgments made across cultural and ethnic boundaries may be invalid unless the values that guide a person's behavior and shape the purposes and goals of that behavior are recognized and understood. In one culture, longevity may be valued more than the richness of contemporary life experience. In some African cultures the number of children in a family may be valued higher than the survival of a single child, since having many children is in part a function of the parents' expectation that some of their offspring will not survive. Similarly, in cultures where disability is viewed as a handicap for the society as well as for the individual, investment in the survival of a disabled person is not highly valued. Cultural groups not faced with the demands of technology and geared to traditions of experimental validation may ascribe less value and precision to measurement, use of language, and observance of time. These and other differences in values idiosyncratic to specific groups significantly affect the behavior and attitudes of culture and ethic group members. The skillful clinician will probe and observe carefully to discover and appreciate these differences in order to adapt prescriptions and treatments to the individual.

Pluralistic Criteria. In the clinician's process of adaptation, problems of pluralistic criteria and the reconciliation of contradictions are crucial factors. Obviously, in some circumstances, a standard criterion must be set. Certain conditions are essential to survival. Practices that greatly increase the risk of ill health, permanent damage, or death must be prevented. Under such circumstances one cannot accept multiple criteria. However, in some cases, a number of different routes will reach the same end. An example would be nutrition, since, within limits, pluralistic criteria are permitted to assure an adequate diet that takes into account cultural differences. In other situations where there is greater tolerance for variation, the manner in which the task is done, the frequency with which the practice is engaged, the precision demanded, as well as the choice of ends may well be left pluralistic so as to accommodate the lifestyles and preferences of the people served. After all, in health matters, which must be self-monitored, general compliance is often better than no compliance at all, and self-directed compliance is thought to be a function of personal identification with and acceptance of the procedure.

RECONCILING CONTRADITIONS

We face a more difficult problem in having to reconcile contradictions born of cultural differences. Here the responsible clinician has fewer degrees of freedom. Again, when the contradiction reflects preference, style, or aesthetic values, the conflict should be resolved in favor of the patient's bias. However, when the issues involve life-threatening or permanent negative sequelae, we turn first to the informed judgments of parents and ultimately to our own responsibilities to respect and advance human development. This may require the imposition of an alien standard, goal, or practice upon a reluctant patient. In these cases, I ask myself the following questions when making professional decisions about a patient's care: Does my decision represent the best-informed and most honest judgment that I can make under the circumstances? Does my decision increase the alternatives for wholesome development rather than reduce them for this person?

15
Supplementation and Supplantation as Alternative Education Strategies

In this chapter written in collaboration with A. Saa Meroe, we present a brief overview of such school reforms as curriculum intensification, the implementation of performance indicators (i.e., standardized testing on national and state levels), and the professional development of teaching staff. We then discuss the core features of promising programs directed towards students of color. Next, we consider the possible strengths and weaknesses of the recent movement for the privatization of schools and the devolution of institutional management from the federal and state levels to individual schools. Finally, we turn to the issue of the need for involving family and community members more vigorously in the support and supervision of academic achievement through various forms of supplementary education as an alternative to the supplantation of public schools with privatization.

Varieties of school reform

Over the past three presidential administrations, there have been a number of proposals for school reforms that bear the stamp of various constituencies' visions for an adequate education. The unanimous assumption underlying these reforms are that public schools are not performing as well as they ought. The distinguishing characteristics between these reforms have to do with a sense of esteem held for the idea of public education and various conceptualizations of the weaknesses and ultimate purposes of public education.

For example, proposals for "intensification" assume that public schools are not offering rigorous and sufficient saturation in core items of traditional curricula (e.g., English literacy, mathematics and the natural sciences). Not only should students be exposed to more course material, but they also should be exposed for longer periods by the extension of the school day and the school year and the assignment of more work to be completed at home.

255

Reforms that go by the names of "accountability" and "performance indicators" advocate the further implementation of standardized testing and other achievement assessments in light of heightened academic standards (supposedly reflected in intensification reforms). Additionally, these new standards can entail stricter codes for student conduct (e.g., behavior and dress, etc.). Systems designed to encourage student compliance with these new regulations include, on one hand, awards and honors for high achievement and, on the other hand, grade retention or reduced academic opportunities and extracurricular privileges if students fail to meet GPA minimums as well as more punitive sanctions for misconduct. Furthermore, school administrations and staff members would also be subject to continuous assessments, rankings, and competitions for financial rewards.

In the course of the narrowing of traditional core curriculums, some reforms have suggested the dismantling of Transitional Bilingual Education (TBE) and the reinstitution of full English Immersion programs. This runs counter to research findings that language minority students in multi-year TBE programs not only develop bilingual literacy but also outperform Immersion cohorts in math and science achievement. Nevertheless, the rationale for the abolition of TBE is that educational institutions should be promoting a homogeneous curriculum (for the production of homogeneous populations) (Berliner & Biddle, 1994; Brisk, 1998; Lucas, Henze, & Donato, 1990; Miller, 1995; Rivera & LaCelle-Peterson, 1993; Trueba, 1989; Zentella, 1997).

In a similar vein, some reforms demonstrate a growing dismissal of the special needs of some students in favor of gifted and talented programs. While this move resonates with the general call for higher standards and core curriculum intensification, countless researchers have called attention to the *de facto* segregation between high SES, Asian- and European American students and low SES African-, Latina/o- and Native American students when it comes to the populations most likely to be served by gifted versus special education curriculums (e.g., Darling-Hammond, 1998; Oakes, 1985; 1996).

These types of school reform proposals have troubling implications for the academic welfare of low SES ethnic minority students who are currently having problems in our educational institutions. As many commentators note, if certain groups of students are presently struggling from underachievement, what likelihood is there that the universal elevation of academic standards will attend to their needs? This is not to say that these students would not benefit from enriched curriculums; however, without sufficient interventions for their present challenges, more rigorous standards have a strong potential for amplifying cycles of failure and the displacement of these students from the mainstream endowments of schooling.

Particular reforms for non-Asian students of color

There are smaller scale programs and interventions that have demonstrated promise in reversing the patterns of underachievement among ethnic minority students. A review by Borman, Stringfield & Rachuba (1998) identifies interventions that target student and school characteristics relevant to enhancing academic performance. Student characteristics include engagement with school events and practices, identification with high achievement values, and personal skills for resiliency such as independence, interpersonal facility, flexibility, and the maintenance of positive ties with adults (typically parents) and peers with high and stable expectations for achievement. High achieving ethnic minority students also tend to come from higher SES backgrounds and experience less housing mobility than lower achieving counterparts.

Features of the school environment that encourage academic success are teachers' positive attitudes and high expectations for students regardless of ethnic or SES group membership and lower percentages of poverty among the student population. Additionally, such schools employ pedagogical strategies that are student-centered, emphasize comprehension and personal relevance (as opposed to rote memorization), and demonstrate instructional flexibility and respect for cultural diversity. Also, students of color who are exposed to gifted and talented curricula tend to develop higher levels of proficiency. It is, of course, unclear whether this is a function of the superior education treatment, a result of selection bias, or a combination of the two.

Reviewing the reforms of the Calvert School, the Comer School Development Model, Core Knowledge, Paideia, and Success for All, Borman et. al, find that programs such as the Comer Model and Success for All take a holistic approach to the well-being of students by focusing on academic, psychological, and social needs. Success for All and Paideia both use cooperative learning strategies between school peers while the latter program uses exploratory and meaning-focused group discussion (of a Socratic style). The Calvert School emphasizes the development of expertise through revisions of student work. Overall, these are programs that offer challenging curricula, student-centered and cooperative pedagogical methods (between students and with teachers), diverse and integrated student bodies (in terms of ethnicity and SES), and shared values for high achievement among peers, family and community members.

Fashola & Slavin (1997) find that, among the variety of national educational reforms implemented in elementary and middle schools, the most effective programs have the following characteristics: they are developed in the context of university-based, national or regional initiatives in contrast to more commercial packages; these programs focus on a well-defined cluster of goals that are pursued with clear guidelines, coherent curricula, and instructional methods; there are clear standards and procedures for professional development among the faculty that involve intensive training, staff cooperation, and technical support; and educational outcomes are repeatedly assessed throughout the course of implementation.

Analyses of the common characteristics of effective school settings (for all grades) argue that smaller class sizes and school populations facilitate stronger interpersonal ties between students and teachers and may promote more interaction between students of different ethnicities; diversified curriculums and learning experiences outside the classroom are more engaging and challenging for students and teachers; cooperative learning strategies and school curriculum and governance procedures, that centrally involve student input, promote a greater sense of students' academic agency, identification, responsibility and community with peers; and extended periods of school-related contacts support interpersonal continuities allow for more comprehensive monitoring of student progress throughout the years (e.g., longer school years, consistent relationships over the years between a group of students and a homeroom teacher, etc.) (Darling-Hammond, 1998; Jones, 1998; McQuillan, 1998; Wang et al., 1995).

The school reforms discussed above point to at least two main issues for reversing minority student achievement. First, such students greatly benefit from exposure to enriched educational environments and practices directed at intellective development. High academic expectation and values, challenging course materials, engaging teaching methods, and sufficient material resources – conditions typically available to our most privileged and academically able young citizens – are equally, if not more critical to the achievement of students of color. Secondly, effective school reforms for minority and low-income students tend to employ holistic approaches for addressing the needs particular to the individual student and the communities from which these students hail. Inventiveness and good intentions alone will not be sufficient for the further propagation of these programs; the effective implementation of these interventions demand adequate financial resources in the way of curriculum, teaching, assessment, and professional development (Borman et al., 1998; Darling-Hammond, 1998a & b; Fashola & Slavin, 1995).

Full funding of education

Compared to other Western countries, the United States evidences a legacy of unequal—and inequitable—funding of education. In contrast to other industrialized nations that establish federal statutes for educational expenditures, most school funding in the United States is generated from local and state tax bases. This translates into significant discrepancies between states and between school districts with healthier tax bases and those in poorer rural and central city locales. As a result, schools districts serving middle to high SES populations can allocate 1.5 to even 5 times more tax dollars per student than poorer districts (Berliner & Biddle, 1994; Darling-Hammond, 1998; Kozol, 1991; Miller, 1995).

In turn the school district's resources also determine the quality of school resources and teaching staff. Consequently, there can be great differences in the quality of educational resources varying across districts and states and almost universally, these disparities impact the poor and people of color. Given that these populations typically arrive at school with greater needs than more socioeconomically privileged students, it is not enough for schools to be funded equally. Schools need to be funded equitably, that is, in proportion to the existing demands of the clientele served (Gordon, 1985; Gordon, 1999; Miller, 1995). As many have noted, future endeavors in educational research, school reforms, and budgetary considerations should incorporate the notion that high achievement should not be dependent upon students' middle or upper class status or the presence of two highly sophisticated parents (with one working solely in the home) (Berliner & Biddle, 1995).

Gordon and Gordon (1999) and Miller (1995) propose even more comprehensive approaches to educational funding. Namely, expenditures to promote high academic achievement should also address the larger issue of the distribution of wealth in the United States. It may not be sufficient to solely ameliorate the poverty-induced disabilities that children bring to their schools. Interventions must enhance these students' chances of growing up in less oppressive communities and familial circumstances and justify their academic efforts with the likelihood of improved life chances.

259

Professional development of administrative, teaching, and counseling staff

The development of high achieving ethnic minority students is certainly related to the professional standards and expertise required of their teachers. We already know that lower SES students are more likely to be taught by less experienced and less capable teachers than student populations from higher SES groups. Compared to other Western countries and other domestic professions, teaching staff in the United States endure middling levels of professionalization, expertise, autonomy/authority, and financial reward. Gordon (1999) suggests that the future professional development of teachers address the following three domains: (a) the content of pre-service and in-service education for teachers; (b) the diversification and flexibility of the methods by which continuing education is made available to teaching staff; and (c) the organizational and logistical characteristics of professionalization programs.

Programs for teacher education have typically focused on the sufficient mastery of particular subjects and the use of newly initiated pedagogical strategies. In addition to these central foci, Gordon encourages the explicit development of teachers' recognition and demonstration of requisite features of intellective competence. In other words, it is both conducive to higher levels of teacher confidence and student comprehension if teachers possess expertise in the subject matter as well as the cognitive competence and disciplinary repertoires that undergird that mastery.

In Darling-Hammond's (1999) terminology, teachers must have expertise in both "pedagogical content knowledge" as well as "pedagogical learner knowledge." That is teachers must develop facility not only with the "art" of teaching but also an understanding of the scientific knowledge and practices underlying pedagogical innovations (e.g., cognitive and developmental psychology). Teachers should be comfortable with employing flexible methods for the ongoing analysis, assessment and documentation of student comprehension and progress as well as the relative efficacy of various teaching approaches according to subject matter, student needs, classroom characteristics and available resources. As far as encouraging student engagement, it is critical that teachers have a wide repertoire for relating to the variety of individual and cultural differences that students bring to the classroom and understanding how these differences may demand diverse strategies for motivating each student (also see Oakes and Lipton, 1998).

Griffin (1999) and Darling-Hammond (1999) are two strong advocates of the refashioning of traditional models of teacher education. In their view, the preparation of teachers should be elaborated beyond what is typically available in undergraduate programs or education. For example, Darling-Hammond (1996; 1999) supports the trend for graduate level teacher preparation, as is the case in many European nations. In addition to years of undergraduate training within the university, prospective teachers would be required to undergo two to three years of graduate training in accord with the standards of other professions.

Furthermore, the professionalization process must involve placing prospective teachers within actual school settings. For example, within an "apprenticeship" mode, student teachers are more likely to effectively integrate pedagogical theory with practice and to be prepared for the constant challenges of teaching once they enter the profession. As is the case with the instruction of students, teacher education itself should diversify its techniques beyond traditional didactic and passive learning methods. Teacher education should involve *in situ* and collaborative problem solving with other teachers and expert supervision. The introduction of novel technical supports, instructional materials and resources should be integrated within performative and hands-on training experiences (Darling-Hammond, 1999; Goodlad, 1990; Griffin, 1999; Whitford & Metcalf-Turner, 1999).

In the case of the logistical features of programs for teacher development, measures should be taken to insure that administration staff and pedagogical experts do not issue educational reforms without the input of teaching and counseling staff (McClure, 1999). The neglect to encourage cooperative efforts with teaching staff and to ensure the provision of additional temporal and financial resources can result in teachers' disenchantment with and resistance to promising innovations. Additionally, pressures on school staff to produce heightened student performances on standardized assessments undermine the possibility of teachers experimenting with and tailoring their expertise according to new pedagogical methods (i.e., the likelihood of "teaching to the test"). The need for closer analysis and supervision of individual student progress (i.e., adaptive education) entails a negotiable teacher-student ratio. Teacher development programs that attend to the range of these demands promise greater intellective gains for student achievement, competence and confidence; nonetheless, without high standards for teachers' proficiency, ongoing training, professional status and agency, any such practices are likely to be less effective (Darling-Hammond, 1999; Griffin, 1995).

School choice and privatization

Issues concerning parental choice in the education of children have emerged among minority populations in response to the perceived crisis in education. African American parents in particular understandably harbor considerable doubts about the extent to which their children are adequately served by public schools. African American pundits for school choice are likely to cite the importance of educational options, increased personal control of the distribution of education-directed revenue, freedom from the political fetters of teachers' unions, more institutional accountability, and the potential for greater parental advocacy (Chubb, 1997; Chubb & Moe, 1990; Fulani, 1999; Vanourek et al., 1997). Among other segments of the population, choice appears to be increasing in popular acceptance as much out of concern for social insulation (from lower SES and ethnic minority groups) as for the pursuit of high-quality education.

Approaches to school choice range from state and federal level proposals for vouchers, tax credits and rebates for parochial and private school tuition expenses to opportunities for parental choice between district-wide public, magnet, charter, and alternative/community schools. Most central to the national debate have been the potential gains and hazards of implementing wide-scale voucher and charter school programs. Although the campaign to introduce voucher programs began more than thirty years ago, the actual distribution of vouchers and the development of charter schools are less than a decade old. As such, assessments of these relatively new interventions are usually inconclusive (Anyon, 1997; Henig, 1994; Sarason, 1998; Whitty, 1997).

In general, proponents of voucher programs claim that parents should have the right to send their children to a public school of their choice or parochial and private facilities if they are dissatisfied with the performance of assigned schools. With Adam Smith-like faith in the tendencies of the free market towards social equilibrium, voucher advocates, starting with Friedman's (1962) proposals in *Capitalism and Freedom,* look to deregulated parental choice as a means for addressing educational resource disparities and encouraging competition between private and public schools. By this logic, access to a sufficient education is less of a universal right than it is a private good for purchase. Intertwined with the appeals for an educational marketplace are the larger trends towards the privatization of social welfare services in generals and the dismantling of federal, state and labor union jurisdiction (Henig, 1997; Whitty, 1998).

Voucher-type options do present a reasonable means for protecting students' interests against those of large, and perhaps inflexible, school-related bureaucracies. However, vouchers, scholarships, and/or tax credits do not necessarily remedy the great disparities between the levels of resources that lower versus higher SES families are able to allocate for educational expenses beyond tuition (e.g., transportation, study aids, etc.). Furthermore, the financial allowances that are provided by vouchers to lower income families typically are insufficient for covering the tuition costs of high quality private institutions. Rather, for lower SES families, these benefits are usually only applicable to parochial school attendance. Research does indicate that students of color demonstrate higher levels of achievement in private institutions, a great majority (approximately 90%) of which are church affiliated. Bryk et al. (1993) find that African American students who attend Catholic schools are more likely to graduate from high school and attend four-year colleges. Available research does not enable definitive causal statements. It is unclear as to whether these schools are better or if the families who choose to use them are more academically motivated and are more active in the support of the academic development of their children. Nevertheless, there are a number of problems with the use of public funds for the support of parochial schools. First, voucher programs present a violation of the Constitutional separation of church and state. The re-direction of public funds to such private institutions not only results in the funding of religious organizations but also the loss of the taxpayer's voice with regard to the particular practices instituted in these schools. Additionally, the transference of funds from public school budgets to those of parochial and private institutions risks weakening the resources available to the least advantaged students who do not enroll in voucher programs (Berliner & Biddle, 1994; Darling-Hammond, 1998; Doerr, Menendez & Swomley, 1996; Whitty, 1997).

In comparison to voucher-type programs, there appears to be even greater public support for charter schools (Berliner and Biddle 1994; Henig 1994). Charter schools are autonomously operated institutions that are funded with public revenue. There are two basic types of charter schools: (1) those that have been converted from formerly public facilities and (2) those that are newly formed by teachers, parents, community residents, school administrators, institutions for higher education (e.g., colleges and universities), not-for-profit institutions (e.g., museums, institutes, etc.), or for-profit business firms. Existing private institutions are usually not eligible for conversion to charter status.

Most charter schools are purportedly based upon the following objectives:

(a) to improve academic achievement especially among "at risk" populations; (b) to increase educational options for families and encourage greater parental involvement; (c) to create wider professional opportunities for administrative and teaching staff; and (d) to shift the accountability systems from those based upon rules to those more attentive to performance. A more tacit assumption about charter schools refers to colloquial notions about the benefits of market competition. The idea is that charter schools, if successful, will drive traditional public schools to improve their own services in order to remain viable.

Supporters of charter schools claim that low-income students of color tend to make greater gains in achievement after enrolling in charter schools (Chubb & Moe, 1990; Vanourek et al., 1997). Charter schools also hold specific attractions for underserved ethnic minority populations given charter schools' liberty to focus on particular educational concerns. For example, some charter schools explicitly target "at risk" students of color, promote the development of advanced proficiency in the sciences, mathematics, arts or business, proactively generate stronger coalitions between school staff, parents and community-based institutions, feature smaller class sizes and overall student bodies, and/or create school environments and curricula that focus on specific ethnocultural worldviews and subject matter (Nathan, 1996; Sarason, 1998).

Critics of the school choice movement voice concern about a few central issues: the dismantling of the public school system and the potential for educational re-segregation (Berliner & Biddle, 1994; Henig, 1996; Orfield, 1996; Orfield & Eaton, 1996; Whitty, 1997). In terms of the distribution of school-allocated funds, the district's per-student allowances follow the student. Therefore, the transfer of students to charter schools also means the loss of funds for the public school that once served these students. If a school is perceived as ineffective, it is more likely to be divested of funds that might otherwise be redirected into its future school-based reforms. If the district-wide demand for charter schools exceeds the supply, students remaining in traditional public schools will be likely to suffer from the depletion of much needed resources.

Admission to charter schools is usually determined by lottery or first-come-first-served policies. At the same time, there are selection mechanisms that undermine universal access to these facilities. Many charter schools actively recruit students according to the particular emphasis of the school and subsequently select the most "appropriate" students—often, this can mean academically or artistically gifted students. As Whitty (1997) observes in his review of the "quasi-privatization" of education in New Zealand, the United Kingdom and the United States, in a marketplace atmosphere, the likelihood for charter schools to resort to "cream-skimming"— choosing the best-prepared students—is high. In demonstrating that their services are among the best available, focus will be given to the quality of the "products," that is, the students themselves. Less attention will be given to the effectiveness of the school in enhancing levels of student performance. Instead, consumers will look to present levels of student achievement (which often reflect the extant strengths that students bring to the school) instead of the gains that students have made since enrolling in the school.

Furthermore, parent consumers tend to approach the educational marketplace with traditional and entrenched conceptions of "a good school." A number of charter school applicants are generated by word of mouth among parents. Parents are also more likely to choose institutions that are conveniently located and pose fewer concerns about social integration. These tendencies present the likelihood that if charter schools open in relatively segregated communities (in terms of ethnicity and SES), the student body will most likely reflect these same characteristics if not closely regulated by the licensing agencies (Henig, 1996; Orfield, 1996; Orfield & Eaton, 1996).

Sarason (1998), drawing upon observations of charter schools in Arizona, Connecticut, Illinois, and Massachusetts, warns that in order for charter schools to meet their goals there must be some understanding of the "contributing factors you seek to prevent." In short, the attitudes and practices of school agents (e.g., administration and teaching staff) in the past have contributed to part of the problem; therefore, those who develop and implement charter initiatives must confront the adverse consequences of their "over learned" and counterproductive repertoires. Sarason anticipates a number of specific problems that charter schools might encounter:

1. In terms of institutional and programmatic planning, there is an underlying presumption that subsequent reforms or improvements will not be necessary for charter institutions. As such, there is no alternative plan required if the charter school encounters difficulties such as changes in leadership or the need for additional resources. Financially, the state aid formulas for per pupil costs are not realistic for the creation of a new school and the expectations of superior outcomes. Without subsidies

from external sources (e.g., for-profit corporations such as Boston's Edison Project), insufficient start-up funds and monies for continuing expenses are among the most central challenges for founders of charter schools (also see Henig, 1994; Nathan, 1996). In short, the re-distribution of funds for education via charter programs is not the same as the investment of greater amounts of financial resources in US education.

2. As for the governance of charter schools, a well-defined structure of decision-making is not required in the application of a charter and, therefore, a wide disparity exists in this area. The reality of a shared power model of governance—offering students, parents, teachers, and administrators equal voices—is much more laborious and time-intensive than initially expected. Schools that envision an environment in which students are also policy makers (and feel a sense of ownership) can lack a clear vision, resulting in difficulty with setting appropriate limits and establishing discipline policies. When parents are among the founders of charter schools, there is the additional dilemma of accommodating parents' private interests in their own children with the welfare of the student body as a whole. Often schools spend so much time addressing pressing organizational issues, educational issues are not given their needed focus. Teachers (who are typically European American, middle-class, young and relatively inexperienced), and principals put in longer hours, increasing the possibility of early burnout. Also, ethnic diversity among the student population is often compromised for smaller classes and autonomy.

3. It is not uncommon for charter schools to operate within a hostile community environment that feels charter schools are taking money away from public schools. Given that most public schools probably will not welcome the presence of new charter schools, this institutional and professional isolation may frustrate many opportunities for collaborative efforts. As such, Sarason suggests that charter schools attempt to create networks amongst themselves for the sharing of important resources such as technical assistance and support.

266

Once reliable data has been collected on the various charter school programs developing around the country, Sarason predicts that we are likely to see an encouraging subset of successful charter programs among a majority of inadequate or failing experiments. Other scholars note that, despite the laudable intentions of charter school founders, a national *laissez-faire* policy with regard to educational reform has the potential to create a new subsets of troubles in addition to those we are already seeking to ameliorate (Berliner & Biddle, 1994; Henig, 1996; Orfield, 1996; Orfield & Eaton, 1996; Whitty, 1997).

The limitations of existing school reforms

Even the best programs are not radically altering minority achievement on a mass scale given the uneven levels of quality and quantity in the delivery of these interventions. Success for All is, perhaps, the most carefully and rigorously engineered and implemented of these reform initiatives. As is true of other interventions, this initiative has been associated with improvements in the achievement of targeted students. However, Success for All and the best of the remaining reform programs still leave 30 percent to 40 percent of the targeted population seriously behind in terms of academic development. Several years ago, Benjamin Bloom introduced "Mastery Learning," a program based upon rigorous teaching and repeated exposure to unlearned material. Bloom boasted about the capacity of mastery learning to bring 65 percent of the targeted population up to grade level. Most of these reform programs do make a difference and are to be encouraged but they have not solved the problems of academic under-productivity in African American, Latino American and Native American children.

If one is to take seriously the importance of human resource development capital, and the extensive use of supplementary educational experiences by more affluent and successful students, it becomes obvious that many of the factors contributing to high levels of academic achievement come from outside the school. Schooling may work because it builds upon a variety of capital resources that children bring with them to school. As such, schooling must build upon or compensate for the absence of these varieties of human resource development capital. Students' exposure to high quality educational programs will be enhanced by economic and social stability in the family as well as familial, peer, and community involvement with and support of academic development. These challenges require more comprehensive public policies that go beyond educational institutions to additionally target raising the quality of living standards for all citizens in the form of employment opportunities, political participation, health care, housing, and the continued implementation of civil/human rights.

Similarly, many affluent and sophisticated parents do not depend alone on what happens in school for the education of their children. These families use a wide range of supplements to schooling to ensure that adequate academic and personal development is achieved. This strategy involves using the public schools for whatever they can provide and to supplement those educational services with the additional services that are deemed necessary to the adequate education of each child. As is discussed later in this paper, these supplements include guidance and tutoring, travel, expectation and demand, modeling, exposure to high culture, supports for academic development in the home, and other factors.

What is clear from a survey of school reform movements is that there are limits to what we can expect. Even if schooling were perfected and distributed equitably, it is possible that low status minorities would still be left behind, in part because it does not appear that schools can be made to function as efficiently as may be needed, and because schooling, at its best, is insufficient to meet the academic and personal development needs of most children. Schooling, public and private, appears to require supplementation by a host of additional educative experiences. We see the need for continued efforts to improve and reform schools and increase access to society's broader range of educative facilities and functions. At the same time, we hold that there are limits to what can be immediately expected from school reform and that there are numerous problems with the supplantation of public schools with private institutions. Below, supplementary education will be discussed as a viable alternative.

The Idea of Supplementary Education and the Development of High-Performance Learning Communities

At least since the first major investigation and assessment of the equality of educational opportunities (Coleman et al., 1966), we have been aware that schools alone cannot ensure high academic achievement. On the other hand, we also know that high academic attainment is related to well-endowed capital resources that are not easily garnered by the populations with which we are most concerned. High levels of parental and community engagement in the active support academic learning typically results in higher morale for the school staff and their student clients. In the case of communities of color, there may exist financial, temporal, and sociocultural barriers to adequate involvement in such supports for schooling. For example, even African-, Latina/o- and Native American students from relatively middle and high SES backgrounds still perform less well than Asian- and European American members of lower SES groups. Nevertheless, we do believe that it is both crucial and possible to develop what resources do exist in less privileged communities of color. One means for addressing this issue involves the development of what Gordon (1997) in general refers to as supplementary education. He has developed, as an example of supplementary education, a proposal for the creation of "high performance learning communities."

The idea of supplementary education is based on the premise that beyond proficiency with the school's primary curriculum, high student achievement is closely correlated with exposure to learning experiences that take place outside of school in family and community-based activities. For low SES and non-Asian students of color, these opportunities are generally underdeveloped in comparison to other ethnic groups. For instance, in the home, students benefit from home computers, collections of books, magazines and journals, and the academic assistance and encouragement of older siblings and/or parents. In terms of community resources, local library privileges, the organization of mentoring and tutoring programs, peer-based study groups, Saturday and/or after-school academies, the attendance of various cultural events and visits to institutes for folk and "high" cultures also aid in the development of proactive and engaged dispositions for learning.

Community leaders and others adept at student advocacy must share their skills and experiences for the further development of parent-teacher-administration alliances. School administration and staff must develop ways to involve parents in the school experience and provide guidance for home-based learning experiences that complement/supplement the primary curriculum. Mentoring and peer group activities and organizations that support academic achievement and development and offer alternatives to risky social behaviors have also proved effective.

In general, high degrees of congruency between values promulgated at school, at home, and in one's immediate community are associated with high academic achievement. What may be important are students' perceptions that what happens at school matters and is consistent with what parents and other family members consider important. This is conveyed through expectations, physical provisions for academic pursuits, attitudes toward intellectual activity, and the models that are available for children to emulate. These supplementary practices contribute to the development of high performance learning communities and shared values for the importance of academic achievement for personal fulfillment, community development, and social and political mobility.

The notion of "high-performance learning communities" refers to the establishment of pro-academic community-based initiatives and cultures that support academic achievement within family/home, peer, community, and school environments. With respect to community as a context for human learning, we proceed from the assumption that community can be thought of as an institution or a locale—people and places where common kinship, purpose, mores and values are shared. Community can also be more symbolic, that is, not identifiable as a concrete place but strongly expressed through association at the level of shared belief and in communal spirit. Community, in this latter sense, functions more like a culture (Gordon and Thomas, 1991). In this proposed initiative, high performance learning communities are not formal institutions (e.g., schools) but close-knit associations between people (families and peer groups) in which relationships are nurtured, where commitment to high academic achievement is a shared purpose, where academic socialization occurs naturally, where pro-academic and pro-social mores and values are promoted, where learning how to support the academic development of each other, and where members are expected to achieve and are rewarded for academic and personal excellence— individual and collective. The idea is to convert the actual families and peer groups to which selected participants belong into high performance learning communities where the application of one's intellective competence to high level academic endeavors is culturally and socially legitimized (Fordham and Ogbu, 1986, Steele, 1992). As should be clear from our descriptions, supplementary education and high performance learning communities are necessarily interpenetrating practices; that is, an effective component of supplementary education would involve the formation of high performance learning communities and a high performance learning community would most likely rely upon a variety of supplementary education practices. These proposals are grounded in three conceptions of human learning:

1. At the core of the initiative is the view of human learning as a social and cooperative endeavor (Vygotsky, 1978, Slavin et al., 1996, Sarason, 1998, Cole et al., 1971, Gordon and Thomas,

1991). We consider that situative—the cultural and social—factors which are associated with academic learning are as important as the substance of what is to be learned and the process by which it is learned. Consequently, attention will be given to the creation of positive social conditions for academic learning such as cooperative learning experiences, organized tutorial, and study groups, the use of athletic style academic coaching, and the creation of ubiquitous high expectations. In addition, attention will be given to reducing the dissonance between hegemonic and ethnic minority identities as is reflected in the phenomenon described as "fear of acting White." (Fordham and Ogbu, 1986) The principal vehicles for addressing the social cooperative nature of learning will be through the creation of high performance learning teams of fifteen students and a coach and teams of parents and teachers who work together in support of the academic and personal development of these teams of students.

2. Human learners are viewed as greatly influenced by the social contexts in which they develop and their achievements are viewed as dependent upon the extent to which social contexts support the aspired ends. Some of these essential contextual supports have been described as various forms of human development resource capital, which enable and facilitate academic learning and personal development. Through the high performance learning community initiative, we seek to strengthen families in their capacities to advocate for and access these varieties of human development resource capital and to place them at the disposal of their children's' academic and personal development.

For example, the Parents for Rockland Youth Supplemental Education (RYSE) is a supplementary education initiative developed by the senior author and Patti Smith. In an effort to address some of these problems, Parents RYSE was created in two suburban communities north of New York City to serve communities of color that were experiencing problems in the academic achievement of their children. The program goals included providing families with some of the human resource and social capital that is naturally available to families from more advantaged homes and making explicit the link between education, cultural integrity, and political power through purposeful attention to political socialization and cultural celebration in the context of a multicultural society. These goals were achieved by providing parent education that focused on: (a) better understandings of the school's curriculum and educational services; (b) familiarity with the respective responsibilities of teachers, counselors, and parents and the importance of developing parent-teacher alliances; (c) facility with implementing educational practices for their children outside of school; and (d) the development of highly effective parenting and student advocacy skills. Supplementary education services in the form of Saturday schools and individual tutoring were also provided for the children of these families. These direct services to students were to elaborate upon the students' schoolwork and to model effective out-of-school academic experiences that were necessary for high academic achievement. Family members involved with the RYSE program participated in trips to colleges, universities and cultural events. Parents organized smaller cottage meetings in their homes for mutual support, collective strategizing, and information sharing. Occasionally, more sophisticated (e.g., academically, profession-ally, etc.) members of ethnic minority communities were invited to share their experiences and act as mentors for RYSE parents and students. Ultimately, this package of parent and student services increased parents' acumen in understanding the scope and breadth of experiences in which their children should participate to succeed and excel in a competitive academic environment.

3. We assume that the students selected to participate in this intervention are already in functioning schools that are at least adequate in fostering reasonable levels of achievement among some students. We assume that these students do not need a different pedagogical approach to their education. What these

students need is the additional support that many children from affluent and more academically sophisticated families receive. As such, components of this initiative should target:

- The practical know-how of parents to advocate for and support their children's academic interests and personal development;
- The development and provision of high-quality supplementary educational activities comparable to those available to more affluent and/or academically savvy populations;
- The facilitation of cooperative learning cadres among student peers and social environments that encourage and nurture academic achievement;
- Specific interventions designed to enhance students' skills in academic socialization, a personal understanding of how one thinks and learns and strategies to boost these capacities, and diagnostically-targeted remediation;
- The development of computer literacy for accessing various types of academically-related information and resources;
- The ongoing use of research and evaluation processes to track the overall progress (e.g., strengths and shortcomings) of this initiative and to develop and distribute accessible and culturally tailored guidelines for the implementation of similar programs.

Academic and political socialization to academic achievement

For low SES students and/or students of color, negative school experiences such as low-level tracking, persistent failure and racism can result in disidentification and the outright rejection of aspirations for academic achievement. These reactions may be ameliorated through school-, community, peer- and family-mediated interventions that allow students to grasp the relevance of education not only for potential individual gains in future careers, but also as a means for developing a well-informed understanding of issues of social justice and inroads to political advocacy.

Furthermore, a familiarity with the history of the role of the use of knowledge and skill in the struggle for emancipation and justice can add an element of politicization as an instrument of pedagogy. In the process, students are socialized to their responsibility for self-empowerment and the empowerment of others as well as an understanding of the potential relationships between academic mastery and one's political objectives. Politicized consciousness can be seen as a particular form of supplementary education and a guiding principle for high performance learning communities.

Summary and Conclusions:
Supplantation versus supplementation in public education

Causing some controversy, Coleman et al.'s (1966) study, *Equality of Educational Opportunity,* concluded that differences in the family backgrounds of students, as opposed to school characteristics, accounted for the greatest amount of the variance in their academic achievement. In later works, Mercer (1966) and Wolf (1967; 1995) posited that it is the presence of family environmental supports for academic development that may explain this association between family status and student achievement. The literature on the relationship between academic achievement and quality of schooling is less definitive for all students, but it is clear that features of schooling account for a considerable portion of the variance in the academic achievement of low income and ethnic minority students. It is reasonable to assume that the most academically successful populations (which in the US are mainly European American, Asian American, and the middle, professional classes) tend to have a combination of strong home and school resources support their academic development. The least successful groups (which are mainly African American, Latina/o American, Native American, and the poor) have, on average, a much weaker combination of home and school resources.

Efforts to improve schools on a widespread basis for students from the least successful groups have produced some good results, but there are formidable obstacles to providing high quality schooling to minority populations on a consistent basis. Available evidence also suggests that racial/ethnic group differences in achievement remain even in schools that are regarded as well resourced and serve mostly advantaged (middle class) students. These differences even exist within classrooms (as is the case with demanding college preparatory courses and Advanced Placement courses).

Reform of School Governance

Most of the action on the school reform front has been directed at changes in the organizational structure and governance of schools. In a number of school systems across the nations, efforts are underway to increase teacher participation in decisions concerning what happens in schools. This notion rests on the logical conclusion that people are likely to work more effectively when they are pursuing goals and actions of their own choosing – when they feel some sense of ownership of the programs and projects in which they are involved. The basic idea is consistent with related developments in the industrial sector and is thought to partially explain the reported differences between the productivity of Japanese and US workers.

Site-based management seems to have become the current panacea for much that it considered to be wrong with schooling despite findings that such efforts to date have done more for teacher morale than for student achievement (Ogawa & White, 1994; Whitty, 1997; Wohlstetter, 1995). Most advocates for this approach to school reform argue that real change cannot occur without support from staff and that site-based management is the supposed route to such involvement and support. But active participation in the decision-making and management of schools requires more than authorization to participate. It requires know-how, resources, and societal commitment—none of which are in adequate supply. With respect to know-how, until we strengthen the pedagogical and substantive competence of our teaching force, their involvement in decision-making and school improvement is likely to be of limited effect. In addition, if the primary goal of many of our efforts at school reform is to reduce the incidence of school failure among these students who present very diverse characteristics to the school and who are currently served poorly by our schools, the current reforms in school governance hardly seem to be the treatment of choice.

Efforts at Accountability and Higher Standards

Many of the states, and certainly the federal government, have staked their hopes for school reform and the improvement of education for students at risk of failure on the imposition of higher standards of academic achievement and some attempts at establishing systems whereby schools can be held accountable for their productivity. Now there is no question but that the standards by which we judge academic achievement and to which we consistently fail to hold schools accountable are too low. They compare poorly to the standards achieved in other technologically advanced countries. However, it can be argued that our standards and achievement are low not simply because our sights are too low, but because our practices of and provisions for education are inappropriate to the requirements of educational excellence.

Among the most prominent efforts at goal and standard setting are the president's National Goals for Education and the non-governmental New Standards Project. While for some the National Goals would be measured by a new educational achievement test, New Standards proposes a new system of education assessment. The latter is headed in the right direction with respect to assessment, but both give woefully little attention to the importance of educational inputs. One cannot argue with the substance of the national education goals:

1. By the year 2000, all children in American will start school ready to learn;
2. By the year 2000, the high school graduation rate will increase to at least 90 percent;
3. By the year 2000, American students will leave grades four, eight and twelve having demonstrated competency in challenging subject matter (e.g., mathematics, science, English, history, and geography) and every school will ensure that all students learn to use their minds well in preparation for responsible citizenship, further learning, and productive employment in our modern economy;
4. By the year 2000, US students will be first in the world in science and mathematics achievement; and
5. By the year 2000, every adult will be literate and will possess the knowledge and skills necessary to compete in a global economy and to exercise the rights and responsibilities of citizenship.

In each instance, we see iterated a rational expectation of what will be required of our students if they are to have meaningful, satisfying and responsible participation in the social order. The values reflected in such goals, especially the third goal listed above, send a powerful message to school systems concerning what the nation expects from its educational institutions. However, an extremely negative message is sent by the promulgation of such goals in the absence of the resources, know-how, and a national commitment to ensure that schools and students are enabled to meet these goals. Nothing in the national efforts speaks to the desperate need for staff development and the improvement of the quality of the labor force in schools. Nowhere in that effort is attention given to the states' responsibility for ensuring that schools have the capacities to deliver the educational services necessary to the realization of such goals. Nowhere is there any recognition of the circumstances beyond the school that are conducive to these objectives. Without attention to these extra-school forces, it is folly to expect that the national effort will address questions of responsibility for ensuring that these enabling conditions will prevail.

In the report of the New York City Chancellor's Commission on Minimum Standards (Gordon, 1986), the case was made for the importance of symmetry in the pursuit of school accountability. After identifying achievement-level targets as standards, the Report proposed that standards also be set for professional practice and institutional capacity. New York City, other school districts, the federal government, and New Standards have yet to seriously engage standards for practice and capacity. Yet, if we are to expect that children at risk of failure (and other children as well) will experience great improvements in their academic performance, it is more likely to come from the imposition of higher standards upon those of us who manage their education and guide their learning. The problem is that it is relatively easy to arrive at agreement on what students should know and know how to do while it is very difficult to agree on what the educational inputs should be to achieve these aims without becoming overly prescriptive or without facing—what is more problematic politically—questions concerning entitlement and the fixing of responsibility for costs. If the field can ever agree on a set of standards for professional practice and school capability, do we then have a basis for asking the courts to hold schools or states responsible for making them available, especially to children at risk of school failure?

The Problem with Supplantation

The most aggressively pursued models for the implementation of choice in elementary/secondary education are efforts directed at the privatization of the delivery of educational services. These efforts would result in the supplantation of public education with a vast array of commercially and privately sponsored deliverers. (To supplant is to take the place of or substitute for.) However, discouragement with the effectiveness of public schools is an understandable response to the failure of these institutions to adequately serve low status populations, but the crisis in public education in this country may indeed be as "manufactured" as Berliner and Biddle (1995) claim. Public schools can and do work: for some people and under conditions of appropriate support. Privatization is not the answer.

A. We object to any retreat from public responsibility for the education of all members of our society.

B. We object to the allocation of public funds to support private endeavors.

C. The dependence on the privatized delivery of health care has left the United States with one of the world's most advanced collection of medical technology and one of the weakest systems of health care delivery.

D. The problem is not one of parental choice of schools but parental and community support of schooling.

E Supplanting public with private schools will not address two of the most neglected problems in education: (1) the inequitable distribution of human resource development capital necessary for investment in the academic and personal development of children--health, polity, social networks, income and wealth, relevant cultural experiences and models, opportunities and rewards; and (2) the underpreparation of the teaching force required for the delivery of adequate and sufficient opportunities to learn.

The Potential of Supplementation

In James Comer's most recent book, *Waiting for a Miracle: Why Our Schools Can't Solve Our Problems – And How We Can* (1997), a persuasive argument is made for the limitations of school reform. An even more cogent argument is made for the importance of families and communities taking responsibility for improving and supplementing what happens in school to ensure that the education of our children is effective. Comer suggests that the maximization of the academic/intellective development of minority groups and the poor will require substantial investments in making available to them supplementary supports comparable to those that are available to better-advantaged students. Supplementary education may be needed for both low and high SES segments of the population. Across ethno-cultural groups, high support for academic achievement is not a universal condition. Supplements to formal schooling may fulfill two roles for minority populations in particular:

- helping to compensate for the weaknesses of the schools attended by these students, and
- providing students access to opportunities for intellective development, academic socialization, and high achievement value orientations in the heart of their social networks - regardless of whether students attend weakly or strongly resourced schools.

16
Affirmative Development of Academic Abilities

The construct, affirmative development, appears to have originated in a presentation by Edmund Gordon at a conference, sponsored by the National Action Committee on Minorities in Engineering, in an exchange between Gordon and Scott Miller concerning the persistent underrepresentation and modest performance of minority students in mathematics and the sciences. This may have been seven years or more before Corta-Robles, Gordon, and Miller teamed up with the College Board to create the National Task Force on Minority High Achievement. The construct first appeared in print in the report of the Task Force, Reaching the Top (The College Board, 1999), as the implicit over arching recommendation of the Task Force:

> The continued educational underdevelopment of so many segments of the African American, Latino, and Native American communities makes a very strong case for expanding their access to good schools and to high quality colleges and universities, the latter of which has been a primary focus of affirmative action. But expanded access does not necessarily translate directly into higher academic achievement. Thus, the Task Force recommends that an extensive array of public and private policies, actions, and investments be pursued, which would collectively provide many more opportunities for academic development for underrepresented minority students through the schools, colleges, and universities that they attend, through their homes, and through their communities. We summarize this as a commitment to *affirmative development*.

In this chapter, I continue that discussion.

280

INEQUALITY OF CAPITAL

In the summer of 1958, in a talk at a public hall on 125th Street and Lenox Avenue in Harlem, W.E.B. DuBois mused about his 1903 claim that the "problem of the twentieth century is the problem of the color line." In 1958, he was beginning to consider the possibility that the line between the haves and the have-nots, greatly confounded by color, could emerge as a more critical problem. I think DuBois was correct in 1903 and in 1958. The century between 1900 and 2000 was marked by considerable turmoil associated with racist values and DuBois' "color line," but, equally significant, it was also marked by a monumental decline in the significance of the "color line." Wilson"s book, *Declining Significance of Race* (1978), documented this radical change in our society and validated the DuBoisian prediction that inequalities in the distribution of income and wealth would emerge as more critical.

Skin color and other sources of cultural identity continue to be the basis for troublesome social divisions in the United States and elsewhere. However, I am increasingly persuaded that it is the unequal distribution of resources and the perceived threat of loss of "my share" of those resources that enable cultural, gender, racial, and religious bias to surface and flourish. We did not eliminate racism with the civil rights movement, but we did make enormous strides in moving this nation and other parts of the world away from the worst expressions of discrimination based on race. During the early part of the movement, when masses of ethnically diverse people saw their life chances improving and the opportunities increasing for their children to have lives better than their own, most people in this country were more willing to share those broadening opportunities. As the perception that life was getting better or that it would be better for our children began to wane, we saw increasing antagonism toward organized labor, equality for women, Blacks, Spanish-speaking persons, and others who seemed alien to whatever was passing for "standard American." It is not surprising that a book like *The Bell Curve* (Hernnstein & Murray, 1994) with its rehash of the notion about the "genetic inferiority" of some of us was published in the final decade of the last century. Nor are the tax revolts and the rescinding of affirmative action unexpected. These are the reactions of a desperate populace who have been frightened into incontinence by deindustrialization, by the exportation of production jobs, by the requirement that two or more members work in the labor force in order to support a family of four; by the downsizing of the work force while profits and the economy soar; and by realistic estimates that the next generations will not live as well as many of us do now. DuBois was right, the line between the haves and the have-nots will challenge the color line as the problem of the twenty-first century.

To understand the magnitude of this problem it is necessary that we look more closely at what it is to have and to have not. In many of the available analyses, income distribution has been the variable of focus. For individuals, inequality in the distribution of, and inadequacy in access to, income comprise a critical factor, but for groups the problem of inequality in the distribution of wealth may be even more critical. This may be true because while income may provide limited access to available resources, it is wealth that provides access to power and control. It is also wealth that provides ready access to essential human resource development capital. Some of us are beginning to believe that without the capital to invest in human resource development it is impossible to achieve meaningful participation in an advanced technological society. What is the nature of that capital? According to Bourdieu (1986), Coleman et al. (1966), Miller (1995), Gordon and Meroe (1989), it includes:

Cultural capital: the collected knowledge, techniques and beliefs of a people.

Financial capital: income and wealth, and family, community and societal economic resources available for human resource development and education.

Health capital: physical developmental integrity, health and nutritional condition, etc.

Human capital: social competence, tacit knowledge and other education-derived abilities as personal or family assets.

Institutional capital: access to political, education and social.

Pedagogical capital: supports for appropriate educational experiences in home, school, and community.

Personal capital: dispositions, attitudes, aspirations, efficacy, and sense of power.

Polity capital: societal membership, social concern, public commitment, and participation in the political economy.

Social capital: social networks and relationships, social norms, cultural styles, and values.

Obviously, wealth is more than money. It is the accessibility and control of resources. Schools and other social institutions seem to work when the persons served bring to them the varieties of capital that enable and support human development. If we are correct in assuming that the effectiveness of schools and other human resource development institutions is in part a function of the availability of such wealth-derived capital for investment in human development, we may have in this relationship a catalyst for pedagogical, political and social intervention.

AFFIRMATIVE ACTION

Until recently, our society has accepted the assignment of preferential treatment to designated categories of persons as special rewards for service to the nation, as compensation for unusual prior disadvantage, or simply as the entitlement associated with one's status. These various forms of affirmative action are currently under increased attack largely because of their public and colloquial association with minority group membership privilege. In all candor, affirmative action is also under attack because of abuses in its practice. Instead of an effort to ensure that qualified persons are not disqualified because of ethnicity or gender, affirmative action is often perceived as a program to privilege "unqualified persons over those who are "qualified." The preoccupation with race may be a part of the problem. In a racist society all social arrangements are designed to reflect racist values. And explicit efforts to subvert those values are bound to come up against open resistance.

I propose a few adjustments. Rather than targeting ethnic or gender groups for affirmative action, I propose targeting larger and more diverse groups: those that are low on wealth and wealth-derived capital resources. Education and employment opportunities could be regarded as instruments of human resource development rather than agencies for the credentialing and rewarding of the "ablest." Rather than protecting the opportunity to enter, let us ensure the opportunity to develop and qualify. In addition to a program of affirmative action, we are proposing a program of affirmative development.

The largest affirmative action effort in the history of the USA was our veterans' preference program. This was also an affirmative development program. The components of that program ensured that veterans had ample opportunities to improve their economic, education, and health status. They were a protected group with respect to vocational skills development and employment. They were assisted in the acquisition of wealth through subsidized business and home ownership. The social ethos even gave them privileged positions in the political arena where they were enabled to access political capital through the jingoistic and patriotic biases of the populists. This national effort may have begun as a reward for service in the nation's defense establishment, but in reality it was a massive human resource development endeavor that positioned the nation's labor force for the economic and technological expansions of the latter half of the twentieth century. The affirmative development of the nation' underdeveloped human resources proved to be in the best interest of the entire United States.

AN AFFIRMATIVE DEVELOPMENT POLICY

A national effort at affirmative development to complement continuing efforts at affirmative action should be much broader than the initiatives directed at improving the effectiveness of education. Within the education establishment, however, we know a great deal about the deliberate development of academic ability. I propose that the education community embark upon a deliberate effort to develop academic abilities in a broad range of students who have a history of being resource deprived and who as a consequence are underrepresented in the pool of academically high achieving students. The deliberate or affirmative development of academic ability should include more equitable access to the variety of capitals referred to above and to such educational interventions as:

1. Early, continuous and progressive exposure to rigorous pre-academic and academic teaching and learning transactions. This should begin with high levels of language, literacy, and numeracy development.

2. Rich opportunities to learn through pedagogical practices traditionally thought to be of excellent quality. We do not need to wait for new inventions: Benjamin Bloom's Mastery Learning, Robert Slavins Success for All, James Comer's School Development, Bob Moses' Algebra Project, Vinetta Jones' Equity 2000; the College Board's Pacesetter, and Lauren Resnick's "effort-based" "thinking curriculum" all attempt to do some of this.

3. Diagnostic, customized, and targeted assessment, instructional and remedial interventions.

4. Academic acceleration and content enhancement.
5. The use of relational data systems to inform educational policy and practice decisions.
6. Explicit socialization of intellect to multiple cultural contexts.
7. Exposure to high performance learning communities.
8. Explication of tacit knowledge, meta-cognition, and meta-componential strategies.
9. Capitalization of the distributed knowledge, technique, and understanding that reside among learners.
10. Special attention to the differential requirements of learning in different academic domains.
11. Encouragement of learner behaviors such as deployment of effort, task engagement, time on task, and resource utilization.
12. Special attention to the roles of attitude, disposition, confidence, and efficacy.
13. Access to a wide range of supplementary educational experiences.
14. The politicalization of academic learning in the lives of sub-altern[1] communities of learners.

INTELLECTIVE COMPETENCE

While my list begins with an emphasis on rigorous academic experiences and achievement, I do not stop there. The mastery of academic learning is, for me, only instrumental to the development of intellective competence. In my vision of teaching, learning and assessment, academic outcome standards are central, but the explication of what we want learners to know about specific disciplines and to be able to do must be considered as instrumental to what we want learners to become. There is no question about the importance of what students learn and are taught. Most of us would agree that teaching and learning independent of content (subject matter) is problematic. However, just as teaching and learning without subject matter are vacuous, teaching and learning should not be so

---

1. Subaltern peoples are groups of persons who have been subordinated by the dominant culture yet have simultaneously adopted aspects, developed alternative forms and strategies of resistance to the dominant culture. Some groups of African-American males are sometimes referred to as subaltern groups.

constrained by content that the purpose of engagement with these pedagogical endeavors is precluded.

I am more and more persuaded that the purpose of learning, and the teaching by which it is enabled, is to acquire knowledge and technique in the service of the development of adaptive human intellect. I see these as being at the core of intellective competence. The old "scholastic aptitudes" may not have been so far from the mark. In the effort to achieve some distance from the actual material covered in the nation's diverse curricula, the scholastic aptitudes were perceived as more generic capacities to handle academic tasks. Those aptitudes should be thought of as generalized developed abilities that not only reflect the capacity to handle academic work, but more importantly, reflect the meta-manifestations of intellective abilities that result from particular kinds of education and socialization. Instead of scholastic aptitudes it may be more appropriate that we think of developed intellective abilities or intellective competencies as the meta-expressions of a wide range of human learning achievements, some of which are related to what happens in schools.

These developed abilities are not so much reflected in the specific discipline-based knowledge a student may have, but in the student's ability and disposition to adaptively and efficiently use knowledge, technique, and values in mental processes to engage and solve both common and novel problems.

James Greeno suggests that what I call intellective competence is really "intellective character." What is intellective competence? I have come to use the term to refer to a characteristic way of adapting, appreciating, knowing, and understanding the phenomena of human experience. I also use the construct to reference the quality with which these mental processes are applied in one's engagement with common, novel, and specialized problems. Intellective competence reflects one's habits of mind, but it also reflects the quality or goodness of the products of mental functioning.

Like social competence, which I feel is one manifestation of intellective competence, it reflects "goodness of fit" or the effectiveness of the application of one's affective, cognitive, and situative processes to solving the problems of living. Fifteen years ago I might have used the term "intelligence" or "intelligent behavior" to capture this characteristic or quality of one's mental capabilities or performance. In 2001, I am concerned with more. I am trying to capture aspects of human capability, developed ability, and disposition to use and appreciate the use of human adaptive processes in the service of intentional behavior. I am not

286

surprised that Greeno calls it a manifestation of character. No matter what we call it, I argue that competence can be created through the deliberate development of academic ability. The task to which I am committed in my next career is the "affirmative development of academic ability" in a broader range of human beings.

CONCLUSION

DuBois was right! Income and wealth have replaced, or greatly reduced the significance of, the color line in our society. Ethnicity continues to be important, but economic, political, and social planning may be more appropriately directed at reducing the growing disparities between the haves and the have-nots. In the twenty-first century, this will require a quantum leap in the development and utilization of all our peoples. It will require the affirmative development of large numbers of persons who, because of the mal-distribution of human resource development capital, have undeveloped academic and other abilities the nation will need.

Such an effort would favor the under classes in which ethnic minorities are congregated, but are by no means the majority. It would be wise, however, to remember that my proposed national program of affirmative development would privilege the development of the lower and under classes in our society. Unfortunately, classism may be an even more recalcitrant illness than racism. It is sometimes acceptable to talk of racial justice. It is generally thought to be subversive to talk about economic justice. In my judgment, however, the pursuit of universal economic justice, together with racial justice, may be the most promising route to universally optimal human development.

It may also be a necessary condition for the survival of our democratic nation. I propose to begin the pursuit of justice with the affirmative development of academic ability in those persons whose natural conditions of life do not permit the easy acquisition of intellective competence. In the twenty-first century, professional educators and pedagogical scientists need to fully engage the challenge posed by James Coleman in his 1965 study, Equality of Educational Opportunity (Coleman et al., 1965). Coleman challenged the nation to seek deliberately to uncouple academic achievement from the social divisions to which our students are assigned (class, ethnicity, gender, and first language). A national commitment to the affirmative development of academic ability may enable such an achievement.

287

17

Establishing a System of Public Education in which all Children Participate, Achieve at High Levels, and Reach their Full Potential

The Covenant with Black America

Educational opportunities and academic achievement for persons of African descent in the United States are at an all-time high point. More of us are in school. Proportionately, fewer of us are dropping out of school. The percentage of Black children whose mothers have obtained a high school education has increased significantly. More of us are attending and completing post-secondary education programs and higher education. More of us hold faculty appointments in non-historically Black institutions. But we seem to have reached a plateau with respect to gains in academic achievement.

Gains made in the 1960s, 1970s, and 1980s have slowed. We have not been able to eliminate or significantly reduce the academic achievement gap between African American, Latina/o, and Native American students and their counterparts who identify themselves as Asian American or European American. Not only has the gap not disappeared, rather it appears to have also increased as academic achievement and/or social-economic-status (SES) rise. That is, the gap is smaller between low-achieving and low-SES Blacks and Whites than it is between high-achieving or high-SES Blacks and Whites. In other words, higher academic achievement and higher social class status are not associated with smaller but rather greater differences in academic achievement. African American males lag behind African American females in academic achievement.[1] Schools that serve predominantly Black student populations are more likely to be under-resourced than are schools serving predominantly White student populations.

Fifty years after the U.S. Supreme Court's decision declaring school segregation unconstitutional, most Black children attend public schools where minorities represent the majority of the student body. Students attending schools

288

in predominantly White neighborhoods are less likely to experience teachers of poor quality than are students attending schools in predominantly Black communities. By almost all the common indicators of academic achievement and school quality, students who identify themselves as Black suffer in the comparisons with students who identify themselves as White.

The continuing shortage of African American, Latino/a, and Native American students who achieve at very high levels academically is the issue that guided the work of the National Task Force on Minority High Achievement, a group organized by the College Board in 1997. The report of the Task Force, *Reaching The Top,* concluded that it would be "virtually impossible to integrate the professional and leadership ranks of our society . . . until many more students from these underrepresented groups become high achievers."[2]

As our nation and schools become increasingly diverse, the issue of closing the achievement gap becomes more urgent. Between 1972 and 1998, the proportion of students of color in public schools increased from 22 percent to 38 percent. The enrollment rates for students of color in the West and South already constitute 47 percent and 45 percent, respectively, of the student population. And what some of us do not realize, or may not even accept, is that these proportional increases suggest that the prosperity of our nation will be increasingly dependent on the knowledge and contributions of students of color. Thus, in our multifaceted roles as educators, policy-makers, parents, and community members, it is important that we stimulate high levels of academic achievement for *all* students, particularly those who have been least well-served by our schools.

Clearly the state of education in Black America is multidimensional and complex. Arguably, the most critical problem in education that faces Black America is the problem of the gap in academic achievement known to exist between Blacks and Whites. Further, as we have indicated, not only is this problem manifested at all achievement and SES levels, but as we go up the ladder with respect to each, the achievement disparity also increases. Obviously, this society has not been able to make education function to optimize and equalize academic development among Blacks.

This failure is not unique to the United States. In other industrialized societies in which caste-like systems are in place, we see comparable differentials in the academic achievement of high-status and lower-status children.[3] There certainly appears to be a ubiquitous association between one's status in the social order and one's level of academic achievement that favors high status and privilege.

289

There are several possible explanations for these widely observed phenomena that are reflected in the academic achievement gap. Persistent explanations place varying degrees of emphasis on assumed cultural and/or genetic differences between Blacks and Whites. In this line of argument, assumed inferiority is the underlying premise, whether it be genetically or culturally determined.[4]

Some liberal scholars argue for cultural and behavioral differences that are not necessarily inferior but are, nonetheless, inappropriate to the demands of high levels of academic achievement, and these differences tend not to be addressed by typical approaches to schooling.[5] Other explanations have focused on the attitudes and behaviors of the students themselves. Here we have the Fordham and Ogbu (1986) finding of "fear of acting White" as a factor that directs the attention and behavior of Black students away from serious academic pursuit.[6] More recently, Steele has advanced the notion concerning "fear of stereotype confirmation" in which Black students' performance is assumed to be impaired by their anxiety concerning the possibility that if they try and do not do well, they will confirm the negative stereotype that others hold concerning them.[7]

From the Black community and other reasonably well-informed sources, we hear the argument that the achievement gap is a reflection of inadequate opportunities to learn. This argument rests on the historic finding of inequality in the educational opportunities available to children in America.[8] It is the inequality in educational opportunity that has been the driving force behind the school desegregation movement and behind much of the continuing effort at school reform.

If that inequality in opportunity to learn and the inequality in achievement are ultimately to be eliminated, we think that the nation must undertake a multifaceted initiative to improve the state of education in Black America. Such an initiative would include interventions directed at:

- Reducing the relatively high levels of academic under-productivity observed in so many of our children and the schools that serve them;

- Stabilizing the social fabric of our families and communities to better protect and support the academic and personal development of our children;

- Reducing inefficiencies in and the under-utilization of the power of schooling and supplemental education in the development of the sizeable group of children of color who now achieve at modest levels or barely survive with minimum performance in many of our schools; and

- Increasing the nurturance and celebration of developed ability in the group that Du Bois called "the talented tenth" of our people upon whom the Black community and the nation must depend for leadership.[9]

The National Urban League, through its former President/CEO Hugh Price, and the College Board have recently advocated that greater attention be given to high academic achievement of students of color.[10] We too have continuously promoted the idea of a national effort at the "Affirmative Development of Academic Ability." [11] This notion was first advanced at a conference sponsored by the National Action Committee on Minorities in Engineering some 20 years ago. In an exchange with Scott Miller, we proposed that for affirmative action to work in a society where opportunities to learn are unequally distributed, a parallel program directed at the affirmative development of academic ability might be needed.[12] The notion was picked up a decade later in the recommendations of the College Board's National Task Force on Minority High Achievement.

> Thus, the Task Force recommends that an extensive array of public and private policies, actions, and investments be pursued, which would collectively provide many more opportunities for academic development for underrepresented minority students through the schools, colleges, and universities that they attend, through their homes, and through their communities. We summarize this as a commitment to affirmative development.[13]

In this line of argument, we have borrowed from Bourdieu (1986) to emphasize the variety of forms of capital upon which effective education rests.[14] (See Table 18:1)

TABLE 18:1 FORMS OF CAPITAL FOR EFFECTIVE EDUCATION

Kinds of Capital	Definition
Health	Physical developmental integrity, health, nutritional condition
Financial	Income, wealth, family, community, and societal economic resources available for education
Human	Social competence, tacit knowledge, and other education-derived abilities as personal or family assets
Social	Social network relationships, social norms, cultural styles, and values
Polity	Societal membership, social concern, public commitment, political economy
Personal	Disposition, attitudes, aspirations, efficacy, sense of power
Institutional	Quality of and access to educational and socializing institutions
Pedagogical	Supports for appropriate educational treatment in family, school, and community

Access to these forms of capital is grossly unequally distributed. Schools and other social institutions seem to work when the persons served bring to them the varieties of capital that enable and support human development. If we are correct in assuming that the effectiveness of schools and other human resource development institutions is in part a function of the availability of such wealth-derived capital for investment in human development, we may have in this relationship a catalyst for pedagogical, political, and social intervention.

If the effectiveness of education rests on such resources and they are unequally distributed, it is reasonable to anticipate that the effects of education will be unequal. The achievement distribution data correlate highly with the data on access to these forms of capital. Our notion of affirmative development is conceptually grounded in possible approaches to offsetting the negative effects of the mal-distribution of access to these forms of education-related capital. While the most direct approach to the solution of the problem of mal-distribution would involve the redistribution of income, wealth, and related resources, it is not reasonable to expect that such a radical solution will resonate with twenty-first century America. It is possible, however, that even a compassionate conservative society will see it to be in the best interest of the nation to organize its social institutions and its services so as to remove the negative effects of such mal-distribution on the academic and personal development of its people.

A national effort at affirmative development to complement continuing efforts at affirmative action should be much broader than the initiatives directed at improving the effectiveness of education. Within the education establishment, however, we know a great deal about the deliberate development of academic ability. We propose that the education community embark upon a deliberate effort to develop academic abilities in a broad range of students who have a history of being resource deprived and who as a consequence are underrepresented in the pool of academically high-achieving students.

The deliberate or affirmative development of academic ability should include more equitable access to the variety of assets and strengths referred to in the chart above as capitals and to such educational interventions that provide early and continuous high-quality learning opportunities, high-quality teaching and school facilities, and rich community supports that are stimulating, encouraging, and supportive of educational excellence. Broad political will, and courageous leadership from the Black community and beyond, must also present a strong and consistent demand for adequate investments to achieve the high-quality education of all children.

The state of education in Black America is considerably better than it was one hundred years ago—better than even fifty years ago. Some evidence suggests that our progress has been uneven during the past half-century. There is no question, nonetheless, that there remain complex and serious problems. These problems are related to the significant gap between the academic achievement levels of peoples of color and the achievement levels of Asian American and European American peoples.

But even more problematic may be the changing and rising demands for intellective competence that are associated with urbanicity and post-modernity, at the same time that Blacks are trying to close the academic achievement gap.

With such a moving target, the challenge may be exacerbated. What we need is a national commitment to the affirmative development of academic ability in Black and other populations that are underrepresented among the high achievers in our society. A cross-section of what is being done in pockets all across America is highlighted in the balance of this chapter.

The Facts
EARLY CHILDHOON EDUCATION

- Early childhood education is key to school readiness and sustained academic achievement, yet at age three, only 45 percent of African American children are enrolled, and at age four just 73 percent are registered.[15]

READING COMPREHENSION

- Just 12 percent of African-American 4th graders have reached proficient or advanced reading levels, while 61 percent have yet to reach the basic level.[16]

- In a national assessment of student reading ability, Black children scored 16 percent below White children.[17]

- Forty-six percent of Black adults, compared with 14 percent of White adults, scored in the lowest category of the National Adult Literacy survey. The results indicate that Blacks have more limited skills in processing information from articles, books, tables, charts, and graphs compared with their White counterparts.[18]

MATHEMATICAL PROFICIENCY

- Many Black 17-year-old students graduating high school have the math skills of White 8th graders.[19]

PROMOTIONS/RETENTIONS, SUSPENSIONS/EXPULSIONS

- While nine percent of White students have repeated a grade, twice as many, or 18 percent, of Black students have been held back at least once.[20]

- One out of three African American students in seventh through twelfth grades has been suspended or expelled at some point, as opposed to 15 percent of White children. [21]

HIGHER EDUCATION

- Of Black 16- to 24-year-olds, 13 percent have not earned a high school diploma or GED; 7 percent of White young people are without a high school credential.[22]

- In 2000, 31 percent of African Americans ages 18 to 24 were enrolled in colleges and universities; nearly two-thirds of these students were female.[23]

- According to the most recent statistics, the nationwide college graduation rate for Black students is only 40 percent, compared to 61 percent of enrolled White students.[24]

What the Community Can Do

Without question, education is the key to progress and prosperity in the United States today. Whether fair or not, educational opportunity and academic achievement are directly tied to the social divisions associated with race, ethnicity, gender, first language, and social class. The level and quality of educational attainment either open the doors to opportunity or close them.

Education starts at home, in neighborhoods, and in communities. Reading to children, creating time and space for homework, and demonstrating—through words and deeds—that education is important are the key first building blocks for high educational achievement. While schools are responsible for what children are taught in school, reinforcement at home is essential. As members of the Black community, we must take responsibility for educating *all* our children—whether ours by birth or otherwise—to uplift our people as a whole.

From the time of slavery to today, Black Americans have struggled to attain high-quality education. During slavery, educating Blacks was forbidden. Today there is a legal right to attend schools, but for many Blacks, a quality education is almost as difficult to obtain as it was more than a century ago. Schools are more segregated than they were 20 years ago, too many of which are pre- dominantly Black and of low quality. We must demand that local communities provide the resources to educate all children, that the state and federal governments provide sufficient resources. The mandate of educating all of America's children rests on all of us.

What every individual can do now

- Read to your children or grandchildren everyday.

- Create clean, quiet spaces for your children to do homework; check to make sure that assignments are completed.

- Get library cards for each member of your family.

- Arrange enriching family and neighborhood activities for children of all ages: museums, educational games, spelling bees, and science fairs.

- Become involved in your children's school—PTA, school committees; attend back-to-school events; if you do not have children in the school, consider becoming a volunteer.

MOST OF ALL
Hold all leaders and elected officials responsible and demand that they change current policy.

Following are some strategies that you may want to consider emulating.

Thelma Harrison's "Mama, I Want to Read"
Thelma Harrison is the founder and director of "Mama, I Want to Read," a program that teaches reading skills to preschoolers and helps them prepare for kindergarten. The 87-year-old veteran of the civil rights movement started the organization in an inner-city neighborhood of Norfolk, VA.

With the skills these young children acquire under Harrison's tutelage, they are prepared to succeed in their early years of elementary school. She has developed relationships with parents, grandparents, teachers, and administrators. From offering teaching advice and curriculum suggestions directly to schools, to offering great wisdom, compassion, and love to families, Harrison has created lifelong bonds. She believes that "it does take a village" for children to succeed and spends each day ensuring that she does her part, as do the people she rallies to the cause, continuing tirelessly to build a strong foundation for our future.

Harlem Children's Zone

The Harlem Children's Zone (HCZ)[25] is one of the largest community-based programs devoted to combining learning in and out of school in the United States. Its mission: to change the odds for children and parents in a 60-block zone in central Harlem, an area with nearly 7,000 children, more than 60 percent of whom live below the poverty line and three-quarters of whom score below grade level on statewide reading and math assessments. President and CEO Geoffrey Canada's strategy focuses on more than academic achievement, however. He has developed a system in which academic excellence is one of the outcomes, achieved in a number of ways, but it also includes nurturing family stability, opportunities for employment, decent and affordable housing, youth development activities for adolescents, and a quality education for children and parents in the zone.

Over the past 15 years, Canada has increased the Harlem Children's Zone annual budget by $34 million by creating a national buzz and an interest for investors everywhere, making the HCZ a model for other growing community organizations across America. If the country is talking about Canada, just imagine the energy on Harlem's streets. Most if not all of the families in Harlem have either a child, a niece, a nephew, or know a young person in one of HCZ's programs.

The Harlem Children's Zone houses Promise Academy Charter School, an institution that strives to provide the highest quality education for up to 700 middle and high school children. Students are fortunate enough to have access to a modern library with research facilities, a state-of-the-art computer lab, a science laboratory, and a gymnasium.[26]

Other HCZ initiatives include: Baby College, a nine-week series of workshops offered to parents of children ages of 0–3; Harlem Gems, a pre-K program; Peacemakers, which trains young people ages 18 to 24 to work with teachers in elementary school classrooms and operate after-school and summer programs; The Family Empowerment Program, which provides home-based supportive counseling as well as individual and family therapy, a parenting group, and an anger management group; and Summer Freedom Schools, described in detail below.[27] Canada and his dedicated staff are determined to touch every single child in Harlem, especially those who would otherwise slip through the cracks.

Children's Defense Fund Freedom Schools®

Each Children's Defense Fund (CDF)[28] Freedom School is a product of the relationships between the CDF and community organizations, churches, universities, and schools. There are at least 70 schools in more than 20 states and 40 cities that "create supportive, nurturing, literature-rich environments that set high expectations for all children through a focus on literacy, cultural heritage, parental involvement, Servant-Leadership, and social action."[29]

The Freedom Schools program was organized during the civil rights movement by the Student Nonviolent Coordinating Committee and the Council of Federated Organizations. The Mississippi Freedom Summer Project of 1964 strived to "motivate young people to become critically engaged in their communities and to help them identify and design authentic solutions to local programs."[30] Proudly rooted in the American Civil Rights Movement, the Children's Defense Fund Freedom Schools® program was reborn in 1993 by Marian Wright Edelman and the Children's Defense Fund Black Community Crusade for Children (BCCC); it draws on the vision, philosophy, and experience of those who conducted Freedom Schools as part of the "Mississippi Freedom Summer Project" of 1964.[31]

The program's key elements are educational enrichment and cultural awareness, parental involvement, intergenerational leadership, community involvement, and social action. These schools are unique because young African American children who would otherwise spend long summer days home alone or out on the streets have the opportunity to connect with other youth, form lasting relationships, sharpen their academic skills, and empower themselves as they learn about their rich heritage. Close to 5,500 children attended a CDF Freedom School in the summer of 2005.

What Black Leaders and Elected Officials Can Do
POLICY RECOMMENDATIONS

- Invest in child and parental development.
- Implement federal support at all levels of education.
- Ensure an education in which students truly amass knowledge and preparedness for the next level of schooling and life.

- Develop a universal, well-rounded, and comprehensive curriculum.
- Provide well-resourced conditions and circumstances for learning in all public schools.
- Adequately train and compensate professional staff that teach in responsible ratios of adults to children and are trustworthy and culturally sensitive.
- Guarantee that all children have access to appropriate and sufficient facilities, curriculum resources, and materials.

Invest in child and parental development

Government resources should be better invested to support the academic and personal maturity of children. Local officials should readily help to develop and fund after-school, mentoring, college preparatory, and collegiate scholars programs and leadership opportunities. School administrators should also identify supplemental enrichment programs for students. Children's learning processes are enhanced only when they have forums to exercise other parts of their ongoing development.

Continuing development of parents to ensure that they are capable of advocating for and orchestrating the supplementary support necessary for the holistic development of their children is also key to a complete, quality education. In large part, many parents are part of a working population that cannot advocate at their leisure because of work or other commitments. In being sensitive to those issues, schools must provide parents with ways to be active without taking time off work, phone conferences, making special arrangements with teachers on how to monitor a child's progress, and creating opportunities for parents to be involved before and/or after work. If schools make it possible and beneficial for parents to participate, every child will benefit.

Implement federal support at all levels of education

The United States government should provide public early childhood education, just as they do elementary and secondary education. It is proven that attending preschool and pre-kindergarten better prepares children to succeed at all levels of schooling. Because many preschools, or other types of early childhood learning programs are not free, parents who cannot afford them simply do not send their children. They enter into kindergarten already at a disadvantage to their peers who have just completed preschool. In order to level the playing field from day one, early childhood education must be a basic right of all children, just as elementary, junior and high schools are.

We must also demand access for all to higher education. Federal and state level officials have to work to greatly extend programs that provide scholarships and support to those who do not have the resources to afford college. Quality community colleges need to be more broadly available, and they should be required to have in-house programs to encourage students to transfer to 4-year institutions. No student should ever be denied federal aid when applying to the higher education institution of his or her choice. In addition, this money should be in the form of grants, as opposed to loans. The fear alone of having to pay back a substantial loan with high interest rates, turns many young people away. There must be nothing daunting about pursuing a higher education.

Ensure an education in which students can learn and grow

Too often teachers and administrators are concerned with national school rank or are simply careless and promote children to the next grade before the students are ready. Every child in America, regardless of school reputation, must be duly educated so that he or she may have a fair and an equal chance of being a productive and successful member of society. We must not allow children to be promoted until they are prepared to move forward; at the same time, we must demand that educators take the time to keep our children learning at least at grade level. It is unacceptable for children to be left behind academically; we must find and offer whatever special resources are needed to help them learn and progress on par with others their age.

The objective of all educational institutions has to be just that, to educate. It is crucial that local officials enforce teaching so that children actually learn, as opposed to memorizing answers for government-issued standardized tests. As national requirements for elementary and secondary schools change, official tests are administered to all students and schools are categorized according to overall scores. This practice encourages teachers to teach the exams, rather than covering a wide range of grade-level appropriate topics. Knowledge must be the end result, not test scores.

Develop a universal, well-rounded, and comprehensive curriculum

Schools must provide for the early and continuous exposure of all children to rigorous, varied, and joyful learning experiences where personal effort is encouraged and rewarded. This includes educating them in the arts, foreign languages, and physical education as well as in all other required academic subjects. Those courses that are now considered to extend beyond basic education should be a part of every child's curriculum. Areas of study that stimulate other parts of a child's brain must not be reserved as a privilege of children who attend private schools or public schools in wealthy districts.

All schools that have been forced to cut music, visual arts, performing arts, and sports must have them restored. If government officials allocate substantive educational funding to all schools equally, then every child will have the opportunity to explore both creative and academic areas of interest. A truly educated child is not only proficient in math, science, history and English, but also in painting, piano, and a foreign language.

Provide an environment for learning
Guarantee adequately compensated and prepared professional staff
in responsible ratios of adults to children

Educating our children is critical to cultivating and sustaining our society. Without education, crime rates would skyrocket; health breakthroughs would be limited, if they existed at all, with no doctors or nurses to cure or care for the sick, and so on. That scenario notwithstanding, teachers are inadequately compensated for their efforts and contributions to the well-being of this country. Logically, a contented teacher makes for a better teacher. While we must acknowledge and be grateful for the educators who are in the profession out of love for youth, many can barely survive on their salaries. Elected officials must raise the starting salary for educators nationwide.

Teachers have a responsibility as well: They should be required to go through yearly training to share and learn new teaching techniques, raise their awareness of cultural current events, and brush up on educative methods. School staff must be responsible for creating and maintaining trust and a safe space between staff members, between staff and students, between staff and parents, and between students and students such that prejudice real or perceived is avoided. In enforcing this policy, school officials must nurture relationships, especially with those parents and students that seem hard to reach.

Many of the nation's classrooms are extremely overcrowded, the worst instances with 40 students to 1 teacher. Schools must divide such classes in half and increase their staff. Focused, individual attention is necessary for students to progress, mature, learn at a healthy pace, and succeed.

Make the necessary tools available

Every child has the right to his or her own desk, textbooks in good condition, new pencils, and other necessary supplies. Local officials must never accept the fact that students are forced to share curriculum resources and learning materials. Administrators have to be responsible for ensuring that they provide teachers with grade-appropriate and up-to-date texts and interactive learning materials that are relevant to today's society. Furthermore, all schools must maintain safe and clean playgrounds, classrooms, hallways, and bathrooms. We cannot allow our schools to house our children in makeshift classrooms or auditoriums. All of these factors contribute to a positive school experience.

• • •

If we are actively engaged in our children's learning and development from an early age, and if we hold our elected officials responsible for providing well-resourced educational facilities, programs, and staff, then we can establish a system of public education in which all children participate, achieve at high levels, and reach their full potential. Education must be guaranteed as a civil right and a civil liberty for every child in America.

Notes

1. J.S. Coleman, E.Q. Campbell, C.J. Hobson et al., *Equality of Educational Opportunity* (Washington, DC: U.S. Government Printing Office, 1966).

2. The College Board, *Reaching the Top: A Report of the National Task Force on Minority High Achievement* (New York: The College Board, 1999).

3. J. Ogbu, *Minority Education and Caste: The American System in Cross-cultural Perspective* (New York: Academic Press, 1978).

4. *See* R.J. Herrnstein and C. Murray, *The Bell Curve: Intelligence and Class Structure in American Life* (New York: The Free Press, 1994); A.R. Jensen, "How much can we boost IQ and scholastic achievement?," *Harvard Educational Review* 39, 1969, pp. 1–23; O. Lewis, *A Puerto Rican Family in the Culture of Poverty* (New York: Random House, 1966); and W. Shockley, "Dysgenics, Geneticity, Raceology: A Challenge to the Intellectual Responsibility of Educators," *Phi Delta Kappa* 53(5), 1972, pp. 297–307.

5. F. Riessman, *The Culturally Deprived Child* (New York: Harper and Row, 1962).

6. S. Fordham and J. Ogbu, "Black Students' School Success: Coping with the burden of 'acting White,'" *Urban Review* 18, 1986, pp. 17–206.

7. C.M. Steele, "A Threat in the Air: How Stereotypes Shape Intellectual Identity and Performance," *American Psychologist* 52(6), 1997, pp. 613–629.

8. See K. Clark, *Dark Ghetto* (New York: Harper & Row, 1965); Coleman et al., *op. cit.*; G.D. Jaynes and R.M. William, eds., *A Common Destiny* (Washington, DC: National Academy Press, 1989); J. Kozol, *Savage Inequalities: Children in America's Schools* (New York: Crown Publishers, 1991); L.S. Miller, *An American Imperative: Accelerating Minority Educational Advancement* (New Haven: Yale University Press, 1995); F.F. Piven and R.A. Cloward, *Regulating the Poor: The Functions of Public Welfare (New York: Pantheon Books, 1971); and V. Sexton, Education and Income Inequalities of Opportunity in Our Public Schools* (New York: Viking Press, 1961).

9. W.E.B. Du Bois, *The Souls of Black Folks* (New York: New American Library, 1969 [1903]).

10. H. Price, *Achievement Matters: Getting Your Child the Best Education Possible* (New York: Kensington Publishing Corporation, 2002); and the College Board, *op. cit.*

11. E.W. Gordon, ed., *Education and Justice: A View from the Back of the Bus* (New York: Teachers College Press, 1999); Gordon, "Affirmative Development of Academic Abilities," *Pedagogical Inquiry and Praxis 2* (New York: Teachers College, Columbia University, Institute for Urban and Minority Education, September 2001); and Gordon, "Affirmative Development: Looking Beyond Racial Inequality," *College Board Review* 195, 2002, pp. 28–33.

12. Miller, *op. cit.*

13. The College Board, *op. cit.*

14. P. Bourdieu, "The Forms of Capital," in J. Richardson, ed., *Handbook of Theory and Research for the Sociology of Education* (Westport, CT: Greenwood, 1986), pp. 241–258.

15. http://www.idra.org/Research/edstats.htm#earlychildhood.

16. "African American Achievement in America," http://www2.edtrust.org/NR/rdonlyres/9AB4AC88-7301-43FF-81A3-EB94807B917F/0/AfAmer_Achievement.pdf, The Education Trust.

17. Llagas, *op. cit.*, p. 48.

18. *Ibid.*, pp. 122, 123.

19. African American Achievement in America," *op. cit.*

20. Llagas, *op. cit.*, p. 38.

21. *Ibid.*

22. *Ibid.*, p. 40.

23. *Ibid.,* pp. 92, 94.

24. http://www.jbhe.com/features/45_student_grad_rates.html.

25. For more information, see http://www.hcz.org/project/mission.html.

26. http://www.hcz.org/project/sites.html.

27. *Ibid.*

28. http://www.freedomschools.org.

29. http://www.freedomschools.org/mission/default.aspx.

30. http://www.freedomschools.org/history/freedomschools1964.aspx.

31. http://www.freedomschools.org/history/default.aspx.

18
The Policy Implications of
Status Variables and Schooling

So eminent is the function of status, that is, one's social class position relative to others that many of the initial sociological treatises to be published in the United States were concerned with the issue. Few topics have aroused more provocative candor, rancor, and research examination than the interrelated phenomena of social class status and schooling and the oft perceived pivotal role of schooling in elevating social class standing. This is due, in part, to the fact that the elites, those of the upper strata in most societies, participate in politics and assume leadership positions because it is expected of them, a sense of *noblesse oblige;* But the paramount issue is one of social class status and what it commands, for not only do those of the upper strata expect to govern and partake of society's bounty, but it is expected of them (Yeakey, 1981).

For those who would argue that status and both the amount and type of schooling which one receives was and is incidental in American society, we hasten to remind the reader that the introduction of public schooling was subsequent, by at least two hundred years, to schooling for the rich, for those of the upper strata. And it was only after repeated attempts by those proponents of egalitarianism and democratization that public schooling, on far from a massive scale, commenced. Even in contemporary America, we view repeated attempts by the lower classes, who hold a somewhat visionary yet sublime faith in the value of schooling, to eradicate existing social and political realities and enhance social mobility, however unwarranted that faith might be. It is as if schooling is the rue du passage, the ladder upon which ambition climbs to privilege (Yeakey, 1981, p. 182).

Research efforts have substantiated the fact that status plays an allocative role in that one's actual school achievement is positively correlated with the socioeconomic status of one's family. The cumulative evidence suggests that the higher a student's social status, the greater one's educational opportunity. The converse is also true (See Conant, 1961; Havighurst, & Loeb, Hollingshead, 1949; 1944; Lynd & Lynd, 1929; Warner, Wylie, 1963). American society is well stratified along the lines of achieved or acquired status as depicted by both the amount and type of schooling one receives, occupation, income, and life-style. Ascribed status is assigned on the basis of one's race, ethnicity, sex, religion, social status, age, and family background. Therefore mentioned factors, in concert, have a circuitous and mutually reinforcing effect on youths' opportunities for achievement and advancement in the larger society.

Given the foregoing, it is the purpose of this chapter to examine the relationship between status, schooling, and social mobility in American society, and to provide an historical as well as a contemporary analysis. Issues are centered around the social, political, and economic impingements which frame the variables under discussion.

STATUS, SCHOOLING, AND THEORIES OF EDUCABILITY

Despite repeated attempts to offset marked inequalities in American society, the society is marred by inequality of opportunity as well as results. The history of American schooling is replete with struggles for equity and social justice to mitigate the catalytic influences of low social class standing, racism, and sexism and to provide more and better schooling for the masses (Bledstein, 1976).

Any contemporary analysis of schooling and its relationship to status must chronicle past views and earlier theories of mental ability, for only the past can provide that longitudinal view which aids in the discriminant interpretation of contemporary phenomena. In the history of the Western world, the powerful have always resisted the demands of the lower classes for schooling for their children, and have yielded reluctantly and only under great pressure. With the introduction of democratic theories and processes, however, denial was rationalized in terms of the intellectual limitations of the lower classes (Schwebel, 1968). It was Plato's theory of educability, differentiating the social classes that became the predominant model from which the democratic nations of the world have scarcely deviated.

How paradoxical that Plato is held with such distinction in the Western world, in those very nations that promulgate justice and equitability. Yet Plato was "a thorough aristocrat" with "a pro¬found contempt for the opinions of the masses, and a true aristocrat's dislike of any taint of the shop or of the workman's bench" (Rogers, 1929, p. 67). Democracy, as Plato conceptualized it, was the least favorable form of government and his distrust of people was exemplified in the kinds of controls he incorporated in the ideal state in the *Republic*. Not only were the arts to be censored, but schooling was differential depending on one's status in life. So stratified a system of schooling was designed to maintain the position of the aristocracy and ensure the permanence of the status quo.

The ensuing explanations for such stratification were couched in terms of the so-called inherent differential abilities of the social classes. In fact, those who are now engaged in contemporary discussions of the educationally disadvantaged could benefit from the debates of the past on the educability of the poor. The educational "haves" and "have-nots" are the economic "haves" and "have-nots" of the society, with achievement closely paralleling a cultural, racial, and economic line.

Much the same is occurring today to the present groups of lower-status persons in the public schools, to the Native Americans, Blacks, lower-status Whites, and Hispanics. Subsequent to both *Brown I* and *II* and other legal mandates, to compensatory efforts, to community control ideologies, skepticism was raised as to whether Blacks and other minorities of color possessed the intellectual ability of Whites. And as will be demonstrated in later sections of this chapter, such doubts have been raised historically about the ability of the lower classes who at various times in American history, have been, for example, English, German, Irish, Italian, Polish, and Jewish. The preponderant characteristic is that all were victims of social circumstances, of lower class status, suffering accumulated disadvantage. Thus the spurious research evidence advanced as to the purported inferiority and ineducability of Blacks and other minorities is but a latter-day version of an old problem in new dress.

Unfortunately, the prevailing theory of educability in our society, upheld by educators, psychologists, and behavioral scientists, is that the limits of educability are predetermined by the genes inherited from one's parents at the moment of conception and the approximate level of lifetime ability is measurable in childhood. America's school system is founded on this belief and the schooling of all children is influenced by a theory of intelligence that has demanded the use of intelligence tests, tracking, ability grouping, and labeling distinctions designed to select and sort out. According to Schwebel (1968),

From the contemporary theory of intelligence, which is little different from the Platonic conception of man, have come such modern derivatives as the IQ test. Though not inherently good or bad, it has become, through the use made of it, an instrument of subtle torture that adversely affects the child's self-expectations and self-concept, and his parents' and teachers' expectations and concepts of him. It has falsely given everyone the belief that it measures something immutable and predictive of the child's powers to develop intellectually. It has done this for individuals of all social classes and for groups in the lower classes, and it has served to justify differential education: high quality academic education for the higher classes and low quality general or vocational education for the lower classes (p. 17).

If one accepts this theory, then the overwhelming degree of academic mediocrity and backwardness in today's schools is to be expected. If the proposition is wrong, as the authors believe it is, if one believes not in the immutability and fixity, but the malleability of intelligence, then man's capacity may be subject to unknown heights of development as a result of intervention in one's life experiences. And if the possibility exists for overcoming handicapping life experiences and under preparedness, then school reform must be both marked and dramatic. Any ensuing failures must be attributed to the natural functioning of the school and its host of allied institutions. Despite the rather wholesale preoccupation with and adherence to the fixity of mental ability, as early as the seventeenth century, attempts were made to dispel the theory of inborn capacity. Godwin (1798, as cited in Simon, 1960) wrote:

How long has the genius of education been disheartened and unnerved by the pretense that man is born all that it is possible for him to become? How long has the jargon imposed upon the world, which would persuade us that in instructing a man you do not add to but unfold Education will proceed with a firm step and with a genuine lustre, when those who conduct it shall mow what a vast field it embraces; when they shall be made aware that ... the question whether the pupil shall be a man of perseverance and enterprise or a stupid and inanimate dolt, depends upon the powers of those under whose direction he is placed, and the skill with which those powers shall be applied (p.49).

The social, political, and educational consequences of choosing between the two dominant conceptions of mental ability--the hereditarily "fixed" and the environmentally "open" have dire ramifications beyond the establishment of educational goals and curricular content supportive of those goals. The attitudes of teachers toward their students (teacher-pupil interaction), and that of pupils' conceptualizations of themselves and the world around them, as well as toward one another (pupil-pupil interaction), aspects of the learning situation now recognized as paramount were largely influenced by the prevailing theories of the day and the social and political prejudices upon which such theories were founded. Suffice it to say that the genetic theory of mental ability is basic to the most important educational policies and practices.

THE IMMIGRANT EXPERIENCE

To understand the significance of status concerns in American society, we deem it appropriate to examine the status phenomenon from a temporal rather than episodic frame of analysis. That is, we will examine in this section the status phenomenon relative to immigrant group populations historically, and assess as well the impact of schooling upon social mobility. Understanding the interlocutory relationship between the schools and other societal institutions, our analysis will be framed in the social, political, and economic realities of the times.

Since the emigration of more than seventy million persons from Europe in the seventeenth century, with more than half settling in the United States, America has been romanticized as an asylum for the oppressed and the downtrodden, as reflected in Lazarus' poem: "Give me your tired, your poor, your huddled masses yearning to be free...." Contrary to what the foregoing would suggest, however, there has been consistent, perpetual preoccupation with the persuasive influence of ethnic diversity upon America's social standards and traditions. Further reading of the inscription on the Statue of Liberty shows a depiction of the "tired, poor, huddled masses" as "wretched refuse," which suggests that, in practice, our nation has been far less benevolent and beneficent than our exaggerated accounts relate.

For much of the nineteenth century, immigrants to the United States were drawn from northern and western European countries (Britain, Germany, France, Scandinavia, Belgium, the Netherlands). Toward the latter part of the nineteenth century, a growing number of immigrants were from southern and eastern Europe (Italy, Yugoslavia, Hungary, Czechoslovakia, Poland, and so forth). There was a malevolent distinction between "new" immigrants (those from southern and eastern Europe) and "old" immigrants (those from northern and western Europe). The prevailing sentiment was that the old immigrants constituted a superior race of tall, blond, blue-eyed Nordics or Aryans, whereas the new immigrants included the inferior darker Alpines and Mediterraneans (Gordon, 1961). And, the respectability of such ideologies was pervasive.

Ellwood P. Cubberley (1909), an educational historian, voiced the prevailing sentiment of the time:

> These southern and eastern Europeans are of a very different type from the north Europeans who preceded them. Illiterate, docile, lacking in self-reliance and initiative, and not possessing the Anglo-Teutonic conceptions of law, order, and government, their coming has served to dilute tremendously our national stock, and to corrupt our civic life.... Everywhere these people tend to settle in groups or settlements, and to set up their national manners, customs, and observances. Our task is to break up these groups or settlements, to assimilate and amalgamate these people as a part of our American race, and to implant in their children, so far as can be done, the Anglo-Saxon conception of righteousness, law and order, and popular government and to awaken in them a reverence for our democratic institutions and for those things in our national life which we as a people hold to be of abiding worth (pp. 15-16).

Between 1895 and 1923, the "new immigrants" so numerically outnumbered the "old immigrants" that in 1917 restrictive discriminatory quota legislation was passed in the form of literacy tests and other equally restrictive measures. Established quotas were designed for each nation in proportion to its "contribution" to the American population. Thus with the great migrations at the end of the nineteenth century and the beginning of the twentieth century, each new wave brought a new addition of at least temporary second-class citizens whose statuses were graduated depending on whether they came from the northern and western parts of Europe or from the eastern or southern part of the continent.

THE PROCESS OF ASSIMILATION

There are three ideologies or explanations as to the manner in which America's largely White, Anglo-Saxon, and Protestant population absorbed over forty million immigrants from highly diversified environs and fused them into the contemporary American populace: The three are Anglo-conformity or Americanization, the melting pot, and cultural pluralism. Assimilation is the blanket terminology, which covers the aforementioned subprocesses, and is defined as the process by which minority and majority groups are merged and welded, in varied ways, into the total societal unit.

Cole and Cole (1954) first coined the concept Anglo-conformity or Americanization as a well-devised plan to divest the immigrant of his native cultural attachments in favor of the behavior and values of the Anglo group. The degree of Anglo conformity required is not enforced uniformly for all groups, for ethnic groups, which are identifiably closer to the Anglo-Saxon prototype are subjected to less cruel and brutal Americanization.

The melting pot theory envisioned a biological merger of the Anglo-Saxons with other immigrant groups and their respective cultures, to create a new indigenous American type (Gordon, 1964). Yet the notion of America as a melting pot is, in reality, a fallacious and spurious one. Racial and ethnic groups have retained much of their distinctive heritage and diversity, albeit with an American flavor, such that "Little Italy" and "Spanish Harlem" are not identical to their European counterparts. Given the role of skin color as an individious discriminating factor in our society, the originators of the concept never intended it to include the racial and ethnic groups of color (Blacks, Native Americans, and Hispanics). The theory, in reality, enveloped only the "old" and "new" immigrants who emigrated to America at the turn of the century.

Gordon and Stewart suggest that what has evolved in America is a transmuting pot where the majority populace experiments with the minority group's culture and refashions it into an Americanized mold (See also Stewart, 1954). It is not inconsequential, therefore, that Whites wear Afro hairstyles, speak in Black dialect, use the "soul brother" handshake, and wear dashikis. A host of similar examples can be derived from the cultural borrowings of almost any ethnic group in America.

A new conception, the triple melting pot theory of assimilation, was posited by Kennedy, who noted that although intermarriage crossed nationality groupings, there was strong propensity to remain within one's religious group

(Kennedy, 1944), the three major religions being Protestantism, Catholicism, and Judaism. Thus while marital endogamy appears to be loosening, religious endogamy persists with future divisions along religious lines.

Horace Kallen (1956) is acknowledged as the leading philosophical exponent of the idea of cultural pluralism, which suggests equality and unity in diversity. Unfortunately, most who use the term do so erroneously. The term, by definition, implies equality of status and opportunity for all racial and ethnic groups who retain their distinct identities. Implied as well is full social, economic, and political integration into American society irrespective of one's racial and ethnic diversity. Of the three models of assimilation, cultural pluralism exacts the least homogeneity from racial and ethnic groups. But if American society cannot be described as a melting pot, it is doubtful that it can be portrayed as pluralistic. To be sure, racial and ethnic minorities preserve and retain much of their ethnic diversity, yet inequality of status and opportunity still persists.

It is significant to note that the ideological shift from the Anglo-conformity and melting pot constructs came not from the immigrants themselves (who were more concerned with survival than with theories of accommodation and adjustment), but from many middle-class visionaries who worked in the settlement house. Most notable among them was Jane Addams who witnessed the deplorable effects of those forces that compelled Anglo-conformity (Addams, 1902, 1914, 1930). The impact was equally as devastating upon the immigrants' children who became estranged not only from their parents, but from their racial and cultural heritage as well. The immigrants, economically confined to the ghettos, were unalterably harmed by the unrelenting, menacing scoffs and attacks on their culture, their language and institutions, and on the very conception of themselves. Worse still was the contemptuous attitude of the children toward their parents' rustic, un-American way.

What followed was an intense ethnic self-hatred with its predictable, debilitating side effects of psychological maladjustment, family disorganization, adult crime, and juvenile delinquency. Adults and youngsters soon learned on the street the skills and values needed to survive. Ironically, the noted social psychologist Kenneth B. Clark (1965) wrote eloquently of these same variables operant in today's urban ghettos now inhabited largely by Blacks, Native Americans, Hispanics, and lower-class Whites, Although the racial and ethnic origin of the ghetto's inhabitants has changed, the common threads of poverty, depressed economics, and the class based nature of urban dwelling remain constant.

As evidence of such social decay and disorganization, there were youth gangs composed of White ethnic immigrants in New York City as early as 1728 (Foster, 1974). And during the 1850s, gang battles were so savage that police had to enlist the aid of the National Guard. Such gangs:

> Were attributed to the cultural dislocations and community disorganization accompanying the mass immigration of foreigners .... The existence of gangs is widely attributed to a range of social injustices: racial discrimination, unequal educational and work opportunities, relevant over inequalities in the distribution of wealth and privilege in an affluent society, and the ineffective or oppressive policies of service agencies such as the police and the schools (Miller, 1969, p. 12).

Those who are appalled at today's youth gang actions or the demonstrations by students, Blacks, Native Americans, and Hispanics should examine the historical research on the draft riots in New York City in 1863. Conservative estimates suggest that 8,000 were wounded and 2,000 were killed. Although the majority of persons in the draft riots were Irish, from many of the ethnic and racial immigrant neighborhoods came the criminals and lawbreakers of the succeeding generations (Asbury, 1970). Intergroup violence resulted not wholly from the divergent life-styles, speech patterns, or other cultural factors. Nor were such problems the result of antagonisms among White ethnic groups. The precipitating factors for the creation of such frustrating, aggressive behavior was an alienating life-style in a hostile environ and the racial and class based nature of their suppression.

Assimilation involves other processes, which have attained distinct labels. The first is acculturation, often called behavioral assimilation, or the absorption of the cultural behavioral patterns of the dominant society. Amalgamation refers to the biological blending or intermarriage across racial and ethnic lines and is based upon the melting pot construct. Structural assimilation relates to the accessibility of the immigrants to the elite social cliques, organizations, institutional activities, and overall civic life of the majority society. To be sure acculturation or behavioral assimilation has taken place; however, structural assimilation, most assuredly, has not.

Structural assimilation was disallowed for the first generation immigrants, yet it was the second and succeeding generations that found a much more subtle yet virulent situation:

Many believed they heard the siren call of welcome to the social cliques, clubs, and institutions of White Protestant America. After all, it was simply a matter of learning American ways, was it not? Had they not grown up as Americans, and were they not culturally different from their parents, the "greenhorns?" Or perhaps an especially eager one reasoned (like the Jewish protagonist of Myron Kaufmann's novel, Remember Me to God, aspiring to membership in the prestigious club system of Harvard undergraduate social life): "If only I can go the last few steps in Ivy League manners and behavior, they will surely recognize that I am one of them and take me in." But, alas, Brooks Brothers suit not withstanding; the doors of the fraternity house, the city men's club, and the country club were slammed in the face of the immigrant's offspring (Gordon, 1964 p. 285).

THE NON-WHITE GROUP EXPERIENCE

The arrival of racial and ethnic groups of color (Blacks, Puerto Ricans, Mexican Americans, and Native Americans) to America cannot be understood under the framework of immigration and assimilation that applied to European ethnic groups. These "people of color" share not only similar historical patterns of racial oppression and exploitation, but contemporary patterns as well. Today, these groups have coalesced and proclaimed themselves a "third world movement" asserting that there is an indisputable connection between the third world nations abroad, that is, Africa, Asia, Latin America and the Caribbean, and America's third world peoples within. By placing the realities of racial oppression and domination within an international frame, a common political fate is implied (Blauner, 1972).

The fundamental issue is historical, political, and economic. There is a basic distinction between immigration and colonization. White immigrant groups entered America voluntarily even though they may have fled their mother country because of dire circumstances. Colonized groups were conquered, enslaved, and pressured to come to America through force or violence. The third world premise boldly attacks the publicized notion of America, a nation whose population increased solely through immigration, reminding us of the fact that along with immigrants and settlers, were colonial subjects (conquered Native Americans, Black slaves, and later, defeated Mexicans) on American soil.

There are three major factors that differentiate the reality of the non-White group experience from that of the European immigrants (Blauner, 1972). The first is forced entry into a society. Second is the subjugation to various forms of unfree labor that restrict the physical and social mobility of the group and its participation in the political arena. The third is a cultural policy that not only constrains, but transforms and destroys the values, traditions, and ways of life of the colonized group.

The historical experiences of non-White groups conform to the colonial model. Africans were captured, enslaved, and transported to the southern United States and other lands in the Western hemisphere. Similarly, the three hundred year process of the virtual annihilation of the Native Americans is a case of classical colonialism, akin to Europe's imperious control over Asia, Africa, and Latin America. The same holds true of the conquest and defeat of the Mexican Southwest and its Spanish speaking population. Puerto Ricans, on the other hand, have undergone a part colonial, part immigrant experience whereby Puerto Rico was arid is exploited by America, yet, at the same time, the inhabitants have some freedom to move and work in the States.

To be sure, European immigrants and non-White groups have shared similar experiences in that both groups were poor and early generations were often employed as unskilled workers. As Blauner (1972) and Litwack (1961) suggest, perhaps the question of how, where, and why new arrivals worked in America is of primary importance. The different types of work available to non-Whites and Whites, is a significant reason why their histories have followed disparate paths, in light of the fact that America's labor forces were based on sexual and racial distinctions.

It has been documented that Americas assimilation processes have been oppressive. But, with the passage of time, most White ethnics blended into the larger society adopting and adapting the characteristics of the dominant culture. The cultural experience of non-Whites in America has been different, for colonization and slavery not only weakened, but destroyed communal ties.

THE IMMIGRANT THEORY OF PROGRESS

Given our shrinking economy with widescale unemployment, high prices, and a scarcity of resources and rewards, White ethnic groups have voiced considerable resentment over what appears to them to be exclusive attention by the federal government to the needs of non-White groups (Novak, 1971). Blacks, Native Americans, Puerto Ricans, and Mexican Americans are being compared with White immigrant groups who emigrated to America and who started at the bottom of the ladder and purportedly "pulled themselves up by their bootstraps" to elevated social standing. Documentation proves, however, that the bottom has by no means been the same for all groups.

A more sophisticated version of the argument explaining how European immigrants improved themselves economically over time is capsulized in what might be called the waves theory. This theory claims that groups of European immigrants came to America at different times, met discrimination and after numerous trials of varying length, overcame adversity, and ascended the social class ladder of American prosperity. This process was repeated time and again by each new wave of immigrants. According to this theory, Blacks, Native Americans, Puerto Ricans, and Mexican Americans are viewed as only the most recent groups of "immigrants" to go through this process; for it is not until the twentieth century that large numbers of these groups moved to the cities and to the North and thereby began to encounter modern social problems of adjustment. The proponents of this view argue further that, in time, these newcomers, just as their European counterparts, will eventually become a part of the mainstream and share in America's riches.

This view overlooks several fundamental aspects of the United States experience, and parts of American history, which if accurately portrayed do permanent damage to such faulty analysis. A cursory examination of the Black man's experience in America provides some interesting insights. For example, after the Native American, and along with the first English immigrants, those who arrived before the Mayflower, Blacks were living in America. The Black man is by no stretch of the imagination a newcomer to America. In terms of language, tradition, mores, and culture--the most important avenues for acculturation into a society--the Black American, even with his distinct cultural identity and diversity, was as qualified for American citizenship as the first or even second generation European immigrant. Certainly this was true as early as 1880 when the major waves of Europeans began to arrive over 25 years after the first African slaves were brought to America. Moreover, this sociological claim to share in America's bounty is made without considering the enormous contribution Blacks have made in winning independence for this nation or their subsequent military participation in preserving it since then. It is made also without mentioning the decisive role Blacks have played in the economic development of the nation. Similar analyses could be made for each non-White group mentioned in this chapter.

Furthermore, notwithstanding the horrendous treatment of the Native Americans, these groups, on the basis of their racial and ethnic diversity, are the most abused and discriminated in America. The Irish, the Italians, the Germans, the Poles, the Jews, and a host of others have come to this country at times when certain of these groups (Blacks, Native Americans) were at the bottom of the economic spectrum. If the wave theory is correct, then all of these European ethnic groups should clearly be below Blacks and Native Americans in terms of social class standing, no matter how well-off economically the former Europeans might be. In reality, however, when the first nineteenth and twentieth century European immigrants initially arrived, at worst, they dislodged non-Whites from their meager hold on the bottom rung of the economic ladder, pushing non-Whites off or beneath them. At best, they began at a level slightly above (Litwack, 1961). Some European immigrants suffered and fought against discrimination; they moved up the ladder and witnessed other White ethnic groups, arriving after them, go through the same process. But the subsequent masses of non-Whites have been kept at virtually the same socioeconomic position—at the bottom of the economic ladder—as their predecessors. The irony is that non-Whites often taught European immigrants the skills, which would, at times, enable White ethnics to replace and even move up and beyond them on the economic ladder. Also, tragically, along with other qualifications for citizenship, far too often these immigrants have manifested racism towards non-Whites as a necessary characteristic of their newly adopted Americanism (Westie, 1965).

Non-White groups in America are not just another urban migrant group with a marked potential for assimilation into the mainstream of American society. Rather, as groups they have failed, for generations, to gain the rewards and statuses attained by others. It is somewhat illusory therefore to characterize contemporary urban problems in employment and schooling as transitory and capable of resolution over time. Many of these problems have grown worse over the years and have been strongly resistant to solution. While the ghettos of White ethnics dissolved as social and economic opportunities increased, today's non-White ghettos have become more isolated and crowded as urban renewal in the city centers and the suburban drift of Whites have depressed opportunities in employment, housing, and schooling. Moreover, most of the earlier immigrants arrived knowing that generations of their predecessors had worked their way out of poverty by diligence, saving, and perseverance, and believed that they could do likewise (Hummel & Nagle, 1973). Today's non-White groups share no such conviction. For too long, they have experienced little in the way of reward for hard work, regularity, and frugality; and they have little optimism for that which the future portends.

Although European immigrants met often with cruel discrimination, given the level of technology at that time, unskilled and semiskilled work was needed, and the opportunities for economic betterment were irrefutable. For most urban non-Whites today, however, jobs are scarce and opportunities elusive. Confined ever more densely in central cities and lacking the qualifications to move up or out, they have become the city's captives. Having little social basis for self-esteem, their ambitions and confidence in the society depressed by continual failure, many have tempted to strike out in anger or turn inward to the solace of fantasy through alcohol, drugs, or violence, as members of European groups have done.

While the non-White employment patterns may have much in common with those of poor lower-class Whites, there is a certain measure of irreducible discrimination against non-Whites that reflects their high racial visibility and the historical condition of oppression. Insofar as skin color is used as a criterion for invidious distinctions in employment, there is a dimension of non-White employment patterns that is both unique and idiosyncratic. Skin color and history, then, introduce a measure of uniqueness in non-White groups employment patterns that have separated the non-White further from his society than any European immigrant. The qualitative and quantitative differences between the extent of discrimination suffered by non-Whites and that suffered by White European ethnic groups signify that the character of the discrimination is also different. Certainly the extreme racists in America are generally anti-Semitic and anti-Catholic as well as anti-Black, and so forth. However, Jews and Catholics have achieved greater acceptance because they are White, whereas non-Whites have not, thus highlighting the fact that the color line in America is far more impenetrable and formidable to cross than any White ethnic, religious, or social line has ever been.

Further, we err in not seeing any difference between the ghettos of White ethnics and the non-White ghettos of today. The ghettos of earlier groups were transitory, perceived as a first step on the road to affluence, and for this reason the squalor and the deprivation could be borne. To the non-White, whose parents and grandparents grew up in similar deprivation, the real or perceived chances of upward mobility are slight, making it burdensome to bear the condition of deprivation. Moreover, many ghettos of White immigrant groups were in close proximity to places of work, and in some cases economic opportunities existed within the geographical limits of the ghetto itself. Today, non-Whites have a far different situation. The movement of industry from the cities to the suburbs has left little other than unskilled service employment in close vicinity.

Similarly, today's ghettos are characterized by a level of resentment and hostility that has little parallel to earlier types of ghettos. Numerous factors contribute to this: (a) the high concentration of the permanently unemployed-old and young-who have years of productive life left but see no possibility for jobs; (b) municipal overburden, the inadequate allocation of resources for social services to supplement needs generated by urban living; (c) the heightened deteriorating relationship between ghetto residents and the police; (d) the restrictive opportunity structure for advancement; (e) the political, social, psychological, and economic alienation-both felt and real-from the mechanisms that might produce needed changes; and, (f) the lack of "success models" and sources of job information (Ferman, Kornbluh, & Miller, 1969, pp. 254-272),

THE ROLE OF SCHOOLING

The old adage that knowledge is power has been extended to imply that schooling is the key to elevated social and economic status. A corollary to this belief is that schooling can prevent many of the social ills referred to in earlier sections of this chapter. As early as 1917, then U.S. Commissioner of Education P. P. Claxton noted:

> Comparatively few are aware of the close relationship between education and the production of wealth, and probably fewer still understand fully the extent to which the wealth and the wealth-producing power of any people depend on the quality and quantity of education...(Ellis, 1917 p.3)

Poverty is not to be pleaded as a reason for withholding the means of education, but rather as a reason for supplying it in larger proportion (Ellis, 1917, p. 3). Underlying this almost impervious faith in the value of schooling, is the notion that schooling provided the means by which European immigrants moved into the social, cultural, and political mainstream while Blacks, Hispanics, and Native Americans have evinced far less prosperity. Yet, research by Greer (1972) and by Cohen (1970) sustains the fact that only with certain notable exceptions, city schools were not the ladders of social class mobility for European immigrants, for in many fundamental respects, city schools related to European working-class immigrants in much the same way as they relate to non-White groups and lower-class Whites. Census data in 1920 and in succeeding decades, up to and including 1960, made it clear that even when immigrants became Americans, neither schools nor society offered quite the social class mobility imagined (Carpenter, 1927; Coles, 1969; Glazer & Moynihn, 1963; Jencks & Riesman, 1969; Laidlaw, 1932; McCarthy, 1970; U. S. Bureau of the Census, 1970).

The belief that schools should act as social levers is attributable, in large measure, to progressive educational ideology. In the latter half of the nineteenth century, progressive education began as part of a larger program of social and political reform called the Progressive Movement. The effort was to recast the school as a ladder for social class mobility and political regeneration, viewing the school as an "adjunct to politics" while simultaneously adding to its functions and gradually transforming it into a multipurpose social service center (Cremin, 1964, p. 88). It was at this juncture that school curricula were expanded to include vocational subject matter and to attract a more diversified clientele, as part of a larger movement toward egalitarianism. It should be noted here that while the foregoing was occurring, the former decentralized school decision-making structure was dismantled and removed from the hands of the local clientele to more centralized authorities. The result was that the progressive education movement was not as benevolent and beneficent as initially perceived. As Katz (1971) and Tyack (1974) argue, progressivism was profoundly conservative, for it sprang from a search for social order and social control by the dominant groups in society.

Cohen's (1970) comparative analysis of large-scale surveys of European immigrants, IQ scores, rates of retardation, and academic achievement from the early 1990s to the present is noteworthy. Cumulatively, the research studies to date are uneven, fragmentary, and often noncomparable. But even preliminary findings suggest that the children from many immigrant groups had far mort hindrances in school than initially perceived. While some immigrant populations fared better than others (for example, Jews and children whose parents emigrated from England, Scotland, Wales, Germany, and Scandinavia), it was essentially central and southern European non-Jewish immigrants, and to a small degree, the Irish and Italians, who experienced severe difficulty in school. Whether it was rates of retardation, achievement scores, IQ, or retention, on almost any index of educational attainment, youngsters from these nationalities were far worse off than native urban Whites.

Speculation exists as to the origin of these ethnic differences and school successes. Did they arise from group differences ill inherited social and economic attributes or are they attributable to differences in culture and motivation? The question is a complex one, for data suggest that the rank order of intelligence among immigrant groups corresponded roughly to their rank order on an index of urbanization (Cohen, 1970). Similarly, there is evidence that those immigrant children who achieved well stood somewhat higher on the occupational scale, sustaining again the influence of social class status on achievement (Bere, 1964).

Relative to the school's response to the immigrants, the arrival of massive numbers of immigrant pupils coincided with the emergence of achievement and IQ testing, vocational guidance, and the movement to diversify instruction and curriculum in city schools. Such practices were employed, if not conceived, as a way of limiting the amount and type of schooling presumed suitable for children of the lower social classes.

It should be noted here that heightened debates centered on the comparative intelligence of immigrants that parallels, quite precisely, the debate over the intelligence of Black Americans. Central to this discussion were the questions of whether measured differences were environmental or genetic and whether the tests utilized were culturally and linguistically biased.

With analytical cogency, Greer (1972) debunks the legend that the schools were an effective antipoverty agency that taught poor immigrant children so well that they eventually became affluent Americans. The reality was quite different, for the actual function of the public school was the reverse of its legendary function: to certify lower-status youngsters as socially inferior at an early age and initiate the process that kept many of them economically and socially inferior in adulthood. In Greer's terminology, the school was coined an agency of negative credentialism. Because the legend is so pervasive, social programs and policies founded on the legend continue to persist. And so unswerving is America's faith in the school as the vehicle for social mobility that the search for more effective vehicles to obviate poverty is neglected.

The unassailed assumption, as evidenced by the school's institutional policies and processes, is that all persons start from roughly the same vantage point. The fact is that the legend has permitted our nation to maintain a high degree of inequality while concurrently thwarting any challenges to the underlying assumptions that are perceptibly false. On a societal scale, a notion of equality has been propagated while the victims, the non-White groups in America, are blamed for their failure to use the school as is envisaged, however erroneously, European immigrant groups have done. So the legend supports a social policy which is secure in its faith that the agency for the amelioration of most social problems already exists and that those problems whose solution eludes us now either will be resolved, or are beyond solution, through no fault of that great nation, but because of deficiencies in particular people who cannot seem to solve their problems as countless other Americans have before them (Greer, 1972).

The legend has persisted because the schools have been viewed altruistically, as apolitical institutions above the self-interests so pervasive in our economy and detached from the very structural alignments that perpetuate inequality (Greer, 1972). It was only in the late 1950s and 1960s that radical critiques of the school's role and relationship to lower-status individuals, as well as attempts to inter the legend, gained currency. The legend endures in part because in the early twentieth century in America, unskilled jobs were plenteous, and immigrant youngsters who failed in schools entered the economy and progressed economically. In the main, this romanticized view of historic slums and social class mobility is mindless of the fact not that some immigrants "made it," but "how."

Cultural patterns and the degree of Anglo-conformity were basic to the degree of success experienced by specific groups. To be sure, what the child brings with him to the public school classroom is not a pure or direct product of an historic land of origin, but the combined product of some of those patterns and the patterns established by the group in order to survive in the social class position assigned to it in America. These factors contribute to one's self-esteem and to the preparedness of children from particular racial and ethnic groups to meet successfully the academic and behavioral demands of the public schools (Greer, 1972).

In America, one's racial and ethnic identity has always been an important leverage for social class mobility as well as a clue to one's social status. As Andrew Greeley described it, a "totemic clan" system was built around which the social order was organized (Greeley, 1971, p. 91). The quest for cultural pluralism, just as the quest for Anglo-conformity, which it succeeded, confirms social class status and patterning in American society. The quest for group diversity is meaningless in a society in which it must exist in relation to a dominant culture, which permits social class mobility and progress only with adjustment and accommodation to the dominant mold. As various groups come to America, the level of social class progress and' mobility is now captured by the racial and ethnic group label. The phenomenon of cultural pluralism must be understood as a phenomenon of class and not wholly the defense of indigenous groups against assimilation and acculturation (Greer, 1972). Groups that have achieved, historically, in American society may be plotted in racial and ethnic terms and the perpetuity of each group's relative status in the social hierarchy suggests the class-based nature of ethnic group designations in America.

Perhaps the most pervasive mythology in social science research has been the use of special methodology for perceiving the lot of non-White groups confined to lower social class status. Inherent is the belief that no sound solutions are possible to alleviate the dire straits of such groups. The public school is deemed powerless. Yet this same logic has been utilized to argue quite the reverse for White immigrant groups. Thus some immigrant groups "made it" because of the school, while other groups have been excluded from America's prosperity through no fault of the school (Greer, 1972, p. 103).

The schools are not failures. They are highly successful enterprises, holding firm to the constancy of their task to select individuals for opportunities according to a hierarchy closely paralleling existing social class patterns. That certain racial and ethnic groups remain the underachievers and the bulk of society's burden, evinces the class-based nature of racial and ethnic group derivations in the society.

Both intelligence and academic achievement follow too closely a cultural-economic line to be held the product of the genes unless, of course, one is prepared to identify specific gene pools in identified ethnic groups, taking full account of intermarriage, when and how often for various subgroups, as if the aforementioned is possible without the convenience of skin color (Mayo, 1913). The unalterable fact in our society is that educational marginality parallels the economic marginality of any racial and ethnic group. And, as the Coleman report indicates, school has a less pervasive influence on students than home background (Coleman, Campbell, Hobson, McPartland, Mood, Weinfeld, et al., 1966). Perhaps the most profound and unheeded implication of Greer's research is that, historically, poor people did not succeed economically through the school, but that as they succeeded economically, they exerted pressure to ensure that their children would succeed. The import of this statement suggests that educational success follows upon the heels of economic success, not the converse (Greer, 1972).

POLICY IMPLICATIONS

What the foregoing has shown is that policy makers and researchers have erred badly in the study of the relationships between status and public schooling. The questions that need to be addressed have never been posed and correct answers will hardly be attained until questions are framed growing out of the social, political, and economic actualities that have given rise to factors influencing social class mobility in our society. Attempts to examine status variables and their impact upon social mobility in the society as though they existed in a vacuum are thwarted by the realities of the interdependence and interchangeability of these variables. The ubiquitous nature of the problem is exacerbated when researchers and policy makers fail to examine their work in this light and proceed imperceptibly, mindless of the blatant anachronisms they tend to perpetuate. The advancement of our conceptual knowledge and the failure of school programs and policies suffer accordingly. What remains is ignorance of the impertinence of much of what we continue to do for and to youngsters.

From the initial efforts at egalitarianism, centuries ago, at attempts to maximize educational opportunities for the European immigrant populace, must be added more contemporary attempts to equalize educational opportunities for the school's present populace of Native Americans, Blacks, Hispanics, low-status Whites, females, and the physically and mentally handicapped. There is a long and uneven history of attention given to the educational problems of these groups. Despite various attempts to effectuate a greater equalization of opportunity, there appears to be only modest progress in both the achievement of equality of opportunity or outcomes. Today's educational problems-cultural and linguistic curricular content, the ethnic and racial mix of schools and their staffs, and the overall ineffectiveness of the-schools in educating lower-status youngsters and those with special needs are indicative of a larger problem with historical antecedents. So far, efforts at equalizing opportunity and freeing achievement from its perennial association with status have been largely unsuccessful.

THE LIMITED CAPACITY OF THE SCHOOL

The reality is that the school is limited in its capacity to respond adequately to the diverse characteristics of people and serves best those youngsters who place the fewest demands upon it. Proponents of this view hold that the roots of inequality in the United States are based in the class structure and in the system of racial, sexual, and group power relationships. The school system is but one of an alignment of institutions serving to perpetuate such privilege. Given this, the school system is relatively powerless to correct economic inequality, for the racial, ethnic, and status biases in schooling do not produce but reflect the pyramidal structure of property, privilege, and power in the larger society (see Bell, 1976; Bowles & Gintis, 1976; Edwards, Reich, & Weisskopf, 1978; Thurow, 1972). It is believed therefore that it is primarily the economic system that reinforces racial, ethnic, and other ascriptive distinctions of birth.

For too long, researchers have tended to focus on differential characteristics of groups that occupy lower-status positions when what may be more relevant is the functional status of the group. It is Greeley's "totemic clan" system in operation that confirms hierarchical social patterning in the United States primarily along racial, ethnic, and sexual lines and ensures the perpetuity of each group's status in the social hierarchy. The foregoing underscores the salience of the caste-like nature of sex and particularly ethnic group designations. Although it is low ethnic or sex group status that so often mediates social disadvantagement—a caste-like phenomenon—it is the ubiquitous and recalcitrant fact of class divisions in the society that ultimately requires that there be privileged and less privileged members of the society. As one can see, the degrees of freedom in decision making for the public schools are really quite limited when one considers society's expectation for the schools, since the school's freedom to educate is restricted by what it will allow of a group depending on its status. Inequality of educational opportunity, therefore, is generated mainly by, the differences in opportunities afforded families according to their socioeconomic background.

The authors would be remiss in failing to note the increasing percentages of lower-status racial and ethnic minorities who have moved into the middle-class ranks. But these increases, primarily attributable to compensatory programs and intensive recruitment efforts, serve to give increased benefits to the few, not the many. The authors do not suggest that the image of former lower-status persons in token positions is totally illusory. It is important to note that minority middle-class professionals serve to refute degrading, humiliating, and offensive stereotypes and give incentive to lower-status youth. On the other hand, such an image has caused frustration and aggression as well. It appears that the drive toward achievement and accomplishment that the token image inspires is overwhelmed and distorted by the social reality it conceals (Yeakey & Johnson, 1979).

And, for those who hope that the increasing technological advancement of the industrial society will enhance equality of opportunity and social class mobility?

The available evidence dispels the notion that inequality decreases as industrial societies become more technologically advanced (see Yeakey, 1983; Boudon, 1974). In fact, it has been shown that educational growth has the effect of increasing rather than decreasing social and economic inequality and distance between the high- and low-status groups. One explanation for this is the fact that individuals, groups, or areas already more developed have an inherent advantage over the less fortunate. Schooling simply fortifies this self-perpetuative propensity among preexisting inequalities. Whereas this propensity may be attributable to a Machiavellian effort by the more advanced to "stay on top," it also reflects the operation of what might be called the law of unequal advantage or disadvantage. Children from the upper strata have greater access to higher education; areas more richly endowed by nature or possessing more development potential tend to attract investment more readily; and groups whose members already have more skills, talents, and schooling have a differential advantage in further development (Yeakey, 1983). The process of uneven development continues according to its own logic and dynamic unless countervailing influences, including ideological shifts and egalitarian social, economic, and political policies, make provisions for equal access to schooling in concert with the deliberate and affirmative reallocation of resources to compensate the less advantaged. A caveat is in order here. The authors would welcome, however incremental, school reform in admissions policies, curricular content, prevailing theories and value standards, among others. But to consider changes in the school system in isolation of other social, political, and economic reform is all too illusory, for the crux of inequality and the mobility dilemma in America is explicitly political and economic. The ills suffered by those of lower status in the school system are indicative of even greater wrongs in the larger sociopolitical order. As we strive to construct policies and programs to alleviate educational disadvantagement, we should bear in mind that despite the massive educational development that has characterized American schooling since World War II, such development has had a negligible effect on equality of opportunity and elevated mobility for lower-status persons in our democratic society. It is time to ask why and to address as well the profound societal dilemmas we must unalterably face.

Carol Camp Yeakey and Edmund W. Gordon
Copyright 1982. Published in A. Lieberman & L. M. McLaughlin (Eds.), Policy making in education: Yearbook for the National Society for the Study of Education (pp. 105-132). Chicago: Chicago Press.

19
Broadening the Concept of Career Education

In a chapter which has reached much too limited an audience, Sidney P. Marland, Jr. (who served as US Commissioner of Education from 1970-1973 during Richard M. Nixon's presidency) has made an eloquent plea for the expansion and enhancement of the comprehensive high school to insure that all young people leave the secondary school with generic competence in general education and specific mastery of some areas of vocational education. The paper speaks primarily to the need for development of assessment instruments and procedures by which such competence and mastery may be measured and recorded. However, it is in this paper (written in about 1968) that Marland used the term "career entry" to refer to the transmission from the truly comprehensive high school to post high school study and/or work. Implicit in that paper is a concern for the achievement of a high degree of symmetry on the attention given to intellectual and vocational development. Both were seen as crucial elements in the educational process but the latter had traditionally been given second-class status. The opportunities for schools to reward wider varieties of talent, to develop curricular that had greater relevance for a wider range of pupils and at the same time contribute to the nation's pool of trained labor were given emphasis. It is out of this kind of thinking that the current concern with Career Education, also introduced by Marland, has emerged (see also Marland, 1973, 1974).

Three factors, however, have contributed to a prevailing view of career education that is too narrow. First, we have traditionally considered all basic education which includes vocational skill mastery as a specific goal to be vocational education. Second, in an effort at redressing the balance to give greater status to preparation for work, the employability potential of the products of career education has been overemphasized. Third, the traditional reservations held by academicians for anything that smacks of vocational education, has enabled experts in vocational education to preempt early developments in the emergence of career education.

327

In the review of much of the contemporary thinking relative to career education, one finds a heavy emphasis given to concern for vocational education and development. As recently as 1971, in searching the Educational Index for references to career education, one is referred to vocational education as if the terms are synonymous. In some discussions of the concept, career education takes on different meanings depending on the level of schooling at which it is introduced. For example, in the primary grades career education would involve introduction to some of the categories of work experience available in the immediate community; in the middle grades youngsters are likely to be exposed to guests who are representatives of varieties of vocations. It is also at that level that some attention might be given to attitudes toward work and exposure to some of the tools and instruments associated with categories of work. At the high school level youngsters would be expected to master the skills of at least one marketable occupation.

There have been some efforts at broadening the concept so as to include college bound as well as non-college bound pupils. In this scheme it is proposed that effort be directed at the achievement of competencies in the content of general education as well as mastery of a marketable skill. Graduates of such programs very much like the comprehensive high school could go on to college, gain admission to technical institutes or enter the labor force. In each of these prevailing concepts, the concern with vocational skill and employability is prominent. However, it may well be that none of these concepts is appropriately responsive to the problems of the society in which the young people we are now training will live. If this is true, a broader conception of career education is indicated.

Career may be defined as a course of continued progress in the life of a person. Since, in the recent history of mankind, one's life has been largely defined by the work that one does; vocation or occupation has become the colloquial connotation for career. In the social order that is emerging, work may no longer be central, but may give way to other processes as the critical concerns of life. In such a social order, our conception of career will be closer to the definition, broadly concerned with continued progress throughout the life span requiring attention to the multifaceted life of man.

Let us examine the direction in which our society is moving and identify some of the implicit educational goals to which schooling must be sensitive. The educational tasks faced by the United States have been greatly complicated and enlarged by three revolutionary developments in our society:

1. the explosion in the quantity and complexity of knowledge available to man,

2. emerging transition from an industrial society to a technological, cybernetic society, and

3. the emergence of radical changes in the realms of political awareness, patterns of social organization, explicit values and economic potential.

In almost every discipline or category of knowledge, we are beginning to recognize overlapping concepts, parallels, and dependencies, which make many of the simplistic concepts of the past now appear to be infinitely complex. Postulates that were once accepted as fact have been brought under serious questioning and many can hardly be stated without extensive qualification. In addition, the mass of knowledge available to man is thought to double itself about every ten years. In the United States some 33,000 new books are published each year, and close to a million articles, reports, and scientific papers are produced. The effect of such complexity and magnitude is confounded by its ready availability and often burdensome dissemination as a function of a phenomenally efficient communication system. This vast amount of knowledge and high prospect of its continual growth have important implications not only for what is learned but also how we learn it.

Recent advances in technology that are rapidly enabling us to combine the power of the machine with the capabilities of the computer are ushering us into the cybernetic era. The changes which will be forced upon the society as a result of this transition from the industrial era to the cybernetic era are likely to be more challenging and dislocating than the transition from the agricultural era into industrial era. Not only will the means of production be changed, but man's involvement in it may be all but eliminated. The industrial era placed greater demands on man for skill and reduced his need for strength. The cybernetic era may reduce man's need for skill and greatly increase man's need for mental facility. The industrial era changed the formerly idiosyncratic and crafted to homogenous and repetitious manipulation. The cybernetic era may not only completely change the nature of man's work, but could eliminate work as an essential human function. The implications of these changes will greatly influence education and practically all other aspects of our society.

As societies become more complex and congested, political processes become more intricate and the requirement for politicalization becomes almost essential to survival. The growing political awareness and social action of significant segments of the society is but a reflection of this phenomenon. As a result of this politicalization and other pressures, patterns of social organization are in a considerable state of flux, with old foci and institutions giving way to new and sometimes none. In addition, institutional ties are being severed and alienation is prevalent. In this period of increasingly rapid change, old values are surrendering to new, contradictions between professed and practiced values are becoming more obvious, and conflicts between values are more disruptive. Among the contradictions, none is more obvious than the fact of hunger and poverty in the midst of affluence. This discrepancy in the distribution of society's wealth is maintained by our technological developments that have brought us to a point where our potential productivity is almost unlimited. Such conditions in the presence of high economic potential could become the basis for radical changes in the political economy of the nation. Prediction of the direction of change is difficult, but the existence of such circumstances make obsolete many aspects of traditional cultures as well as the current predominant trend toward political and social conservatism.

To enable our educational efforts to match the demands of these developments, attention must be focused on remodeling the concepts and structure of education so that schools of the future will not only be more appropriately aligned with the needs of that future society, but will also be a positive force in facilitating societal transition. The vast amount of knowledge available to man, together with the demands of the advanced technology by which our society moves, will require of our student-future-citizens skill in the management of knowledge; just as changes in the politico-social sphere will make more necessary than ever before competencies and skill in intrapersonal management and interpersonal relations.

A society that approaches education with these concerns might appropriately give attention to five specific educational goals.

1. Mastery of basic communication skills: Education for all in our society must be built upon the mastery of basic skills in symbolic representation and utilization. The survival tools of the cybernetic era are communication skills including speech, reading, writing, and arithmetic computation.

2. Problem solving: The movement from anxiety, confusion and disorder to problem formulation involves competence in the analysis of data and experience leading first to problem identification followed by competence in the synthesis of concepts and postulates to the end that strategic approaches to problem solution may be generated.

3. The management of knowledge: Knowledge of the physical, biological, and social sciences is so vast as to preclude complete content mastery by any single person. Knowledge of the dimensions of these fields, mastery of their principle, skill in the creation or discovery of order or pattern in their data, and competence in the management and utilization of this knowledge are urgently needed competencies. The emerging technology for the retrieval and technical management of information make knowledge content mastery a far less compelling goal for our citizens of the future.

4. Employment, leisure, and continuing education: Theobald (1963) sees the world of the future as one where achievement through physical work will no longer be a prime requirement in our society. Utilization of leisure will emerge as a central problem. Rapidly changing technology is destroying the lifetime career in a single vocation. Today's children may, as adults, often change not only jobs but also kinds of work, and will be required to make quick adaptation to radically different work situations. The demand will be for trainability and continuing education throughout one's lifespan. However, if some of the projections hold true many, of today's young people as adults will live in a society that no longer rewards physical work. The new society may reward, instead, self-expression through art, through inter action with nature, through social interchange and through symbolization and ideation as art forms. Creative self-expression

may become important for vocational utilization as well as for aesthetic purposes.

5. Self-management: The achievement of goals such as these will involve the schools in activities more explicitly directed at personal, social, and character development. It may require a more adequate understanding of self and others than has usually been achieved. It may make essential the wider adaptations to multi-ethnic and multi-cultural societies. It may require a high degree of flexibility and capacity to accommodate to change as a primary survival tool. It may give added urgency to conflict resolution through avenues of non-violence and the development of appreciative and respectful relationships with the worlds of nature of man-made objects, of ideas, and of values. Thus, the most crucial demand for competence may be in self-management.

The achievement of a high degree of communicative skill, skill in seeking and managing information, and competence in the transfer of knowledge and skills to new situations requires school systems to focus on a wide variety of developmental needs of students rather than on more specialized contents and skills mastery. In this context, career education is perceived not as a substitute for some other aspect of education or as an appendage to the existing content, but as an integral part of all basic educational programs. Career education must be concerned more with facilitating the processes of living, and less with the preparation for making a living—more with the development of a meaningful life than with earning a good livelihood. This view of education, then, does not involve a separate emphasis on one's educational or vocational development, but a comprehensive concern with career development, in which 'career' is defined as the course by which one develops and lives a responsible and satisfying life.

By defining "career" in terms of man's lifespan, we must include one's role as a learner, producer, citizen, family member, consumer, as well, for example, as one's role as a social-political being. Throughout the lifespan these roles are in a constant state of change in relative importance. At one point, an individual may perceive the role of a citizen as his highest priority. At another time, the role of producer may be most important. Although the assignment of permanent pre-eminence to any one of these roles must be avoided, temporary emphasis on one or another may be justified. In that sense, some concern with vocational education may be justified since the vocational role is one for which we must prepare, at least in the immediate future. However, vocational skill development may be inappropriate for long-term goal fulfillment. It is no longer appropriate to focus entirely on one's vocational skills and role, for it may be appropriate to too small a portion of the human lifespan. One's career should be concerned with several roles. Preparation for all of these roles is essential so that one can move in and out of work, politics, institutions; relate in a variety of settings; utilize knowledge and skill for appropriate social adjustments; assign values and make choices in unanticipated situations requiring decisions; and develop appreciation for aesthetic and humane values in preparation for many roles as an expressive and compassionate being.

One of the reasons for this shift in concern is the fact that man increasingly devotes less of his time to the production of things and services, and more to leisure. Leisure is thought of as the varying periods in the lifespan when one is free from the requirements of productive work or service, and free to devote energies to voluntary self-expression. In leisure, gratification comes from doing things relevant to one's own voluntary pursuit of life's idiosyncratic meanings. Thus, one's involvement in self-fulfilling activities is essential to the living of a meaningful and satisfying life.

In earlier stages of our society, most people were able to give meaning to their lives through the work of their vocations. For many, the search for meaning and satisfaction was not engaged. The society did not extend that privilege to them. But one of the contradictions of the present period, one likely to extend into the next, is found in societal conditions that constantly stimulate man to search for meaning and satisfaction, but provide limited resources for fulfilling that search. What is the essential ingredient necessary to the living of a meaningful and satisfying life? Probably nothing is more important to this process than is intellect. It is through man's intellect that all else becomes possible. It is the development of intellect that has enabled man to rise above lower forms of animal life. It is also intellect that prevents man from being reduced to robot status by the technology of his own creation. Yet, it is the intellect of man that receives so little attention in almost all our efforts at schooling.

According to Anthony Wallace (1968), what a man should learn is a function of his culture. What is expected of education depends upon whether it occurs in a revolutionary, conservative or reactionary society. No society is exclusively based on one of these value orientations although one does predominate in a given group during a particular period. According to Wallace (1968), any one society will repeatedly progress through this tripartite cycle of revolutionary, conservative, and reactionary stages.

A particular philosophy of education that determines what is to be learned is associated with each stage. Priorities for learning are assigned and classified into three categories: the development of intellect—the ability to critically analyze transmitted culture to generate or create something more; the development of morality— capability of establishing values and discerning meaning from them; the development of skills—the mechanics or operations used to achieve morality, intellect and productivity. It is interesting to note that none of the stages (revolutionary, conservative, or reactionary) rank intellect as the top learning priority for the society.

Learning priorities for a revolutionary society support a process of cultural transformation by converting the population to a new code of morality, as its primary concern. The first task for this society is to fill positions of leadership with intellectually resourceful people who adhere to the new morality. These personnel are designated to develop and carry out a program that will convert the populace to its revolutionary ethic. Intellect serves a secondary but important function in a stage of cultural, moral transformation.

In a conservative society, since code formation is established, intellect has no special use or political influence. Schools have no reason to emphasize intellect, and responsibility for intellectual education is left to the individual. Pseudo-intellectualism and pretentious amateurs flood academia with incompetencies. The pure intellect utilizes his talents in contributing to amoral production of new weapons, new philosophies, and new curricula. The system rewards technological advancement and places technical skill training as the highest educational priority and intellect that is separated from morality, as the lowest.

In a post-conservative or reactionary society learning centers around two matters: (1) renewal of enthusiasm for a once pure, revolutionary morality, (2) suppression of contradictory doctrine. It should be noted that a common phenomenon in revolutionary and reactionary societies is the paramount concern with morality. However, there are severe discrepancies in their designs for achieving it. In the former, morality and intellect are viewed jointly to achieve predetermined behavior; while in the latter, intellect is viewed as an enemy. In the conservative society, intellect is simply ignored. Most alarming, however, is that a moral or skill-based education is forced upon the young at the expense of personal and intellectual development. Clearly, then, it seems that in all stages of societal development, technique and socialization are stressed, while intellectual cultivation is assigned low priority.

For the emerging social order, it is crucially important that the paradigm described by Wallace (1968) be changed to ensure that the development of intellect is raised to the highest priority. Skills and imposed morality will leave man insufficiently equipped to deal with the most critical problems of twenty-first century man. Even now, the advanced technology of modern communications has created a condition in which: the contradictions of complex social order, the atrocities of interpersonal, intertribal, and international conflicts, the inequities inherent in practically all of our social systems, as well as the richness of our cultural and technical accomplishments, constantly bombard the human spirit with relentless assault and stimulation. Human beings, accustomed to far simpler social environments, have reached to these inputs with habitation or adaptation. As these inputs increase in complexity and intensity, the process of habitation is likely to accelerate, and the processes of adaptation must become more complex. These processes are reflected in a growing insensitivity to social and moral indignation or shock, increasing insulation and isolation in personal-social interchange, alienation from the concepts, institutions, and affiliations which heretofore have provided stabilizing points of reference, and disaffection or loss of a sense of faith in nature, in society, in authority figures, or in oneself as continuing influential forces.

Under such conditions the survival of man will increasingly depend on the capacity of man to use his intellectual power to adapt to his changing environment as well as on his ability to adapt the environment to his special needs. Such capacities are likely to be the product of learning experience designed to cultivate the mind and spirit of man, in ways that combine competence in the use of knowledge, compassionate and empathetic appreciation of values, and mastery of selected skills. It is then these three, which must comprise the dimensions of career education—education that prepares for continued progress in the life of a person. Obviously, such an education must be concerned with mastery of basic communication skill; competence in problem solving; competence in the management of knowledge; preparation for continuing education, employment, and leisure; and competence in self management. The specific content to be emphasized will vary as the emphases of the society change. For a number of years that content will probably include some concern with mastery of a marketable skill along with other content specialties. However, if that education is appropriately managed, it will not have as its purpose mastery of that specific skill or content. Its purpose will be to use that content as the vehicle by which intellectuality--the capacity to understand and to adapt--is developed and enhanced. For if career education, or any education, does not do that, it is inadequate education.

References

References for chapter 1:
Education, Excellence and Equity

American Council on Education (2003). *Minorities in Higher Education 2002-2003: Twentieth Annual Status Report.* Washington, DC: American Council on Education (ACE)

American Council on Education (2000). *Minorities in Higher Education 1999-2000: Seventeenth Annual Status Report.* Washington, DC: American Council on Education (ACE)

Bandura, A. (2001). Social Cognitive Theory: An Agentic Perspective. *Annual Review of Psychology,* 54(1), 1-26.

Bloom, B. (1985). *Developing Talent in Young People.* Ballantine Books, Inc.

Bourdieu, P. (1986). The forms of capital. In J. Richardson (Ed.), *Handbook of theory and research for the sociology of education* (pp. 241-258). Westport, CT: Greenwood Press.

Bransford, J., Brown A., and Cocking, R., Eds. (1999) *How People Learn: Brain, Mind, Experience and School.* Committee on Developments in the Science of Learning, Commission on Behavioral and Social Sciences and Education, National Research Council Washington, D.C. National Academy Press.

Brown v. Board of Education, 347 U.S. 483, 74 S. Ct. 686, 98 L. Ed. 873 (1954).

Bryk, A. S., et. al. (2003). Trust in Schools: A Core Resource for School Reform. *Educational Leadership,* 60(6), 40-44.

Carroll, J.B. (1989). The Carroll model: A 25 year retrospective and prospective view. *Educational Researcher,* 18(1), 26-31.

Carter, D. J., & Wilson, R. (1996). Minorities in higher education. ACE Sixteenth Annual Status Report. Washington, DC: American Council on Education.

Clark, K. B. (1950). "Effect of prejudice and discrimination on personality development." Paper presented at the Midcentury White House Conference on Children and Youth.

Coleman, J. S. (1987). "Families and Schools." *Educational Researcher,* 16, 32-38.

Coleman, J. S. (1966). "Equal schools or equal students?" *The Public Interest,* 60-75.

Cole, M., J. Gay, G. Glick and D. Sharp (1971). *Cultural Context of Learning and Thinking.* New York: Basic Books.

Cole, M. & S. Scribner (1974). *Culture and Thought.* New York: Wiley.

Achievement, N. T. F. o. M. H. (1999). *Reaching the top: A Report of the National Task Force on Minority High Achievement* New York: College Board.

Cremin, L. (1975/2007) Public Education and the Education of the Public. Teachers College Record 109 (7), 1545-1558

Duran, R.P. (1983). *Hispanics' education and background: Predictors of college achievement.* New York: College Entrance Examination Board.

Everson, H.T., & Dunham, M.D. (1996). Signs of Success: Equity 2000-Preliminary Evidence of Effectiveness. New York, NY: College Board. (ERIC Document Reproduction Service No. ED 455 109)

Flavel, J.H. (1979) Metacognition and Cognitive monitoring: a new area of cognitive developmental inquiry, American Psychologist, 34, pp. 906-911.

Fullilove, R. E., & Treisman, P. U. (1990). Mathematics achievement among African American undergraduates at the University of California, Berkeley: an evaluation of the mathematics workshop program. *Journal of Negro Education,* 59(3), 463-478.

Gordon, E.W., & Associates (1988) *Human Diversity and Pedagogy.* New Haven, CT: Yale University, Center in Research on Education, Culture and Ethnicity. Institution for Social and Policy Studies.

Gordon, E. W., & Bhattacharya, M. (1994). Race and intelligence. In Robert J. Sternberg (Ed.), *Encyclopedia of human intelligence.* New York: MacMillan Publishing Company.

Gordon, E. W. & E. Armour-Thomas (1991). Culture and cognitive development. In L. Okagaki & R. Sternberg (Eds.), *Directors of Development: Influences on the Development of Children's Thinking.* Hillsdale, NJ: Erlbaum and Associates.

Greeno, J. (1991). Number sense as situated knowing in a conceptual domain. *Journal for Research in Mathematics Education,* 22(3), 170-218.

Hoffman, K., Lieges, C. & Snyder, T. (2003). *Status and Trends in the Education of Blacks.* Washington, D.C.: National Center for Education Statistics.

Hunt, J. M. (1966). Black genes - White environment. Transaction, 6, 12-22.

Ianni, F.A.J. (1988). *The search for structure: A report on American youth today.* New York: The Free Press.

Jaynes G. D. & R. M. Williams (Eds.) (1989). *A Common Destiny.* Washington, D.C.: National Academy Press.

Martinez, M. E. (2000). *Education as the cultivation of intelligence.* Mahwah, NJ: Lawrence Erlbaum Publishers.

Mercer, J. R. (1973). *Labeling the Mentally Retarded: Clinical and Social System Perspective on Mental Retardation.* Berkeley: University of California Press.

Miller, L. Scott (1995), *An American Imperative: Accelerating Minority Educational Advancement.* New Haven, Ct. Yale University Press.

Piven, F. F., & Cloward, R. A. (1993). *Regulating the Poor: The Functions of Public Welfare.* New York: Vintage./Piven, F. F., & Cloward, R. A. (1971). *Regulating the poor:* The functions of public welfare. New York: Pantheon Books.

Plessy v. Ferguson, 163 U.S. 537 (1896).

Ramist, L., Lewis, C., and McCamley-Jenkins, L. (1994). *Student Group Differences in Predicting College Grades: Sex, Language, and Ethnic Groups.* New York: The College Board.

Resnick, L. B. (1987). Learning in and out of school. *Educational Researcher,* 16(9), 13-20.

Sexton, P. (1969). *Income and education.* New York: Viking Press.

St. John, N., & Smith, N. (1975) School Desegregation: Outcomes for Children. New York: Wiley

Steele, C.M., Aronson, J. (2000). Stereotype threat and the intellectual test performance of African Americans. In *Stereotypes and prejudice: Essential readings,* C. Stangor (Ed), 369-389, Philadelphia, PA: Psychology Press/Taylor & Francis. Steele, C. M., & Aronson, J.(1995). Stereotype threat and the intellectual test performance of African-Americans. Journal of Personality and Social Psychology,69, 797-811.

Steinberg, L., Bradford, B., & Dornbusch, S. (1996). *Beyond the classroom: Why school reform has failed and what parents need to do.* New York: Simon & Schuster

Vygotsky, L.S. (1978). *Mind and society: The development of higher mental processes.* Cambridge, MA: Harvard University Press.

Weiss, H. B., Bouffard, S.M., Bridgall, B.L., & Gordon, E.W. (2009). Reframing Family Involvement in Education: Supporting Families to Support Educational Equity *Equity Matters: Research Review* (Vol. 5). New York: The Campaign for Educational Equity.

Wilson, W.J. (1978). *The declining significance of race: Blacks and changing American institutions.* Chicago: University of Chicago Press.

Wolf, Richard. (1995). The measurement of environments, in A. Anastasi (ed.), Testing problems in perspective. Washington, D.C.: American Council on Education.

References for chapter 2:
Compensatory Education

American Council on Education, "Higher Education as a National Resource." School and Society, Vol. 91, May 4, 1963, pp. 218-221.

Anastasi, Anne, and D'Angelo, Rita Y. "A Comparison of Negro and White Preschool Children in Language Development and Goodenough Draw-A-Man IQ." *Pedagogical Seminary and Journal of Genetic Psychology (Journal of Genetic Psychology],* Vol. 81, December 1952, pp. 147-165.

References

Ausubel, David P., "How Reversible Are the Cognitive and Motivational Effects of Cultural Deprivation? Implications for Teaching the Culturally Deprived Child." *Urban Education,* Vol. I, No. I, Autumn 1964, pp. 16-38.

Beckey, Ruth Elizabeth, "A Study of Certain Factors Related to Retardation of Speech." *Journal of Speech Disorders,* Vol. 7, September 1942, pp. 223-249.

Bellamy, Edward, *Looking Backward.* Cleveland, Ohio: The World Publishing Company, 1945, 3II pp. (out of print). Available through Modern Library, Inc

Bernstein, Basil, "Language and Social Class." *British Journal of Sociology,* Vol. 11, September 1960, pp. 271-276.

Bernstein, Basil, "Social Class and Linguistic Development: A Theory of Social Learning," Chap. 24, pp. 288-314 in Halsey, A. H.; Floud, J.; and Anderson, C. A.; eds., *Education, Economy and Society.* New York: Free Press of Glencoe, Inc., 1961, 640 pp.

Bernstein, Basil, "Social Class, Linguistic Codes and Grammatical Elements." *Language and Speech,* Vol. 5, 1962, pp. 221240•

Birch, Herbert G., *Brain Damage in Children: Biological and Social Aspects.* Baltimore, Md.: Williams and Wilkins Co., 1964, 199 pp.

Birch, Herbert G., and others, "Reactions to New Situations - An Index of Individuality in Childhood." *American Journal of Orthopsychiatry,* Vol. XXXII, No.2, March [962, pp. 341-342.

Board of Education of the City of New York, Bureau of Educational Research and Bureau of Educational and Vocational Guidance, *Demonstration Guidance Project: Fourth Annual Report,* 1959-60. New York: Board of Education, 68 pp.

Brazziel, William F., and Terrell, Mary, "An Experiment in the Development of Readiness in a Culturally Disadvantaged Group of First Grade Children." *Journal of Negro Education,* Vol. 31, Winter 1962, pp. 4-7.

Carroll, Rebecca Evans, "Relation of Social Environment to the Moral Ideology and the Personal Aspirations of Negro Boys and Girls." *School Review,* Vol. 53, January 1945, pp. 30-38.

Carson, Arnold S., and Rabin, A. I., "Verbal Comprehension and Communication in Negro and White Children." *Journal of Educational Psychology,* Vol. 51, April 1960, pp. 47-51.

References

Clark, Kenneth B., "Segregated Schools in New York City." Paper read at conference, "Child Apart," North Side Center for Child Development, New Lincoln School, New York, April 1954.

Clark, Kenneth B., and Plotkin, Lawrence, *The Negro Student at Integrated Colleges.* New York: National Scholarship Service and Fund for Negro Students, 1963, 59 pp.

Clarke, A. D. B., and Clarke, A. M., "Cognitive Changes in the Feebleminded." *British Journal of Psychology,* Vol. 45, 1954, pp. 173-179.

Coles, Robert, *The Desegregation of Southern Schools: A Psychiatric Study.* New York: Anti-Defamation League, July 1963, 25 pp.

Davidson, Kenneth S., and others, "A Preliminary Study of Negro and White Differences on Form I of the Wechsler Bellevue Scale." *Journal of Consulting Psychology,* Vol. 14, October 1950, pp. 489-492.

Davis, Allison, "The Future Education of Children from Low Socio-Economic Groups," pp. 27-54, in Elam, Stanley, ed., *New Dimensions for Educational Progress.* Bloomington, Ind.: Phi Delta Kappa, 1963, 190 pp.

Davis, Paul H., "Changes Are Coming in the Colleges." *Journal of Higher Education,* Vol. 33, March 1962, pp. 141-147.

Day, R. E., *Civil Rights U.S.A.; Public Schools, Southern States,* 1963: *North Carolina.* Staff report submitted to the United States Commission on Civil Rights. Washington, D. C.: Government Printing Office, 60 pp.

Deutsch, Cynthia, "Auditory Discrimination and Learning: Social Factors." *Merrill- Palmer Quarterly,* Vol. 10, July 1964, pp. 277-2 96.

Deutsch, Martin, *Minority Group and Class Status as Related to Social and Personality Factors in Scholastic Achievement.* Society for Applied Anthropology, Monograph NO.2. Ithaca, N. Y.: Cornell University, 1960,32 pp.

Deutsch, Martin, "The Disadvantaged Child and the Learning Process," pp. 163179 in Passow, A. Harry, ed., *Education in Depressed Areas.* New York: Bureau of Publications, Teachers College, Columbia University, 1963, 359 pp.

Deutsch, Martin, "The Role of Social Class in Language Development and Cognition." *American journal of Orthopsychiatry,* Vol. XXXV, January 1965, pp. 7888.

342

References

Dreger, Ralph Mason, and Miller, Kent S., "Comparative Psychological Studies of Negroes and Whites in the United States." *Psychological Bulletin,* Vol. 57, September 1960, pp. 361-402.

Educational Policies Commission, *Universal Opportunity for Education Beyond the High School.* Washington, D. C.: National Education Association, 1964, 36 pp.

Ferry, H., "College Responsibilities and Social Expectations." *Teachers College Record,* Vol. 65, November 1963, pp. 99-111.

Gallagher, J. J., "Social Status of Children Related to Intelligence, Propinquity and Social Perception." *Elementary School journal,* Vol. 58, January 1958, pp. 225231.

Goff, Regina M., "Some Educational Implications of the Influence of Rejection on Aspiration Levels of Minority Group Children." *journal of Experimental Education,* Vol. 23, December 1954, pp. 179-183.

Gordon, Edmund W., "A Review of Programs of Compensatory Education." *American journal of Orthopsychiatry,* Vol. XXXV, July 1965, pp. 640-651.

Gordon, Edmund W., "Counseling Socially Disadvantaged Children," pp. 275-282 in Riessman, Frank; Cohen, Jerome; and Pearl, Arthur; eds., *Mental Health of the Poor.* New York: Free Press of Glencoe, Inc., 1964, 648 pp.

Gordon, Edmund W., *Educational Achievement in the Prince Edward County Free School,* 1963-64. New York: Ferkauf Graduate School of Education, Yeshiva University, 1965, 63 pp. Mimeographed.

Gould, Rosalind, "Some Sociological Determinants of Goal Strivings." *journal of Social Psychology,* Vol. 13, May [941, pp. 461 -473.

Haeusserman, Else, *Developmental Potential of Preschool Children: An Evaluation of Intellectual, Sensory and Emotional Functioning.* New York: Grune & Stratton, Inc., 1958, 285 pp.

Hager, Walter E., "Challenges to Public Higher Education." *School and Society,* Vol. 91, April 20, 1963, pp. 200-201.

Hansen, Carl F., "The Scholastic Performances of Negro and White Pupils in the Integrated Public Schools of the District of Columbia." *Harvard Educational Review,* Vol. 30, o. 3, Summer 1960, pp. 216-236.

343

References

Harrington, Michael, *The Other America: Poverty in the United States*. New York: The Macmillan Company, 1962, 191 pp.

Hieronymus, A. N., "Study of Social Class Motivation: Relationships Between Anxiety for Education and Certain Socio-Economic and Intellectual Variables." *Journal of Educational Psychology*, Vol. 42, April 1951, pp. 193-205.

Hilliard, George H., and Troxwell, Eleanor, "Informational Background as a Factor in Reading Readiness and Reading Progress." *Elementary School journal*, Vol. 38, December 1957, pp. 255-263.

Hunt, Joseph McV., *Intelligence and Experience*. New York: Ronald Press Company, 1961, 416 pp.

Irwin, Orvis C., "Infant Speech: The Effect of Family Occupational Status and of Age on Use of Sound Types." *journal of Speech and Hearing Disorders*, Vol. 13, September 1948, pp. 224-226.

Jensen, Arthur R., "Learning Ability in Retarded, Average, and Gifted Children." *Merrill-Palmer Quarterly*, Vol. 9, April 1963, pp. 123-140.

John, Vera P., and Goldstein, Leo S., "The Social Context of Language Acquisition." *Merrill-Palmer Quarterly*, Vol. 10, July 1964, pp. 265-276.

Katz, Irwin, "Review of Evidence Relating to Effects of Desegregation on the Intellectual Performance of Negroes." *American Psychologist*, Vol. 19, June 1964, pp. 381-399.

Keller, Suzanne, "The Social World of the Urban Slum Child: Some Early Findings." *American journal of Orthopsychiatry* Vol. XXXIII, October 1963, pp. 823-831.

Kendrick, S. A., "College Board Scores and Cultural Bias." *College Board Review*, No. 55, Winter 1964-65, pp. 7-9.

Keppel, Francis, "In the Battle for Desegregation What Are the Flanking Skirmishes, What is the Fundamental Struggle?" *Phi Delta Kappan*, Vol. 46, September 1964, PP.3-5.

Kirk, Samuel A., *Early Education of the Mentally Retarded: An Experimental Study*. Urbana: University of Illinois Press, 1958, 216 pp.

Klineberg, Otto, "Negro-White Differences in Intelligence Test Performance: A New Look at an Old Problem." *American Psychologist* Vol. 18, April 1963, pp. 198-203.

Lee, Everett S., "Negro Intelligence and Selective Migration," pp. 669-676, in Jenkins, James J., and Paterson, Donald S., eds., *Studies in Individual Differences.* New York: Appleton-Century-Crofts, 1961, 774 pp.

LeShan, Lawrence L., "Time Orientation and Social Class." *journal of Abnormal and Social Psychology,* Vol. 47, July 1952, pp. 589-592.

Lopez, Leo, and Thomas, Donald, *Recommendations for Expansion by the California State Legislature of the State Compensatory Education Program Based on the McAteer Act.* Sacramento, Calif.: Advisory Committee on Compensatory Education, 46 pp. Mimeographed.

McGrath, Earl J., *The Predominantly Negro Colleges and Universities in Transition.* New York: Bureau of Publications, Teachers College, Columbia University, 1965, 204 pp.

McKendall, Benjamin W., Jr., "Breaking the Barriers of Cultural Disadvantage and Curriculum Imbalance." *Phi Delta Kappan,* Vol. 46, March 1965, pp. 307-311.

Meister, Morris; Tauber, Abraham; and Silverman, Sidney, "Operation Second Chance." *junior College journal,* Vol. 33, October 1962, pp. 78- 88.

Montague, David O., "Arithmetic Concepts of Kindergarten Children in Contrasting Socioeconomic Areas." *Elementary School journal,* Vol. 64, April 1964, pp. 393-397·

Niemeyer, John, "Some Guidelines to Desirable Elementary School Reorganization." *Programs for the Educationally Disadvantaged.* U.S. Office of Education Bulletin 1963, No. 17 (OE-35044). Washington, D. C.: U.S. Department of Health, Education, and Welfare, 1963, pp. 80-85.

Pasamanick, Benjamin, and Knobloch, Hilda, "The Contribution of Some Organic Factors to School Retardation in Negro Children." *journal of Negro Education,* Vol. 27, February 1958, pp. 4-9.

Plaut, Richard L., *Blueprint for Talent Searching: America's Hidden Manpower.* New York: National Scholarship Service and Fund for Negro Students, 1957, 41 pp.

Plaut, Richard'L., "Increasing the Quantity and Quality of Negro Enrollment in College." *Harvard Educational Review,* Vol. 30, No. 3, Summer 1960, pp. 270-279.

Plaut, Richard L., "NSSFNS and Volunteers Create New Program for Disadvantaged Students." *ACAC Newsletter,* Vol. 2, No. 4, October 1964.

References

Pringle, M. L. Kellmer, and Tanner, Margaret, "The Effects of Early Deprivation on Speech Development: A Comparative Study of Four Year Olds in a Nursery School and in Residential Nurseries." *Language and Speech,* Vol. I, October December 1958, pp. 269-287.

Riessman, Frank, *The Culturally Deprived Child.* New York: Harper & Row, Publishers, 1962, 140 pp.

Rockefeller Panel Reports, *Prospect for America.* New York: Doubleday & Company, Inc., 1961,486 pp.

Rosen, Bernard C., "The Achievement Syndrome: A Psychocultural Dimension of Social Stratification." *American Sociological Review,* Vol. 21, April 1956, pp. 20321 I.

Rosenthal, Robert, *Research on Experimenter Bias.* Paper read at the American Psychological Association, Cincinnati, September 1959·

Sells, S. B., "An Interactionist Looks at the Environment." *American Psychologist,* Vol. 18, November 1963, pp. 696-702.

Sewell, William H.; Haller, Archie 0.; and Straus, Murray A., "Social Status and Educational and Occupational Aspiration." *American Sociological Review,* Vol. 22, February 1957, pp. 67-73.

Siller, Jerome, "Socioeconomic Status and Conceptual Thinking." *Journal of Abnormal and Social Psychology,* Vol. 55, November 1957, pp. 365-371.

Silverman, Susan B., *Self-Images of UpperMiddle Class and Working Class Young Adolescents.* Unpublished master's thesis, University of Chicago, 1963

Smith, Sherman E.; Mathamy, Harvard V.; and Milfs, Merele M., *Are Scholarships the Answer?* Albuquerque: University of New Mexico Press, 1960, 89 pp.

Southern School News, Untitled. *Southern School News,* Vol. 7, No.2, Columns 1-2, August 1960.

Stallings, Frank H., "A Study of the Immediate Effects of Integration on Scholastic Achievement in the Louisville Public Schools." *Journal of Negro Education,* Vol. 28, Fall 1959, pp. 439-444.

Strauss, Alfred A., and Kephart, N. C., *Psychopathology and Education of the Brain-Injured Child. Vol. 2, Progress in Theory and Clinic.* New York: Grune & Stratton, Inc., 1955,266 pp.

Strodtbeck, Fred L., "The Hidden Curriculum of the Middle Class Home," pp.

1531, in Hunnicutt, C. W., ed., *Urban Education and Cultural Deprivation.* Syracuse, N. Y.: Syracuse University Press, 1964, 126 pp.

Templin, Mildred C., *Certain Language Skills in Children; Their Development and Interrelationships.* Institute of Child Welfare Monograph Series No. 26. Minneapolis: University of Minnesota Press, 1957, 183 pp.

Templin, Mildred C., "Norms on Screening Test of Articulation for Ages Three through Eight." *Journal of Speech and Hearing DisorrJers,* Vol. 18, December 1953, pp. 323-331.

Theobald, Robert, *Free Man and Free Markets.* New York: Crown Publishers, Inc., 1963, 203 pp.

Thomas, Dominic Richard, *Oral Language, Sentence Structure and Vocabulary of Kindergarten Children Living in Low SocioEconomic Urban Areas.* Doctoral thesis. Detroit, Mich.: Wayne State University, 1962, 393 pp. Abstract: Dissertation Abstracts, Vol. 23, NO.3, 1962, p. 1014.

Trueblood, Dennis L., "The Role of the Counselor in the Guidance of Negro Students." *Harvard Educational Review,* Vol. 30, Summer 1960, pp. 252- 269.

Turkewitz, G.; Gordon, E. W.; and Birch, Herbert G., "Head Turning in the Human Neonate: Spontaneous Patterns." *Journal of Genetic Psychology,* Vol. 107, September 1965, pp. 143-158.

Wax, Murray L.; Wax, Rosalie H.; and Dumont, Robert V., *Formal Education in an American Indian Community.* Society for the Study of Social Problems Monograph, Spring 1964, 126 pp.

Wax, M. L., Wax, R. H., & Dumont, R. V. Jr. (1989). Formal education in an American Indian community: Peer society and the failure of minority education. Long Grove, IL: Waveland

References for chapter 3:
Individualization and Personalization in Pedagogy

Applebee, A., Langer, J., Nystrand, M., & Gamoran, A. (2003). Discussion-based approaches to developing understanding: Classroom instruction and student performance in middle and high school English. *American Educational Research Journal,* 40, 685–730.

References

Bandura, A. (1991b). Self-regulation of motivation through anticipatory and self-regulatory mechanisms. In R. A. Dienstbier (Ed.), Perspectives on motivation: Nebraska symposium on motivation (Vol. 38, pp. 69-164). Lincoln: University of Nebraska Press.

Bandura, A. (1986). *Social Foundations of Thought & Action: A Social Cognitive Theory.* Englewood Cliffs, NJ: Prentice-Hall.

Bandura, A. (1988). Self-regulation of motivation and action through goal systems. In V. Hamilton, G. H.

Bandura, A. 2001. "Social Cognitive Theory: An Agentic Perspective." *Annual Review of Psychology* 52(1): 1-26

Bangert-Drowns, R. L., Kulik, C. C., Kulik, J. A., & Morgan, M. (1991). The instructional effect of feedback in test-like events. *Review of Educational Research,* 61, 213-238.

DeMarrais, K. Bennett and LeCompte. M.D. (1990). The Way Schools Work: A Sociological Analysis of Education, 301 pages. (2nd edition, 1995, 365 pages; 3rd edition, 1998, 382 pages) White Plains, NY: Longman.

Bennett, A., Bridglall, B.L., Cauce, A. M., Everson, H.T., Gordon, E.W., Lee, C.D, et. al (2004). All students reaching the top: Strategies for closing academic achievement gaps. A report of the National Study Group for the Affirmativ Development of Academic Ability. Naperville, IL: Learning Point Associates, Central Regional Educational Laboratory.

Bolvin, J. & Glaser, R. 1968 Developmental Aspects of Individually Prescribed Instruction. Pittsburgh University, PA Learning Research and Development Center. Sponsor Agency: Office of Education (DHEW), Washington, DC. Bureau of Research.

Bourdieu P. (1986). The form of capital. In J.G. Richardson (Ed.), *Handbook of theory and research for sociology of education* (pp. 241-258). New York: Greenwood Press.

Brandt, D. (2003). Changing literacy. *The Teachers College Record,* 105(2), 245-260.

Bridglall, B. L., & Gordon, E.W. (2004). The nurturance of African American scientific talent. *Journal of African American History,* 89(4), 331-347.

Bryk, A.S. & Schneider, B. (2002). *Trust in schools: A core resource for improvement.* New York, NY: Russell Sage Foundation.

References

Fletcher, R. (1991). The Burt Case: Another Foray. (Book Reviews: Science, Ideology, and the Media. The Cyril Burt Scandal.). *Science, 253,* 1565-1566.

Callahan, R. E. (1962). Education and the cult of efficiency. *Chicago: University of Chicago.*

Carver, C. S., & Scheier, M. (1998). *On the self-regulation of behavior.* Cambridge, UK: Cambridge University Press.

Chess, Stella, and Alexander Thomas. *Goodness of fit: Clinical applications from infancy through adult life.* Psychology Press, 1999.

Chronbach and Richard Snow (1977) Aptitudes and Instructional Methods: A handbook for Research on Interactions. New York: Irvington.

Coleman, J. (1988). Social capital and the creation of human capital. *American Journal of Sociology, 94,* 95-120.

Connor-Smith, Jennifer K.; Compas, Bruce E.; Wadsworth, Martha E.; Thomsen, Alexandra Harding; Saltzman, *Heidi Journal of Consulting and Clinical Psychology,* Vol 68(6), Dec 2000, 976-992. doi: 10.1037/0022-006X.68.6.976

Esposito. (1966). *Dynamic Blending and Adaptations to Differential Human Charatericstics.* New York, New York: Yeshiva University.

Finch, Shanahan, Mortimer, and Ryu 1991 as cited in Heinz, W. R. (Ed.). (1999). *From education to work: cross national perspectives.* Cambridge University Press.

Flanagan, J. C. (1971, January). "The Plan System for Individualizing Education," NCME: Measurement in Education. 2

Eccles, J. S., Roeser, R. Wigfield, A., & Freedman-Doan, C. (1999). Academic and motivational pathways through middle childhood. In L. Balter and C. S. Tamis-Lemonda (Eds.), Child psychology: A handbook of contemporary issues (pp.287-317). New York: Taylor & Francis;

Fabes, R. A., Shepard, S., Guthrie, I., & Martin, C. L. (1997). The roles of temperamental arousal and same-sex play in children's social adjustment. *Developmental Psychology, 33,* 693-702

Garner and Cole 1989 see Cole, P. M., Martin, S. E., & Dennis, T. A. (2004). Emotion regulation as a scientific construct: Methodological challenges and directions for child development research. *Child development, 75*(2), 317-333.;

Gardner, H. (2006) The development and education of the mind: the selected works of Howard Gardner. New York, Routledge

349

Gerris, Dekovic and Janssens 1997 as cited in Ratner, C. (2002). *Cultural psychology: theory and methods.* Springer.

Glaser, R. (1977) Adaptive Education: Individual Diversity and Learning. New York, Holt, Rinehart & Winston

Glaser, R. (1966). The Education of Individuals. PA, University of Pittsburgh: Learning Research and Development Center

Gordon, E. W. (2000). Production of Knowledge and Pursuit of Understanding. In Y. C.C. (Ed.), *Producing Knowledge Pursuing Understanding.* Stamford, CT: Advances in Education Divers Communities: Research Policy and Praxis.

Gordon, E. W. (1992) Implications of Diversity in Human Characteristics for Authentic Assessment. Los Angeles, University of California, Los Angeles, National Center for Research on Evaluation, Standards, and Student Testing (CRESST): 11

Graham, S., & Weiner, B. (1996). Theories and principles of motivation. In D. C. Berliner & R. Calfee (Eds.), Handbook of educational psychology (pp. 63-84). New York: Macmillan.

Greeno, J. G. (2005) Toward the development of Intellective character. Affirmative Development: Cultivating Academic Ability. B. L. E. W. Gordon, Bridglall. Lanham, Rowman & Littlefield Publishers: 17-47

Hogan and Pressley 1997; Rogoff 1990; Wood et al. 1976 as cited in Reiser, B. J. (2004). Scaffolding complex learning: The mechanisms of structuring and problematizing student work. *The Journal of the Learning Sciences,* 13(3), 273-304

Hughes, M., & Demo, D. H. (1989). Self-perceptions of Black Americans: Self-esteem and personal efficacy. *American Journal of Sociology,* 132-159.

Kagen, J., 1998. Three Seductive Ideas. Cambridge, MA: Harvard University Press

Kelly, George (1955) The psychology of personal constructs. 2 vols., New York: Norton

Kliebard, H. M. (1995). The Tyler rationale revisited. *Journal of Curriculum Studies,* 27(1), 81-88.

Knapp, M. S., Shields, P. M., & Turnbull, B. J. (1995). Academic challenge in high-poverty classrooms. *Phi Delta Kappan,* 76, 770-770.

Kohn, M. L. (1983). On the transmission of values in the family: A preliminary formulation. *Research in sociology of education and socialization,* 4(1), 1-12.

Kornhaber, M. (1994). The theory of multiple intelligences: Why and how school we it. Qualifying paper, Graduate School of Education, Harvard University, Cambridge, MA

LeDoux 2000 as cited in Radin, J. L. (2012). Creating Enriched Learning Environments: Lessons from Brain Research.

Lewis, S. K., Ross, C. E., & Mirowsky, J. (1999). Establishing a sense of personal control in the transition to adulthood. *Social Forces,* 77(4), 1573-1599.

Liu, X., Kaplan, H. B., & Risser, W. (1992). Decomposing the reciprocal relationships between academic achievement and general self-esteem. *Youth & Society.*

Locke, E. A., & Latham, G. P. (1990). *A theory of goal setting & task performance.* Prentice-Hall, Inc.

Masten, A. S. G., N. (1985) *Risk, vulnerability and protective factors in developmental psychology. Advances in child clinical psychology.* B.B. L. A. E. Kazdin. New York: Plenum Press: 1-52

Messick, D. M., & Schell, T. (1992). Evidence for an equality heuristic in social decision making. *Acta Psychologica,* 80(1), 311-323.

Mirowsky, John and Catherine E. Ross. 1998. "Education, Personal Control, Life Style and Health: A Human Capital Hypothesis." Research on Aging 20:415-49.

Mirowsky and Ross 1989 as cited in Mirowsky, John and Catherine E. Ross. 1998. "Education, Personal Control, Life Style and Health: A Human Capital Hypothesis." Research on Aging 20:415-49.

Mirowsky and Ross 1986; 1989 as cited in Mirowsky, John and Catherine E. Ross. 1998. "Education, Personal Control, Life Style and Health: A Human Capital Hypothesis." Research on Aging 20:415-49.

Mone, M. A., Baker, D. D., & Jeffries, F. (1995). Predictive validity and time dependency of self-efficacy, self-esteem, personal goals, and academic performance. *Educational and Psychological Measurement,* 55(5), 716-727.

Lin, N., Cook, K. S., & Burt, R. S. (Eds.). (2001). *Social capital: Theory and research.* Transaction Publishers.

Noddings; Caring: A feminine approach to ethics and moral education. University of California Press, Berkeley (1984).

Pianta, R. C., Cox, M. J., Taylor, L., & Early, D. (1999). Kindergarten teachers' practices related to the transition to school: Results of a national survey. *Elementary School Journal,* 100, 71–86.

Portes, Alejandro. 1998. "Social Capital: Its Origins and Applications in Modern Sociology," *Annual Rev. Sociology* 24, pp. 1-24.

Pintrich, P. R. & B. Schrauben. (1992). "Students' motivational beliefs and their cognitive engagement in classroom tasks." Pp. 149-183 in Student perceptions in the classroom: Causes and consequences, edited by D. Schunk & J. Meece. Hillsdale, NJ: Erlbaum.

Pintrich, P. R., & Zusho, A. (2002). The development of academic self-regulation: The role of cognitive and motivational factors. In A. Wigfield & J. S. Eccles (Eds.), Development of achievement motivation (pp. 249–284). San Diego, CA: Academic.

Pressley, M., Levin, J. R., & Miller, G. E. (1982). The keyword method compared to alternative vocabulary-learning strategies. *Contemporary Educational Psychology,* 7(1), 50-60.

Dolezal, S. E., Welsh, L. M., Pressley, M., & Vincent, M. M. (2003). How nine third-grade teachers motivate student academic engagement. *The Elementary School Journal,* 239-267.

Rosenberg, Morris. 1979. Conceiving the Self. Malabar,FL:RobertE. Krieger.

Rosenberg et al. 1989. Society and the Adolescent Self-Image. Rev. ed. Middletown, CT: Wesleyan University Press.

Rosenberg, Morris and Roberta G. Simmons. 1972. Black and White Self-Esteem: The Urban School Child. Washington, D.C.: The American Sociological Association. Siegel, Sidney.

Ross, C. E., & Broh, B. A. (2000). The roles of self-esteem and the sense of personal control in the academic achievement process. *Sociology of Education,* 270-284.

References

Ross, Catherine E. and John Mirowsky. 1992. "Households, Employment, and the Sense of Control." Social Psychology Quarterly 55: 21 7-35.

Ross, Catherine E., and Jaya Sastry. 1999. "The Sense of Personal Control: Social Structural Causes and Emotional Consequences." Pp 369-94 in The Handbookof the Sociology of Mental Health and Illness, edited by Carol S. Aneshensel and Jo C. Phelan. New York: Plenum

Rotter, J. B. (1966). Generalized expectancies for internal versus external control of reinforcement. Psychological Monographs, 80 (Whole No. 609).

Schwalbe, M. L., & Staples, C. L. (1991). Gender differences in sources of self-esteem. *Social Psychology Quarterly*, 158-168.

Schunk, 1995

Sizer, T. (1973). *Places for learning, places for joy: Speculations on American school reform.* Cambridge, MA: Harvard University Press.

Sternberg, R. J., & Horvath, J. A. (Eds.). (1999). Tacit knowledge in professional practice: Researcher and practitioner perspectives. Psychology Press.

Thomas, J. W., Iventosch, L., & Rohwer Jr, W. D. (1987). Relationships among student characteristics, study activities, and achievement as a function of course characteristics. *Contemporary Educational Psychology*, 12(4), 344-364.

McLaughlin, M. W., & Talbert, J. E. (1993). Contexts that matter for teaching and learning: Strategic opportunities for meeting the nation's educational goals.

Thomas, A., & Chess, S. (1977). Temperament and development. New York: Brunner/Mazel.

Thomas, A., Chess, S., Birch, H., Hertzig, M., & Korn, A. (1971). Behavioral Individuality in Early Childhood. New York, New York University Press.

James Toliver (2003) personal communication between Gordon. University of Maryland, Baltimore County.

Ergene, T. (2003). Effective interventions on test anxiety reduction a meta-analysis. *School Psychology International*, 24(3), 313-328.

Wade, T. J., Thompson, V., Tashakkori, A., & Valente, E. (1989). A longitudinal analysis of sex by race differences in predictors of adolescent self-esteem. *Personality and Individual Differences*, 10(7), 717-729.

Wallston, K. A., Wallston, B. S., & DeVellis, R. (1978). Development of the multidimensional health locus of control (MHLC) scales. *Health Education & Behavior,* 6(1), 160-170.

Wheaton, B. (1980). The sociogenesis of psychological disorder: An attributional theory. *Journal of health and Social Behavior,* 100-124.

Wiske, S., Moore, J., Sweeney, L.B., Grogan, D., Strumminger, R., Williams, A. (1997) Designing a Networked Learning Environment: A Working Paper. Retrieved from http://learnweb.harvard.edu/ent/library/avd_paper1.html .

Wolters, C. A. (2003). Regulation of motivation: Evaluating an underemphasized aspect of self-regulated learning. *Educational psychologist,*38(4), 189-205.

Yabiku, S. T., Axinn, W. G., & Thornton, A. (1999). Family Integration and Children's Self-Esteem 1. *American Journal of Sociology,* 104(5), 1494-1524.

Zimmerman, 1994 as found in Zimmerman, B. J. (2002). Becoming a self-regulated learner: An overview. *Theory into practice,* 41(2), 64-70.

Bransford, J., Brown, A. L., & Cocking, R. R. National Research Council. Committee on Developments in the Science of Learning. 1999. How people learn: brain, mind, experience, and school.

References for chapter 4:
A Curriculum of Cultural Interdependence and Plural Competence

Banks, J.A. (1992). *African American Scholarship and the Evolution of Multicultural Education.*

Banks, J.A. & McGee Banks, C.A. Editors (1994). *Handbook of Research on Multicultural Education.* New York: Macmillan.

Bloom, A. (1987). *The Closing of the American Mind.* New York: Simon & Schuster.

Case, R. (1985). *Intellectual Development: A Systematic Reinterpretation.* New York: Academic Press.

Ceci, S.J. & Liker, J. (1985). *Academic and Nonacademic Intelligence and Experimental Separation.* In R.J. Sternberg & R.K. Wagner (Eds.), New York: Cambridge University Press.

References

Coleman, J. (1968). The concept of Educational Opportunity. *Harvard Educational Review,* 38, pp. 7-22.

Coleman, J.S. (1973). Equality of Opportunity an Equality of Results. *Harvard Educational Review,* 43, pp. 129-137.

Cremin, L. (1989). *Education and its Discontents,* Cambridge, MA: Harvard University Press.

Cronbach, L.J., & Snow, R.E. (1977). *Aptitudes and Instructional Methods,* New York, NY: Irvington.

D'Sousa, D. (1991). *Illiberal Education: The Politics of Race and Sex on Campus.* New York: Free Press.

Geertz, C. (1983). *Local Knowledge.* New York: Basic Books.

Glaser, R. (1977) *Adaptive Education: Individual Diversity and Learning.* New York, Holt, Rinehart & Winston.

Gollnick, D.M. & Chinn, P.C. (1990). *Multicultural Education in a Pluralistic Society,* 3rd ed. Columbus, OH: Merrill.

Gordon, E. W. (1991). Human Diversity and Pluralism. *Educational Psychologist,* 26(2), 99-108.

Gordon, E. W., Bhattacharyya, M. (1992). Human Diversity, Cultural Hegemony, and the Integrity of the Academic Canon. *The Journal of Negro Education,* 61(3), 405-418.

Gordon, E. W., Roberts, F., & The New York State Social Studies Review and Development Committee. (1991, June). *One Nation, Many Peoples: A Declaration of Cultural Interdependence.* Albany, NY: State Department of Education.

Guess, R. (1981). *The Idea of a Critical Theory.* Cambridge: Cambridge University Press.

Harris, M.D. (1992). *Africentrism and Curriculum: Concepts, Issues and Prospects.*

Hart J. K. (1924). *The Discovery of Intelligence.* New York: Century Co.

Hirsch, E.D. (1987). *Cultural Literacy, What Every American Needs to Know.* Boston: Houghton Mifflin.

McCarthy, C. (1988). Rethinking Liberal and Radical Perspectives on Racial Inequality in Schooling: Making the Case for Nonsynchrony. *Harvard Educational Review,* 58, 265-279.

McGuire, W.J. (19   ). *A Contexualist Theory of Knowledge: Its Implications for Innovation and Reform in Psychological Research.*

Ravitch, D. (1990). Multiculturalism, *The American Scholar,* Summer, pp. 337-354.

Schlesinger, A. M., Jr. (1991). *The Disuniting of America.* Knoxville, TN: Whittle Direct Books.

Sherman, J. (1978). *Sex Related Cognitive Differences.* Springfield, IL: Charles C. Thomas.

Stanfield II, John H. (1992). Ethnic Pluralism and Civic Responsibility in Post-Cold War America. *Journal of Negro Education.*

Tedeschi, J. T. (Ed.) (1974). *Perspectives on Social Power.* Chicago: Aldine.

Van Gelden, L. (1985, January). *Help for Technophobes.* Ms., pp. 89-91.

References for chapter 5:
Dynamic Assessment and Pedagogy

Armour-Thomas, E. (2008). In search of evidence for the effectiveness of professional development: An exploratory study. *Journal of Urban Learning, Teaching and Research* 4, 1-12.

Armour-Thomas, E., Chatterji, M.,Walker, E., Obe, V., Moore, B., & Gordon, E. W. (2005). *Documenting classroom processes and early effects of dynamic pedagogy: A study in selected elementary classrooms in New York.* Paper presented at the annual meeting of the American Educational Research Association, Montreal, Canada.

Armour-Thomas, E., Walker, E. N., Dixon-Roman, E., Mejia, B. X., & Gordon, E. W. (2006). *An evaluation of dynamic pedagogy effects on 3rd grade mathematics achievement of ethnic minority children from low income backgrounds.* Paper presented at the annual meeting of the American Educational Research Association, San Francisco, CA.

References

Armour-Thomas, E., Walker, E. N., Manoff, F., & Goldfischer, T. (2006). *Supporting high quality teaching through staff development: Lessons learned from a university-school partnership.* Paper presented at the annual meeting of the National Council of Supervisors of Mathematics, St Louis, MO.

Armour-Thomas, E., Walker, E. N., Mejia, B. X., & Gordon, E.W. (2004). *The relationship between teacher-student classroom interactions and mathematics achievement.* Poster presented at the American Psychological Association Annual Convention, Honolulu, Hawaii.

Armour-Thomas, E., Walker, E. N., Mejia, B. X., Toro, M, Gordon, E. W. (2005). *Using methodological triangulation to study autonomous learning among children from ethnically diverse backgrounds.* Paper presented at the annual meeting of the American Educational Research Association, Montreal, Canada.

Armour-Thomas, Walker, E. Obe, V., Toro, M., Mejia, B. X. & Gordon, E. W. (2007). *Using discourse analysis to study teacher-student interactions in the classroom.* Paper presented at the Annual Conference of the American Educational Research Association, Chicago, IL.

Birch, H. (1958). Introduction. In E. Hausserman, *Developmental potential of preschool children: An evaluation of intellectual, sensory, and emotional functioning* (pp. ix-xvii). New York: Grune & Stratton.

Bonilla-Bowman, C. (1999). *Systematizing portfolio assessment in a bilingual, bicultural middle school: Building upon the PACE model.* (Doctoral dissertation, Columbia University, 1999). *Dissertation Abstracts International, 60,* 2337.

Campione, J. C. (1989). Assisted assessment: A taxonomy of approaches and an outline of strengths and weaknesses. *Journal of Learning Disabilities, 22* (3), 151-165.

Chatterji, M., Koh, N., Everson, H., & Solomon, P. (2008, March). *Mapping cognitive pathways in mastering long division: A case study of grade 5-6 learners supported with a dynamic model of proximal assessment and learner diagnosis.* Paper presented annual meeting of the American Educational Research Association, New York.

Gickling, E. & Havertape, J. (1981). Curriculum-based assessment (CBA). Minneapolis: *National School Psychology In-service training Network.*

References

Gordon, E. W. (1970). *Access and appraisal: Continuing education, higher education, career entry. The Report of the Commission on Tests to the College Entrance Examination Board. IRCD Bulletin,* 6(4). (ERIC Document Reproduction Service No. ED049324).

Gordon, E. W. & Armour-Thomas, E. (2006). *The effects of dynamic pedagogy on the mathematics achievement of ethnic minority students* (RM06224). Storrs, CT: The National Research Center on the Gifted and Talented, University of Connecticut.

Hausserman, E. (1958). *Developmental potential of preschool children: An evaluation of intellectual, sensory, and emotional functioning.* New York: Grune & Stratton.

Skinner, B. F. (1957). *Verbal behavior.* New York: Appleton-Century-Crofts.

Skinner, B. F. (1969). An operant analysis of problem solving. In B. F. Skinner, *Contingencies of reinforcement* (pp. 133-157). New York: Appleton-Century-Crofts.

Slavin, R. E. (2001). *Educational psychology: Theory and practice.* New York: Allyn & Bacon.

Sternberg, R. J. (1985). *Beyond IQ: A triarchic theory of human intelligence.* Cambridge, MA: Cambridge University Press.

Sternberg, R. J. (1988). *The triarchic mind: A new theory of human intelligence.* New York: Viking.

Vygotsky, L. S (1978). *Mind in society: The development of higher psychological processes.* Cambridge, MA: Harvard University Press.

Walker, E. N. (2007). Rethinking professional development for elementary mathematics teachers. *Teacher Education Quarterly,* 34 (3), 113-134.

Walker, E. N., Armour-Thomas, E., & Gordon, E. W. (2007) Dynamic pedagogy in diverse elementary classrooms: A comparison of two teachers' instructional strategies. *National Council of Teachers of Mathematics* (NCTM) *Mathematics for All Book Series.*

References for chapter 6:
Thinking Comprehensively about Education

Bernstein, B. (1961). Social Class and Linguistic Development: A Theory of Social Learning. *Education, Economy and Society.* A. H. Halsey, Floud, J, and Anderson, C. A. New York, Free Press of Glencoe, Inc.: 288-314.

Birch, H. G., and J. D. Gussow. (1970). Disadvantaged Children: Health, Nutrition and school failure. New York: Harcourt Brace and World.

Bourdieu P. (1986). The form of capital. In J.G. Richardson (Ed.), Handbook of theory and research for sociology of education (pp. 241-258). New York: Greenwood Press.

Bridglall, B & Gordon, E. W. (Editors) (2001). Academic Ability & Affirmative Development: Cultivating Academic Ability in *Pedagogical Inquiry and Praxis.* No 2. New York: Institute for Urban and Minority Education at Teachers College, Columbia University & The College Board.

Clark, K. B (1954). Segregated Schools in New York City. Child Apart. Northside Center for Child Development, New Lincoln School NY.

Coleman, J., Campbell, E., Hobson, C., McPartland, J., Mood, A., Weinfeld, F.D. et al. (1966). *Equality of educational opportunity.* Washington D.C.: Department of Health, Education and Welfare.

Comer, J.P. (1997). *Waiting for a miracle: Why schools can't solve our problems -and how we can.* New York, NY: Dutton.

Cremin, L. (1975/2007). Public Education and the Education of the Public. Teachers College Record 109 (7), 1545-1558.

Dewey, J. (1916). *Democracy and Education.* New York, NY: Macmillan.

Feuerstein, R., Rand, Y., & Hoffman, M., & Miller, R. (1980). Instrumental Enrichment: An intervention program for cognitive modifiability. Baltimore, MD: University Park Press.

Frazier, F. E. (1965). *Black Bourgeoisie.* New York: Free Press.

Gordon, E.W. (1965). Characteristics of Socially Disadvantaged Children. *Review of Educational Research* 35(5): 377-388.

Gordon, E.W. and D. Wilkerson. (1966). Compensatory Education for the Disadvantaged: Programs and Practices, Preschool through College. New York, College Entrance Examination Board.

Gordon, E. W. (1995). Performance Assessment Collaborative in Education. A Report to the Rockefeller Foundation. New York City: The Rockefeller Foundation.

Gordon, E.W. (1999). *Education and justice: A view from the back of the bus.* New York: Teachers College Press.

Gordon, E. W., Bridglall, B. L., & Meroe A. S. (Eds.). (2005). *Supplementary Education: The hidden curriculum of high academic achievement.* Lanham, MD: Rowman and Littlefield.

Gordon E. W., Bridglall, B.L. (2007). *Affirmative Development: Cultivating Academic Ability.* Boulder, CO: Rowman & Littlefield.

Heath S. B., M. W. McLaughing, eds. (1993). Identity and Inner city Youth: Beyond Ethnicity and Gender. New York: Teachers College Press.

Hunt, J. M. (1961). *Intelligence and Experience.* New York, Ronald.

Katz, I. (1964). Review of evidence relating to effects of desegregation on the intellectual performance of Negroes. *American Psychologist* 19:381-399.

Martinez, M. E. (2000). *Education as the Cultivation of Intelligence.* Mahwah. Lawrence Erlbaum Publishers

Mercer, J. R. (1973). *Labeling the mentally retarded: Clinical and social system perspective on mental retardation.* Berkeley: University of California Press.

Miller, L and E. W. Gordon. (1974). Equality of Educational Opportunity: Handbook of Research. New York: AMS Press.

Miller, S. (1995). *An American Imperative: Accelerating Minority Educational Advancement.* New Haven, CT: Yale University Press

National Task Force on Minority High Academic Achievement. (1999). *Reaching the top: A report of the National Task Force on Minority High Academic Achievement.* New York: The College Board.

Price, H. (2002). *Achievement Matters: Getting your Child the Best Education Possible.* New York, NY: Kensington.

Proctor, D. S. and G. S. Weiss. (1966). "Wealth Accumulation of Black and White Men: The Case of Housing. Equity." *Social Problems,* 30: 199-211.

Rebell, M. and J. Wolff. (2008). *Moving Every Child Ahead.* New York: Teachers College Press

Riessman, F. (1962). *The Culturally Deprived Child.* New York: Harper and Row

Steele, C. M. & J. A (2000). Stereotype Threat and the Intellectual Test Perfomance of African Americans. *Stereotypes and Prejudice: Essential Readings.* C. Stangor. Philadelphia, PA, Psychology Press: 369-89

Sternberg, R.J. (1999). "The theory of successful intelligence." Review of General Psychology 3(4): 292-316

Strodtbeck, F. L. (1964). The Hidden Curriculum of the Middle Class Home. Urban Education and Cultural Deprivation. C. W. Hunnicutt. Syracuse, NY: Syracuse University Press: 15-31

The College Board. (1999). Reaching the top: A report of the National Task Force on Minority High Achievement. New York: The College Entrance Examination Board.

Tiedeman, D. V. (1965). A symposium on existentialism in counseling: Prologue. Personnel and Guidance Journal, 43, 551-552.

Varenne, H. (2007). Difficult collective deliberations: Anthropological notes towards a theory of education. *Teachers College Record* 109 (7), 1559-1587

Weiss, H.B, Bouffard, S.M., Bridgall, B.L., & Gordon, E.W. (2009). Reframing Family Involvement in Education: Supporting Families to Support Educational Equity. Equity Matters: Research Review No. 5. New York: The Campaign for Educational Equity.

Weiss, H., Dearing, E., Mayer, E., Kreider, H. & McCartney, K. (2005). Family educational involvement: Who can afford it and what does it afford? In C. Cooper, C. García Coll, W. Bartko, H. Davis, & C. Chatman (Eds.), *Developmental pathways through middle childhood: Rethinking context and diversity as resources* (pp.17-40). Mahwah, NJ: Lawrence Erlbaum.

Weiss, H., Caspe, M., & Lopez, M. E. (2006). Family involvement makes a difference: Family involvement in early childhood education. Cambridge, MA: Harvard Family Research Project.

References

Wilkerson, D. (Ed.) (1979). *Educating All Our Children: An imperative for Democracy.* Westport, CT: Mediax, Inc.

Wolf, M. M. (1966). The measurement of environments. In A. Anastasi (Ed.), Testing problems in perspective (pp. 491-503). Washington, D.C.: American Council on Education.

References for chapter 7:
Democratizing the American Educational Research Association

Allen. P. G. (1989). *The Sacred hoop.* Boston; Beacon Press.

Asante, M. K (1990). *Kemet, Afrocenrtricity, and Knowledge.* Trenton, NJ: Africa World Press.

Banks. J. A. (1993). The canon debate, knowledge construction, and multicultural education. *Educational Researcher,* 22(5), 4-14.

Banks, J. A. (1995). The historical constuction of knowledge about race: Implications for transformative teaching. *Educational Researcher.* 24(2), 15-25.

Campbell, D. T., &: Stanley. C. (1963). *Experimentaland quasiexperimental designs for research.* Chicago: Rand McNally.

Collins. P. H. (1991). *Black feminist thought: Knowledge. Consciousness, and the politics of empowerment.* New York: Routledge.

Eisner, E. W. (1993). Forms of understanding and the future of educational research. *Educational Researcher.* 22(7), 5-11.

Gordon, B. M. (1990). The necessity of African-American epistemology for educational theory and practice. *Journal of Education,* 172(3), 88-106.

Gordon. E. W. (1995). Culture and the sciences of pedagogy. *Teachers College Record,* 97(1). 32-46.

Gordon, E. W., &: Meroe, A. S. (1991. January). Common destinies-continuing dilemmas. *Psychological Science,* 2(1).

Gordon, E. W., Miller. E, &: Rollock. D. (1990) Coping with communicentric bias in knowledge production in the social sciences. *Educational Researcher* 19(3), 14-19.

Harding. S. (1991). *Whose science? Whose knowledge? Thinking from women's lives.* Ithaca, NY; Cornell University Press

Heshusius, L. (994). Freeing ourselves from objectivity: Managing subjectivity or turning toward a participatory mode of consciousness? *Educational Researcher,* 23(3), 15-22

Keto, C. T. (1989). *The Africa Centered Perspective of History.* Blackwood, NJ: K. A. Publications.

Ladson-Billings, G. (199S). Toward a theory of culturally-relevant pedagogy. *Ameria2n Educational Researcher Journal,* 32(3).465-492.

Ladson-Billings. G., &: Tate, W. E, IV. (1995). Toward a critical race theory of education. *Teachers College Record,* 97(1).47-68

Magee. B. (973). *Karl Popper.* New York: The Viking Press

Miller. L S. (995). *An American Imperative: Accelerating minority educational advancement.* New Haven, CT: Yale University Press.

Rosaldo, R. (1989). *Culture and Truth.* Boston: Beacon Press.

Said, E. W. (1979). *Orientalism.* New York: Vintage Books.

Scheurich, J. J., &: Young, M. D. (in press). *Coloring epistemologies: Are our research epistemologies racially biased?*

Stanfield, J. H., 11 (1985). The ethnocentric basis of social science knowledge production. *Review of Research in Education,* 12. 387-415.

Young, R. (1990). *White Mythologies: Writing history and the West.* New York: Routledge.

References for Chapter 8:
Diverse Human Populations and Problems in Educational Program Evaluation via Achievement Testing

Calfee, R. (1976). *Practical uses of assessment for individual reading instruction.* Proceedings of the Conference on Beginning Reading Instruction. University of Pittsburgh, IRDC.

Glaser, R. (1976, May). *On intelligence and aptitude.* Paper presented at the Work Conference on Exploring Alternative to Current Standardized Tests. University of Pittsburgh.

Haeusserman, E. (1958). *Developmental potential of preschool children: An evaluation of intellectual, sensory and emotional functioning.* New York: Grune and Stratton.

Hayden, R. C. (976). *Project Torque: A new approach to the assessment of children's mathematical competence.* Newton, Mass: Educational Development Center.

Hebb, D. O. (1972). What psychology is about. *American Psychologist,* 29(2), 71-79.

Suchman, E. A. (1969). *Evaluation research: Principles and practice in public service and social action programs.* New York: Russel Sage.

Williams, R.L. (1975). The Bitch-100: A cultural specific test. *Journal of Afro-American Issues,* 3(1), 103.

References for chapter 9:
Education of the Disadvantaged:
A Problem of Human Diversity

American Institutes for Research in Behavioral Sciences (1969a). *Diagnostically based curriculum: A compensatory program; an evaluation.* Washington, DC: U.S. Government Printing Office.

American Institutes for Research in Behavioral Sciences (1969b). *Perry Preschool Project, Ypsilanti, Michigan. One of a series of successful compensatory education programs.* Palo Alto, CA: Author.

Bereiter, C., & Englemann, S. (1966). *Teaching disadvantaged children in the preschool.* Englewood Cliffs, NJ: Prentice-Hall.

Birch H.G. (1967, April). *Health and the education of the socially disadvantaged children.* Presented at the conference on Bio-Social Factors in the Development and Learning of Disadvantaged Children. Syracuse, N.Y.

Birch H.G., & Gussow, J.D. (1970). *The disadvantaged child—health, nutrition and school failure.* New York: Harcourt, Brace and World.

References

Bloom, B. (1965). *Stability and change in human characteristics.* New York: John Wiley.

Board of Education (1967). *Camden City Schools, New Jersey: Title I: E.S.E.A., 1966-67, Projects of the Camden City Board of Education–Evaluative report.* Camden, NJ: Author. (ERIC Document Reproduction Service No. ED018473).

Campbell, J. (1964). *Testing culturally different groups.* College Entrance examination Board Research and Development Report 63-4 (14). Princeton, NJ: Educational Testing Service.

Channon, G. (1967). The more effective schools: An evaluation. Urban Review, 2. (ERIC Document Reproduction Service No. ED013845).

Cleary, T. A., & Hilton, T. L. (1966). *An investigation of item bias.* College Entrance Examination Board Research and Development Report 65-6 (12). Princeton, NJ: Educational Testing Service. (ERIC Document Reproduction Service No. ED011267).

Cleary, T. A. (1966) *Test bias: Validity of the Scholastic Aptitude Test for Negro and White Students in integrated colleges.* College Entrance Examination Board Research and Development Report 65-6 (18). Princeton, NJ: Educational Testing Service. (ERIC Document Reproduction Service No. ED018200).

Cohen, D. (1967, November*). Policy for the public schools: Compensation or integration?* Paper presented at the National Conference on Equal Educational Opportunity in America's cities. Washington, DC.

Coleman, J.S., Campbell, E.Q., Hobson, C.J., McPartland, J., Mood, A.M., Weinfeld, F.D., et al. (1966). Equality of educational opportunity. Washington, DC: U.S. Government Printing Office. (ERIC Document Reproduction Service No. ED012275).

Cravioto, J., Delicardie, E.R., & Birch, H. G. (1966). Nutrition, growth, and neurointegrative development: An experimental and ecologic study. *Pediatrics, 38* (2), 319-372.

Davidson, H. H., & Greenberg, J. W. (1967). *Traits of school achievers from a deprived background.* New York: City University of New York, City College. (ERIC Document Reproduction Service No. ED013849).

Esposito, D. (in press). *The relationship between ability grouping and ethnic and socioeconomic separation of children.* New York: Teachers College, Columbia University, ERIC Information Retrieval Center on the Disadvantaged.

Flaxman, E. (1969). *A selected bibliography on teacher attitudes.* ERIC-IRCD Urban Disadvantaged Series No. 1. New York: Teachers College, Columbia University, ERIC Clearinghouse on the Urban Disadvantaged. (ERIC Document Reproduction Service No. ED027357).

Glasser, R. (1966). *The education of individuals.* PA: Learning Research and Development Center, University of Pittsburgh. (ERIC Document Reproduction Service No. ED014785).

Glasser, R. (1967). *Objectives and evaluation: an individualized system.* PA: Learning Research and Development Center, University of Pittsburgh. (ERIC Document Reproduction Service No. ED015844).

Goldstein, B. (1967). *Low income youth in urban areas: A critical review of the literature.* New York: Holt, Rinehart & Winston.

Gordon, E. W. (1965). A review of programs of compensatory education. *American Journal of Orthopsychiatry,* 35(4), 640-651.

Gordon, E. W. (1965). Help for the disadvantaged. *American Journal of Orthopsychiatry,* 35(3), 445-448.

Gordon, E. W., & Jablonsky, A. (1968). Compensatory education in the equalization of educational opportunity: II. *Journal of Negro Education* 37(3), 280-290.

Gordon, E. W., & Wilkerson, D. (1966). *Compensatory education for the disadvantaged: Programs and practices, preschool through college.* New York: College Entrance Examination Board.

Gray, S. W., & Klaus, R. A. (1965). *An experimental preschool program for culturally deprived children.* Child Development, 36, 887-898.

Guerrriero, M. A. (1968). *The Benjamin Franklin High School Urban Leagues Academies Program. Evaluation of ESEA Title I Projects in New York City, 1967-68.* New York: Center for Urban Education. (ERIC Document Reproduction Service No. ED034000).

References

Hawkridge, D. G., & et al. (1969). *A study of selected exemplary programs for the education of disadvantaged children: Part II, final report.* Palo Alto: American Institutes for Research in the Behavioral Sciences. (ERIC Document Reproduction Service No. ED023777).

Hess, R. D., & Shipman, V. (1966). *Maternal attitudes toward the school and the role of pupil: Some class comparisons.* Paper presented at the Fifth Work Conference on Curriculum and Teaching in Depressed Urban Areas, Teachers College, Columbia University.

Hirsh, J. (1969, Fall). Behavior genetic analysis and its biosocial consequences. *IRCD Bulletin,* 5(4), 3-4, 16-20.

Hunt, J. M. (1969). Black genes? White environment. *Transaction,* 6, 12-22.

Jablonsky, A. (1969, January). *A selected ERIC bibliography on individual instruction, ERIC-IRCD Urban Education Series No. 2.* New York: Teachers College, Columbia University, ERIC Information Retrieval Center on the Disadvantaged. (ERIC Document Reproduction Service No. ED027358).

Jensen, A. (1966). Cumulative deficit in compensatory education. *Journal of School Psychology,* 4, 37-47.

Jensen, A. (1968). Social class, race, and genetics: Implications for education. *American Educational Research Association Journal,* 5, 1-42.

Jensen, A. (1969). How much can we boost IQ and scholastic achievement? *Harvard Educational Review,* 39, 1-23. (ERIC Document Reproduction Service No. ED023722).

Katz, I. (1967). *Desegregation or integration in public schools: The policy implications of research.* New York: Teachers College, Columbia University, ERIC Information Retrieval Center on the Disadvantaged. (ERIC Document Reproduction Service No. ED015974).

Kennedy, W. A., Van De Riet, V., W. J. C. (1963). Normative sample of intelligence and achievement of Negro elementary school children in the Southern United Status and Chicago. Serial No. 98, 28(6), 1-5,7, 11, 13-41, 43-57, 59-63, 65-112.

Khanna, J. L. (1969). *An evaluation of the human relations training program.* (ERIC Document Reproduction Service No. ED013845).

References

Klaus, R., & Gray, S. (1968). *The Early Training Project for Disadvantaged Children? A report after five years* (Monograph, Vol. 33 (4). Chicago: Society for Research in Child Development.

Kravetz, N. (1966). *The more effective schools program.* New York: Center for Urban education.

Leacock, E. B. (1969). *Teaching and learning in city schools: A comparative study.* New York: Basic Books.

Lewis, H. (1967). Culture, class, and family life among low-income urban Negroes. In A. M.

Ross & H. Hill (Eds.), *Employment, race, and poverty* (pp.149-172). New York: Harcourt, Brace and World.

Lilienfeld, A. M., Pasamanick, B., & Rogers, M. (1955). The relationship between pregnancy experiences and the development of certain neuropsychiatric disorders in childhood. *American Journal of Public Health, 45,* 637-643.

Lopate, C., Flaxman, E., Bynum, E., & Gordon, E.W. (1970, February). *Some effects of parent and community participation on public education: Review of research.* ERIC-IRCD Urban Disadvantaged Series, Number 3. (ERIC Document Reproduction Service No. ED027359).

McPartland, J. (1968). *The segregated student in desegregated schools: sources of influence on Negro secondary students: Final report.* Baltimore, MD: Center for the Study of Social Organization of Schools, Johns Hopkins University. (ERIC Document Reproduction Service No. ED021944).

Minuchin, P. (1965). *Patterns and correlates of achievement in elementary school children.* New York: Bank Street College of Education.

Moynihan, D. P., & Barton, P. (1965). *The Negro family in the culture of poverty?* San Juan and New York. New York: Random House.

Orfield, G. (1969). *The reconstruction of Southern education. The schools and the 1964 Civil Rights Act.* New York: Wiley-Interscience.

Pasamick, B., & Lilienfeld, A. M. (1955). Association of maternal and fetal factors with the development of mental deficiency, I: Abnormalities in the prenatal and perinatal periods. *Journal of the American Medical Association, 159*(3), 155-160.

Passow, A., Goldberg, M., & Tannenbaum, A. J. (1967). *Education of the disadvantaged: A book of readings.* New York: Holt, Rinehart and Winston.

Rigrodsky, S. (1967, Sept.). *Speech therapy for disadvantaged pupils in non-public schools: An evaluation of the New York City Educational Project 1966-1967.* New York: Center for Urban Education, Committee on Field Work and Evaluation.

Rodger, H. (1969). *Poverty and mental retardation: A causal relationship.* New York: Vantage Books.

Rosenthal, R., & Jacobson, L. (1968). *Pygmalion in the classroom: Teacher expectation and pupil's intellectual development.* New York: Holt, Rinehart and Winston.

Schwager, S. (1967). *An analysis of the evaluation of the More Effective Schools Program conducted by the Center for Urban Education.* New York: United Federation of Teachers.

Schwebel, M. (1968). *Who can be educated?* New York: Grove Press.

Scrimpshaw, N., & Gordon, J. (1967). *Malnutrition, learning and behavior.* Cambridge, MA: MIT Press.

Shaw, M. C., & Rector, W. (1968, July). *Influencing the learning environment by counseling with teachers.* Monograph No. 6. (ERIC Document Reproduction Service No. ED022233).

Shuey, A. M. (Ed.). (1966). *The testing of Negro intelligence* (2nd ed.). New York: Social Science Press.

Skodak, M., & Skeels, H. M. (1945). A follow-up study of children in adoptive homes. *Journal of Genetic Psychology, 66,* 21-58.

Smilansky, S. (1965). Promotion of preschool, culturally deprived children through dramatic play. *American Journal of Orthopsychiatry, 35,* 201.

Smilansky, M. (1966, October). Fighting deprivation in the promised land. *Saturday Review, 82,* 85-86, 91.

St. John, N. H. (1968). *Minority group performance under various conditions of school ethnic and economic integration: A review of research.* New York: Teachers College, Columbia University, ERIC Clearinghouse on the Disadvantaged. (ERIC Document Reproduction Service No. ED021945).

Stodolsky, S. S., Lesser, G. S. (1967). *Learning patterns in the disadvantaged.* New York: Yeshiva University. ERIC Information Retrieval Center on the Disadvantaged. (ERIC Document Reproduction Service No. ED012291).

Thorndike, R. L. (1967). *Head Start Evaluation and Research Center annual report, September 1966-August 1967.* New York: Teachers College, Columbia University. (ERIC Document Reproduction Service No. E 020781).

Thorndike, R. L. (1927). *The measurement of intelligence.* New York: Teachers College, Columbia University.

U.S. Commission on Civil Rights (1967). *Racial isolation in the public schools.* Washington, D.C.: U.S. Government Printing Office (Vol. I: ED012 740; Vol. II: (ERIC Document Reproduction Service No. ED015959).

Valentine, C. A. (1968). *Culture and poverty: Critique and counter-proposals.* Chicago: University of Chicago Press. (ERIC Document Reproduction Service No. ED035707).

Webster, S. W. (Ed.). (1966). *The disadvantaged learner: Knowing, understanding, educating.* San Francisco, CA: Chandler. (ERIC Document Reproduction Service No. ED013266).

Weinberg, M. (1968). *Desegregation research: An appraisal.* Bloomington, IN: Phi Delta Kappa, Commission on Education and Human Rights.

Weinberg, M. (1968). *Integrated education: A reader.* Beverly Hills, CA: Glencoe Press.

Westinghouse Learning Corporation & Ohio University (1969). *The impact of Head Start. An evaluation of the effects of Head Start on children's cognitive and affective development* (Vol. 1: Report to the U.S. Office of Economic Opportunity). Athens: Author.

Wolf, M., & Stein, A. (1966a). *Long range effects of preschooling on reading achievement, study III.* New York: Yeshiva University, Ferkauf Graduate School. (ERIC Document Reproduction Service No. ED015 027).

Wolf, M., & Stein, A. (1966b). *Six months later, a comparison of children who had Head Start with their classmates in kindergarten—a case study of kindergartens in four public elementary schools, study I.* New York Yeshiva University, Ferkauf Graduate School. (ERIC Document Reproduction Service No. ED015 027).

References for chapter 10:
Educational Reforms for Students at Risk: Cultural Diversity as a Risk Factor in the Development of Students

Cole, M. and Gay, J. and Glick, J. and Sharp, D.W. *The Cultural Context of Learning and Thinking,* NY: Basic Books, 1971.

Coleman, J et al. *Equalization of Educational Opportunity,* Washington: US Government Printing Office, 1966.

Geertz, C. Interpretation of Cultures, New York: Basic Books, 1973.

Goffman, E. *Stigma: Notes on the Management of Spoiled Identity.* New York: Simon & Schuster, 1963.

Gordon, Edmund W. *Human Diversity and Pedagogy,* Center in Research on. Education, Culture, and Ethnicity Institution for Social and Policy Studies, Yale University, New Haven, CT, 1988.

Gordon, Edmund W. *Foundations for Academic Excellence,* NYC Chancellor's Commission on Minimum Standards, NYC Board of Education, Brooklyn, NY, 1986.

Gordon, Edmund W. and Song, Lauren Dohee. "Variations in the Experience of Resilience," for the Conference on Resilience, Temple University Center for Research on Human Development and Education Philadelphia, January 30-31, 1992.

Gordon, Edmund W. and Rollock, David and Miller, Fayneese. "Coping with Communicentric Bias in Knowledge Production in the Social Sciences." Educational Researcher, 19, 19, 1990.

Gordon, Edmund W. Report of Consultant Panel: Mid-Course Review of Project Canal:

Chicago Public Schools, spring, 1991. Gordon and Gordon Associates, Pomona, NY.

Greenough, W.T. and Black, J.E. and Wallace, C.S. "Experience and Brain Development," *Child Development,* 58, 539-559, 1987.

Hebb, Donald. *The Organization of Behavior: A Neuropsychological Theory.* New York: Wiley, 1949.

Ogbu, J. *Minority Education and Caste: The American System in Cross Cultural Perspective*, NY: Academic Press, 1978.

Rawls, John. *A Theory of Justice.* Cambridge, MA: The Belknap Press of Harvard University Press, 1971.

Rosehan, D.L. *Cultural Deprivation and Learning: An Examination for Learning.* In H.L. Miller (ed) Education for the Disadvantaged pp 38-42. NY: Free Press. Students at Risk in at Risk Schools: Improving Environments for Learning. Editors

Hersholt C. Waxman, Judith Walker de Felix, James E. Anderson, and H. Prentice Baptiste, Jr. California: Corwin Press Inc. A Sage Publications Company, 1992.

Tyler, R.W. *Basic Principles of Curriculum and Instruction.* Chicago: Chicago University Press, 1949.

Vygotsky, L.S. *Mind in Society,* Cambridge, MA: Harvard University Press, 1978.

References for chapter 11:
Some Theoretical and Practical Problems in
Compensatory Education as an Antidote to Poverty

Gurin, G. (1970). An expectancy approach to job training programs. In V.L. Allen (Ed.), *Psychological Factors in Poverty* (pp. 277-297). Chicago: Markham Publishing.

References for chapter 12:
Commentary: Group Differences versus Individual Development
in Education Design

Berg, I. (1970). *Education and jobs: The great training robbery.* New York: Praeger.

Greenfield P. M. & Bruner, J. S (1969). Culture and cognitive growth. In D. Goslin (Ed.) *Handbook of socialization theory and research* (pp. 633-657). Chicago: Rand McNally

Lesser, G.S., Fifer, G., & Clark, D.H. (1965). Mental abilities of children from different social class and cultural groups. *Monographs of the Society for Research in Child Development,* 30, 279-325.

Witkin, H. A. (1973). The role of cognitive style in academic performance and in teacher-student relationships. Princeton, NJ: Educational Testing Service.

References for chapter 13:
Characteristics of Learning Persons and the Adaptation of Learning Environments

Bracht, G. H. (2977). Experimental factors related to aptitude-treatment interactions. *Review of Educational Research,* 40, 627-645.

Cronbach, L. & Snow, R. E. (1977). *Aptitudes and instructional methods.* New York: Irvington.

Endler, N. S., & Magnusson, D. (Eds.) (1976). *Interactional psychology and personality.* New York: Wiley.

Esposito, D. (1971). *Homogeneous and heterogeneous groupings: Principal findings and implications of a research of the literature.* New York: Teachers College, Columbia University. ED056150.

Gagne, R. M. (1974). *Essentials of learning for instruction.* Hinsdale, Ill.: Dryden Press.

Glaser, R. (1977). *Adaptive education: Individual Diversity and Learning.* New York: Holt, Rinehart & Winston.

Glaser, R., & Rosner, J. (1975). *Adaptive environments for learning: Curriculum aspects.* In H. Talmage (Ed.), Systems of individualized education (pp 84-135). Berkeley, CA: McCutchan.

Gordon, E. (Ed.). (1985). *Human diversity and pedagogy.* Pomona, N.Y.: Ambergis Family Press.

Gordon, E., Wang, M. C., & DeStefano, L., (1982). *Temperament characteristics and learning.* Pittsburgh: Learning Research and Development Center, University of Pittsburgh. Mimeographed.

References

Hunt, D. E. (1975). Person-environment interaction: A challenge found wanting before it was tried. *Review of Educational Research,* 45, 209-230.

Hunt, J. M. (1961). *Intelligence and experience.* New York: Ronald Press.

Mercer, J. (1973). *Labeling the mentally retarded: Clinical and social system perspectives on mental retardation.* Berkeley, CA: University of California Press.

Messick, S. (1970). The criterion problem in the evaluation of instruction: Assessing possible, not just intended, outcomes. In C. Wittrock and David W. Wiley (Eds.), *The evaluation of instruction: Issues and problems* (pp.183-220). New York: Holt, Rinehart & Winston.

Messick, S. (1982). *Cognitive styles in educational practice.* Paper presented at the Annual Meeting of the American Educational Research Association, New York.

Nojan, M., Strom, C. D., & Wang, M. C. (1981). *Measures of degree of implementation and program evaluation research.* Paper presented at the Annual Meeting of the American Educational Research Association, New York.

Ogbu, J. U. (1978). *Minority education and caste: The American system in cross cultural perspective.* Carnegie Council on Children Monograph. New York: Academic Press.

Rothkopf, E. Z. (1978). The sound of one hand plowing. *Contemporary Psychology,* 123, 707-708.

Shipman, S., & Shipman, V. (in press). Cognitive styles: Some conceptual, methodological, and applied issues. In E. W. Gordon (Ed.), *Human diversity and pedagogy.*

Snow, R. E. (1977). Individual differences and instructional theory. *Educational Researcher,* 6, 11-15.

Talmage, H. (Ed.). (1975). *Systems of individualized education.* Berkeley, CA: McCutchan.

Tyler, L. E. (1978). *The psychology of human differences.* New York: Appleton-Century Crofs.

Wolf, R.(1966). The measurement of environments. In A. Anastasi (Ed.), *Testing problems in perspective* (pp. 491-503). Washington, D.C.: American Council on Education.

References for chapter 14:
Culture and Ethnicity

Banks, C. (1975). Delay of gratification in Black adolescent boys. *IRCD Bulletin,* 12, (3).

Berry, B. (1951). *Race and ethnic relations.* Boston: Houghton-Mifflin Co.

Erikson, E. (1951). *Childhood and society.* New York: Harper Brothers.

Goffman, E. (1971). *Relations in public.* New York: Basic Books.

Harrington, C. (1978). Culture as a manifestation of human diversity. In E. W. Gordon (Ed.), *Human diversity and pedagogy* (pp. 6.1-6.51). Westport, CT: Yale University, Center in Research on Education, Culture and Ethnicity, Institution for Social and Policy Studies.

Isajiw, W.W. (1974). Definitions of ethnicity. *Ethnicity,* 1, 111.

Jensen, A. (1969). *Harvard Education Review,* 39, 1-123.

Kluckholn, C. (1965). *Culture and behavior.* New York: The Free Press.

Ogbu, J. (1978). *Minority education and caste: The American system in cross cultural perspective.* New York: Academic Press.

Tylor, E. B. (1891). *Primitive culture (Vol. I, 3rd* ed.). London: John Murray. (First edition, 1871).

References for chapter 15:
Supplementation and Supplantation as Alternatives Education Strategies

Anderson, E. & Keith, T. 1997. A longitudinal test of a model of academic success for at-risk high school students. *Journal of Educational Research,* 90, 5, 259-268.

Anyon, J. 1997. *Ghetto schooling: A political economy of urban educational reform.* New York: Teachers College Press.

Bates, T. 1995. Rising skill levels and declining labor force status among African American men. *Journal of Negro Education,* 64, 3, 373-383.

References

Battle, J. 1997. The relative effects of married versus divorced family configuration and socioeconomic status on the educational achievement of African American middle-grade students. *Journal of Negro education,* 66, 1, 29-42.

Berliner, D. & Biddle, B. 1995. *The manufactured crisis: myths, fraud, and the attack on America's public schools.* New York: Addison-Wesley.

Bernstein, B. 1977. *Class, codes and control.* New York: Routledge.

Blau, Z. 1981. *Black children/White children: Competence, socialization and social structure.* New York: Free Press.

Borman, G., Stringfield, S. & Rachuba, L. 1998. Advancing minority high achievement: National trends and promising programs and practices. Johns Hopkins University Center for Social Organization of Schools.

Bourdieu, P. 1974. The school as a conservative force. In J. Eggleston (Ed.), *Contemporary research in the sociology of education,* (pp.32-38). London: Methuen. _____.1977. Cultural reproduction and social reproduction. In A. Halsey & J. Kaubel (Eds.), Power and ideology in education. New York: Oxford University Press.

Bowles, S. & Gintis, H. 1976. *Schooling in capitalist* America. New York: Routledge.

Brisk, M. 1998. *Bilingual education: From compensatory to quality schooling.* Mahwah, NJ: Lawrence Erlbaum.

Brophy, J. 1983. Research on the self-fulfilling prophecy and teacher expectations. *Journal of Educational Psychology,* 75, 633-647.

Bryk, A.., Lee, V. & Holland, P. 1993. Catholic schools and the common good. Cambridge, MA: Harvard University.

Caldas, S. & Bankston, C. 1997. Effect of school population socioeconomic status on individual academic achievement. *Journal of Educational Research,* 90, 5, 269-277.

Chen, C. & Stevenson, H. 1995. Motivation and mathematics achievement: A comparative study of Asian-American, Caucasian-American, and East Asian high school students. *Child Development,* 66, 1215-34.

Chen, H. & Lan, W. 1998. Adolescents' perceptions of their parents' academic expectations: Comparison of American, Chinese-American, and Chinese high school students. *Adolescence, 33,*130, 385-390.

References

Chubb, J. & Moe, T. 1990. Politics, markets and America's schools. Washington DC: Brookings Institute.

Chun, K. 1995. The myth of Asian American success and its educational ramifications. In D. Nakanishi & T. Nishida (Eds.), *The Asian American educational experience* (pp. 95-112), New York: Routledge.

Clark, R. 1983. *Family life and school achievement: Why poor Black children succeed or fail.* Chicago: University of Chicago Press.

Cole, M., Gay, J., Glick, J. & Sharp, D. 1971. The cultural context of learning and thinking. New York: Basic Books.

Coleman, J. 1988. Social capital and the creation of human capital. *American Journal of Sociology,* 94, 95-120.

Coleman, J., Campbell, E., Hobson, C., McPartland, J., Mood, A., Weinfeld, R. & York, R. 1966. *Equality of educational opportunity.* Washington DC: Government Printing Office.

Coleman, J. & Hoffer, T. 1987. *Public and private high schools: The impact of communities.* New York: Basic

Comer, J. 1997. *Waiting for a miracle: Why schools can't solve our problems–and how we can.* New York: Dutton.

Cordero-Guzman, H. 1997. Why do some children score higher than others? An empirical study of the role of the family, school, and community level resources on racial/ethnic differences in standardized test scores (AFQT). Paper presented at The National Economic Association.

Darity, W. 1997. Programmed retardation and the theory of noncompeting groups. Unpublished monograph.

Darling-Hammond, L. 1994. *The current status of teaching and teacher development.* New York: National Commission on Teaching and America's Future.

_____.1995. Cracks in the bell curve: How education matters. Journal of Negro Education, 64, 3, 340-353.

_____.1996. *The right to learn: A blueprint for creating schools that work.* San Francisco: Jossey-Bass.

_____. 1998. *Unequal opportunity: Race and education.* Brookings Review, 16, 2, 28-32.

_____. 1999. Educating teachers for the next century: Rethinking practice and policy. In G. Griffin (Ed.) *The education of teachers*, (pp.221-256). Chicago: University of Chicago Press.

Datnow, A. & Cooper, R. 1996. Peer networks of African American students in independent schools: Affirming academic success and racial identity. *Journal of Negro Education*, 65, 4, 56-72.

Delgado, R. (Ed.) 1995. *Critical race theory: The cutting edge.* Philadelphia: Temple University Press.

Delpit, L. 1988. The silenced dialogue: Power and pedagogy in educating other people's children. *Harvard Educational Review*, 58, 3, 280-298.

Dewey, J. 1916/1966. *Democracy & education.* New York: Free Press.

Dixon-Floyd, I. & Johnson, S. 1997. Variables associated with assigning students to behavioral classrooms. *Journal of Educational Research*, 91, 2, 123-126.

Doerr, E., Menendez, A. & Swomley, J. 1996. *The case against school vouchers.* Amherst, NY: Prometheus Books.

Dusek, J. & Joseph, G. 1983. The bases of teacher expectations: A meta-analysis. *Journal of Educational Psychology*, 75, 327-346.

Farkas, G. 1996. *Human capital or cultural capital? Ethnicity and poverty groups in an urban school district.* New York: Aldine de Gruyter.

Farkas, G., Grobe, R., Sheehan, D., & Shuan, Y. 1990. Cultural resources and school success: Gender, ethnicity and poverty groups within an urban district. *American Sociological Review*, 55: 127-142.

Fashola, O. & Slavin, R. 1997. Promising programs for elementary and middle schools: Evidence of effectiveness and replicability. *Journal of Education for Students Placed at Risk*, 2, 3, 251-307.

Fejgin, N, 1995. Factors contributing to the academic excellence of American Jewish and Asian students. *Sociology of Education*, 68, 18-30.

Ford, D. & Harris, J. 1996. Perceptions and attitudes of Black students toward school, achievement, and other educational variables. *Child Development*, 67, 1141-1152.

Fordham, S. 1988. Racelessness as a factor in Black students' school success: Pragmatic strategy or pyrrhic victory? *Harvard Educational Review,* 58, 1, 54-84.

Fordham, S. & Ogbu, J. 1986. Black students' school success: Coping with the burden of acting White. *Urban Review,* 18, 176-206.

Friedman, M. 1962. *Capitalism and freedom.* Chicago: University of Chicago Press.

Fulani, L. 1999. Reform Party reflects views of Black America on education options. Committee for a United Independent Party.

Fuligni, A. 1997. The academic achievement of adolescents from immigrant families: The roles of family background, attitudes, and behavior. *Child Development,* 68, 2, 351-363.

Fuller, B., Burr, E., Huerta, L., Puryear, S. & Wexler, E. 1999. *School choice: Abundant hopes, scarce evidence of results.* Berkeley, CA: Policy Analysis foe Calfornia Education, University of California, Berkeley and Stanford University.

Gibson, M. & Ogbu, J. (Eds.) 1991. *Minority status and schooling: A comparative study of immigrant and involuntary minorities.* New York: Garland.

Giroux, H. 1983. *Theory and resistance in education: A pedagogy for the opposition.* New York: Bergin & Harvey.

Goodlad, J. 1984. *A place called school: prospects for the future.* New York: McGraw-Hill.

_____. 1990. *Teachers for our nation's schools.* San Francisco: Jossey-Bass.

Gordon, E. W. 1985. Social science knowledge production and the Afro-American experience. *Journal of Negro Education,* 54, 117-133.

_____. 1986. *Foundations for academic excellence.* Brooklyn, NY: NYC Chancellor's Commission on Minimum Standards, New York City Board of Education.

_____. 1995. Toward and equitable system of educational assessment. *Journal of Negro Education,* 64, 3, 360-372.

_____. 1996. Toward an equitable system of educational assessment. *Journal of Negro Education,* 64, 3, 1-13.

_____. (Ed.) 1999. *Education and justice: A view from the back of the bus,* (pp. 71-88). New York: Teachers College Press.

Gordon, E.W. & Armour-Thomas, E. 1991. *Culture and cognitive development.* In L. Okagaki & R Sternberg (Eds.), *Directors of development: Influences on the development of children's thinking* (pp.83-100). Hillsdale, NJ: Erlbaum & Associates.

Gordon, E.W. & Bowman, C. 1999. Equity and social justice in educational achievement. In Gordon (Ed.), *Education and justice: A view from the back of the bus.* New York: Teachers College Press.

Gordon, E.T., Gordon, E.W., & Gordon-Nembhard, J. 1994. Social science literature concerning African American men. *Journal of Negro Education,* 63, 4, 508-531.

Gordon, E.W., Miller, F. & Rollock, D. 1990. Coping with communicentric bias in knowledge production in the social sciences. *Educational Researcher,* 19, 3, 14-19.

Gordon, E.W. & Shipman, S. 1979. Human diversity, pedagogy, and educational equity. *American Psychologist,* 34, 1030-1036.

Gordon, E.W. & Yowell, C. 1994. Cultural dissonance as a risk factor in the development of students. In R.J. Rossi (Ed.), Schools and students at risk, (pp. 51-69).

Graham, S., Taylor, A. & Hudley, C. 1998. Exploring achievement values among ethnic minority early adolescents. *Journal of Educational Psychology,* 90, 4, 606-620

Gramsci, A. 1971. *Selections from prison notebooks.* New York: International Publishers.

Griffin, G. 1999. Changes in teacher education: Looking to the future. In G. Griffin (Ed.) *The education of teachers,* (pp.1-17). Chicago: University of Chicago Press.

Guha, R. & Spivak, G. (Eds.) 1988. *Selected subaltern studies.* New York: Oxford University Press.

Hanushek, E. 1989. The impact of differential expenditures on school performance. *Educational Researcher,* 18, 48.

Hao, L. & Bonstead-Bruns, M. 1998. Parent-child differences in educational expectations and the academic achievement of immigrant and native students. *Sociology of Education,* 71, 175-198.

Harris, J. & Ford, D. 1999. Hope deferred again: Minority students underrepresented in gifted programs. *Education & Urban Society*, 31, 2, 225-237.

Hemmings, A. 1998. The self-transformation of African American achievers. *Youth & Society*, 29, 3, 330-368.

Henig, J. 1994. *Rethinking school choice: Limits of the market metaphor.* Princeton, NJ: Princeton University Press.

Henig, J., Hula, R., Orr, M. & Pedescleaux, D. 1999. *The color of school reform: Race, politics and the challenge of urban education.* Princeton, NJ: Princeton University Press.

Herrnstein, R. & Murray, C. 1994. *The bell curve: Intelligence and class structure in American life.* New York: Free Press.

Hofferth, S., Boisjoly, J. & Duncan, G. 1998. Parents' extrafamilial resources and children's school attainment. *Sociology of Education,* 71, 246-268.

Illich, I. 1971. *Deschooling society.* New York: Harper & Row.

Jensen, A. 1967. Varieties of individual differences in learning. In R.M. Gagne (Ed.), *Learning and individual differences* (pp.165-187). Columbus, OH: Charles Merrill.

_____. 1969. How much can we boost IQ and scholastic achievement? Harvard *Educational Review,* 39, 1-123.

Jones, V. 1998. Improving Black student performance on a large scale: The lessons of Equity 2000 program. In *The state of Black America.* (pp. 173-194.) National Urban League.

Jordan, W., Lara, J. & McPartland, J. 1996. Exploring the causes of early dropout among race-ethnic and gender groups. *Youth & Society*, 28, 1, 62-92.

Kao, G. & Tienda, M. 1995. Optimism and achievement: The educational performance of immigrant youth. *Social Science Quarterly*, 76, 1-19.

Keith, T., Keith, P., Quirk, K., Sperduto, J., Santillo, J., & Killings, S. 1998. Longitudunal effects of parent involvement on high school grades: Similarities and differences across gender and ethnic groups. *Journal of School Psychology*, 36, 3, 335-363.

Kozol, J. 1991. *Savage inequalities.* New York: Harper Collins.

LaCelle-Peterson, M. & Rivera, C. 1994. Is it real for all kids? A framework for equitable assessment policies for English language learners. Washington DC: George Washington University Center for Policy Studies.

Ladson-Billings, G. 1998. Just what is critical race theory and what's it doing in a nice field like education? *Qualitative Studies in Education,* 11, 1, 7-24.

Lagemann. 1996.

Lau v. Nichols. 1973. 414 U.S. 563, 566.

Lucas, T., Henze, R., & Donato, R. 1990. Promoting the success of Latino language-minority students: An exploratory study of six high schools. *Harvard Educational Review,* 60, 3, 315-340.

Mahiri, J. 1998. *Shooting for excellence: African Americans and youth culture in new century schools.* New York: Columbia University Press.

McClure, R. 1999. Unions, teacher development, and professionalism. In G. Griffin (Ed.) *The education of teachers,* (pp.18-62). Chicago: University of Chicago Press.

McQuillan, P. 1998. A proposal for reform. *Educational Administration Quarterly.*

Mickelson, R. 1990. The attitude-achievement paradox among Black adolescents. *Sociology of Education,* 63, 44-61.

Miller, L.S. 1995. *An American imperative:* Accelerating minority educational advancement. New Haven, CT: Yale University Press.

Moe, T. 1995. *Private vouchers.* Palo Alto, CA: Hoover Institution Press.

Moore, E. 1988. Family socialization and the IQ test performance of traditionally and transracially adopted Black children. *Developmental Psychology,* 22, 317-326.

Myrdal, G. 1944/1962. *An American dilemma: The Negro problem and modern democracy.* New York: Harper & Row.

Nakanishi, D. 1989/1995. A quota on excellence? The Asian American admissions debate. In D. Nakanishi & T. Nishida (Eds.), *The Asian American educational experience* (pp. 273-284), New York: Routledge.

Nakanishi, D. & Nishida, T. (Eds.) 1995. *The Asian American educational experience.* New York: Routledge.

References

Nathan, J. 1996. *Charter schools: Creating hope and opportunity for American education.* San Francisco: Jossey-Bass.

National Center for Education Statistics. 1996. *NAEP 1994 reading report card for the nation and the states.* Washington DC: US Department of Education.

National Commission on Excellence in Education. 1983. *A nation at risk: The imperative for educational reform.* Washington, DC: Department of Education.

National Commission on Teaching and America's Future (NCTAF). 1996. *What matters most: Teaching for America's future.* New York: Author.

Nyberg, K., McMillin, J., O'Neill-Rood, N. & Florence, J. 1997. Ethnic differences in academic retracking. A four-year longitudinal study. *Journal of Educational research,* 91, 1, 33-41.

Oakes, J. 1985. *Keeping track: How schools structure inequality.* New Haven: Yale University Press.

Oakes, J. & Lipton, M. 1998. *Teaching to change the world.* Boston: McGraw-Hill.

Ogawa, R. & White. P. 1994. School-based management: An overview. In S.A. Mohrman, P. Wohlstetter & Associates (Eds.), School-based management: *Organizing for high performance* (pp.53-80). San Francisco: Jossey-Bass.

Ogbu, J. 1978. *Minority education and caste: The American system in cross-cultural perspective.* New York: Academic Press.

Ogbu, J. & Simons, H. 1998. Voluntary and involuntary minorities: A cultural-ecological theory of school performance with some implications for education. *Anthropology & Education Quarterly,* 29, 2, 155-188.

Okagaki, L. & Frensch, P. 1998. Parenting and children's school achievement: A multiethnic perspective. *American Educational Research Journal,* 35, 1, 123-144.

Orfield, G. 1996. Public opinion and school desegregation. In E. Lagemann & L. Miller (Eds.) *Brown v. Board of Education: The challenge for today's schools.* New York: Teachers College Press.

Orfield, G. & Eaton, S. (Eds.). 1996. *Dismantling desegregation: the quiet reversal of Brown v. Board of Education.* New York: The New Press.

Osborne, J. 1995. Academics, self-esteem, and race: A look at the underlying assumptions of the disidentification hypothesis. *Personality and Social Psychology Bulletin,* 108, 330-333.

_____. 1997. Race and academic disidentification. *Journal of Educational Psychology,* 89, 4, 728-735.

Plomin, R. 1989. Environment and genes: Determinants of behavior. *American Psychologist,* 44, 105-106.

Polite, V. & Davis, J. (Eds.).1999. *A continuing challenge in times like these: African American males in schools and society.* New York: Teachers College Press.

Rawls, J. 1971. *A theory of justice.* New York: Oxford University Press.

Reich, R. 1991. *The work of nations.* New York: Knopf.

Rivera, C. & LaCelle- Peterson, M. 1993. Will the national education goals improve the progress of English language learners? Washington DC: George Washington University, Evaluation Assistance Center.

Rofes, E. 1998. *How are school districts responding to charter laws and charter schools?* Berkeley, CA: Policy Analysis for California Education.

Rose, F. & Kamin, L. 1984. *Not in our genes: Biology, ideology and human nature.* New York: Pantheon.

Rumberger, R. & Larson, K. 1998. Toward explaining differences in educational achievement among Mexican American language-minority students. *Sociology of Education,* 71, 69-93.

Sanders, M. 1997. Overcoming obstacles: Academic achievement as a response to racism and discrimination. *Journal of Negro Education,* 66, 1, 83-93

Sarason, S. 1998. *Charter schools: Another flawed educational reform?* New York: Teachers College Press.

Scarr, S. & Weinberg, R. 1978. The influence of "family background" on educational attainment. *American Sociological Review,* 43, 674-692.

Schneider, B. & Lee, Y. 1990. A model for academic success: The school and home environment of East Asian students. *Anthropology & Education Quarterly,* 21, 358-377.

Secada, W., Chavez-Chavez, R., Garcia, E., Munoz, C., Oakes, J., Santiago-Santiago, I. & Slavin, R. 1998. No more excuses: The final report of the Hispanic Dropout Project.

Shor, I. & Freire, P. 1987. *A pedagogy for liberation.* New York: Bergin & Garvey.

Slavin, R., Madden, N., Dolan, L., Wasik, B. Ross, S., Smith, L. & Dianda, M. 1996. Success for all: A summary of research. *Journal of Education for Students Placed at Risk*, 1, 41-76.

Solomon, R. 1992. *Black resistance in high school*. Albany, NY: State University of New York.

Stanfield, J. 1995. The myth of race and the human sciences. *Journal of Negro Education*, 64, 3, 218-231.

Steele, C. 1997. A threat in the air: How stereotypes shape intellectual identity and performance. *American Psychologist*, 52, 613-629.

Steele, C. & Aronson, J. 1995. Stereotype threat and the intellectual test performance of African Americans. *Journal of Personality and Social Psychology*, 69, 797-811.

Steinberg, L., Dornbusch, S. & Brown, B. 1992. Ethic differences in adolescent achievement: An ecological perspective. *American Psychologist*, 47, 728.

Sternberg, R. (Ed.) 1994. *The encyclopedia of human intelligence*. New York: Macmillan.

Sue, S. & Okazaki, S. 1995. Asian American educational achievements: A phenomenon in search of an explanation. In D. Nakanishi & T. Nishida (Eds.), *The Asian American educational experience*, (pp. 133-145), New York: Routledge.

Sun, Y. 1998. The academic success of East-Asian American students – An investment model. *Social Science Research*, 27, 432-456.

Suzuki, B. 1995. Education and the socialization of Asian Americans: A revisionist analysis of the "model minority" thesis. In D. Nakanishi & T. Nishida (Eds.), *The Asian American educational experience* (pp. 113-132), New York: Routledge.

Tapia, J. 1998. The schooling of Puerto Ricans: Philadelphia's most impoverished community. *Anthropology & Education Quarterly*. 29, 3, 297-323.

Trueba, H. 1989. *Raising silent voices: Educating the linguistic minorities for the 21st century*. New York: Harper Collins.

Updegraff, K., McHale, S. & Crouter, A. 1996. Gender roles in marriage: What do they mean for girls' and boys' school achievement? *Journal of Youth & Adolescence*, 25, 1, 73-88.

References

Valencia, R. 1991. (Ed.) *Chicano school failure and success.* New York: Falmer Press.

Vanourek, G., Manno, B., Finn, C. & Bierle, L. 1997. Charter schools as seen by those who know them best. Executive summary of a Hudson Institute Report.

Villanueva, I. 1996. Change in the educational life of Chicano families across three generations. *Education & Urban Society,* 29, 1, 13-34.

Vygotsky, L. 1978. *Mind in society.* Cambridge, MA: Harvard University Press.

Wacquant, L. & Wilson, W.J. 1989. The cost of racial and class exclusion in the inner city. *The Annals of the American Association of Political and Social Science,* 501, 10, 16-17.

Wang, L. 1976/1995. Lau v. Nichols: History of a struggle for equal and quality education. In D. Nakanishi & T. Nishida (Eds.), *The Asian American educational experience* (pp. 58-94), New York: Routledge.

Wang, M., Oates, J. & Weishew, N. 1995. Effective school responses to student diversity in inner-city schools: A coordinated approach. *Education & Urban Society,* (pp.484-503).

Watkins, T. 1997. Teacher communications, child achievement and parent traits in parent involvement models. *Journal of Educational Research,* 91, 1, 3-14.

Weinberg, M. 1977. *A chance to learn: A history of race and education in the United States.* New York: Cambridge University Press.

Wells, A.S. 1993. *Time to choose: America at the crossroads of school choice.* New York: Hill & Wang.

_____. 1998. *Beyond the rhetoric of charter school reform: A study of ten California school districts.* Los Angeles, CA: University of California, Los Angeles.

Whitford, B. & Metcalf-Turner, P. 1999. Of promises and unresolved puzzles: Reforming teacher education with professional development schools. In G. Griffin (Ed.) *The education of teachers,* (pp.257-278). Chicago: University of Chicago Press.

Whitty, G. 1997. Creating quasi-markets in education: A review of recent research on parental choice and school autonomy in three countries. *Review of Research in Education,* 22, 3-47.

Williams, R. 1993. Race, deconstruction, and the emergent agenda if feminist economic theory. In M.Ferber & J. Nelson (Eds.), *Beyond economic man.* Chicago: Chicago University Press.

Willis, P. 1977. *Learning to labour.* London: Saxon House.

Wilson, W.J. 1978. *The declining significance of race.* Chicago: University of Chicago Press.

_____. 1987. *The truly disadvantaged: The inner city, the underclass and public policy.* Chicago: University of Chicago Press.

Wohlstetter, P. 1995. Getting school-based management right: What works and what doesn't. *Phi Delta Kappan, 77,* 1, 22-26.

Wolf, R. 1967. The measurement of environments. In A. Anastasi (Ed.), *Testing problems in perspective* (pp. 491-503). Washington, DC: American Council in Education.

_____. 1995. The measurement of environments: A follow-up study. *Journal of Negro Education, 64,* 3, 354-359.

Wollenberg, C. 1978/1995. "Yellow peril" in the schools. In D. Nakanishi & T. Nishida (Eds.), *The Asian American educational experience,* (pp. 3-29). New York: Routledge.

Wong, M. 1983. Model students? Teachers' perceptions and expectations of the Asian and White students. *Sociology of Education, 53,* 236-246.

Zentella, A. 1997. Latino youth at home, in their communities and in school: The language link. *Education & Urban Society, 30,* 1, 122-130.

Zigler, E. & Seitz, V. 1982. Social policy and intelligence. In R. Sternberg (Ed.) *Handbook of human intelligence* (586-641). New York: Cambridge University.

References for chapter 16:
Affirmative Development of Academic Abilities

Bourdieu, P. (1986). The forms of capital. In J. Richardson (Ed.), *Handbook of theory and research for the sociology of education* (pp. 241-258). Westport, CT: Greenwood.

Coleman, J.S., Campbell, E.Q., Hobson, C.J., McPartland, J., Mood, A.M., Weinfeld, F.D., & York, L.R. (1966). *Equality of educational opportunity.* Washington, DC: U.S. Government Printing Office.

The College Board. (1999). *Reaching the top: A report of the National Task Force on Minority High Achievement.* New York: Author.

Gordon, E.W., & Meroe, A.S. (1989, January). *Common destinies—Continuing dilemmas. Psychological Science,* 2(1).

Hernnstein, R.J., & Murray, C. (1994). *The bell curve: Intelligence and class structure in American life.* New York: Free Press.

Miller, L.S. (1995). *An American imperative: Accelerating minority educational advancement.* New Haven, CT: Yale University Press.

Wilson, W.J. (1978). The declining significance of race: Blacks and changing American institutions. Chicago: University of Chicago Press.

References for chapter 18:
The Policy Implications of Status Variables and Schooling

Addams, J. (1902). *Democracy and social ethics.* Cambridge, MA: Harvard University Press.

Addams, J. (1914). *Twenty years at Hull House.* New York: Macmillan.

Addams, J. (1930). *The second twenty years at Hull House.* New York: Macmillan.

Asbury, H. (1970). The gangs of New York: An informal history of the underworld. New York: Capricorn Books.

Bell, D. (1976). *The cultural contradictions of capitalism.* New York: Basic Books.

Bere, M. (1964). *A comparative study of the mental capacity of children of foreign parentage.* New York: Teachers College Press.

Blauner, R. (1972). *Racial oppression in America.* New York: Harper.

Bledstein, B. J. (1976). *The culture of professionalism.* New York: W. W Norton.

Boudon, R. (1974). *Education, opportunity, and social inequality.* New York: John Wiley.

Bowles S. & Gintis, H. (1976). *Schooling in capitalist America.* New York: Basic Books.

Carpenter, N. (1927). Immigrants and their children, 1920. Census Monograph NO.7 (vol. I, Table 16). Washington, DC: U.S. Government Printing Office.

Clark, K. B. (1965). *Dark ghetto.* New York: Harper.

References

Cohen, D. K. (1970). Immigrants and the schools. *Review of Educational Research,* 40, 13-27.

Cole, S. G. & Cole, M. W. (1954). *Minorities and the American promise.* New York: Harper and Brothers.

Coleman, J. S., Campbell, E.Q., Hobson, C.J., McPartland, J., Mood, A.M., Weinfeld, F.D., et al. (1966). *Equality of educational opportunity.* (Washington, DC: U.S. Government Printing Office.

Coles, R. (1969). *Still hungry in America.* New York: New American Library.

Conant, J. B. (1961). *Slums and suburbs.* New York: McGraw-Hill.

Cremin, L. A. (1964). *The transformation of the school.* New York: Vintage Books.

Cubberley, E. P. (1909). *Changing conceptions of education.* (New York: Houghton Mifflin.

Edwards, R., Reich, M., & Weisskopf, T. E. (Eds.). (1978). *The capitalist system.* Englewood Cliffs, NJ: Prentice Hall.

Ellis, A. C. (1917). *The money value of education.* Bulletin No. 22. Washington, DC: U.S. Bureau of Education.

Ferman, L. A.., Kornbluh, J. L., & J. A. Miller, (Eds.). (1969). *Negroes and jobs.* Ann Arbor, MI: University of Michigan Press.

Foster, H. L. (1974). *Ribbin', jiving', and playin' the dozens: The unrecognized dilemma of inner city education.* Cambridge, MA: Ballinger.

Glazer, N. Moynihan, D. P. (1963). *Beyond the melting pot: The Negroes, Puerto Ricans, Jews, Italians, and Irish of New York City.* Cambridge, MA: MIT Press.

Gordon, M. M. (1961). Assimilation in America: Theory and reality. *Daedalus,* 90, 263-285.

Gordon, M. M. (1964). *Assimilation in American life: The role of race, religion and national origins.* New York: Oxford University Press.

Greeley, A. (1971). *Why can't they be like us? America's White ethnic groups.* New York: Dutton.

Greer, C. (1972). *The great school legend.* New York: Basic Books.

Hollingshead, A. (1949). *Elmtown's youth.* New York: John Wiley.

Hummel, R. C. & Nagle, J. M. (1973). *Urban education in America: Problems and prospects.* New York: Oxford University Press.

Jencks, C. & Riesman, D. (1968, Winter). *On class in America.* Public Interest, No. 10. Washington, DC: Bureau of the Census.

Kallen, H. M. (1956). *Cultural pluralism and the American idea.* Philadelphia, PA: University of Philadelphia Press.

Katz, M. B. (1971). *Class, bureaucracy, and schools.* New York: Praeger.

Kennedy, R. J. (1944). Single or triple melting pot? Intermarriage trends in New Haven, 1870-1940. *American Journal of Sociology,* 49, 331-39.

Laidlaw, W. (1932). *Statistical sources for demographic studies: Greater New York, 1910 and 1920.* New York: New York Census Committee.

Litwack, L. (1961). *North of slavery.* Chicago: University of Chicago Press.

Lynd, R. S., & Lynd, H. M. (1929). *Middletown: A study in American culture.* New York: Harcourt, Brace.

Mayo, M. J. (1913). The mental capacity of the American Negro. *Archives of Psychology, No. 28.* New York: Science Press.

McCarthy, C. (1970, July 13). 40 million Americans and a broken odyssey. *The Washington Post,* p.29.

Miller, W. B. (1969, Sept.). White gangs. *Trans-Action,* 6, 12.

Novak, M. (1971). *The use of the unmeltable ethnics.* New York: Macmillan.

Rogers, A. K. (1929). *Student's history of philosophy.* New York: Macmillan.

Schwebel, M. (1968). *Who can be educated?* New York: Grove Press.

Simon, B. (1960). *Studies in the history of education* 1780-1870. London: Lawrence and Wishart.

Stewart, G. R. (1954). *American ways of life.* New York: Doubleday.

Thurow, L. C. (1972, Summer). Education and economic inequality. *Public Interest,* No. 28, 66-81.

Tyack, D. (1974). *The one best system: A history of American urban education.* Cambridge, MA: Harvard University Press.